Of Passionate Intensity

Right-Wing Populism and the Reform Party of Canada

Of Passionate Intensity looks at the problems faced by liberal democracies worldwide from the unique perspective of Canadian history and politics. In this timely book, Trevor Harrison examines the historical, social, and ideological forces that give rise to changing political formations, particularly populist parties and movements.

The federal election of 25 October 1993 was a watershed in Canadian political history. While the Liberal party regained power, the real election story was the near eclipse of two of Canada's traditional parties, the NDP and the Progressive Conservatives, and the rise to prominence of two neophyte parties, the Bloc Québécois and the Reform party. Founded in 1987, the Reform party has achieved extraordinary popularity. What factors explain Reform's success? Who supports the party? And what is likely to be its long-term political future? Harrison provides an empirical and theoretically informed response to these questions and others.

Drawing from Canadian history, economic developments, and political and cultural contexts, Harrison incorporates a broad range of sources. He uses a historical-sociological methodology, employing surveys, interviews, newspaper accounts, and primary documents. On a theoretical level, the text uses the 'case' of the Reform party as a means of addressing the questions Why do populist parties arise? and What factors influence their ideological orientation? *Of Passionate Intensity* concludes with a discussion of the nature of populist politics and the promise of popular democracy in the future.

TREVOR HARRISON is a professor in the Department of Sociology, University of Alberta.

For Terri, Jayna, and Keenan

Of Passionate Intensity

Right-Wing Populism and the Reform Party of Canada

TREVOR HARRISON

UNIVERSITY OF TORONTO PRESS
Toronto Buffalo London

© University of Toronto Press Incorporated 1995
Toronto Buffalo London
Printed in Canada

ISBN 0-8020-0600-0 (cloth)
ISBN 0-8020-7204-6 (paper)

Printed on acid-free paper

Canadian Cataloguing in Publication Data

Harrison, Trevor, 1952–
  Of passionate intensity : right-wing populism
  and the Reform Party of Canada

  Includes bibliographical references and index.
  ISBN 0-8020-0600-0 (bound) ISBN 0-8020-7204-6 (pbk.)

  1. Reform Party of Canada. 2. Populism – Canada.
  3. Canada – Politics and government – 1984–1993.*
  4. Canada – Politics and government – 1993–   .*
  I. Title.

JL197.R34H37 1995   324.271'0983   C94-932611-9

University of Toronto Press acknowledges the financial assistance to its
publishing program of the Canada Council and the Ontario Arts Council.

Turning and turning in the widening gyre
The falcon cannot hear the falconer;
Things fall apart; the centre cannot hold;
Mere anarchy is loosed upon the world,
The blood-dimmed tide is loosed, and everywhere
The ceremony of innocence is drowned;
The best lack all conviction, while the worst
Are full of passionate intensity.

(W.B. Yeats, 'The Second Coming')

Contents

Preface

All the money in the world can't spark a movement if the time isn't right, and all the money in the world can't stop one when it gets rolling.

Preston Manning, the Western Assembly, 1987[1]

The federal election of 25 October 1993 was a watershed in Canadian political history. Of course, the Liberal party – Canada's 'natural party' of governance for much of the century – was once more in power. But the real election story was the near eclipse of two of Canada's traditional parties, the New Democratic Party (NDP) and the Progressive Conservatives, and the rise to prominence of two neophyte regional parties, the Bloc Québécois in Quebec and the Reform party, centred primarily in western Canada. This is the story of the latter.

The Reform Party of Canada was founded in 1987. In the 1988 federal election, while failing to win a seat, Reform nonetheless received a credible 15 per cent of the popular vote in the province of Alberta, and 7 per cent of the vote in British Columbia. The next spring, a Reform party candidate won a federal by-election in the Alberta riding of Beaver Lake. Later that fall, a Reform party candidate won an Alberta election held to nominate a representative to the federal Senate.

Over the next three years, the party's popularity continued to soar throughout English-speaking Canada. In 1991, the party expanded beyond its western base. That same year, several national polls placed Reform in third place, behind the Liberals and NDP, but ahead of the governing Tories. By early 1992, Reform was boasting an unconfirmed membership of over a hundred thousand and financial backing in the

millions of dollars. And, although its popular support dropped noticeably in the early months of 1993, the party remained in position to
stage the assault on parliament that would finally see 52 Reformers
elected to the House of Commons later that year.

Reform's impact on the Canadian political scene, however, cannot be
measured by numbers alone. By 1993 the Reform party had already
had a major influence upon Canadian politics, altering the terms of
discourse and shifting the ideological terrain on which Canada's political battles are fought to one occupied by the neo-conservative right.
Reform's presence led the federal Tory government of the time to impose
more restrictive immigration policies. In the context of a real rise in
government expenditures, Reform's single-minded emphasis on deficit
reduction also swayed the Tories to withdraw support for universal
social programs and to cap medicare expenditures. But Reform's influence was not limited to the federal Tories. Both the federal Liberals and
New Democrats, including their provincial counterparts, have been
forced by Reform's articulation of Canada's problems to re-evaluate the
role of government in the economy, the political rights of citizens, and
the policies of the welfare state. Finally, the Reform party also played
an instrumental role in the public's rejection of both the Meech Lake
Accord in 1990 and the Charlottetown referendum in 1992.

How did the Reform party phenomenon come about? A number of
popular books have attempted to answer this question.[2] Whether critical or supportive, however, these texts (in common with various magazines and newspaper articles) tend to portray Reform as a 'white, Anglo-
Saxon, male' western rump of the federal Tories, welded together by its
leader, Preston Manning. Moreover, and with few exceptions, these
texts are largely atheoretical and ahistorical.[3]

In the main, I do not quarrel with the arguments put forward by
previous authors, and readers familiar with these works will recognize
in this account a necessary repetition of some material. Research breeds
further studies. Subsequent analyses of Reform might well provide more
empirical data regarding Reform's recent success. I welcome these
studies. What readers will find in this text, however, and what I believe
will stand the test of time, is a carefully textured and theoretically
informed analysis that focuses on the historical, social, and ideological
forces that give rise to changing political formations.

In particular, this book situates the rise of the Reform party in the
problems of liberal democracy since the 1960s and the unique political
cultures of Alberta and British Columbia that made those provinces a

fertile seed-bed for a conservative revolt. I further show that at least some of Reform's appeal can be traced to a peculiarly Anglo-Canadian form of nativism with firm roots in Canada's history. I suggest also that Reform's early rise was in part the result of economic instability in Alberta and British Columbia during the 1980s. I show how together these sources of disenchantment, in consort with other events occurring in Canada, conspired to fragment the electoral coalition forged by Brian Mulroney in 1984, leading at last to the formation of the Reform party. Along the way, I provide a more empirically grounded portrait of Reformers' class, age, gender, education, and other characteristics than has been detailed previously. Although not disavowing Preston Manning's substantial influence within the party, I provide also an examination of other key members of the Reform party as well as its organizational structure and finances.

At a deeper level, I employ the 'case' of the Reform party in an attempt to answer two specific theoretical questions: Why do populist parties arise? What factors influence the ideological orientation of populist parties? These questions lie at the heart of this book.

Additionally, a sub-plot runs through this text: What is the nature of populist politics – and the promise of popular democracy generally – at this stage of the late twentieth century? The question is topical, given the apparent rise in demands by people the world over – whether taxpayers in California or Britain, peasants in an impoverished Mexican state, or newly liberated peoples in Eastern Europe – for a greater say in running their lives. Where economies experience 'globalization,' what does popular democracy mean? Is popular democracy, in a meaningful sense, even possible?

Acknowledgments

In the course of writing this book, and the doctoral thesis upon which it is based, I have acquired numerous debts that I gladly acknowledge. First and foremost, I want to thank generally those members and supporters of the Reform party who engaged me in a dialogue. I wish to acknowledge specifically the contribution of certain individuals. Francis Winspear was candid, friendly, and helpful in our face-to-face conversations. I am also indebted to Stephen Harper and Ted Byfield, who took time to be interviewed. Unfortunately, I am unable to thank personally Alfred Hooke, who has since passed away. Nonetheless, I acknowledge his contribution to my work. I would also like to note the contributions of Robert Grbavac, Neil and Pia Roberts, Gordon Gibson, Tom Flanagan and Ian McLelland.

Special mention also must be given to Gordon Laxer, my academic supervisor and a good friend during the period in which the thesis was written. It would be difficult to overestimate Gordon's contributions to the thesis and the book, both academically and stylistically.

I would be severely remiss if I did not also give specific mention to Harvey Krahn. Harvey made significant contributions to the analysis of much of the data used here. Above all, however, I want to publicly thank Harvey for his unswerving support and friendship over the years. My debts to both Gordon and Harvey are surpassed only by my respect for them.

I would also like to take this opportunity to thank John Richards, Stephen Kent, Larry Pratt, and Linda Trimble. Their advice, comments, and criticisms during the stages of writing the thesis were unerringly perceptive and invaluable. Additional thanks are owed to Murray Dobbin, William Stanbury, Keith Archer, and Michael Percy. Further thanks are extended to Virgil Duff, Mary McDougall Maude, and all the staff of the University of Toronto Press, and to the anonymous reviewers for their helpful comments.

I would also like to thank those organizations that supported me financially during the period of my doctoral studies – the University of Alberta and, particularly, the Department of Sociology; the Social Science and Humanities Research Council of Canada; and the Charles Camsell Hospital of Edmonton.

I also wish to thank my mother, brother, and numerous friends who supported – and tolerated – me during this period. A special thanks goes to John Hartsen. Last but not least, I want to express public thanks and gratitude to my wife, Terri, my daughter, Jayna, and my son, Keenan, for their emotional support and numerous sacrifices during the period in which this book was researched and written. I could not have done it without them.

Any errors, omissions, or distortions contained herein are, of course, my responsibility alone.

T.W.H.
December 1994

Of Passionate Intensity

Right-Wing Populism and the Reform Party of Canada

1. The 'Problem' of Populism

At a certain point in their historical lives, social groups become detached from their traditional parties ... [which are then] no longer recognized by their class (or fraction of a class) as its expression.

Italian political theorist Antonio Gramsci[1]

The Reform party emerged at the end of a tumultuous decade in Canadian politics, a period that featured, among other events, the fracturing of support for the traditionally dominant Liberal and Progressive Conservative parties, the rise of Quebec (and other) nationalist sentiments, and a series of divisive constitutional and policy debates (over the National Energy Program, free trade, and the Meech Lake Accord). Even in the context of these occurrences, however, the success of the Reform party may appear incongruous, particularly given the situation of western Canadian politics earlier in the decade.

In 1979, the federal Progressive Conservative party, headed by a western (Albertan) leader, Joe Clark, won election. Clark's minority government held office, however, for only eight months. The subsequent election in 1980 saw the return of a majority government headed by Liberal leader Pierre Trudeau, whose previous tenure in office (1968–79) had ended in defeat and retirement only a few months earlier. Particularly galling for many western Canadians was the fact that the Liberals won a majority government despite winning only two of seventy-seven seats in Manitoba, Saskatchewan, Alberta, and British Columbia.

In the weeks and months that followed, right-wing populist parties emerged like locusts out of the prairie landscape. Some were openly separatist, such as Western Canada Concept and West-Fed. Others, like the Unionest party (whose name joins 'union' and 'west'), called for the region to join the United States. These parties seemed to represent the widespread frustration of many western Canadians with the federal political system, a frustration that increased as the left-of-centre Liberal party enacted nationalist and state-centralist policies, such as the hated National Energy Program (NEP). During the same period, Canada's economy entered into a prolonged recession. The economic downturn was particularly emotionally scarring for many Albertans, contrasting as it did with the oil-fed prosperity of the late 1970s. Many blamed the NEP for the impact of the recession, if not for its cause. The right-wing populist parties failed to thrive, however, despite these political advantages. By the end of 1983, beset by internal squabbles and lacking widespread public support, most had faded from significance on the political scene.

The following year, the federal Progressive Conservative party under Brian Mulroney gained a resounding victory, winning 211 of 282 seats, 58 of 77 in the western region. Within a short time, the Tories disman-tled state-nationalist economic policies, decentralized political author-ity and control, and generally followed a pro-business agenda. What was the effect of this political change upon the western region? Though the left wing, headed by the New Democratic Party, organized labour, and other groups, was able to mount sporadic opposition to this agenda, ironically right-wing populism gained in momentum!

The fall of 1987 saw the formation of both the religiously oriented Christian Heritage Party (CHP) and the Reform Party of Canada. Al-though the Mulroney Tories won again in the federal election of 1988, taking 169 of 295 seats, 48 in the West, each of these new right-wing parties received significant popular electoral support, the CHP in On-tario and the Reform party in the West. Thereafter, the Reform party continued to gain in popularity and influence, thus setting the stage for the unprecedented rout in the federal election of 1993 that would see the once-proud party of Sir John A. Macdonald reduced to a mere 2 seats, none west of Quebec, while the upstart Reformers garnered 52 seats, all but one in the West.

In summary, other right-wing populist parties sputtered and fell at a time of apparently conducive political circumstances, yet the Reform party gained its success in opposition to, and during the time in office of, the right-wing federal Progressive Conservative party. How can this apparent incongruency be explained?

An answer to this question must be sought within a wider examination of populist movements and their causes.

POPULISM: WHAT IS IT?

'Populism' is a notoriously slippery concept.[2] As David Laycock has noted, the term has almost been rendered analytically useless by the journalistic practice of assuming that 'any folksy appeal to the "average guy," or some allegedly general will, is evidence of populism.'[3] On this basis, writers in the past have referred to Hitler, Mao, Juan Peron, Huey Long, and Father Coughlin as populists, while, more recently, such diverse personalities as Ronald Reagan, George Wallace, Jesse Jackson, Bill Vander Zalm, and Ross Perot have received the same label.

But if, as Laycock asserts, populism cannot be reduced to merely a type of political leadership style what, then, is it?

For Laycock, the essential feature of populist movements is their mass-organizational nature, a view elaborated upon by others who have stated that the core notion underlying populism is that of 'a people' defined by its historic, geographic, and/or cultural roots.[4] Perhaps the clearest definition of populism, however, is provided by Peter Sinclair.[5] According to Sinclair, a populist movement frequently 'stresses the worth of the common people and advocates their political supremacy,' rejects 'intermediate associations between the mass and leaders,' and directs its protests 'against some group which lies outside the local society.'

In short, populism constitutes an attempt to create a mass political movement, mobilized around symbols and traditions congruent with the popular culture, which expresses a group's sense of threat, arising from presumably powerful 'outside' elements and directed at its perceived 'peoplehood.' In this sense, populist movements occupy a middle ground between traditional sources of collective identity, such as 'nation' and 'ethnic group,' which primarily revolve around (real or imagined) notions of consanguinity, and modern territorially based forms of nationalism. While populist movements are in theory more inclusive than the former, they are in practice more exclusive than the latter, thus allowing populist movements to include among their entry qualifications such things as class, occupation, and/or status.

The notion of what groups lie 'outside' the movement is problematic, however, and goes beyond mere geographic location. Hence, while populism often gains its power through appeals that cross class and ethnic lines, the notion of peoplehood is not all-encompassing. Indeed, the identification of a group 'not of the people,' possessing illegitimate political and economic power in opposition to 'the people,' serves to bind the latter closer.[6]

Finally, concrete expressions of populism frequently vary.[7] What is the particular source of such movements? And what factors determine their ideological orientations and political actions? These questions have lain at the heart of debates on populism for over a century.

Although examples of populist revolt can be found in earlier periods – Watt Tyler and the Luddites in England, for example – the concept of populism is primarily associated with the various agrarian movements that arose throughout North America, Russia, and parts of Western Europe in the late nineteenth century. Indeed, American journalists coined the term 'populism' in 1896 to describe the People's party that contested the American election that year.

The American social historians who attempted to explain the rise of that party (and earlier manifestations) began a series of debates, which have continued to the present time. Drawing on Frederick Turner's 'frontier theory,' American theorists of this earlier period tended to explain populist movements as resulting from regional economic factors.[8] In particular, populism was defined as a regional agrarian response to the increasing scarcity of free land under advancing settlement. As land became more scarce, the farmers and, to a lesser extent, the labourers of the American west became increasingly pressed by the power of monopoly interests, in particular 'the manufacturers, the railroads, the moneylenders, the middlemen – plutocrats all.'[9] Farmers at first formed cooperative associations through which to press their political interests. When lobbying alone did not bring about the desired results, these organizations created their own political party, the People's party.

In Canada, William L. Morton's study of the Progressive party and Seymour M. Lipset's study of the Co-operative Commonwealth Federation (CCF) similarly contended that populist parties resulted from the uncertainty of regional hinterland economies.[10] Like their American counterparts, Morton and Lipset also were generally positive in their portrayals of populism as egalitarian, democratic, and reformist.

Shortly after Morton's and Lipset's analyses of populism entered the public domain, a negative critique of populism was launched by American historian Richard Hofstadter. Although Hofstadter gave perfunctory credit to populism ('There is indeed much that is good and usable in our Populist past'), on the whole, he tended to view the agrarian movements as irrational, regressive, anti-intellectual, and paranoid.[11] According to Hofstadter, the world-view of the populists ultimately was narrow and ethnocentric – a position to which he returned in later texts.[12]

Hofstadter's thesis essentially deals with a particular form of populism: nativism.[13] Nativism is a belief system forged out of the conjunction of nationalism with ethno-cultural, religious, and/or racial prejudice.[14] Nativist attitudes are most likely held by people in social groups that have the same racial, ethnic, and/or religious characteristics as the dominant class, but not the economic or political power. Such attitudes emerge most frequently during periods of social, political, or economic crisis, the latter form of crisis suggesting that nativism also may be linked to a feeling of 'relative deprivation.'[15] However caused, the crisis nonetheless results in the emergence of a sense of 'calling' among the heretofore-identified social groups to defend the country against perceived internal threats posed by various minority groups.[16]

Until recently, few theorists have applied the notion of nativism to Canadian studies. Carl Berger's study of nineteenth-century Canadian imperialism, Howard Palmer's application of the concept to an historical examination of prejudice in Alberta, and Martin Robin's recent examination of extreme right-wing groups in Canada between 1920 and 1940 provide three exceptions.[17] Notably, however, the concept has not been applied explicitly to populist movements in Canada – an apparent lacuna given the American experience.

A third stream within theories of populism draws its impetus from Marxism. A few years before Hofstadter's work appeared, political scientist C.B. Macpherson used Marxist class concepts in an effort to explain the rise in 1935 of the Social Credit party in Alberta.[18] In particular, Macpherson returned to Marx and Engels's depiction of the predicament of the petite bourgeoisie under modern capitalism first elaborated in *The Communist Manifesto*.[19]

In that text, Marx and Engels had outlined their theory of class struggle. Under modern capitalism, they said, the essential class struggle is between the proletariat and the owners of the means of production, the bourgeoisie. Caught between these two classes are other classes, most notably the petite bourgeoisie comprising small manufacturers, shopkeepers, artisans, and peasants. Although it is destined ultimately to sink into the proletarian class, the petite bourgeoisie nonetheless plays an important role in the larger struggle between capital and labour insofar as it 'fight[s] against the bourgeoisie, to save [itself] from extinction.' But, warned Marx and Engels, the petite bourgeoisie elements are 'not revolutionary, but conservative. Nay more, they are reactionary, for they try to roll back the wheel of history. If by chance they are revolutionary, they are so only in view of their impending transfer into the proletariat.'[20]

Lenin elaborated upon this theory of the 'reactionary bourgeoisie' in his study of the Narodist movement in Russia.[21] In contrast to Marx and Engels, Lenin recognized the positive attempts of Russia's agrarian petite bourgeoisie to create a better, more democratic society.[22] Nonetheless, Lenin, like his Marxist predecessors, viewed Narodism as a movement 'based on backward theories,' 'a romantic and petty bourgeois criticism of capitalism,' and 'a disregard for the cardinal facts of Russian history and reality.' Narodism, said Lenin, wanted to replace capitalist development with 'a fiction of the pre-capitalist order' and, as such, stood in opposition to the historical necessity of capitalist development.[23] Ultimately, populist movements were unable to transcend their petit bourgeois class circumstances with a radical critique of capitalism:

the small producer ... looks with one face to the past ... without knowing or wishing to know anything about the general economic system and about the need to reckon with the class that controls it – and with the other face to the future, adopting a hostile attitude to the capitalism that is ruining him.[24]

In short, Lenin diagnosed Russian populism as displaying the 'typical' ideology and behaviour of a group occupying what is now commonly termed a 'contradictory class position.'[25]

Macpherson's study of Alberta Social Credit borrowed heavily from Marx and Engels's and Lenin's view of populism. Macpherson contended that Alberta's class structure was relatively homogeneous, dominated by 'independent commodity producers,' primarily the agrarian petite bourgeoisie, whose economic circumstances rendered them incapable of developing a class consciousness. But his work was also distinctly Canadian, drawing on the staples tradition established by Harold Innis, in contending that a hinterland-metropolis relationship existed between western farmers and the rest of North America, a relationship that consigned the West to a 'quasi-colonial' status.[26] In effect, Macpherson overlaid regional economic factors with Marxist class analysis in diagnosing the causes underlying the rise of Social Credit.

Like Macpherson, Maurice Pinard applied a class analysis to the sudden rise to prominence of Social Credit's Quebec counterpart, the Créditistes, during the federal election of 1962. According to Pinard, the Créditistes were a rural-based party supported primarily by small businesspeople, farmers, and workers, whose class positions had declined precipitously, relative to the province as a whole, during the recession of the early 1960s. Pinard contended, however, that economic and social strains alone were insufficient to result in the rise of a third party. Rather, the social and political situation must also be conducive to a third party's emergence. Frequently, this means the weakness of existing parties. Finally, Pinard contended that people's resultant sense of grievance and alienation must be mobilized into political action. The weakness of the federal Tories in Quebec's rural hinterland, combined with support generated for the Créditistes through pre-existing organizational structures, notably farmers' organizations and the media, proved conducive to the rise of Réal Caouette's party.[27]

Like Hofstadter's account, both Macpherson's and Pinard's analyses tend to depict populist parties as reactions to structural changes imposed from outside. After the 1960s, however, many North American theorists began countering these negative, and largely impotent, views of populism. In the United States, Norman Pollack and Lawrence Goodwyn, in particular, aimed their rebuttals at Hofstadter, whom Pollack specifically accused of unempirical and ahistorical revisionism of the populist experience.[28] In Canada, counter-claims were also pressed against Macpherson by scholars asserting the essentially radical nature of Social Credit policies and otherwise debunking the contention that Social Credit was supported primarily by the petite bourgeoisie.[29]

By the late 1970s, North American debates about populism had reached an impasse. On one side were theorists who, usually relying on regional economic arguments, contended that early populist movements had been moderately left-wing and democratic attempts at redirecting the trajectory of capitalist development through political means. On the other side were those theorists who, using nativist or class arguments, viewed these movements as tending towards right-wing extremism and reactionism. Both sides shared only a common tendency to 'historicize' populism. That is, each viewed populist movements as largely an agrarian phenomenon that was disappearing rapidly from North American political life.[30]

The civil rights movement and Vietnam protests of the 1960s, however, and the neo-conservative counter-revolution of the late 1970s, which eventually led to the election of Ronald Reagan as president in

1980, made apparent that populist politics had re-emerged, albeit in an altered form (urbanized, more 'high-tech'). As a result, many theorists returned to an examination of earlier populist movements, hoping that a better understanding of the new populism might emerge. An offshoot of this 'return' was the attempt by several theorists to come to terms with the many faces of populism.

Canovan's typology, for example, distinguished between 'agrarian' populism, defined by 'a particular kind of socioeconomic base (peasants or farmers), liable to arise in particular socioeconomic circumstances (especially modernization of one sort or another), and perhaps sharing a particular socioeconomic program'; and 'political' populism, defined as a 'particular kind of political phenomenon where the tensions between the elite and the grass roots loom large.'[31]

Canovan's work is interesting and provocative. The asymmetry of her categories is, however, problematic. The best typologies always consist of implicit comparisons, oppositions, and continuities between the categories. Beside this ideal, Canovan's classification begs the question, why not non-agrarian economic populism? Similarly, the reader is left to ask, in what sense is agrarian populism not also political?

In contrast to Canovan's typology, and in direct opposition to her assertion that any attempt 'to label populism as either Right or Left is a lost cause,'[32] other theorists have presented typologies based on just such a traditional division. In his seminal work on populism, John Richards listed a series of characteristics defining right- and left-wing populist movements in Canada.[33] Richards specifically noted that, historically, left populist movements in Canada tended to be class alliances (farm-labour); to present a general critique of corporate capitalism; to demand greater state involvement as a countervailing force to the corporate sector; and to spring from rural cooperative organizations. In contrast, right populist movements tended to mobilize along regional rather than class lines; to narrow their critique to the power of banks, the money supply, and credit; to view big government as the primary enemy; and to eschew participatory democracy in favour of plebiscites. It is important to note that Richards's work not only describes differences between left and right populist movements, but also, at least implicitly, suggests that structural and organizational factors underlie the differences.

Richards's typology was subsequently applied by Alvin Finkel to his examination of the Social Credit party in Alberta and expanded by

David Laycock into four categories: social democratic populism, radical democratic populism, plebiscitarian populism, and crypto-Liberalism.[34] A similar right-left typology is also used throughout this text.

Despite these recent efforts, an adequate theory of populism remains elusive. Is it possible to construct a theory of populism that is both sensitive to particular empirical detail yet broad enough to illuminate the populist experience in general? Can such a theory, moreover, make sense of the various permutations of populism? I think so.

A THEORY OF POPULISM

Populist unrest results from delegitimation crises and the resultant decomposition of previous political alliances. The type of populism that emerges (right- or left-wing) is a product of the social, political, and ideological elements set adrift by this process and the consequent reconfiguration of alliances designed to resolve the crisis.

Underlying such alliances is what Antonio Gramsci terms 'hegemony.'[35] Hegemony refers 'to the use by the dominant class of its political, moral, and intellectual leadership to shape the world view of subordinate classes in conformance with its own long-term interests.'[36] Thus, hegemony is the capacity of a dominant class to construct an overarching concept of reality. This constructed reality neutralizes conflicts over the ownership, distribution, and use of socially produced capital either by reducing such conflicts to simple 'differences' or, alternatively, displacing the source of antagonisms.[37] Under this resultant illusion of a congruency of interests, a political coalition of social elements – in Gramsci's words, an 'historic bloc' – is formed that in turn shapes the general contours of society at that particular moment.[38]

Such alliances are particularly necessary in states where political decisions are ostensibly decided through electoral politics.[39] In capitalist societies, where the fundamental conflict remains between capital and labour, yet where neither class is objectively large enough to form a majority, class interests must necessarily be pressed into an often uneasy alliance with each other or with other classes, groups, or fragments of these social elements.

Class alliances are further attenuated by other production, consumption, and distribution influences. Together, these varied influences result in the situating of individuals within social locations of which class is only one part.[40] Within these social locations, themselves existing in real historical time, ideologies are produced and reproduced, creating habits of mind that guide, though never determine, the possibilities for political action.

The form of hegemonic alliances arising in a given time and place depends upon (1) the relative power of the two fundamental classes as determined by their objective size, subjective consciousness, internal cohesion, and access to resources; (2) the relative power of those in contradictory social locations who, lacking a class consciousness, construct their politics around ostensibly non-class issues that may, nonetheless, favour either capital or labour; (3) the historically existing political culture in which definitions of reality and consequent decisions are made; and (4) the organizational capacity of the two fundamental classes and their leadership to form coalitions with each other or with the remaining classes.

Political parties, especially the governing party, are both the practical embodiment of these hegemonic alliances and the major instrument for their construction. All members of the existing polity – that is, the government and contenders for power with routine, low-cost access to political resources – tailor their policies and actions to the existing possibilities for alliance construction.[41] Hence, to some extent, even opposition parties reaffirm the legitimacy of the existing hegemony by their participation in the political process.

Hegemony, however, is a dynamic process. This is particularly the case in modern capitalist countries. Marx and Engels noted that [modern capitalism] 'cannot exist without constantly revolutionizing the instruments of production, and thereby the relations of production, and with them the whole relations of society.'[42] While crude interpretations of Marx often have limited the meaning of 'instruments' to material-economic factors, I would suggest – and I think a full reading of Marx's writings bears this out – that he also viewed ideology and politics as essential factors in production. Thus, any significant change in the political, economic, or ideological spheres of society rapidly spreads to other spheres, creating 'organic crises.'[43] In the midst of such crises, previously submerged, real or imagined conflicts between various social groups are likely to re-emerge. The system of political alliances that arose out of, yet simultaneously underpinned, the previous hegemony begins to unravel.

History, particularly since the late eighteenth century, provides numerous examples of this process of unravelling. The political reforms of 1861 in Russia, conceived by the élite as the first stage in modernizing that country, neither freed the serfs, except in a legalistic way, nor proletarianized them. Instead, the reforms tied the peasantry even more to the land, while making them poorer. Lacking exposure to other social classes and/or an alternative vision of social organization, the Russian peasants fell back during their period of discontent upon traditional solutions; hence, the emergence of a kind of reactionary populism.[44]

American agrarians of the same period formed associations and alliances with elements of other classes, notably labour, to lobby for government protections against the declining price of wheat, the perceived illegitimate power of railroads and bankers, and, later, the cost of land. The result was the rise of a series of populist movements that were, sometimes simultaneously, both reactionary and progressive.[45]

A frequent result of an organic crisis is the delegitimation of the existing social order and, as a consequence, the existing polity among various social elements.[46] Legitimacy crises are signalled by increased challenges to the ideas and practices of the dominant hegemony. In mild instances, these challenges may appear as political protests lodged on T-shirts, in grafitti, or in jokes. In more significant cases, such challenges may result in the rise in production and sales of anti-establishment books and tracts, or in radical experimentation in the visual arts and literature. In a more extreme form, legitimation crises may lead to labour, civil, and/or political unrest, as occurred in western Europe during the 1920s, 1930s, and again in the 1960s, and recently in the formerly communist states of eastern Europe. Finally, at its most extreme, the breakdown of political legitimacy may result in revolution, as occurred in Russia, Hungary, Germany, and Italy following the First World War.

Particularly vulnerable to the effects of delegitimation are individuals and groups within social locations that have previously remained relatively insulated from dominant ideological messages or those whose political, economic, or ideological interests have been abruptly and negatively affected by the organic crisis.[47] Although the properties of these 'vulnerable' locations are empirically specific and cannot be exactly determined a priori, it might be expected, for example, that certain regions (for example, hinterland areas) or occupations (for example, those in primary or declining industries), classes (the petite bourgeoisie or unorganized labour, often in secondary job markets), or previously privileged status groups will be most susceptible to delegitimation. Members of vulnerable locations may subsequently attempt to construct a counter-hegemony.

In this regard, it is analytically useful to distinguish between the peripheral elements of any society – a group commonly termed 'the fringe' – and these vulnerable elements. Social disorganization theorists have long insisted upon the centrality of fringe elements to the rise of political movements.[48] While fringe elements may provide, however, the clearest expression of ideas latent in the society, and may even be found politically useful by those interested in establishing a counter-hegemony, we cannot look to the fringe as the source of organized political discontent. Rather, successful political movements require the mobilization by an organized and capable leadership, often through existing organizational structures, of the growing discontent with the existing polity.[49] In order to understand the rise of populist parties we must look, therefore, to those social elements who are directly threatened by the organic crisis.

Why do these vulnerable elements collectively mobilize in support of an alternative from outside of the existing polity, that is, a 'third party'? Why do they not turn to existing political alternatives? In part, the answer lies in a combination of objective political interests and political socialization or, more broadly, the historical political culture within which the vulnerable elements construct their view of the crises' causes and solutions. Thus, the ostensible range of political choices perceived as legitimate by vulnerable elements may, in practice, be quite limited.

In large measure, however, the rise of a third party also results from what might be termed a 'political lag' occurring within the existing polity. Like all organizations, political parties can be prone to inertia.[50] That is, the policies, ideologies, and alliances created by a party in the past may become obstacles to adapting to the changed circumstances brought about by an organic crisis. The existing political parties may lack the agility to construct new coalitions able either to reincorporate or to suppress the 'freed' social elements. By contrast, the nascent third party appears to have no historical obligations. It has only a goal: to preserve and protect 'the people' in the moment of the organic crisis.

Despite this appeal to the people, it is important to keep in mind that populist movements never incorporate all the residents of an area. Indeed, both 'the people' and the particular 'dominant classes,' or 'power bloc,' which must be opposed, are fundamentally contested concepts.[51] The shaping of these concepts within the real historical, political, and ideological circumstances at hand constitutes a major role of the party's emergent leadership. This leadership's shaping of and appeal to the people is strategically useful in attempting to recruit other freed elements and in blunting the appeal of other parties. Moreover, the notion that one represents the people provides a psychological justification for those already-recruited members in pursuing future policies and actions.

Whether populist parties are successful depends on a number of factors. The size, strength, and strategic location of individuals and groups cast off from the existing parties determine the third party's potential limits of political support. In turn, organizational factors, including the party's leadership and material resources, primarily labour and money, affect the party's capacity to mobilize these freed elements.[52] Finally, the party's success is also affected by the ability of its leadership to construct a counter-ideology that speaks to the freed social elements – 'the people' – in a language congruent with culturally and historically accepted symbols, while stating the alleged causes of the crisis, the nature of the 'power bloc' opposing them, the injustices that the former has wrought, and the solutions to be pursued.[53]

Even where all of these factors are in place, the political success of populist parties is not assured. Indeed, their success is in most cases fortuitous. For example, the existing polity, or at least a dominant party within it, might rapidly adapt to the new social and political realities and so construct a new system of alliances that reincorporates the freed elements. Alternatively, the causes of the legitimacy crisis might be resolved satisfactorily before the existing hegemony is irreparably damaged. Finally, other events (wars, natural catastrophes) might intervene to again change the existing political dynamics.

There remains, however, a question: Why do populist parties take on either right-wing or left-wing trajectories? The answer is contingent on the interplay of several factors, the primacy and directional influence of any particular factor being historically specific. Some of these factors are endogenous to the geographic territory in which the party arises. Endogenous factors include the region's historically existing political culture within which understandings of the crisis, including definitions of the people/power bloc antagonism, are constructed; the class configuration of the freed elements; the fortuitous timing of economic crises; and the degree of legitimacy of organizations and potential leaders capable of mobilizing a counter-hegemonic party. But exogenous, world-historical circumstances also are likely to be important. In particular, the dominance of either right-wing or left-wing ideology at a given moment likely will influence the contours of debate in specific areas. The factors resulting in the formation of a particular type of populist party thus cannot be determined a priori, but must be located in the concrete historical circumstances in which the party emerges.

The rise of the Reform Party of Canada provides an opportunity for applying this general theory and otherwise exploring some of the questions raised by previous studies of populist movements.

THE CASE OF REFORM

The ebb and flow of populism in Canadian history generally can be explained only as the end product of a series of historically situated economic, political, and ideological crises. To the extent that these crises result in a fragmentation of the country's hegemonic alliances in general, and its political coalitions in particular, and where these fragmentations are not immediately reversed within the existing polity, the result is the rise of new vehicles of political representation. To substantiate this more general thesis, it is necessary to examine briefly how political alliances have risen and fallen in Canada in response to various crises.

For much of this century, beginning with Wilfrid Laurier's ascent to power in 1896, the Liberal party governed Canada. It did so primarily through an alliance of the conservative (and secular) French-speaking élites in Quebec, agrarians in English-speaking Canada, and big business. Along the way, the Liberal party's dominance was maintained through an adept blend of political savvy, such as Mackenzie King displayed in absorbing most of the Progressives in the 1920s, and sheer fortuitousness, such as being out of power when both the First World War and the full force of the Depression began.

The Depression and the Second World War radically transformed the political and economic order of Canada and other western countries. At the heart of this transformation was 'the great compromise' between labour and capital, overseen and supported by the state's administrative apparatuses, resulting in both the creation of the welfare state and, concomitantly, the increased legitimation of the power and authority of the liberal state.

But the war also transformed Canada in another important way. For years, English-speaking Canadians had struggled to define their own identity in relation to their British colonial past and their powerful neighbour to the south. While the demise of the British empire following the war started the final process of Canada's separation from its British roots, the country was drawn even more tightly into the American sphere of influence by continentalist economic policies and the politics and ideology of the Cold War. By the early 1960s, Canada was a typical liberal democracy, confident in its self-proclaimed belief in equal opportunity for all.[54] Among liberal democracies, in general, Canada seemed particularly immune to class voting.[55] Class, and other potential sources of social and political conflict, had been transformed into insubstantial 'differences.'[56]

Then, slowly, imperceptibly at first, cracks began to appear in 'the great compromise' and, hence, in liberalism's hegemonic edifice throughout the western world. By the end of the 1950s, some people were coming to doubt the promises of liberal democracy. Even as the welfare state grew in size and power, social inequalities seemed to grow more entrenched. Statistics Canada figures show, for example, that the percentage of income earned by each quintile of the Canadian population remained virtually static from 1951 to 1985.[57] Moreover, and contrary to the 'human capital' arguments embedded in liberal economic theory, evidence suggested that differences of income and wealth redounded as much to class of origin, ethnic, gender, and other 'collective' attributes as to individual market capacities.[58]

These results also suggested, however, that traditional class theories alone did not go far enough to explain the problems of modern capitalist societies. Rejecting both totalitarian communism and liberal democratic capitalism, intellectuals during the late 1950s, such as the late E.P. Thompson, began to fashion an alternative vision of politics soon known as the New Left. During the next few years, the New Left came to embrace other expressions of popular discontent, beginning in the 1950s with the anti-nuclear movement in Britain and the civil rights movement in the United States, the later rise of feminism, and finally the Vietnam protests and widespread labour unrest of the mid and late 1960s. The essence of all these movements was a challenge to the structural inequalities and authority relationships embedded within liberal democratic theory.

Canadians were politicized in a vicarious way by all these events. At the same time, the rise of a left-wing counter-hegemony was the result of circumstances and events particular to Canada. The structural changes that had been taking place prior to the Second World War, particularly in eastern Canada, only intensified in the years following that conflict. Like the East, much of the West was also transformed from an agricultural to a manufacturing and service economy. A second major change, begun during the war but accelerated through the 1960s, involved the unprecedented entry of large numbers of women into the workforce. These structural changes led, among other things, to demands by Canadian workers, women, and other minority groups for an expansion of their democratic rights. These demands often were coupled with increased unionization, particularly in the public sector.

The formation in 1961 of the New Democratic Party (NDP) out of an alliance of the CCF and the Canadian Labour Congress brought a further challenge to Canadian liberalism as espoused by the Liberal party. By the late 1960s, in the wake of the Vietnam War and the evident problems of the American economy, New Left elements of the NDP, notably 'the Waffle,' began lobbying for active federal government policies to further the goal of economic nationalism. In doing so, the NDP introduced a more active and independent approach to Canadian development than had been expressed by the laissez-faire 'rentier' mentality of previous Liberal administrations.

Quebec's Quiet Revolution of the 1960s, however, created the major challenge to continued Liberal dominance. The demands of a wide coalition of Quebecers for greater autonomy – demands bolstered by increased political violence within the province against persons and symbols of the Canadian state – made the Liberal government under Lester Pearson abandon its traditional policy of symmetrical federalism. Quebec was allowed greater jurisdiction over its own affairs. At the same time, the Liberal government attempted to manufacture a new kind of 'pan-Canadian' identity through such controversial policies as the installation of the Maple Leaf flag as Canada's official flag in 1965.

In 1968, Pierre Trudeau replaced Pearson as leader of the Liberal party and as prime minister. Trudeau opposed Quebec nationalism – indeed, any other form of nationalism – on the grounds that it was a retrograde identification with collective, rather than individual, rights. He further opposed the recognition of Quebec 'exceptionalism' as practised under Pearson. Returning to the Laurier policy of provincial equality, Trudeau granted increased political and economic powers to all the provinces.[59]

In a further effort to blunt Quebec nationalism, the Liberal government in 1969 enacted the Official Languages Act which guaranteed Canadian citizens the right to deal with federal institutions in either English or French.[60] These events and policies, however, had several unintended consequences.

The rise in Quebec nationalism contrasted markedly with a growing sense of lost identity felt by many English-speaking Canadians after the end of the Second World War. In a process that would only increase over the next three decades, the 1960s saw English Canada's cultural homogeneity challenged by the arrival of non-Anglo immigrants from Asia, Africa, and the Caribbean.[61] The installation of the new flag only added to the growing sense of unease felt by many anglophone Canadians. Designed to create a sense of pan-Canadianism, the new flag was denounced instead by many anglophones as an attack on their cultural heritage. Likewise, the federal government's implementation of official bilingualism in 1969 and of a policy of multiculturalism in 1971 was viewed by many in English-speaking Canada, particularly the West, as a needless and expensive intrusion into their lives.[62] Far from assuaging concerns, federal government policies thus exacerbated the sense of cultural drift felt by many Anglo-Saxon elements.[63]

The federal state, the polity, and Canadians in general failed to construct an overarching national vision that would take into account both French-speaking Quebecer's legitimate aspirations and English-speaking Canada's equally legitimate fears and concerns. At the same time, this failure was exacerbated by the federal government's granting of greater powers to all of the provincial governments. Combined with the election of aggressive new governments in many of the provinces, particularly in the West and Newfoundland, the result was a further denigration of the symbolic and actual powers of the federal state along with a heightening of the quasi-nationalist and regionalist identifications of people residing in these areas. Conflicts increased between the federal and provincial levels of power over political, economic, and social jurisdictions.[64]

Increasingly lacking any real political or economic power, stripped of its symbolic role in uniting the nation state, the federal government faced a crisis of legitimacy.[65] Two events in particular exposed Canada's federal government as a monarch without clothes.

In 1973, the Yom Kippur War, and the subsequent oil crisis created by the Organization of Petroleum Exporting countries (OPEC), brought to a head the long-simmering crisis of western capitalism.[66] Over the next few years, a phenomenon occurred throughout the western industrialized countries that Keynesian economic doctrine had averred was impossible: the simultaneous existence of high inflation *and* high unemployment ('stagflation'). The effect of these political and economic events was the unravelling of the 'post-war Keynesian welfare state consensus.'[67] More than most western countries, however, Canada's ability to deal with the economic crisis was confounded by several unique internal factors. A high level of foreign (especially American) owner-ship, particularly in strategic industries, rendered Canadian govern-ments less able than those of other countries to manage the effects of the economic crisis.[68] The derogation of economic and political power to the provinces further hindered the federal government's ability to manage the economy.[69] In the end, the Canadian federal state was left with responsibility for the increasing debt-load, caused by the reces-sion, while lacking real control over either expenditures or revenues.

The second event that served to reveal the increasing weakness of the federal Liberal government was the election in 1976 of the Parti Québécois. Despite real political power in Ottawa and the implementa-tion of bilingualism, and perhaps because of real economic growth, Quebec increasingly was asserting itself as an independent nation state.

For decades, the Liberal party had portrayed itself as the party that could both manage the economy and bridge the country's historic divi-sions between French and English. It could no longer make either claim. The Liberal party's dominance was ending.

By the late 1970s, however, the New Left was no longer the main challenger to the ruling parties in most liberal democracies. Having pro-moted the expansion of the welfare state, the left was unable to answer criticisms that the state was increasingly remote, costly, and inefficient. Equally, the left was stung by revelations that many 'socialist' models were no more – and often much less – democratic and progressive than liberal democracies.

Finally, the cohesiveness of the left was shattered by internal con-flicts. In the United States, the unravelling began with the Vietnam War. But, as the 1970s progressed, other divisions emerged everywhere between the New Left's feminist, environmentalist, and civil rights wings and the left's traditionally conservative union constituency. In Canada, the left's problems were further exacerbated by the failure of political parties and other social organizations (such as the unions) to transform class, and other objective conditions, into subjective identifications with New Left politics.[70] The result was that the left wing failed to establish during the 1970s and early 1980s a politically marketable counter-hegemony to the faltering hegemony of postwar liberalism.

Instead, the challenge to liberal democracy came from a coalition of right-wing elements, fearful of the emerging economic crisis, sickened by what they viewed as a civic culture dominated by moral laxity and excessive individualism, and resentful of the gains previously made by the New Left. The name given to this right-wing response was 'the New Right,' and its ideology was termed 'neo-conservatism.'

What is neo-conservatism? The literature is fairly consistent in defining it as an amalgam of classical liberal economic and political theory with traditional conservative social and moral doctrine. Specifically, neo-conservatism is said to promote capitalist socio-economic structures and beliefs (the free-market system, individualism, a minimal state, and the private ownership of property) while espousing a belief in natural inequalities and natural authorities (the Christian church, the family, and the state).[71]

In practice, however, the term 'neo-conservatism' is much less precise. For example, the economic policies of both nominally left-wing governments in Australia and New Zealand and right-wing governments in Denmark, the Netherlands, and Germany were fiscally conservative. Equally, while the German variant of neo-conservatism seems to involve a romantic return to Hegelian notions of the role of 'archaic-natural institutions' in regulating society, former British prime minister Margaret Thatcher's version, except when she opposed Britain's further integration into Europe, might more accurately be termed 'neo-liberal.'[72]

Only in the United States, under Ronald Reagan and later George Bush, does the full definition of neo-conservatism as a fusion of liberal economic doctrine with conservative morality seem to hold. Espousing populist rhetoric, Ronald Reagan rode into Washington in 1980 on a promise to get government 'off the backs of the people.' Supporting him was a broad-based coalition of traditional Republicans, Southern Democrats, unionized workers, and disenchanted liberals.[73] Shortly thereafter, Reagan made good on his new 'get tough' approach to public sector unions by smashing the air traffic controllers. Early on, the Reagan administration also began a massive upward redistribution of wealth based on the belief that capital accumulation at the top would eventually result in the 'trickling down' of benefits to the bottom. Social program expenditures, as a percentage of total government expenditures, decreased. Meanwhile, policing and military expenditures escalated, the latter fuelled by an arms race with the Soviet Union.[74]

The actions of the Reagan/Bush administrations, both at home and abroad, were encouraged and supported by 'moral entrepreneurs' such as evangelist Jerry Falwell. Falwell and others in turn were supported by Washington in their attacks on moral permissiveness and their demands for a return to law, order, and traditional values.[75] Often, this espousal of liberal economics and moral conservatism converged, as witness the critique that welfare programs undermine the role of the male breadwinner and thus inadvertently aid in the disintegration of poor families.

Given its conceptual malleability, what are we to make of neo-conservatism? In general, I would suggest that it consists of an uncertain cluster of ideas, varying over time and space, wrapped in a 'tone' of political discourse. At the centre of this discourse is a belief in limits, enforced either through moral edicts or the 'discipline of the market,' in opposition to the 'excesses of democracy' that arose in the 1960s.[76] Specifically, I employ heuristically the term 'neo-conservatism' throughout this text to describe an uneasy coalition of right-wing political interests united in their opposition to modern welfare state liberalism. One measure of how dominant this coalition of interests had become in the United States by the late 1980s was that George Bush's derisive discounting of liberalist discourse as the – presumably unspeakable – '"l" word' during that country's 1988 election went virtually unchallenged. Having crushed and dismembered its principal ideological opponent, neo-conservatism in the United States not only became the ideological basis for the Republicans' winning coalitions between 1980 and 1992, but also shaped and constrained the ideological landscape upon which the Clinton Democrats gained victory in 1992.

Given Canada's geographic proximity and social and economic links to the United States, it is not surprising that political ideas similar to those brought together by the Republicans should also have arisen in Canada during these years. Provincial governments in Manitoba (1977–81) and British Columbia (1982–6) implemented economic and social policies that returned power to the market and reduced government expenditures, while a host of right-wing organizations rose also to promote the economic and social aims of the New Right.[77] Despite this trend, however, neo-conservatism still was only a secondary tributary to the country's hegemonic currents when the Liberal party returned to power in 1980, following the brief interregnum of Joe Clark's Tories.

By then, the twin threats of Quebec separatism and a declining economy, in particular, convinced Trudeau that the traditional bases of Liberal dominance were untenable. The path to Canada's – and the party's – salvation, he believed, lay through a series of constitutional changes that would make the federal government and the courts the guarantor of individual and collective rights, and other policies that would return to the federal government the powers necessary to direct the economy.[78] Above all, the new Canada would be a bilingual, formally egalitarian, and decidedly centralized state.

This change in Liberal policy was not entirely abrupt. After the OPEC crisis of 1973, the federal government had attempted to claw back its power through a series of economic measures, such as the creation of a national oil company, Petro-Canada.[79] On these and various other issues, the Liberals were in continuous combat with many of the provincial governments throughout the 1970s.

Still, the single-mindedness with which Trudeau pursued his objectives after the 1980 election astonished even his most fervent opponents. The patriation of the Constitution in 1982, without Quebec's signature, enraged that province's nationalist element, including most of the provincial Liberal party. Likewise, the implementation of the National Energy Program (NEP) without the agreement of the producing provinces, and affecting primarily the people of the West where the Liberal party had only won two of seventy-seven seats, led to intense political alienation. The result was a hastening of the final collapse of Liberal dominance and the rise to power in 1984 of the Tories under Brian Mulroney.

That year, Mulroney's Tories drew support throughout Canada in winning the election. At the core of their support, however, were Quebec nationalists, big business, and traditional Conservative voters in western Canada, particularly in Alberta and British Columbia. For years, Canada's right wing, particularly in the West, had complained of its exclusion from the corridors of power. Throughout these years, the right wing had waited, confident that the time would come when ideological shifts and economic and political crises would once more return it to the centre of Canada's political life. Now, at last, it seemed its time had come.

Yet, within a couple of years, much of the right wing abandoned Mulroney. Particularly in western Canada, it faulted Mulroney's government for failing to implement the kind of policies enacted in Britain and, more especially, the United States. Indeed, in the eyes of much of the right wing, Mulroney's Tories seemed little better than the hated Liberals: cynical and dishonest spendthrifts, catering to the whims of Quebec and assorted other 'special interests.'[80] In 1987, the fragmentation of Conservative support in the West resulted in the creation of the Reform Party of Canada. Six years later, the latter would act as gleeful pallbearer at the Progressive Conservatives' funeral.

How can this series of events be explained? And what can the rise of the Reform party tell us about the rise of populist parties and movements generally? These questions, and others, lie at the heart of this book.

- What factors, for example, ensured the Reform party's emergence as a right-wing party? Was a left-wing alternative possible?
- What was the influence, in general, of economic factors in creating popular discontent in the West during the 1980s?
- What precisely are the ideological roots of the Reform party? Is Reform merely a northern offshoot of American neo-conservatism?
- What was the structural, ideological, and political relationship between the fringe parties that sprang up in the West during the early 1980s and the Reformers?
- What are the structural locations of Reform party supporters? Why does the party's support appear to be higher in Alberta and British Columbia than in Saskatchewan and Manitoba? Is the Reform party supported by a particular class or elements of a particular class?
- Alternatively, are there aspects of nativism in the Reform party? What other social characteristics underlie Reform party support?
- What was the role of political-institutional and/or organizational factors in the rise of the Reform party? And, finally, what is the likely fate of Reform?

The remaining chapters proceed as follows. Chapter 2 examines the ideological and structural roots of Reform party support in the West, and some of the people and organizations who were instrumental in the party's formation. Chapter 3 examines the causes of western disenchantment with the Progressive Conservatives following that party's victory in 1984, and how this disenchantment led to the creation of the Reform party in 1987.

Chapter 4 deals with Canada's constitutional crisis of 1990 and the recession that began the same year and how these, and other, events were used by the Reform party as a springboard for its becoming a national party. Preston Manning's interpretation of Canadian history is critically examined. The chapter details evidence suggesting that the Reform party possesses strong elements of a peculiarly Anglo-Canadian form of nativism.

Chapter 5 looks at Reform's influence upon the Canadian political scene and examines changes occurring in the party itself since 1987. Profiled also in the chapter are the background and ideological characteristics of Reform's leadership, membership, and supporters, as well as the party's organizational structure and sources of financial support. Finally, Reform's notion of populism, and some of the problems encountered by the party, are also examined.

Chapter 6 examines the momentous events of 1992–3, particularly the Charlottetown referendum, the subsequent resignation of Brian Mulroney, and the federal election of 1993. The chapter concludes with an examination of the problems and potential facing Reform as it begins its role as a major player in the House of Commons. Chapter 7 provides a synopsis of the study's findings, while returning to more general questions regarding populism. In particular, the limitations of both right-wing and left-wing populism at this stage of the twentieth century are examined.

2. The Roots of the Reform Party

... if the Canadian political situation continues to degenerate and if the cause of conservatism continues to suffer and decline ... a whole new political party committed to the social conservative position [will emerge].

Ernest Manning, 1967[1]

Populist parties arise out of an organic crisis and the resultant delegitimation of the dominant hegemony, in general, and of the existing political parties, in particular. This process of delegitimation, however, does not affect all individuals and groups equally or simultaneously. Rather, it affects certain social elements, or their fragments, in ways and under circumstances that are themselves historically determined. Those social elements that have previously remained relatively insulated from dominant ideological messages or whose political, economic, or ideological interests have been abruptly and negatively affected by the organic crisis (that is, vulnerable elements) constitute the basis of later populist parties.

The years leading up to the formation of the Reform party mirror this process of growing alienation by certain social elements from the dominant hegemony and the existing political parties. Particularly alienated were four people whose ideas and long-time efforts would later result in the rise of the Reform party: Francis Winspear, a Victoria millionaire and former bagman for the federal Liberal party; Stanley (Stan) Roberts, a left-of-centre Liberal and former president of the Canada West Foundation; Preston Manning, the technocratic son of a former Alberta Socred premier; and Edward (Ted) Byfield, the colourful, Toronto-born owner/ editor of a controversial right-wing weekly magazine.

This chapter weaves the biographies of these four individuals into an account of the period from the 1960s until the electoral defeat of the federal Liberal party in 1984. Along the way, I examine the political culture of the western provinces, and the events, characters, organizations, and ideas that radicalized many in the region during this period, leading them eventually to seek a political alternative. The chapter begins, however, with a brief historical account of the political cultures of each of the four western provinces.

THE POLITICAL CULTURES OF THE WEST

The West, including British Columbia, entered Confederation late, as 'add-ons' to the existing political system. Apart from this, however, the subsequent development of each province was very different. By 1960, the particular historical, ideological, economic, and political circumstances of each province had created in Manitoba, Saskatchewan, Alberta, and British Columbia distinctive political cultures.[2]

By that time, the radical currents that had carried the Red River Rebellion and Manitoba's entry into Confederation in 1870, and bathed the province in anger during the early farmer protests and in blood during the Winnipeg General Strike of 1919, had been reduced to a slow stream. The development of an increasingly cautious small 'l' liberalism was signalled in the 1920s by a breach within the Progressive party between its Manitoba section and more radical elements centred primarily in Alberta.[3] For many years thereafter, Manitoba's political outlook was shaped, in particular, by three things: a staple-based economy, a strong union presence, and a business community that was never strongly provincial in its outlook. Until 1959, these three factors resulted in provincial politics constantly being pushed towards the centre. When, in that year, the middle ground finally gave way to a rejuvenated Tory party under Duff Roblin, the effect was to reawaken the left-wing in the province.[4]

An NDP government under Ed Schreyer took office in 1969 and held power until 1977 when, in the midst of the recession, the Tories under Sterling Lyon gained power. Lyon's reign, however, was brief. His attempt to introduce certain neo-conservative policies (union and civil service restrictions, cuts in government programs) was opposed massively by the electorate, and in 1981 he was defeated by the NDP.[5]

Like people in the other western provinces, Manitobans have not been entirely immune to reactionary political expression. The Manitoba Schools Question of 1890, the recent bilingualism debate of 1983, and the substantial vote for the anti-bilingual Confederation of Regions (COR) party in the 1984 federal election attest to this. Nonetheless, the diversified political culture of Manitoba has generally prevented extreme right-wing politics from having an unopposed field.

By contrast, the settlement of Alberta and Saskatchewan in the late nineteenth century as extensions of central Canada created very different political cultures. From the start, this quasi-colonial status instilled a deep resentment among the region's inhabitants, a hostility that did not subside with the granting of provincial status to the two in 1905. If anything, a sense of eastern persecution became more ingrained in each province's collective psyche. This sense of persecution was reinforced by some real injustices, such as the federal government's keeping control of their natural resources until 1930. But the West's hinterland economy, exposed to sometimes disastrous cyclical fluctuations in world commodity prices, also kindled imaginary injustices for which central Canada was blamed. By the 1920s, a sense of alienation from the central government had become part of western consciousness, informing the broader political culture of the West and facilitating the proliferation of anti-establishment parties and movements. The United Farmers of Alberta won election in 1921. In the federal election of that same year, the Progressives took sixty-five seats, thirty-eight in the wheat-growing areas of the West, in finishing second to Mackenzie King's victorious Liberals. The following year, the United Farmers of Manitoba also won provincial office. These farmers' parties, particularly elements in Alberta, later spawned two further parties, the semi-agrarian Social Credit and the CCF parties.

The emergence of the latter two populist parties in the 1930s has presented scholars with something of a dilemma ever since. Debate has particularly raged over why two such apparently different populist movements – the right-wing Social Credit party in Alberta and the left-wing CCF in Saskatchewan – could have arisen in provinces contiguous in geography and ostensibly similar in their economies and population.

C.B. Macpherson suggests that Social Credit in Alberta arose out of its primarily petit bourgeois class structure and a general history of one-party rule.[6] By contrast, both Seymour M. Lipset and John Richards contend that the CCF in Saskatchewan was the product of a broad-based coalition of agrarians, socialists, and labourites with strong roots in local cooperative organizations.[7] Others, however, suggest that the idea of a direct break between Alberta's and Saskatchewan's political cultures is in fact overstated.[8] In particular, M. Johnson contends that the failure of Alberta to elect the CCF in that province was merely an 'accident of history.'[9] Similarly, Finkel has recently shown that, at least initially, both the CCF in Saskatchewan and Social Credit in Alberta were fundamentally left-wing parties, and that the later divergence resulted primarily from the Social Credit leadership of Ernest Manning.[10]

There is an element of insight in each of these contentions. Despite recent work suggesting the contrary, class differences (and fractures within classes) may well have underlain (and subsequently been reinforced by) the provinces' different political trajectories.[11] But the role of organization, leadership, and ideology in alliance construction must also be considered. Finally, previous studies have perhaps given insufficient credit to the particular role played by Calgary's political and economic élites in shaping the political cultures of both provinces.

Howard and Tamara Palmer note that, around 1905, '[t]he economic and cultural presence of Anglo-Canadian and British ranchers and professionals and the CPR contributed to Calgary's [voting] Conservative.' The conservative (and Conservative) strain was to last for years, culminating in Calgary lawyer R.B. Bennett's becoming the national Tory leader in 1927.[12] By this time, however, a new element had been added to Calgary's political mix. Immigrants from the United States began arriving in southern Alberta, carrying with them populist ideas of direct democracy while simultaneously blunting the anti-Americanism latent in the previous Tory culture. The resultant amalgam of differing ideological impulses led, in subsequent years, to Calgary's being the mainspring for such diverse populist movements as the Non-Partisan League, the Progressives, the CCF, and Social Credit.

Whatever left-wing tendencies the city's political culture had began to change, however, following the election of Social Credit in 1935. In 1943, premier William Aberhart died and was succeeded by a devout follower, Ernest Manning, who even more fervently preached a linkage between religious fundamentalism and right-wing free enterprise. The oil boom, which occurred shortly thereafter, further reinforced the political acceptability of Manning's ideology. Moreover, the boom also brought the considerable influence of the largely American-owned oil and gas industry to bear upon Alberta's political culture. Nowhere was this more the case than in Calgary. Note Palmer and Palmer:

The relatively few Americans who came to Alberta in the postwar era had a notable social and political impact. In the early years of the boom, a majority of the senior management of the major oil companies ... were from California, Oklahoma, Texas, and Louisiana. From 1955 to 1970, nine of the fifteen presidents of Calgary's exclusive Petroleum club were Americans.... Like their counterparts in the United States, they often held strong right-wing views.[13]

In short, the American-owned oil and gas industry held considerable influence in Calgary.

By the 1970s, Calgary's skyline was dominated by the head offices of the oil and gas sector while the city's political culture was dominated by a strictly free-enterprise ethos.[14] This ethos, and the powerful role increasingly played by Calgary's corporate sector in the economic and political affairs of the province during the repeated oil-crisis years of the 1970s, further reinforced Alberta's right-wing political culture. It is not accidental, therefore, that many of the right-wing think-tanks, lobby groups, and parties that formed in the 1970s and 1980s had strong connections to the city of Calgary and its oil and gas industry.

As the years passed, Social Credit's blend of petit bourgeois conservatism (limited government involvement, limited distribution of wealth, and a heavy reliance on the private sector), combined with Manning's particularly severe fundamentalist Christian belief in individual struggle as the route to salvation, became entrenched in Alberta's political culture.[15] Even after Social Credit was replaced by Peter Lougheed's Tories in 1971, and despite the fact that Alberta's demographic profile was increasingly diverging from its Anglo-Saxon and Protestant roots, this style of political thinking remained a haven to which future governments could, and did, return when economic times grew hard in the 1980s and again in the early 1990s.[16]

During this period, Saskatchewan's political culture took a different turn. In 1944, the CCF gained power. During its next twenty years in power, governing a chronically 'have-not' province, the party displayed a remarkable capacity for fiscal management and political savvy. Along the way, it managed also to institute North America's first public health care insurance program and was responsible for some of the most progressive labour legislation in the country, while simultaneously displaying a pragmatism that won approval from the province's electorate.[17]

It would be wrong, however, to suggest that social democratic ideals had free reign in Saskatchewan. During its time in power, the CCF faced frequent and intense opposition. Highlighting this conflict was the CCF's controversial implementation of provincial medicare in 1962. Finally, however, in 1964, the CCF/NDP went down to defeat at the hands of the reorganized Liberals led by Ross Thatcher.[18]

Thatcher had once been a member of the CCF, winning his seat in three consecutive provincial elections, beginning in 1945, before leaving the party in 1955. Described by historian J.A. Lower as 'primarily a businessman and a "free enterpriser,"' Thatcher subsequently joined the Liberal party and became its leader in 1959.[19] The years of Thatcher's government (1964–71) presaged, in some respects, the style of fiscal conservatism practised by other Prairie governments over the next two decades – opposition to the welfare state and unions, combined with an extreme faith in free enterprise.

Despite Thatcher's rhetoric, however, his government made no serious attempt to dismantle the the the CCF's social programs.[20] Similarly, the years of Liberal reign did not fundamentally move Saskatchewan's political culture towards outright acceptance of right-wing solutions. In 1971, widespread discontent with Liberal resource and agricultural policies resulted in the NDP's return to power under Allan Blakeney.[21] The NDP remained in power for the next eleven years until, in the midst of the recession of the early 1980s, the electorate turned to Grant Devine's Tories. Nonetheless, the roots of a kind of 'commonsensical' left-wing opposition remained deep in the political culture of Saskatchewan, as shown in 1991 by the overwhelming election of an NDP government led by Roy Romanow.

By the 1960s, a very different political culture had formed in British Columbia. From the time British Columbia decided to become a province of Canada in 1871, it was a thriving, very British colony, economically wealthy but dependent on its natural resources, and isolated geographically from the rest of Canada by the Rocky Mountains. In the years that followed, the almost hermetically sealed province developed a political culture marked by an absence of moderation and by intense social and political conflict, particularly between workers and owners. That political conflict between the left and the right, which had long been like two scorpions trapped inside a glass jar, intensified after 1952.

In that year, BC's Socreds came to power. The party was almost solely created by W.A.C. ('Wacky') Bennett, a prominent Tory during the 1940s, as a coalition of the right designed to prevent a victory by the CCF. In the years that followed, Bennett systematically reinforced the already polarized nature of BC politics by regularly warning of the 'socialist threat.'

Like those of Manning's Socreds, Bennett's policies emphasized balancing the budget and creating a favourable climate for private enterprise, while limiting the powers of labour and resisting any real redistribution of wealth. Unlike Manning and Aberhart, however, Bennett (a devout Presbyterian) and his government (many members of which had equally strong religious views) generally did not confuse religion and politics. In some respects, Bennett may also have been more pragmatic than his more ideological counterparts in Alberta, although too much should not be made of this. In a pinch, both Socred governments showed a willingness to abandon ideological purity, as witnessed by Manning's creation of the Alberta Gas Trunk Line Company in 1954 and Bennett's placing of BC Electric under public ownership in 1961.[22] In at least one respect, however, Bennett and Manning were certainly in agreement. By the 1960s, each had developed a profound dislike of bilingualism and the 'socialist' economic policies that they saw emanating from Ottawa.

Bennett's dislike of socialism was not confined to policies on the federal scene. In the midst of the 1972 provincial election, Bennett issued dire warnings that the 'socialist hordes' also were at the province's gates. The warnings failed, however, to sway the voters sufficiently. Bennett's right coalition split, and the NDP led by Dave Barrett, a former social worker, formed BC's first socialist government. But, in 1975, Social Credit rebounded under Bennett's son, Bill Bennett Jr, to win a majority government.[23] The way was thus paved for the test of neo-conservative policies that would follow in the early 1980s, to which I will return later.

In summary, by 1960 each of the western provinces had developed a unique political culture through which socio-economic-political problems were filtered in search of solutions. While Manitoba and Saskatchewan politics were moderate or even mildly left-wing, eschewing radically ideological formulations, British Columbia's politics had become heavily partisan and dominated by the right wing. In Alberta, politics had become dominated by Social Credit's religiously informed free enterprise ethos, heavily influenced by the largely American-owned oil and gas industry. What Dorothy Parker once acerbically remarked about the acting ability of a certain starlet – that it ran the full gamut from a to b – increasingly became applicable to political discourse in Alberta.

Even as the right wing remained dominant in the West's two 'have' provinces (Alberta and British Columbia), however, its ideas became increasingly isolated from the dominant hegemony emerging in Canada after the Second World War. Sensing its increasing weakness, the right wing in the 1960s began to try to regain the ideological and political terrain. Not surprisingly, the impetus for these attempts came from the two Socred provinces.

THE MANNINGS AND SOCIAL CONSERVATISM

By the 1960s both W.A.C. Bennett and Ernest Manning had become increasingly concerned that Canada was threatened by economic and moral ruin, and that only radical political reform could avert disaster.[24] They were especially concerned by what they saw as the socialist policies, such as medicare, emanating from Ottawa.

Particularly disheartening for Manning was the fact that, while he was convinced that Social Credit policies could save the nation, the national Social Credit party was itself in disarray. In 1963, the party disintegrated into two factions, one headed by Réal Caouette, the Quebec leader, the other led by Robert Thompson from Alberta. In light of the seeming political impotence of the national party, Manning proposed at the 1964 Social Credit convention that there should be a political realignment of the right in order to defeat the forces of 'socialism.'[25] The result of this realignment would be a new political force combining free enterprise with social concern, which Manning termed 'social conservatism.' In the years that followed, Ernest Manning continued to investigate the possibilities of implementing this idea. In his effort, Manning was helped by his son, Preston.[26]

Ernest Preston Manning was born on 10 June 1942, a year before his father became premier of Alberta. His first few years were spent in the Garneau area of Edmonton, and the family moved when he was in grade six to a 900-acre farm northeast of the city. There, looked after by housekeepers and nannies, Preston Manning lived a life sheltered from much of the political atmosphere that went with his father's position. He was raised a devout Baptist, and religion remains an important aspect of his life.

After completing high school, Manning returned to Edmonton in

1960 to attend the University of Alberta, where he began pursuing a career in physics. During the summer of 1962, however, his father's political contacts secured a job for Preston working for a Californian division of Canadian Bechtel. The experience led Manning to switch from physics to economics, the field from which he eventually graduated with a BA in 1964.

In 1965, Manning ran as the federal Social Credit candidate in Edmonton East, finishing second (with 6752 votes) to the Progressive Conservative candidate, William Skoreyko (13,596 votes). During the election, Manning came to know David Wilson, a former fundraiser and strategist for the Social Credit party. Wilson recently had been named director of a newly formed organization known as the National Public Affairs Research Foundation (NPARF). Manning was soon hired as (in his words) a 'policy researcher.'

What was the NPARF? Manning himself has variously described the organization as 'a private research foundation engaged in public policy studies'[27] and as a 'foundation ... organized by a number of business people ... interested in developing policy ideas that might be useful to both the Alberta Social Credit Party and the federal Progressive Conservative Party.'[28] A report by columnist Don Sellar in the *Calgary Herald* on 21 July 1967 described the NPARF as a somewhat secretive, staunchly right-wing, lobby group funded by several prominent businessmen, including R.A. Brown, president of Home Oil, Cyrus McLean, chairman of B.C. Telephone, Renault St Laurent, lawyer and son of the former prime minister, Ronald Clarke, an Edmonton architect, R.J. Burns, a Calgary lawyer, and A.M. Shoults, president of James Lovick Ltd. of Toronto, all of whom were close friends of the elder Manning.[29]

Working out of the foundation's small downtown Edmonton office building, Preston Manning was involved with three projects.[30] The first involved assisting a friend and university colleague, Erick Schmidt, to put together *A White Paper on Human Resources Development* for the Socred government. The paper was presented to the legislature in the spring of 1967.

Historian Alvin Finkel has described the language of the *White Paper* as 'turgid, technocratic, and secular' and its author (Manning) as a 'systems-analysis devotee.'[31] Manning would likely agree with the latter description.[32] Read today, it is equally hard to disagree with the description of the text's writing. What is perhaps most striking about the *White Paper*, however, is the list of value judgments explicitly stated early on:

- Human resources will be treated as being intrinsically more important than physical resources.
- Prior consideration will be given to human beings individually (persons), rather than to human beings collectively (society).
- Changes and adjustments to changes will be proposed, but these will always be related to fundamental principles.
- A free enterprise economy, in which all individuals have maximum opportunity to participate, will be regarded as more desirable than a state regimented economy.
- A supporting function, rather than a domineering function, will be ascribed to the state relative to resources development.[33]

In short, the *White Paper* advocated a principled but humane society, based on free enterprise, in which individuals are given priority over collectivities and where the role of government is kept to a minimum. These same values lie at the heart of Preston Manning's political judgments even today.

Manning's second project with the NPARF was 'an investigation of the possibility of putting together the aging Social Credit Party of Alberta ... with the up-and-coming Progressive Conservative Party of Alberta under its new leader, Peter Lougheed.'[34] Erick Schmidt and Preston Manning met with Lougheed's group, represented by Joe Clark and Merv Leitch (later energy minister in the Lougheed cabinet), on several occasions, and eventually produced a draft plan for amalgamating the two parties under the banner of the Social Conservative party. The idea was quickly rejected, however, by officials both within the Manning government and the Lougheed camp.[35]

Nonetheless, the idea of a realignment of right-wing forces stayed with the Mannings, and resulted in Preston's third project with the NPARF: assisting his father in writing *Political Realignment: A Challenge to Thoughtful Canadians*.[36] The book, written in the same style as the *White Paper*, expressed Ernest Manning's contention that real political choice had disappeared from the federal Canadian scene because the parties – particularly the Liberals and the Progressive Conservatives – were not ideologically distinct. Hence, Ernest Manning proposed that political choice be re-established through a realignment/polarization of political thinking and organization. The end product of such a political realignment would be social conservatism, an ideology that Manning defined as welding 'the humanitarian concerns of those with awakened social consciences to the economic persuasions of those with a firm conviction in the value of freedom of economic activity and enlightened private enterprise.'[37]

And what party could bring about a realignment that would enunciate the social conservatism? After a brief discussion of the limitations of all of the existing parties, Manning hesitantly placed his faith in the Progressive Conservative party, noting somewhat prophetically, however, that 'if the Canadian political situation continues to degenerate, and if the cause of conservatism continues to suffer and decline ... a whole new political party committed to the social conservative position [will] emerge.'[38]

Political Realignment was not entirely a set of philosophical musings. In 1967 the federal Conservatives were about to choose a new leader. Ernest Manning was under some pressure from Conservative supporters in the West and Ontario to enter the race.[39] The book therefore can be seen as a political stratagem employed by Manning who had let it be known that, although he was not formally entering the race, he was open to a draft by the party delegates.

After *Political Realignment* appeared, Preston Manning and Erick Schmidt attended both the Progressive Conservative's Thinkers' Conference held in Montmorency, Quebec, in August, and the Conservative party convention held a month later. Their attendance at these meeting appears to have been designed to test both Ernest's support and support for the more general idea of political realignment.[40] In the end, however, neither a draft nor realignment came about. The Tories chose Robert Stanfield, former Nova Scotia premier and heir to the woollen dynasty, as leader.

In the fall of 1967 Preston Manning took a leave of absence from the NPARF to work for TRW Systems of Redondo Beach, California, a company 'heavily involved in systems development for the U.S. defence and aerospace programs.'[41] He apparently never returned to the NPARF, which continued its work as a research-cum-lobby group until its dissolution in December 1973.

In 1968 Ernest Manning stepped down as premier. The elder Manning's resignation raised the immediate problem of succession. A number of Young Socreds at the University of Alberta, including Owen Anderson and Erick Schmidt, attempted to persuade Preston Manning to contest the leadership. Despite his youth and inexperience, the younger Manning had several attributes that might have been found attractive to a party increasingly perceived by the public as out of step with the times and hard-pressed by the opposition Tories headed by the youthful Peter Lougheed. In John Barr's words:

Fair and slight, like his father, on the platform [Preston] was transformed into an even better speaker than his father – he had the Manning voice and technique of marshalling his arguments, but more forcefulness. More important, he was young ... and a prolific generator of ideas. A brilliant student in high school, he was slightly less conservative than his father ideologically, and brought to his study of politics a real gift for synthesizing ideas and searching out new interfaces between intellectual disciplines.[42]

As an insider and unofficial chronicler of the Socred dynasty, Barr's description of Preston Manning may be somewhat biased. Nonetheless, it is apparent that many people saw the younger Manning, from an early age, as an individual with unique qualities for leadership.

In the end, however, Preston's name was never put before the delegates. Approached by the members of the Young Socreds, the elder Manning suggested that, although Preston had many good qualities, he was still too young and politically inexperienced to control a cabinet. Moreover, Ernest feared the accusation of a Manning 'dynasty.' Ernest hinted that a better successor would be Harry Strom. Strom won the subsequent leadership convention on the second ballot.[43]

Strom was a wealthy, fifty-two-year-old farmer from southern Alberta. His reputation as a religious (Evangelical Free Church) family man appealed to the older members of the party, while his moderate approach to social issues and receptivity to new ideas won support from its younger members.[44] Outside the party, however, Strom was viewed as colourless and ineffectual. Compared with the resurgent Tories under a young Peter Lougheed, Social Credit as a whole seemed a tired party. As a result, the Socreds were defeated in the election of 1971 by the Tories.[45]

Following the election, Strom resigned and was replaced as Socred leader by Werner Schmidt, an 'educational administrator whose religiosity and reactionary views endeared him to the Manning generation of Social Creditors.'[46] The 1975 Alberta election saw the Socreds decimated, taking only 18 per cent of the popular vote. Schmidt resigned and was replaced by Bob Clark, a popular and moderate MLA from Olds-Didsbury, but the die was cast. In the subsequent 1979 election, Social Credit won only four of the province's seventy-nine legislative seats. Symbolically, the Camrose radio station, CFCN – the station on which Aberhart had begun broadcasting 'The Back to the Bible Hour' in 1925 – announced in September of the same year that it was dumping the show because of low ratings.[47]

As its support declined, Social Credit in Alberta increasingly became a refuge for right-wing 'fringe' elements. The party's nadir occurred in 1983 when its provincial vice-president, Jim Keegstra, was found guilty on charges of spreading hatred against Jews.[48] By the early 1980s, Social Credit remained a power only in British Columbia.

Social conservatism, the refurbished Socred vehicle by which the Mannings had hoped to save Canada, had by then become a seemingly dead issue. By the 1970s, however, another element had re-emerged to vie for prominence in the political mix of the West: regionalism.

THE REBIRTH OF REGIONALISM

Regional alienation, of course, has always been an underlying thread in the West's political culture. From the earliest days, westerners often expressed anger over their perceived colonial status. The push for provincial status towards the end of the last century expressed the desire of westerners to escape colonialism. During the 1930s, regional alienation even resulted in the formation of separatist parties.[49] Clearly, also, regional alienation underlay many of the grievances expressed by the Progressive, Social Credit, and CCF parties.

As sociologist Janine Brodie has pointed out, however, regionalism is a social-psychological concept affixed, with varying degrees of intensity, to a concept of region which itself moves over time and space.[50] In the West, by the early 1960s, the concept of region had been replaced by the political concept of provinces while the degree of intensity associated with regional strains had been merged into other sources of conflict. Hence, Ernest Manning's opposition to federal policies was based more on ideology than regionalism.[51] Likewise, in Saskatchewan the schism between Thatcher's Liberals and the Liberal government in Ottawa redounded more to ideological differences and electoral strategy than to regional alienation.[52] In Manitoba, meanwhile, regionalism had been contained, at least in part, by the identification of much of that province's ruling class with its eastern counterparts.[53] Perhaps only in British Columbia, isolated by geography and affluent but economically insecure, was there a strong sense of regional 'difference' before 1970. Yet, even here, the political value of regionalism was minor insofar as everyone recognized and accepted the province's 'eccentricity.'

While regionalist sentiments may lie dormant for a time, however, they do not necessarily disappear. Rather, regionalism and regional protests develop out of a cumulative process as 'new symbols, forms, and tensions are layered onto older ones.'[54] Throughout the 1960s, transformations in western Canada's economic, political, and ideological spheres, combined with increasing conflicts with Ottawa, resulted in a strengthening of regionalist identifications.[55] In Alberta, in particular, the coming to power of Harry Strom coincided with the demands of that province's rising indigenous bourgeoisie, centred in the oil and gas industry, for a release from the domination of central Canada.[56]

In his opening address to the federal-provincial constitutional conference in 1969, Strom noted approvingly the role of French Quebecers in bringing to public attention their sense of inequality and injustice: 'We welcome the resurgent spirit and consciousness of our French-speaking citizens, and their understandable desire for a new cultural and economic role in Confederation.' But, he went on to say:

We must recognize the deep feelings of alienation and inequality of treatment that are felt by regional groups in Canada which are neither of French extraction, French-speaking, or resident in the province of Quebec. These feelings may not be cultural in nature, but could prove to be just as dangerous to Confederation as friction between the English and the French cultures.[57]

In short, Strom, no doubt influenced by Alberta's Young Socreds who included Preston Manning, warned the central Canadian political establishment of becoming too preoccupied with Quebec's needs while forgetting those of the other regions, particularly the West.

If Strom's warning was dismissed, the publication in 1971 of *The Unfinished Revolt: Some Views on Western Independence*, a collection of essays edited by two prominent Alberta Social Credit supporters, Owen Anderson and John Barr, hammered it home.[58] In lucid and comprehensive fashion, their book put into words the regional resentments and sense of alienation felt by many westerners. But the book also went beyond traditional gripes concerning tariffs, freight rates, and the price of wheat – although economic arguments remained a big part of it – to extend its critique to a largely central Canadian–based cultural and communications establishment.

As Strom had noted, the rise of quasi-nationalism in the West had its mirror, and at least some of its impetus, in events transpiring in Quebec.[59] The Quiet Revolution had resulted in a renewed sense of that province's sense of cultural identity, leading to popular demands for a reconfiguration of Canada's political and symbolic structure by Pearson's federal government.

While Quebec continued to 'find itself,' however, English-speaking Canada remained trapped between its receding British past and the seemingly irresistable force of American assimilation. The efforts of the Pearson and Trudeau governments to create a pan-Canadianism (through a new flag, implementing bilingualism and multiculturalism) not only failed to win the hearts of Quebecers but angered many English-speaking Canadians, particularly in the West, who were disturbed by the changes in the region's traditional 'symbolic order.'[60]

The resultant anger, and demands for recognition and respect of the West's own identity and culture, went hand in hand with the election of new parties to office in Manitoba (1969), Alberta (1971), and Saskatchewan (1971) during this period. These governments increasingly engaged in 'province-building' policies, through demands for equal political status with the federal government in areas involving foreign trade, and through direct intervention in the economy, particularly in creating growth through mega-projects.[61] They also demanded from the Liberal government increased powers over economic and social programs. Eager to re-establish the equality of all the provinces in the face of Quebec's increasing autonomy, the Liberals acceded to these demands.[62]

Often, however, there remained an entanglement of federal and provincial jurisdictions, objectives, and economic costs. The result was ongoing conflict between the federal and provincial governments. The effects of this conflict were not confined to the political classes, but spilled over into the general public and the western business class, many of whom began to withdraw support from the federal Liberal party. Why did this occur? A brief discussion of the reasons for this change follows.

THE BUSINESS CLASS IN WESTERN CANADA

During the early years of Confederation, the Conservatives were Canada's party of big business and privilege. By contrast, the early Liberals were a mix of agrarian populism and some sections of big business. The Liberal party's ties with big business began to increase, however, during Canada's industrialization, reaching a kind of critical mass with the advent of the Second World War. By this time, Mackenzie King had made what conservative historian George Grant once termed his 'great discovery': If the Liberals were a friend of business, they could remain in power indefinitely.[63] Henceforth, the Liberal party, and King's chief lieutenant, C.D. Howe, overtly pursued an expansion of corporate interests through continentalism. In return for political support, the Liberal party offered business in Canada a relatively peaceful and non-interventionist business environment. During the 1960s, however, many businessmen in western Canada began to turn against the federal Liberal party.

Several factors explain their withdrawal of support. First, the party's pursuit of liberalized trade, particularly with the United States, was not wholehearted enough for many business people in the West. As an underdeveloped, primary-resource region, the West had always relied on external capital and external markets. Tariffs and other policies enacted by the federal government were viewed by western businessmen and politicians as hindering the region's development in the name of protecting the inefficient manufacturing industries of central Canada. As a result, many western businessmen became increasingly supportive of the province-building efforts of their local governments.[64]

A second reason for increased western business hostility to the Liberals came more predominantly from the established, largely Anglo-Saxon élites, which viewed with alarm the cultural-political changes occurring in the country.[65] The adoption of a new flag in 1965 and the implementation of official bilingualism, combined with the apparent rise of francophone power in Ottawa, particularly signalled a radical change in Canada's symbolic order. Indeed, James Richardson, a millionaire and scion of a prominent Winnipeg family, even resigned from the cabinet in 1976, complaining of the 'Gallicization' of the country.

The main concern of many conservative businessmen in the West, however, was the growth of the welfare state and, more generally, what they perceived as socialism. Increasingly, business began to speak its concerns to the political community.

We have already seen some evidence of the links between business and Social Credit through the National Public Affairs Research Foundation (NPARF). Alfred Hooke, a long-time Alberta Socred MLA and personal friend of Ernest Manning, relates the following story:

On at least two occasions Mr. Manning told me in his office that he had been approached by several very influential and wealthy Canadians and that they wanted him to head up a party of the right with a view to preventing the onslaught of socialism these men could see developing in Canada. They apparently had indicated to him that money was no object and they were prepared to spend any amounts necessary to stop the socialist tide.[66]

Ernest Manning, of course, declined the offer, opting instead to press for the vision of 'political realignment' described in his book and pushed by his son in discussions with people in the Progressive Conservative party. For his part, Hooke never discovered the names of the 'influential and wealthy Canadians' but continued to believe years later that they were associated with the NPARF.[67]

Still, on the whole, western businessmen remained generally supportive of the Liberal party throughout the 1950s and 1960s. This began to change, however, with the coming to power of Pierre Elliott Trudeau.

Trudeau came from a 'suspicious' background. Many claimed that he was a socialist before joining the party in 1965. His rapid ascension thereafter to the Liberal leadership in 1968 made many long-time Pearson Liberals uneasy, especially as he had previously been a vociferous opponent of the Liberal party. Nor was the belief that Trudeau was an extreme left-winger particularly assuaged by his appointment to his first cabinet of such strong business supporters as Paul Hellyer, Paul Martin Sr, and John Turner, or (equally) his refusal to appoint Walter Gordon, an economic nationalist. This mistrust was seemingly vindicated by 1971 when both Eric Kierans and Paul Hellyer resigned over disputes with Trudeau. (Hellyer's break was particularly dramatic, and in 1976 he ran for the leadership of the federal Tories, losing to Joe Clark.)

Despite these harbingers, however, the first few years of Trudeau's reign saw the Liberals continue their traditional support of free enterprise and the business community. Two events changed this. The first was the election of 1972. Though re-elected, the Liberal party had fallen to minority status. The Liberals continuance in power depended upon the support of at least one of the other parties. Over the next two years, the NDP under David Lewis supported the Liberal party.

This support, however, was conditional. In return for 'propping up' the Liberal government in the House of Commons, the NDP pushed for policies of increased nationalization or, at least, Canadianization of the economy. The result was the creation of the Canada Development Corporation (CDC) and the Foreign Investment Review Agency (FIRA), the first designed to assist Canadianization, the second to ensure that foreign investment benefited Canadians.[68] NDP pressure was also instrumental in the formation of a government-owned oil company,

Petro-Canada, and the implementation of a tax on oil exported to the United States.[69] In truth, however, the NDP did not have to push some Liberals very hard. Many Liberals, such as Herb Gray, whose report decrying the level of foreign investment in Canada came out in 1972, had already become convinced of the need for a more active role by government in the Canadian economy.

The second event that altered the Liberal government's thinking was the OPEC crisis of 1973. The crisis revealed in dramatic fashion the vulnerability of the Canadian economy to foreign events. Despite Canada's relatively high standard of living, its economy remained resource-dependent, heavily foreign-owned, and overly tied to the American economy.[70] Moreover, since the provinces owned their resources, the federal government was unable to institute a national economic strategy for recovery, as had Germany and Japan after the Second World War. In short, the federal government lacked an effective means of managing the Canadian economy.

In September 1973, with the rapid rise in world oil prices following the Yom Kippur war, the Liberal government made its first major postwar foray into the economy. As was frequently to prove the case, this intervention involved the oil and gas sector and the economies of the western provinces. The federal Liberals froze the price of Canadian domestic crude at four dollars per barrel. Subsequently, the Liberals also announced an export tax on the differential between the domestic and the world price on all oil shipped to the United States in order to subsidize the costs of fuel imported into Quebec and Atlantic Canada.[71] The moves were immediately denounced by American officials, the premiers of the oil-producing provinces (the PC's Lougheed in Alberta and the NDP's Blakeney in Saskatchewan), and the private oil companies.

The Liberal government, however, had widespread support among the consuming public for taking measures that were presumed to ensure protection against future oil crises. Under pressure once more from the NDP, and propelled by nationalists such as Gray within the cabinet, Trudeau announced in December 1973 the creation of a single Canadian market for oil, completion of an oil pipeline to Montreal, intensified research into oil-sands development, and the creation of a publicly owned petroleum company, later to be called Petro-Canada.[72]

Trudeau's minority Liberal government fell in the spring of 1974, before many of these policies could be enacted. A few months later Trudeau was returned to power with a majority government. Many expected that, unencumbered by NDP demands, the Liberal government would now revert to its pre-1972 stance of minimal intervention in the economy. But such was not the case.

Instead the Liberals implemented wage and price controls in an attempt to control inflation.[73] The implementation of controls – which the Liberals had campaigned against during the election – soured both labour and business against the government. The Liberals also proceeded with their plans to create Petro-Canada.[74] Then, in an end-of-1975 interview, broadcast on CTV, Trudeau publicly mused that the free market was no longer working and that government might have to take a larger role in managing the economy. His remarks, in journalist Christine McCall-Newman's words, sent 'the business community into a mild hysteria and [caused] a flight of investment capital.'[75]

The economy continued to fail. In Canada, as elsewhere during the 1970s, the Keynesian consensus fell apart, the victim of a seeming impossibility – the simultaneous occurrence of both high prices and high unemployment. Economists coined the term 'stagflation' to describe the condition, and it rapidly became part of the public vocabulary.

As the economic crisis proceeded, Canada's liberal welfare state found itself caught between an increasing demand for services and a decreasing capacity to fund them. Then, in 1979, the Iranian revolution occurred. Once again, the volatility of world oil and gas prices played havoc with international economies. In Canada, the resource-producing provinces of the West were once more pitted against the industrial heartland of central Canada. A massive transfer of jobs, capital, and – ultimately – political power to the West seemed inevitable.

The costs of cushioning this social dislocation fell to the federal government, which had entered into a series of contractual and moral obligations (such as unemployment insurance) since the Second World War. At the same time, the Canadian government had limited means, primarily taxation and tariffs, of increasing its revenues to meet these costs. Jean Chrétien, who was minister of finance from September 1977 until June 1979, would later remark: 'so much federal money had to be passed on automatically under the federal-provincial arrangements that Ottawa lost effective control over its deficit.'[76]

Chrétien's statement, while partially correct, does not entirely absolve successive Liberal governments. It is true that any explanation for the rise in the public debt must consider, among other things, federal commitments, the role of various levels of government, the demands of special interest groups, the destabilizing effect of recurrent recessions, and Canada's economic relations with the outside world, in particular the United States. Nonetheless, the Liberals also continued to create new public programs and agencies throughout the 1970s, often with apparently little long-term regard for the balance sheet.

The end of the Second World War saw Canada faced with a massive gross federal debt (GFD), larger than the country's entire gross domestic product (GDP). Over the subsequent decades, however, Canada had gradually decreased its debt. In 1977, the ratio of gross federal debt to gross domestic product hit its postwar low of 35.8 per cent (nearly $113 billion).

Thereafter, however, the ratio of GFD to GDP began to rise. By 1980 the gross federal debt, in constant dollars, had risen to $140 billion and was once again consuming 41 per cent of Canada's gross national product.[77] Although the economy was still expanding relative to overall expenditures, the Liberals viewed the overall trend of the last few years as ominous.

Rising with the federal debt was apprehension in the business community over how Trudeau Liberals planned to deal with the fiscal crisis. Business people had already been shaken by a series of resignations from the Liberal cabinet of people they respected (notably James Richardson and John Turner). Trudeau's remarks in 1975 concerning the failure of the free market system had only intensified the fears of private business. By the time of the 1980 election, the business community was viewing even more nervously Trudeau's 'vigorous speeches promising an industrial strategy and a more interventionist approach to the auto industry, to foreign investment, and, above all, to energy self-sufficiency.'[78] Added to this concern was increased consternation among some in the largely Anglo-Saxon business community with the increased power of francophones in Ottawa. McCall-Newman describes this loss of private business support, as seen through the eyes of John Turner:

Trudeau had wrecked the Liberals' old alliance with business. The English-Canadian ministers who had any serious connections with that world had left his cabinet ... the only businessmen left ... were ... from the small-business world ... [Moreover] Trudeau had alienated the West, ignoring its new economic power, so much so that nobody out there of much stature businesswise would think of becoming a Liberal.[79]

One of the western businesspeople who withdrew support from the Liberals was Dr Francis Winspear.[80]

Francis G. Winspear was born in Birmingham, England, on 30 May 1903. The family moved to Canada in 1910 and settled in the small town of Namaka, forty miles east of Calgary. The family lived there until 1919. Winspear later attended school in Calgary, then worked in a bank for four years before articling in accountancy with George A. Touche. He subsequently joined Peat, Marwick, Mitchell and Co., managing their Edmonton office for two years.

In 1930, Winspear started his own accounting firm which eventually expanded to twenty-six offices across Canada. The same year, he became a sessional instructor at the School of Commerce at the University of Alberta. In 1951, he received an honorary doctor of laws from the same institution, and was director of the school in 1954.

Winspear is past president of both the Edmonton and Canadian chambers of commerce, former chairman of the Rhodes Scholarship Committee of Alberta, and a past member of the Economic Council of Canada. In 1967, he was named an officer of the Order of Canada. In 1982, the Faculty of Business at the University of Alberta gave him the Canadian Business Leader Award. The same university also named Winspear professor emeritus in 1983.

He is also a millionaire and a noted philanthropist. Besides his accounting firms, Winspear at various times has owned major interests in such companies as Northwest Industries, Swanson Lumber, Premier Steel, and Gormans Ltd. Over the years, he has been generous in giving money to the University of Alberta (over a million dollars) and various arts organizations, such as the Edmonton Symphony.

In short, Dr Winspear is a kind of 'elder statesman' among the western business class, a man who could write with ease in 1969 that '[c]apitalism is a modern phenomenon [the] characteristics [of which] are often misunderstood, particularly by those not active in the business world.' At the time, he might well have been speaking for many in the business establishment regarding their view of the Liberals in adding that '[t]here are those, *among them politicians* who lust for power, who speak of predatory, selfish businessmen.'[81]

He had, perhaps, not always been as cynical of politicians. A lifelong Liberal, he had once even been a self-admitted 'bag man' for the party under Pearson.[82] Even then, however, it seems that disillusionment with that party was setting in, as evidenced by Winspear's remark at the Western Assembly in Vancouver in 1987 (which led to the founding of the Reform party): 'This country has not been properly governed since the days of Louis St. Laurent.'[83] But any hopes of a rapprochement between Winspear and the Liberal party were irrevocably dashed with the coming to power of Trudeau in 1968:

I thoroughly disliked Pierre Trudeau ... I sized him up immediately as an intellectual snob and a reclusive self-satisfied introvert. He made a series of errors in judgement. He almost wholly ignored the West whilst he blatantly courted Quebec. He centralized the power base in Ottawa whilst ignoring local party officials ... He made a foolish marriage to a much younger woman, invited actresses to the galleries of the House, and pirouetted behind the Queen, thereby offending millions of Canadians. His crowning blunder was the invocation of the War Measures Act for the Province of Quebec. This was worse than the Duplessis Padlock Law.[84]

Francis Winspear was not alone in his estrangement from the Liberal party, a fact reflected in declining financial contributions from the private business community.

Between 1975 – the year Petro-Canada was created and Trudeau made his famous remarks about the economy – and the election years of 1979 and 1980, private business gradually turned away from the Liberals and towards the Tories. In 1975, for example, the Liberals received $524,000 from private corporations compared with the Tories' $445,000. In 1979, however, private corporations gave the Tories $3,287,000 and the Liberal party $2,076,000. The following year, they gave $2,734,000 to the Tories and $2,002,000 to the Liberals.[85]

Unfortunately, we do not know whether the business sector was split along the same east-west lines that otherwise occurred in the elections of 1979 and 1980. The available evidence does suggest, however, that the ties of the private business sector to the Liberal party, in general, had been severely loosened.

The federal Liberal party's loss of business support resulted from its social, economic, and political decisions during the 1960s and 1970s, combined with the rise of regional affiliations. In a wider sense, however, the general withdrawal of even tacit business support for the liberal welfare state was also connected to the worldwide crisis of capitalism which occurred during the 1970s, in the midst of which arose a new ideology: neo-conservatism. This ideology found resonance in Canada, particularly in the historical traditions of the West, and was to play a part in the later rise of the Reform party.

THE RISE OF NEO-CONSERVATISM IN WESTERN CANADA

In the United States, during the 1980s, the Republican Party successfully forged a political coalition in opposition to the type of liberalism fashioned by the Democrats since the 1960s. Under the ideological umbrella of neo-conservatism, Ronald Reagan and later George Bush won support not only from the Republican's traditional conservative constituency, but from workers, the southern poor, disenchanted liberals, and some blacks as well. Given its historical, cultural, and geographical proximity to the United States, it is not surprising that similar elements also began to mobilize a counter-hegemony to liberalism in Canada.

The 1970s and 1980s saw the rise in Canada of several organizations dedicated to neo-conservative values.[86] As happened in the United States, these organizations often displayed a varying emphasis upon either moral conservatism or economic liberalism. Some of these, such as REAL Women (Realistic, Equal, Active for Life), also shared obvious consonance with conservative organizations to the south. Similarly, an Ontario evangelist, Kenneth Campbell, created Renaissance Canada in 1974 as the Canadian counterpart to Jerry Falwell's Moral Majority movement. In 1976, the Business Council on National Issues (BCNI) was created as a counterpart to the U.S. Business Roundtable. The period also saw the formation of such right-wing organizations as Paul Fromm's Citizens for Foreign Aid Reform (CFAR), the Canadian Association for Free Enterprise (CAFE), and a Libertarian political party.

Yet other organizations, such as the Association for the Preservation of English in Canada (APEC), were distinctly Canadian. APEC was founded in 1977 by Irene Hilchie, a federal civil servant in Halifax who felt that official bilingualism was discriminating against unilingual anglophones. In 1980, the organization was taken over by Ron and Pauline Leitch of Toronto, who have run it ever since.

One of APEC's chief supporters has been J.V. (Jock) Andrew, a former lieutenant commander in the Canadian Navy and author of *Bilingualism Today, French Tomorrow*.[87] Published in 1977 by BMG Publishing of Richmond Hill, Ontario, a small firm specializing in such titles as *Red Maple – How Canada Became the People's Republic of Canada in 1981*, *Bilingualism Today* was destined to become BMG's biggest seller.[88] Despite its incredible thesis – that bilingualism is the first step towards the imposition of a unilingual French state – Andrew reports that *Bilingualism Today* had sold 120,000 copies by 1988. He has since written two other books, *Backdoor Bilingualism* (which the author implies was the victim of, first, a mysterious warehouse fire and, second, systematic neglect by the Canadian media) and *Enough (Enough French, Enough*

Quebec).[89] Each of Andrew's texts repeats the thesis that there is a conspiracy occurring to have 'the French' take over Canada.

Except for the BCNI, however, most of these individuals and organizations remained on the fringe of political respectability. By contrast, two organizations formed in the 1970s were to have increasing influence in shifting Canada's – and the West's – public policies sharply to the right.

The National Citizens' Coalition (NCC) was the creation of Colin Brown, a wealthy London, Ontario, entrepreneur with ties to the old boy network, particularly in Ontario and Quebec.[90] Brown made most of his money as a life insurance agent with London Life, but over the years also cultivated broader connections within the political and corporate worlds. Brown was a long-time Tory, but by the late 1960s had apparently come to believe that both John Diefenbaker and Robert Stanfield were socialists. In the wake of the latter's election as leader of the Tories in 1967, Brown formed the NCC. Since then, the NCC has fought consistently for smaller government, more restrictive immigration laws, reduced social programs, balanced budgets, the deregulation of businesses, right-to-work legislation, the privatization of health care, and an end to public insurance, bilingualism, and multiculturalism.

In 1975, Brown transformed the NCC into a non-profit organization secretly funded by private corporate donors, many of them in the oil and gas industry. Like many other right-wing organizations in Canada, the NCC was modelled on American organizations, in this case the Conservative Opportunities Society and the Heritage Foundation. The first board of the NCC included several high-ranking Tories and Socreds, including Ernest Manning and Robert Thompson.

In the late 1970s, Colin Brown read *Trudeau Revealed*, an 'exposé' of Pierre Trudeau's socialist inclinations written by a former *Toronto Sun* reporter, David Somerville. Somerville, the son of a Toronto lawyer, was born in 1951 and received his education at St Andrew's College (in Aurora, Ontario), in Switzerland, and at the University of Toronto.[91] *Trudeau Revealed* was published in 1978 (again by BMG Publishing) and eventually sold 27,000 copies.[92] Brown was so impressed with Somerville's dissection of Trudeau's 'secret agenda' that he offered him a job as vice-president and chief spokesperson for the NCC.[93] Somerville soon became a major figure in the organization, orchestrating the many legal battles of the 1980s which propelled the coalition to its current fame. Nonetheless, the NCC was still a minor force in 1980. Rising much more quickly was another right-wing organization, the Fraser Institute.

The Fraser Institute was founded in British Columbia in November 1974 by Michael Walker, the son of a Newfoundland miner. Walker, holder of a doctorate in economics from the University of Western Ontario, started the institute with the monetary support of BC's business community, which was still reeling from the NDP's election in 1972. By 1984 the institute was operating on an annual budget of $900,000, funded by some of Canada's largest business interests, including Sam Belzberg of First City Trust, Sonja Bata of Bata Limited, A.J. de Grandpré of Bell Canada, and Lorne Lodge of IBM Canada.[94]

The Fraser Institute also boasts impressive conservative credentials. The institute's authors include Milton Friedman and Herbert Grubel, while its editorial board includes Sir Alan Walters, former personal economic adviser to Margaret Thatcher. Finally, William F. Buckley Jr, brother-in-law of BC Socred bagman Austin Taylor, is a favourite guest speaker of the institute.[95]

In short, the Fraser Institute is a conservative think-tank heavily funded by the corporate sector. Like the National Citizens' Coalition, the Fraser Institute has steadfastly used its position to advance the neo-conservative agenda, an agenda liberally sprinkled with such Reaganite buzzwords as fiscal restraint, downsizing, and privatization.[96]

While these various organizations gained in stature throughout the 1970s and early 1980s, their views were not immediately accessible to the general public. At about this time, however, a magazine emerged in western Canada which fulfilled the role as chief disseminator of neo-conservative ideology: *Alberta Report*.[97]

Alberta Report is the creation of Ted Byfield. The son of a *Toronto Star* reporter, Byfield was born in Toronto in 1928. He received most of his education in Ontario, but later attended George Washington University in Washington, DC. In 1946, he joined first the *Washington Post* as copy boy and later became a reporter for the *Ottawa Journal*. In 1952, following stints as editor of the *Timmins Daily Press* and the *Sudbury Star*, Byfield moved west to join the *Winnipeg Free Press*. In 1957, he won the National Newspaper Award for political reporting.

In the late 1950s, Byfield and a group of other laymen at St John's Cathedral in Winnipeg formed St John's Cathedral Boys' School in Selkirk, Manitoba. Conservative in orientation, the private school's curriculum emphasized firm discipline, including the use of corporal punishment. In 1962, Byfield left the newspaper business to become a teacher at the school. In 1968, he oversaw the establishment of a second

St John's School in Genesee, Alberta. A third school has since opened at Claremont, Ontario.

In 1965, in response to the publication of Pierre Berton's *The Comfortable Pew*, a book that attacked the failure of mainstream Christianity to address social issues, Byfield wrote *Just Think, Mr. Berton*.[98] The book defended traditional religious morality and practice and denounced the increasing attempts of Christian churches to become socially 'relevant.' This foray into journalism reawakened Byfield's appetite for the news business, and in 1973 he convinced the other members of the Genesee board to begin publishing a weekly newsmagazine, *St. John's Edmonton Report*.

Edmonton Report was followed into production four years later by *St. John's Calgary Report*. In 1979 both magazines were merged into *Alberta Report*. By 1986 an identical but renamed version of *Alberta Report*, the *Western Report*, was produced for sale in the three remaining western provinces. This was followed, in 1989, by the creation of a somewhat distinctive version, BC *Report*.

Circulation of the three magazines varies. In June 1991 BC *Report* had a paid circulation of 21,000, *Alberta Report* approximately 40,000, and *Western Report* about 1500. The magazine is a typical family business. Since 1981 it has been owned by Ted Byfield and his brother, Dr John Byfield of San Diego, California. Besides Ted, his wife, daughter (Virginia), and two sons (Link and Michael) work for the magazine.

Articulate and controversial, the *Alberta Report* has been, since its inception, western Canada's most prominent and consistent organ for the dissemination of conservative values. In articles and, more especially, editorials and columns (written by Ted and, in recent years, his son Link and other guest writers), the magazine has stood firmly for corporal and capital punishment, the teaching of fundamentalist Christian religion in schools, the rights of the family (that is, the parents), and free enterprise, while espousing an often virulent hatred of metrification, pro-choice advocates, feminism in general, public school curriculums and methods of discipline, divorce, human rights commissions, 'mainstream' Christianity, homosexuality, penal reform, sex education, unions, public ownership, teachers' associations, and rock music.

During their existence, the various *Reports* have reserved particular scorn for government agencies or programs, such as 'the eastern-based' CBC (and most other media), multiculturalism, bilingualism, the Foreign

Investment Review Agency (FIRA), and the National Energy Program (NEP). Indeed, *Alberta Report*'s view of the role of government can be summed up in the headline of one Ted Byfield editorial: 'Legislate morality? Yes, and that's all we should legislate.'[99]

Along the way, Byfield has expressed an intense dislike and mistrust of Canadian nationalism, opposing it to what he sees as the 'true' (right-wing) values of the western region:

The clear goal of the Toronto media propagandist is to reshape what we are, into something we are not. Every one of the values out of which the country has emerged he repudiates. He debunks our religion and he undermines our families. He tells our women that raising children is contemptible, and aborting them an act of heroism. He plumps and pleads every cause from state day care to pansy parsons. He lets the killer stalk the streets while jailing parents who spank their children, and he has helped create governments so bloated and beyond control that more than 50 cents of every dollar we earn is required to feed and pamper them.[100]

In short, Byfield's world-view highlights the increasing links, occurring in the early 1980s, between conservative ideology and western regionalism.

Despite its increased media prominence, corporate support, and general social respectability, neo-conservative ideology began the 1980s lacking direct access to federal decision-making. Shortly thereafter, however, it did begin to make inroads into provincial politics. Not unexpectedly, the two provinces where this occurred were Alberta and British Columbia, whose political cultures contained the two essential elements underlying neo-conservatism – free enterprise combined with traditional morality.

By 1975, B.C.'s right-wing had once more coalesced, this time under W.A.C. Bennett's forty-four-year-old son, Bill Bennett. Barrett's NDP was defeated by the Socreds. In 1979, the Socreds won again – just as the recession began. As Socred fortunes began to wane, Bennett's political advisers decided upon a marketing strategy that would present Bill Bennett as the 'tough guy' who would straighten out BC's economic problems. The result was his announcement in 1982 of a curb on public sector wages and a freeze on government spending. The economy, however, continued to crumble.[101] An election was set for 5 May 1983, during which Bennett promised that, if elected, he would continue the policies of moderate restraint practised in 1982.

On election night, Bennett's Social Credit party took thirty-five seats (49.8 per cent of the vote) to the NDP's twenty-two seats (44.9 per cent of the vote).

Before the opening of the new legislature, the Socred cabinet was advised by the Fraser Institute's Michael Walker of the policies it should take to turn the economy around. Guided by Walker's advice, the Socreds set about making British Columbia the 'testing ground for neo-conservative ideology.'[102]

On 7 July 1983, Bennett's government introduced both a budget and an astonishing twenty-six bills. Among other things, the bills removed government employees' rights to negotiate job security, promotion, job reclassification, transfer, hours of work and other working conditions; enabled public sector employers to fire employees without cause; extended public sector wage controls; repealed the Human Rights Code; abolished the Human Rights Branch and Commission, the Rentalsman's Office, and rent controls; enabled doctors to opt out of medicare; removed the right of school boards to levy certain taxes; and dissolved the Alcohol and Drug Abuse Commission.[103]

Public reaction was immediate. Commented some political analysts: 'It was remarkable how many different groups the government managed to offend at once.'[104] Only four days after the budget announcement, a coalition of these disparate groups was formed to fight the legislation.

Operation Solidarity, as the coalition was called, organized mass demonstrations throughout the summer, ending with a rally of 40,000 on 10 August at Empire Stadium in Vancouver. The fall sitting of the legislature deteriorated into mayhem as the Socreds forced through legislation. On 15 October an angry crowd, estimated at between 50,000 and 60,000, marched on the Hotel Vancouver, where the Socreds were holding their convention. Following adjournment of the legislature on 20 October, Operation Solidarity began a series of escalating strikes, starting with government employees on 1 November. This strike was followed within days by strikes in other sectors; a general strike seemed imminent. The strike was only narrowly averted by an agreement between Jack Monro, regional president of International Woodworkers of America, and Bennett on 13 November, which protected public sector workers from some of the more onerous aspects entailed in the government bills.[105]

The settlement between the government and the union, combined with crumbling public support for the strikers, eroded the wider coalition of left-wing elements.[106] Largely unopposed, Bennett pressed ahead with the agenda set out by the Fraser Institute. In 1984 more bills were passed that severely restricted union powers and otherwise shifted power away from the socially disadvantaged. By the time he stepped down in 1986, Bennett was disliked by many British Columbians, in large measure because of the cold aloofness with which he had pursued his agenda. Nonetheless, many voters also viewed him as a hero who had put unions, social activists, and government workers in their place.

Bennett's conservative measures, while pursued with extreme gusto, were not entirely unique in the recession-torn Canada of the 1980s. Faced with declining revenues, governments of all political stripes resorted to policies of fiscal restraint. In 1982 the federal Liberals limited public sector wage increases by decree. Ontario's Conservative government passed similar legislation during the same period. Similarly, the recession saw Quebec's left-leaning Parti Québécois and Saskatchewan's NDP face bitter public strikes in 1982–3 over fiscal restraint. In 1985 Alberta, never known for its progressive labour legislation, introduced compulsory arbitration and severely limited the rights of some workers to strike.[107] And in 1987 Bill Bennett's successor in BC, Bill Vander Zalm, introduced an anti-labour bill that, in a half-hearted sequel to Solidarity, saw 250,000 workers stage a one-day strike.[108]

The events in BC in 1982–4 highlight, in particularly dramatic fashion, both the growing influence of fiscal conservatism in the West and the uncompromising limits to which its adherents would go in waging a kind of Hobbesian war against other ideas and people. At the same time, it is important to keep in mind that the possibility of creating a neo-conservative counter-hegemony in Canada still seemed remote as the 1980s began. The elections of 1979 and 1980, and their aftermath, however, set the stage for greater right-wing influence through a linkage with regional discontent.

THE ELECTIONS OF 1979 AND 1980 AND THEIR AFTERMATH

The elections of 1979 and 1980 brought to a head federal-provincial conflicts that had been brewing for nearly a decade. As we have seen, the rise of regionalism in the West had been buttressed by the election of strong provincialist governments in the late 1960s and early 1970s. No more so was this the case than in Alberta, where, encouraged by the province's urban business elites, Lougheed's Tory government actively involved itself in capital investment and public ownership in the province – even as government officials paid lip service to free enterprise – and expanded government services. The Tories' efforts at 'province building' were assisted by a rise in oil and gas revenues following the OPEC crisis of 1973.

The OPEC crisis, however, immediately resulted in increased federal-provincial conflict. The source of this conflict lies in the provisions of the Canadian Constitution. Under the Constitution, producing provinces have exclusive ownership of natural resources, but the federal government controls their sale price when they move across provincial or international borders. (Either level of government can levy taxes on the resource.)

The federal Liberals' response to the crisis was to implement wage and price controls and to create Petro-Canada, much to the displeasure of the producing provinces, particularly Alberta. This conflict was repeated in 1979 when the Iranian revolution caused the price of a barrel of oil to jump dramatically, going from U.S. $14.82 in January 1979 to U.S. $34.50 by January 1980. Armand Hammer, the president of Occidental Petroleum, predicted that the price of oil would be U.S. $100 per barrel by 1990.[109] Such a scenario, if it occurred, would see a massive transfer of economic and political power from eastern Canada to the West, particularly Alberta. For Albertans, long accustomed to having a 'boom or bust' economy, it seemed that their time in the sun had arrived at last.

In the midst of these events, Alberta officials and the federal Liberals attempted throughout 1978–9 to negotiate a new pricing agreement on oil and gas. Understandably, both sides wanted to maximize their economic rents. Beset by an increasing federal deficit, and concerned that Alberta's growing wealth might 'unbalance' Confederation, the Liberals proved to be tough bargainers.

The Alberta government, therefore, greeted with some elation the 1979 election of a Tory government headed by a fellow Albertan, High River–born Joe Clark. Lougheed's hopes that a better agreement might be reached with the Tories than the Liberals proved to be justified. In the months that followed, an oil-pricing agreement was arrived at which would have allowed for a $4 per barrel increase in 1980, $4.50 per barrel increase each ensuing year of the agreement, as well as price adjustments in the last two years of the four-and-a-half-year agreement.[110] Clark's government, however, lost a budget vote dealing with the agreement, and his government fell.

The subsequent election polarized Canadian politics. Despite the impending Quebec referendum on sovereignty (scheduled for 20 May 1980), the budget quickly became the central issue of the campaign, openly pitting the oil-producing provinces against the manufacturing heartland of Ontario in particular. In Alberta, which (along with Saskatchewan) had been denied ownership of its own resources until 1930, the conflict rekindled historical regional grievances. It seemed to many Albertans in 1980 that the federal Liberals were prepared to seize the province's resources in a bid to redistribute Alberta's new-found wealth to the more populated region of central Canada. Many Albertans felt that their future prosperity was being robbed to protect the less efficient industries of the East.

Conversely, many easterners viewed as a threat the massive shift of economic and political power to the West entailed by the sudden rise in world oil prices. Prior to the OPEC crisis of 1973, Ontario had subsidized western oil producers through a guaranteed market. Up to this point, the price of Canadian crude had historically been slightly higher than the world price.[111] Having sustained the western industry until it was viable, Ontario was now being asked to accept the higher world price – a price dictated by a foreign cartel that, moreover, would likely make uncompetitive that province's manufacturing industries. Some nationalists were further concerned that windfall returns to the largely foreign-owned oil industry would be used to buy up other key sectors of the economy or would flee the country altogether.

The federal Liberal party, increasingly bent on a political strategy that required government intervention in the economy, appeared to side with central Canada – much to the anger of westerners, particularly Albertans. In contrast, the federal Tory party was strongly influenced by its western members, particularly its powerful Alberta caucus, many of whose members had strong ties to the oil and gas industry. (The Tories had not lost a federal seat in Alberta since 1972, taking all twenty-one in 1979.) In contrast to the interventionist role for government espoused by the Liberals and NDP, the Tories had become increasingly supportive of market-driven economics.

The battle lines were starkly, if rather simplistically, drawn. When they appeared on stage for the election of 1980, the Tories were cast in the role of defenders of western-provincialist and 'free enterprise' interests, the Liberals as protectors of the eastern-centralist and 'socialist' interests. In the end, although the actual issues were more complex than this, involving national and regional development, resource ownership, and distributive justice, among other things, the 1980 election results, based on a first-passed-the-post electoral system, seemed to reflect and even add to the mythology of a simple-minded polarization of regional political interests.

In 1979 the Progressive Conservatives won election primarily on the basis of an Ontario-West axis, taking fifty-seven of ninety-five seats in Ontario and fifty-seven of seventy-seven seats in the West. In 1980, by contrast, the Tories lost seats in every province except Alberta. Tory losses were particularly high in Ontario, where the oil-pricing issue was foremost in voter's minds. In 1980, the Tories took only thirty-eight seats in Ontario, nineteen fewer than in the previous election. The loss of seats reflected a drop in electoral support from 41 per cent in 1979 to 35 per cent in 1980.

As for the Liberals, they were virtually shut out in the West in both elections, taking only three seats in the 1979 election and two seats (both in Manitoba) in 1980, but the 126 seats they took in Quebec and Ontario in 1980 ensured them of victory. In the end, the elections of 1979 and 1980 revealed and accentuated Canada's regional cleavages in a particularly dramatic way. Highlighted against the rise and fall of the abbreviated Tory reign, the 1980 election aroused immediate anger and concern in the West.

In Alberta, a sixty-year-old Edmonton millionaire and car dealer, Elmer Knutson, sent an angry letter to the *Edmonton Journal* the day after the election.[112] The letter, which has acquired an almost mythic stature in western separatist folklore, adumbrated a series of themes which were to be the staples of western separatists and other right-wing elements in subsequent years.[113] It especially complained of a French-dominated Ottawa, as exemplified in such policies as bilingualism, and the fear that Trudeau's majority Liberal government would now proceed with constitutional reforms which would reinforce French domination of the rest of Canada. Knutson's solution to this perceived threat was simple: Quebec must be made to leave Canada.

Knutson was not a stranger to political matters. In the late 1970s he had been co-chair of the One Canada Association, an organization 'committed to increasing police powers, ending bilingualism, and tightening immigration policies.'[114] Then, in December 1979, Knutson lost the Edmonton South Tory nomination to incumbent Douglas Roche, whom Knutson once described as 'a socialist masquerading as a conservative.'[115] But the response to his *Journal* letter – 'One lousy little letter,' in Knutson's words – astonished even him. In one month, Knutson received 3800 replies, most of them positive.[116] As a result of this public response, Knutson formed the Western Canada Federation (West-Fed) in March 1980.[117]

At almost the same time, the results of the federal election breathed new life into the faltering political career of a thirty-four-year-old Victoria lawyer, Doug Christie. Christie, a Manitoba-born monarchist who is reported to have climbed to the roof of the Winnipeg college he was attending to hoist a nine-foot Red Ensign when the Canadian flag was first raised in 1965, had been a committed separatist since at least 1975.[118] Like Knutson, Christie had once tried unsuccessfully to win candidacy for the Conservative party. Following this failure, he formed the openly separatist Committee for Western Independence (CWI) in 1976, an association which gained some notoriety by attracting prominent lawyer Milt Harradance to its fold.[119]

For a time, the CWI was joined by the Independent Alberta Association (IAA), an organization formed in the early 1970s by John C. Rudolph, a Calgary oilman, 'to examine the feasibility of, and if necessary to promote the formation of, an independent Alberta state.'[120] The result was a study produced in 1973 by University of Calgary economist Warren Blackman, later a supporter of West-Fed, and four colleagues. The study contended that an independent Alberta would not only survive but would be economically better off.[121] By 1979, however, Christie had formed another party, the Western Independence Party (WIP). In the provincial election of that year, he contested the Esquimalt–Port Renfrew riding, receiving 280 votes compared to the winner's 24,146 votes.[122]

Six days after the federal election of 1979, Christie and fifty followers of the CWI created the Western National Association (WNA). Within a few months, however, internal bickering among the association members resulted in Christie's leaving. His political career seemed to have reached a dead end – until the 1980 election occurred. The re-election of Trudeau and the backlash it created in the West led Christie to found yet another separatist party, Western Canada Concept, in June 1980.

Meanwhile, in March 1980, the former leader of Saskatchewan's Progressive Conservative party, Dick Collver, resigned to sit as an independent with the intent of working towards western Canada's annexation by the United States.[123] Said Collver: 'The people are ready to express their dissatisfaction with compulsory bilingualism and all of the other centralist dogma which is being perpetrated on our region.'[124] Collver was soon joined in his protest by a fellow PC MLA, Dennis Ham.

Together they formed the short-lived Unionest party. The party never got off the ground, however, and in a final act of personal annexation, Collver moved to the United States.

The emergence of these various right-wing parties and organizations was the most glaring symptom of political discontent arising out of the election, but there were other signs as well. The day after the election, for example, Vancouver radio hot-line host Jack Webster was deluged with phone calls, the majority (67 of 109) saying they were in favour of the West separating. At nearly the same time, the Canada West Foundation, a regional think-tank, received almost 150 calls from people who assumed that the purpose of the foundation was to promote separatism.[125] 'But,' said Stan Roberts, president of the foundation, 'most of our callers have been really concerned about one question: who will speak for the West in Ottawa.'[126]

Negative reaction to the election results might have disappeared in time except that major decisions and policies were in the offing and could not wait. The impending Quebec referendum would require a new constitutional arrangement, no matter what the outcome. And there was the necessary oil-pricing agreement.

In the days and months following the 1980 election, the Alberta government waited to see what Ottawa would do regarding an oil-pricing agreement. By the fall of 1980, Premier Lougheed thought he knew, and proceeded to warn Albertans of the impending rape of their resources by the federal government acting on behalf of eastern, primarily Ontario, interests.[127]

On 28 October 1980, Finance Minister Allan MacEachen brought down his first budget. The budget's major announcement, however, was the creation of the National Energy Program (NEP), a program described by political economist James Laxer as 'the most significant act of government intervention in the Canadian economy since the Second World War.'[128]

The NEP and its companion legislation (the Petroleum Incentives Program [PIP], the Natural Gas Export Tax [NGET], and the Petroleum and Gas Revenue Tax [PGRT]) aimed at increasing Canadianization of the petroleum industry through both public and private sector strategies. The programs also aimed at increasing the federal share of petroleum rents, necessarily at the expense of the producing provinces and the petroleum companies. Specifically, the NEP set the rise in the price of oil at $1 per barrel every six months beginning in January 1981 until the

end of 1983. After that, until the end of 1985, the price would rise at
$2.25 per barrel every six months. After January 1986 the price of oil
would rise at $3.50 per barrel every six months.[129]

The Alberta government's reaction was immediate. Premier Lougheed
went on television to denounce the legislation as an interference in provincial jurisdiction. He further rejected the pricing schedule as too low.
In response, said Lougheed, Alberta would cut back on oil production.
The province would also put on hold decisions concerning the development of the oil sands.

The NEP was also attacked, of course, by the large multinationals.
They were aided in their attack by the election of Ronald Reagan as
president of the United States, a week after the budget announcement.[130]
The intervention of the White House was lauded by Ted Byfield in his
editorial in *Alberta Report* on 25 January 1982:

In the course of the conflict between the Reagan administration and Ottawa, we
Albertans are expected as loyal Canadians to cheer for the victory of Mr. Trudeau
and his thug government. Some of us will find this very hard. We will wave
the flag, of course. But deep in our hearts we will be hoping that the Americans
whip the hell out of him.

In the months and years that followed, Byfield's *Alberta Report* continued to mythologize the intent and the impact of the NEP. The NEP was
opposed, of course, not only by the right wing. At least some on the
left, particularly in western Canada, saw the NEP as politically and economically unfair, a tax imposed upon the West (particularly Alberta
but also Saskatchewan) to protect the slow-to-adapt manufacturing industries of central Canada. As such, the NEP was not a truly 'national'
policy, but rather a short-sighted political stratagem that neglected Canada's real long-term political and economic interests. The most virulent
and public attacks upon the NEP, however, were launched by Alberta's
Conservative government and the western right wing, particularly those
in the private oil and gas industry.

The most outspoken of these critics was Carl Nickle, a prominent oilfield executive and former Tory MP, who publicly condemned the entire
budget outright as discriminatory and repressive. 'I believe short term
political gain for central Canada will foster more alienation, possible
[sic] even lead to splitting the nation apart,' he said.[131] Federal Tories,
such as John Crosbie and Calgary Centre MP Harvie Andre, concurred
with Nickle's assessment.

To the extent that popular culture reflects public sentiment, the numerous anti-Liberal, anti-Trudeau, and anti-eastern bumper stickers, lapel pins, T-shirts, and other paraphernalia that deluged western Canada, particular Alberta, during this period provide additional evidence that many westerners were angry.[132] Nor is it a coincidence that John Ballem, a corporate lawyer with strong ties to the oil and gas industry and former law partner of Peter Lougheed, should in 1981 write *Alberta Alone*, a fictitious novel that revolves around Alberta's separation from Confederation.[133]

In short, the NEP was a red flag for nascent separatists, aggrieved regionalists, private business, and assorted right-wingers in western Canada. Its impact in heightening fear and anger among these elements was accentuated by Trudeau's announcement only a month before its introduction that his government would proceed unilaterally with patriation of the Constitution.

By 1980, the goal of constitutional renewal had become for some Canadian academics and politicians almost a Holy Grail – both compelling and unobtainable in equal parts. Canada's constitutional existence derived from the British North America Act of 1867. The new country, however, was not entirely sovereign, as the British government withheld authority over foreign affairs, judicial appeals, and constitutional amendments. The Statute of Westminster (1931) proclaimed Canada (as well as Australia, New Zealand, and South Africa) sovereign and equal to Great Britain, but Canada declined to take back control over its own Constitution because the federal and provincial governments could not agree on a formula by which it could be amended. Although many Canadian civil servants and politicians thereafter pressed for complete patriation of the Constitution, the lone result was the establishment in 1950 of the Supreme Court of Canada instead of the British Privy Council as the final court of appeal.[134]

It is an irony of his political life that Trudeau should have been the one to finally pursue the goal of patriating and amending the Constitution. Prior to the late 1960s, he had been antipathetic to constitutional change, believing instead that Quebec – and, for that matter, the other provinces – had sufficient powers and lacked only the will to make Confederation work. By the time of the Victoria federal-provincial conference in 1971, Trudeau had begun to change his mind.

That meeting saw the various premiers, including Robert Bourassa of Quebec, decide upon a new Constitution. Faced, however, with strong opposition by Quebec nationalists, trade unionists, business groups, and the media, who viewed the deal as centralizing Canadian authority and otherwise reducing Quebec to the status of the other provinces, Bourassa later withdrew his support for the deal. Now, after a hiatus of nearly a decade, Trudeau returned to the constitutional question as a means of reconstituting Canadian federalism. The immediate impetus for his return was the Quebec referendum of 20 May 1980.

Prior to its election in 1976, the Parti Québécois, led by René Lévesque, had stated that, if elected, it would hold a referendum on sovereignty-association sometime during its mandate. In November 1979, following Trudeau's announcement that he was retiring as leader of the Liberal party, Lévesque announced that the sovereignty referendum would be held on 20 May 1980. Lévesque's timing was quite intentional: he believed that his old nemesis would now be ineffectual in the debate to follow. Lévesque's announcement backfired, however, as it rekindled Trudeau's political desires and played a major part in his decision to lead the Liberal party into the 1980 election.

When the referendum campaign began the following spring, the pro-sovereigntists appeared certain of victory. In the weeks preceding the vote, however, pro-federalists returned to traditional arguments that a vote for sovereignty would result in Quebec's economic ruin, since no one could ensure that economic association with the rest of Canada would necessarily follow. At the same time, various federal politicians, including Trudeau, suggested that a 'no' vote would be followed by constitutional changes that would meet Quebec's demands within Confederation. The federalist arguments won out. The 'no' side received 60 per cent of the vote, although, significantly, the vote among francophone Quebecers was split 50–50. The day following the referendum vote, Trudeau announced his plans to patriate the Constitution.

A draft resolution of the federal government's constitutional position was unveiled in September, but the federal-provincial conference held later that month ended in heated argument and constitutional deadlock over the issue of an amending formula, among other things. It was then that Trudeau announced his government would move unilaterally to patriate the Constitution.

Shortly thereafter, a draft resolution of the Constitution's proposed Charter of Rights and Freedoms went to a joint House of Commons–Senate committee. The committee held hearings throughout November and December, and received briefs or heard testimony from 914 individuals and 294 groups. The committee also accepted over half of 123 proposed amendments. The Charter was then returned to the House of Commons for further debate.

Meanwhile, the legality of the federal government unilaterally patriating the Constitution was challenged before the Supreme Court by Quebec, Newfoundland, and Manitoba. In September 1981 the Supreme Court ruled that the federal government had the legal right to patriate the Constitution, but that convention suggested that it required the consent of the majority of the provinces. The decision was the Supreme Court's polite way of telling Trudeau that he should return to constitutional discussions with the provinces. It had been over a year since their last meeting. But, in November 1981, the first ministers met once more to hammer out a new constitutional deal.

Many of the premiers, particularly Manitoba Premier Sterling Lyon, strongly opposed certain elements of the federal package. In particular, they disliked the proposed Charter of Rights and Freedoms, which they viewed as increasing the powers of the judiciary at the expense of the provincial legislatures. At an earlier meeting of the first ministers, in April 1981, Premier Lévesque had made an important concession, agreeing to surrender Quebec's traditional veto over constitutional matters. Now, at the meeting in November, Lévesque agreed to Trudeau's proposal to hold a national referendum on the Charter. The solidarity of the opposing premiers dissipated. They had no wish to fight the Charter, which they knew had wide support across the country, including in Quebec. All of the premiers, except Lévesque, agreed to the new constitutional arrangement. The meeting broke up.

On the basis of presentations made by groups representing women and aboriginals, some modifications to the deal were made by federal and provincial government officials during subsequent days. Essentially, however, the new Constitution had been formulated. An angry Lévesque, still complaining that he had been betrayed by the other premiers, announced that Quebec would neither sign the Constitution nor take part in future constitutional meetings. Quebec nationalists received another blow to their aspirations in December 1981, when the Supreme Court announced its unanimous decision that Quebec had no constitutional veto. The deal was done. A few months later – 17 April 1982 – the Queen proclaimed Canada's new Constitution.

Trudeau had what he had long wanted, a patriated Constitution with a Charter of Rights and Freedoms, although the latter included a 'notwithstanding clause' that the western premiers, particularly Lyon and

Blakeney, had forced upon him. The clause – Section 33 – allows both provincial and federal legislatures to override court decisions based on certain sections of the Charter. Although Trudeau feared that the clause had opened the door for provincial premiers to override individual protections, it seemed to be a necessary compromise. And – after all – half of a Charter was better than no Charter. On balance, there seemed less of a chance subsequently that a patchwork quilt of individual rights would emerge across the country.

The deal also met certain demands of the provinces. An amending formula had at last been arrived at that could pave the way to future constitutional changes. Moreover, although they had agreed to the inclusion of the Charter in the Constitution, the provinces felt they had limited its effect through the 'notwithstanding clause.' In general, it was understood that the patriation of the Constitution was merely a step in ongoing negotiations over provincial-federal powers.

What did Canadians think of the new Constitution? Quebec nationalists were not to be placated. But would Lévesque's PQ government have signed any deal, short of one that granted Quebec sovereignty-association? Likely not. Certainly, Trudeau, the provincial premiers, and a Tory-leadership hopeful named Brian Mulroney took this view. Women and natives remained displeased that the Constitution did not go far enough in ensuring their rights. Others denounced the élitist process by which the Constitution had been created.[135]

On the whole, however, the new Constitution was well received throughout Canada. A Gallup poll conducted in early May 1982 asked the question: 'The Canadian constitution was proclaimed in Ottawa on April 17, 1982. In the long run, do you think this will be a good thing or not a good thing for Canada?' The results? Nationally, 57 per cent of Canadians thought it would be a good thing; 14 per cent thought it would be a bad thing; 30 per cent didn't know. Regionally, greatest support for the new Constitution was found in Ontario (65 per cent). The least support was in Quebec at 49 per cent, though only 16 per cent thought it was a bad thing. Significantly, however, the most polarized results were found in the Prairies, with 53 per cent of respondents viewing the new Constitution as a good thing compared with 21 per cent who viewed it as bad.[136]

It is unclear which elements in the West comprised this 21 per cent. Certainly, however, the extreme right wing in western Canada opposed the new Constitution. An advertisement placed in the *Alberta Report* by the Alberta Branch of the Canadian League of Rights in May

1981 asked readers to consider that '[t]he Trudeau "constitutional" scheme and so-called "charter of rights" fails to safeguard individual property rights; and takes effective control of natural resources away from the provinces.' The reasons for Trudeau's actions, stated the advertisement, could be found by purchasing a tract put out by the League, *Trudeau's Master Plan for the Betrayal of Canada.* The information in this tract, informed the advertisement, was 'absolutely essential to the defence of our Christian heritage.'[137]

Combined with the enactment of the NEP, the proposed Constitution confirmed for many right-wing separatist elements in the West the notion that the Trudeau Liberals were attempting to create a centralized, socialist, and francophone state. In retrospect, this belief may appear absurd. It should be remembered, however, that similar beliefs were frequently stated by the *Alberta Report*, as well as many prominent members of the western business and political establishment, such as Carl Nickle.

The response of many people in the western business community during this period to the Liberals' economic and political initiatives provides telling evidence of just how completely it had abandoned the Liberal party. A comparison of two conferences held by the influential Canada West Foundation (CWF) in 1978 and 1980 is particularly instructive of the collapse of business support for the Liberal party in western Canada. Moreover, it provides a glimpse into one of the organizations through which the future founders of the Reform party were linked.

THE CANADA WEST FOUNDATION

The CWF grew out of the One Prairie Province conference held in Lethbridge in 1971. Funded by individual memberships and corporate, institutional, and provincial/territorial grants, the foundation conducts research into the economic and social characteristics of the West and the North, and to make proposals regarding the regions' development. From its inception, the foundation has cultivated important political and business connections. Duff Roblin, former Tory premier of Manitoba, and the Liberal MP James Richardson were early members of the foundation's council.[138] Other prominant members in later years have included Izzy Asper and Gordon Gibson, former provincial Liberal leaders in Manitoba and British Columbia, respectively; Edward Schreyer, former Manitoba NDP premier and former governor general of

Canada; and Jim Gray, vice-president of Canadian Hunter Exploration. The foundation's first and only chairman is Arthur Child.

Child was born in England in 1910, the son of a steelworker. The family soon moved to Canada and settled in Ontario. After completing a BA in languages at Queen's University, Child eventually got a job with Canada Packers. He rose to the position of vice-president, before leaving to complete both a masters and PhD. In the mid-1960s he took over as president of Burns Foods Ltd.[139] By 1971, Child was a millionaire and, according to writer Peter Newman, a member of Calgary's 'nouveaux riches,' a club which also included R.A. Brown, founder of the NPARF.[140]

In the climate of the 1970s, the foundation soon found itself increasingly involved in the constitutional debates occurring in the country. These debates became particularly intense following the election in Quebec of the Parti Québécois under René Lévesque in 1976. In response to the PQ's election, the federal Liberals commissioned the Task Force on National Unity headed by former Liberal cabinet minister Jean-Luc Pepin and former Ontario premier John Robarts. The announcement of the commission set off a spate of similar hearings throughout the country. In the West, these hearings were spearheaded by the Canada West Foundation and its high-profile president, Stan Roberts.[141]

Roberts was born in Winnipeg on 17 January 1927 but raised in the bilingual community of St Adolphe in the Red River Valley, where his father owned a grain farm and established a nation-wide reputation as a breeder of Percheron draft horses. Stan Roberts later received post-secondary education at the University of Manitoba (agricultural economics) and the University of Western Ontario (business administration). After a trip to Europe in the early 1950s, during which he met, and soon married, his wife Pia, Roberts returned to Canada and got a job with Canada Packers. In 1954 the Roberts family returned to St Adolphe to manage the family's 2000-acre farm.

In 1958 Roberts entered politics and was elected Liberal MLA for La Verendrye. Young, vigorous, and bilingual, he soon got a reputation for getting under the skin of Duff Roblin's Tory government. Roberts resigned his seat in 1963 but retained important contacts with the Liberal party. He was Manitoba adviser to Prime Minister Lester B. Pearson, a man he respected, until 1968. Roberts then became president and acting leader of the Manitoba party (1969–70).

This was a difficult time for Liberals in the West. The middle ground had disappeared from Manitoba politics with the Tory victory of 1959 and the later resurgence of the left-wing NDP, which won election in 1969. Federally, although Trudeau was elected prime minister in 1968, and even took twenty-seven seats in the West, party support nonetheless remained fragile in the region. Some notes scribbled by Roberts, likely in 1970, describe why he remained a Liberal, both federally and provincially, even during this difficult period. The same notes provide some insight also into his concept of liberalism.

On the federal situation:

If NDP had been elected two years ago – inflation. If PCS had been elected two years ago – 2 countries.

On the provincial scene:

We have Rightwing protectionist Conservatives, championing free enterprise – with no interest in social reform. We have Leftwing socialism trying to build reform. There is a large intelligent mass at the centre that is demanding a more enlightened approach – Fiscal responsibility + social reform. Free to own, free to achieve, free to grow and to change *but* who want their government to take responsibility for stimulating growth ... Only thru liberalism can we have both a free society and a quality of life.

In short, Roberts favoured neither unfettered capitalism nor centralized socialism, advocating instead what might be termed capitalism with a human face.

During this period, Roberts was an executive officer of McCabe Grain Co. Ltd., later National Grain Co. Ltd. He quit this post in 1971, however, to move to British Columbia where he became vice-president of Simon Fraser University. In 1976, Roberts left the university to take a position as the Canada West Foundation's first president following the illness of the foundation's executive director, Leroy ('Chick') Thorssen. Under Thorssen, the foundation had maintained a generally low public profile. Roberts, however, immediately set about changing this. By 1978, he had become convinced that western Canada had to become more involved in the constitutional process. In his own words: 'What has happened in Quebec may have precipitated the crisis, but it's not an Ontario-Quebec debate. It's a Canadian debate and we in the west have a part in it.'[142]

In truth, signs that the foundation was considering a more directly political role were evidenced two years earlier. At that time, it had commissioned a report by M & M Systems Research Ltd. of Edmonton examining how a new balance of national and regional interests and aspirations could be achieved within Canada, 'while maintaining the unity and integrity of Canadian Confederation.'[143]

M & M was owned and managed by Ernest and Preston Manning. They had founded the company, later renamed Manning Consultants Limited, in 1969, a year after the elder Manning's resignation as Alberta premier. In subsequent years, neither of the Mannings had been far from the political arena. Preston Manning had met frequently with Joe Clark whom he had known since university. Clark even attempted to convince Manning to run as a Conservative in the 1972 election, but the latter refused in part because of 'reservations' about the Tory party and Canada's political system in general, and in part because of commitments to his company.[144]

During the same period, the Mannings had also secured their already substantial contacts with the business establishment. Even before the creation of the NPARF, Ernest Manning had cultivated his relationship with big business.[145] Shortly after his retirement as premier in 1968, and much to the astonishment of his loyal followers, Manning had even taken a seat on the board of directors of the Imperial Bank of Commerce.[146] At about the same time, as we have seen, he also joined the board of the National Citizens' Coalition.

In 1970, M & M produced its first paper, entitled *Requests for Proposals and Social Contracts*. Based on the system of contracting used by such American agencies as the National Aeronautics and Space Administration (NASA), and written in the now familiar language of systems theory, the paper advocated the provision of social programs by private industry and commerce.[147] The ideas thus anticipated by nearly a decade neo-conservative solutions to the increasing fiscal problems of the liberal welfare state.

Over the next few years, the Mannings continued to expand their business contacts. In 1977 the Mannings obtained money from the newly formed Business Council on National Issues 'to finance the drafting and promotion of a property rights clause for possible inclusion in the Canadian constitution.'[148] The same year, M & M released the report commissioned by the Canada West Foundation.

Entitled *A Realistic Perspective of Canadian Confederation*, the paper argued that Confederation is an ongoing 'deal' struck between provinces and the federal government. Reflecting Preston Manning's dual interests in history and the application of technical reasoning to problem solving, the study recommended use of a matrix ('the National Unity Matrix') to update systematically Confederation's success in addressing regional concerns and aspirations.[149]

The Mannings' paper was used as the basis for discussions held at public meetings throughout western Canada, the Yukon, and the Northwest Territories during September and October 1977. Then, in December 1977, the foundation commissioned three reputable political scientists – David Elton and Peter McCormick, of the University of Lethbridge, and Fred Engelmann, of the University of Alberta – to study federal systems of government existing elsewhere in the world.

Their study, entitled *Alternatives: Towards the Development of an Effective Federal System for Canada*, came out in February 1978, and made several specific proposals, notably that the Senate be replaced by a House of Provinces consisting of delegates from the provincial governments. The intent of this proposal was to bring the regions into the federal decision-making process, while not fundamentally weakening or decentralizing federal authority. The study also made clear where the authors stood on the Parti Québécois's proposal of sovereignty-association:

There is no question but that French Canadians have legitimate grievances ... [However, the] fuzziness of political independence and economic association would generate feelings of exploitation of both sides of the new divide ... Quebec would [succeed] in creating in political reality that which until now has seldom existed outside her nightmares – a politically unified English Canada facing an isolated Quebec.[150]

This study subsequently became a discussion paper at the CWF's Alternatives Conference held in Banff, Alberta, on 27–9 March 1978.

Among the many funders of that conference was the Winspear Foundation, named after Francis Winspear, the disenchanted former Liberal. The conference attracted 300 delegates from across the country, including 50 from Quebec, and several high-profile speakers, including Flora MacDonald, the federal Tory critic for federal-provincial relations, Alberta premier Peter Lougheed, and Saskatchewan premier Allan Blakeney. In the end, Elton, Engelmann, and McCormick's proposals were generally endorsed by the delegates. Stan Roberts noted: '[w]ith a clear consensus the delegates supported the concept of a strong central government.'[151]

The conference received wide public praise at the time for its moderate tone and success in bringing Canadians together. An editorial in the *Financial Post* of 8 April 1978 read: 'Mighty good sounds out of the West.' Richard Gwyn, in the *Montreal Star* on 31 March, wrote an article titled: 'Western conference generates some fresh perceptions.' And the *Vancouver Province* of 7 April ran an article headed: 'Banff was valuable first step.' Other newspapers such as the *Edmonton Journal* and the *Calgary Herald* were similarly positive in their reviews.

In short, the foundation presented itself during its 1978 Banff conference as a moderate voice within the business community. There was no inference of regionalist or separatist leanings, nor was there a discernible anti-French sentiment. Indeed, the bilingual Roberts had frequently suggested that, while he opposed Quebec separatism, the election of the Parti Québécois had provided a service by forcing a much-needed rewriting of the Constitution for the betterment of all Canada.

In June 1978 the federal government introduced Bill C-60, a bill to amend the Canadian Constitution. In January 1979 the Canadian government's report on Canadian unity was released to the public. It called for a more decentralized and flexible federation.[152] Trudeau immediately dismissed the report, however, suggesting that its recommendations would lead to disunity, fragmentation, and the eventual disintegration of the country. But, if not Pepin-Robarts, what was the alternative?

As we have seen, Canada's political system was in particular crisis by 1980. Joe Clark had won and then lost election to a tired Liberal party, headed once more by Pierre Trudeau. Meanwhile, the governing Parti Québécois had announced that a referendum on sovereignty would be held on 20 May 1980. It was widely believed that the 'yes' side would win the vote.

In the midst of these events, Francis Winspear held a series of meetings at his Victoria home to discuss the current political situation. Present at these meetings were the late Dr Douglas Ross of Sidney, BC, a 'country physician and surgeon ... a musician, an amateur astronomer, and a well-read philosopher,' Trevor Davis, the former mayor of North Saanich, BC, and Dr Andrew Stewart, former president of the University of Alberta and retired economic consultant of the WCF.[153]

Out of these meetings a paper was prepared dealing with the current political crisis. Winspear subsequently presented the paper to several members of the foundation, including Ernest Manning and Stan Roberts. The key points of Winspear's paper were as follows:

a. The Senate of Canada ... should be elected and have equal representation ...
b. All provinces and peoples in Canada should be treated equally.
c. We concurred on bilingualism and equality between the two founding races, but we could not agree with unilingualism in Quebec and bilingualism in the rest of Canada.
d. Part of the checks and balances of the constitutional monarchist parliamentary form of government had been destroyed ...
e. The national budget should be balanced and the debt reduced.
f. Members of parliament should be in closer touch with their constituents.

Ernest Manning listened, apparently unimpressed. Roberts, however, was much more interested. According to Winspear, Roberts's response to the paper was to call

a series of study group meetings throughout the four western provinces, culminating in a massive meeting at the Banff School which was attended by many Quebec citizens and a goodly number from other eastern provinces. We felt that the conference did its bit to assure a favourable outcome of the plebiscite.[154]

Since neither Roberts nor the Canada West Foundation were strangers to setting up conferences, Winspear may be overstating his role in instigating the conference. Nonetheless, it is true that Winspear was an ardent financial supporter of the Alternatives Conferences in 1978 and 1980.

In any case, in December 1980, after Trudeau's declaration that his government would unilaterally patriate the Constitution and shortly after MacEachen's budget announcing the NEP, the Canada West Foundation's Alternatives Conference took place, again at Banff. The keynote address for the conference was made by the foundation's chairman, Arthur Child. Standing before the conference delegates, many of whom were federal Liberals, Child declared, among other things, that the budget was a 'non-budget' and 'irresponsible,' that central Canadians who had voted for the Liberal party had been rewarded with cheap oil, and that the federal government's discriminatory policies had reduced Canada to a 'banana republic.'

Child went on to state that the proposed Charter of Rights and Freedoms should not be entrenched in the Constitution since it favoured the principle of the Napoleonic code that citizens have no rights except those granted by the state. Equally, westerners were opposed to the entrenchment of language rights in the Constitution. Finally, Child stated that Westerners did not elect Liberals federally because they believe that the Liberal party is Quebec-based and generally insensitive to western concerns.[155]

Child's blunt evaluation of Ottawa's, or at least the Liberal party's, treatment of the West had been shared increasingly by Stan Roberts. For several months before the October federal budget, Roberts had travelled the country warning of separatism. The *Alberta Report* of 12 December 1980 noted, however: 'the warnings had become so strong and so eloquent, they were almost making separatism look attractive.' Some of Roberts's friends and colleagues with the foundation even began to refer to him as 'the separatist.'[156]

Many supporters of the foundation were put off, however, by Child's and Roberts' statements. Like the country, the foundation appeared to be in danger of splitting up. Two days before Child's speech, Roberts announced he was resigning as president of the foundation. He was replaced by David Elton who immediately promised to re-establish the foundation's reputation for political neutrality. Child, meanwhile, returned to a lower profile.[157] Nonetheless, the series of incidents reveals in stark fashion the way in which the actions of the federal Liberal party had radicalized a prominant voice of business in the West.

In summary, the political/business class in western Canada – even some of its most moderate representatives – had become increasingly disenchanted during the 1970s and 1980s by the policies of the Trudeau Liberals. The decline of business and institutional support for the Liberal party, combined with increased regional, political, and ideological alienation from central Canadian political life, resulted over the next two years in a revival of right-wing extremism in the West.

THE RISE AND FALL OF THE RIGHT-WING 'FRINGE'

The days and weeks following the announcement of the NEP saw a resurgence of support for the right-wing 'fringe' parties that had been born the previous election day. Advocating an independent western Canada defined by, among other things, one official language, the protection of property rights, the use of citizens' referendums, and free enterprise, Doug Christie's Western Canada Concept (WCC) attracted an estimated 2500 people to a meeting held at Edmonton's Jubilee Auditorium on 20 November 1980.[158] In December a similar WCC rally in Calgary drew over 1000 people.

By the end of that month, the party boasted 2500 members.[159] In-

cluded among these was a fifty-one-year-old Edmonton realtor, Allan
R. Maygard, who became the party's first Alberta leader; Gordon Kesler,
a thirty-four-year-old oil scout and rodeo rider who would later win
a provincial by-election; Hilton (Wes) Westmore, a Calgary geologist
who subsquently became president of the party; and sixty-one-year-old
James Garfield Peever 'a onetime farm boy from Acme, northeast of
Calgary and retired provincial assessment officer.'[160] Both Westmore
and Peever had belonged previously to another separatist organization,
J.C. Rudolph's Independent Alberta Association (IAA). The idea of creating an independent, right-wing western state was suddenly becoming
respectable.

During this same period, the fortunes of WCC's counterpart, West-
Fed, rose even faster, particularly in Alberta's rural community. Unlike
WCC, West-Fed downplayed its support for separation. It also portrayed
itself as a lobby group rather than a party. Nonetheless, West-Fed's
policies were virtually identical to those of the WCC, opposing bilingualism and metrification, while decrying what it viewed as the systematic
degrading of traditional British values and symbols, and the replacement of free enterprise with socialism.[161]

In early October 1980 West-Fed attracted 400 people to a meeting in
Red Deer. In November, a crowd of over 425 people in Airdrie heard
University of Calgary economist Warren Blackman attack Trudeau's
'centralist socialism' as incompatible with the West's 'free enterprise
zeal.'[162] A similar West-Fed rally held at Henry Wise Wood High School
in Calgary attracted nearly 1500 people.[163]

West-Fed's biggest coup, however, came the same month during a
luncheon speech given in Calgary by oilman Carl Nickle. Nickle told
the assembled crowd of 800: 'No matter what the federal government
does now, I am a confirmed separatist.'[164] During the following weeks,
West-Fed twice obtained crowds of over 1000 people in Calgary, and
continued to receive support in the smaller communities. By December
West-Fed claimed an estimated membership of about 25,000.

Any suggestion that separatism had peaked was quashed in early
February when 1000 people showed up at Edmonton's Jubilee Auditorium to hear Elmer Knutson, Blackman, and British-born Edmonton
architect Peter Hemingway denounce the centralist and socialist policies of the Trudeau government. Notably, the meeting was also marred
by several hostile verbal confrontations between the crowd and a few
hecklers. One particularly nasty episode saw a Canadian of East Indian
descent told by some in the crowd to 'go back to Pakistan.'[165]

More separatist rallies occurred throughout the province, and else-where, in the weeks and months that followed. A wcc rally in Rimbey, sixty-four kilometers from Red Deer, attracted 600 people to listen to a debate between Christie and former Liberal MP Jack Horner.[166] Knutson, meanwhile, took his crusade to Manitoba where, on 26 Feburary, he spoke to a crowd of 600 in Brandon. The meeting proved to be a public relations disaster.

The following day, the CBC national news reported that Knutson's speech went beyond western alienation to attack federal immigration policies (which he reportedly said favoured 'Wops and Chinks'), metrification, the human rights commission, and 'francophone power.'[167] By this time, dissent was brewing within West-Fed over Knutson's leadership. In early March, he failed to appear at a fund-raising dinner, apparently in response to the cancellation of Jock Andrew's appearance as guest speaker. The cancellation had been precipitated by the recently elected West-Fed president, Calgarian Fred Noyes, after he read Andrew's *Bilingualism Today, French Tomorrow*. A short while later, West-Fed's executive, including Noyes, resigned, as did the organization's communications director, Michael Byfield, son of Ted Byfield.[168] The low estate to which West-Fed had fallen was reinforced in early April, when a meeting at Henry Wise Wood High School in Calgary, site of a major rally only months earlier, attracted only two dozen people.[169]

There remained, however, many deep feelings of alienation in Al-berta over the implementation of the NEP, as shown by a poll released by the Canada West Foundation in May 1981. The poll showed that 15 per cent of Albertans were in favour of a separate country. Even more revealing, however, was that 49 per cent agreed with the statement that 'Western Canadians get so few benefits from being part of Canada that they might as well go it on their own.'[170] West-Fed, however, was un-able to mobilize this discontent. On 21 May, the night after the Canada West Foundation report was released, only 200 people showed up at a West-Fed fund-raising barbeque in Calgary. Guest speakers at the barbeque were Andrew and former Conservative MP Stan Shumacher. Shumacher, who had recently joined West-Fed, urged people to sup-port Peter Lougheed.[171]

West-Fed was in decline. Under increased attack from his support-ers, Knutson decided in March 1982 to dissolve West-Fed, encouraging his followers instead to join WCC and pursue western independence.[172] By this time, however, Knutson's admonition to his followers was largely redundant; perhaps as many as 80 per cent of West-Fed members were simultaneously members of WCC.[173]

As it happened, many of the same problems that dogged West-Fed were also beginning to beset WCC. A series of speeches by Christie to audiences in rural Alberta were condemned by supporters as arrogant and dictatorial.[174] In October 1981 Maygard and Westmore ousted Christie as leader, ultimately denying him a membership in the Alberta branch of WCC. They were joined on the party executive by Kesler and Howard Thompson. Thompson, a sixty-one-year-old Innisfail grain farmer and brother of former national Social Credit leader Robert Thompson, promptly reorganized the party and turned its policies away from separatism towards proposals for constitutional reform.[175]

Under the leadership of Maygard, Westmore, Kesler, and Thompson, WCC became better organized while stepping up its attack on the NEP. Alberta was then entering a recession, which the WCC and other right-wing elements blamed upon the hated policy. As evidence, they pointed to the number of drilling rigs that had fled the province since the program's inception. On 30 October 1979, 306 rigs were drilling in Alberta. On 21 October 1980, just before the budget announcement and still at the time of the oil-pricing boom, 372 rigs were operating in the province. A year later, on 27 October 1981, only 233 rigs were drilling.[176] Most of the others had fled to the United States or been shut down indefinitely.

Lougheed and Trudeau had signed a pricing agreement in September 1981, a month before Maygard and company took over WCC. The Liberals reduced their export tax to zero in return for Lougheed's agreeing to a two-price system on new and existing oil that in fact provided the province with an immensely better deal than that previously offered by Clark's Tories.[177] A photographer captured the moment: Lougheed and Trudeau toasting, with champagne, the long-awaited agreement.[178]

Unfortunately for both Alberta and the federal Liberals, the agreement had come too late. The members of the OPEC cartel were already cheating on each other, undercutting the world oil price. Moreover, the high energy costs had strangled the economies of the western industrialized world, and much of the Third World, resulting in a major recession and a drop in the demand for oil. Finally, the price of oil also fuelled the renewed efforts of various countries to change to alternative energy sources. All of these factors led to the price of oil dropping to $15 per barrel. Alberta's day in the sun suffered an eclipse.

In the weeks and months following the Ottawa-Alberta oil-pricing agreement, and in the midst of a mounting recession, WCC shifted its criticisms away from federal politics to Peter Lougheed's handling of the Alberta economy. Many in the oilpatch viewed the provincial Conservatives as having sold them out. The photograph of a smiling Lougheed drinking a champagne toast with Trudeau after signing the oil-pricing agreement now came back to haunt the Conservative leader; wcc reported that it was attracting its largest crowds in those rural areas of Alberta hardest hit by layoffs resulting from the drop in oilfield work.[179] There were also increasing complaints that Lougheed's government was preaching, but not practising, free enterprise.[180]

To this point, the right-wing fringe had been denied the possibility of expressing itself in an election. In June 1981, however, Social Credit MLA Bob Clark, former leader of the provincial party, announced that he would be resigning his seat in Olds-Didsbury later in the year. Two days after this announcement, wcc became registered as a political party in the province, thereby making it eligible to contest the expected by-election.

When the by-election finally occurred in February 1982, Gordon Kesler won resoundingly, receiving 4015 votes compared with the Social Credit candidate Lloyd Quantz who took 2669 votes and the Tory candidate Stephen Stiles who took 2346 votes. By-elections are, of course, notorious as opportunities for people to vent anger at ruling parties. Popular opinion in the case of Olds-Didsbury attributed Kesler's victory to 'simmering western rage over the NEP and the September 1981 Alberta-Ottawa energy agreement.'[181] The party claimed (unconfirmed) 12,000 members that year, most of them in Alberta.[182] wcc, and the western right wing in general, appeared to be on the move.

In April the party's executive issued a *Statement of Independence* outlining the party's intentions should it win a forthcoming provincial election. The party intended, said the *Statement*, to 'prepare for independence in a peaceful and democratic manner' and otherwise to pursue policies of unilingualism, fixed electoral terms, the protection of property rights, the right of referendum, a simplified tax system, the rescinding of the NEP, and the elimination of marketing boards. Elsewhere, wcc appeared to be gaining strength in British Columbia, as indicated by a rally in Abbotsford which attracted 1700 people.[183]

In April, however, rumours emerged of dissension between Kesler and Maygard. A while later, Maygard was thrown out as president. Maygard and Westmore left the party, charging that wcc had been taken over by Mormons, led by Kesler, and that Kesler and Howard Thompson were not committed separatists.[184]

The party was soon also rift by other petty scandals. A leadership convention in August 1982 revealed further splits within the party. When the provincial election was held in early November, wcc was not prepared for the challenge. Lougheed's Tories won seventy-five seats with just over 62 per cent of the votes cast, while Kesler (and all other wcc candidates) lost. Nonetheless, wcc received 111,131 votes – nearly 12 per cent of the total vote – indicating a solid base of support for the party's policies.

Both Kesler and Howard Thompson resigned from the party shortly after the election. A former RCMP officer and committed separatist, Jack Ramsay, took over as leader, while Dr Fred Marshall, an Edmonton urologist, became president. The right-wing separatist (or semi-separatist) western parties, however, were in decline. Though many of the parties' members would remain on the political scene, the right-wing fringe parties had virtually disappeared by 1983.

One significant exception to this pattern of decline occurred in Manitoba in 1984. Manitoba has a long history of language disputes, dating back to the end of the last century. The Manitoba Act of 1870 had ensured the rights of French-speaking Roman Catholics in that province. In 1890, however, the provincial Liberal party, encouraged by the English-speaking majority, passed legislation making English the only official language. The resultant political conflict destroyed Sir John A. Macdonald's federal Conservative party, while strengthening Sir Wilfrid Laurier's Liberal party that deferred to provincial jurisdiction in the matter. The dispute between the English-speaking majority and the French-speaking minority continued to fester over the years, even as the percentage of francophones in the province declined.

In 1979, the Supreme Court of Canada ruled that Manitoba's legislation denying bilingualism was unconstitutional. The practical result of this ruling was that Manitoba was faced with translating into French all laws passed since 1890. The Tory government of the day under Sterling Lyon, backed by older, wealthy, and rural elements who tended to be opposed to bilingualism, was reluctant to act on the Supreme Court's decision.

Upon its election in 1983, however, Howard Pawley's NDP decided to meet the court's stipulations. During 1984–5, the government pressed forward with legislation to extend French-language services in the province, despite wide opposition led by the Tories under their new leader, Gary Filmon. Much to the displeasure of Tory leader Brian Mulroney, who denounced opposition to the extension of rights as based in prejudice, Filmon fought vehemently against the legislation. The debate was extremely divisive and frequently racist. When the Tories shut down the legislature by ringing the bell to order and then not attending session, the NDP was trapped. Reluctant to force passage of the legislation, the NDP withdrew it altogether.

The debate was still going on, however, when the federal election was held in 1984. That August Elmer Knutson had finally bowed to pressures from former WCC and West-Fed members in founding and registering a new political party, the Confederation of Regions party (COR). In the election which followed, the COR party was able to parlay anti-French sentiment into 34,384 votes (6.7 per cent of all votes cast) in the province of Manitoba, most of this vote occurring in the southwestern, rural part of the province.

Among COR's more esteemed converts was an aging Douglas Campbell, the last Liberal premier of Manitoba (1948–58). Another notable COR supporter was Fred Debrecen. During the 1986 provincial election, Debrecen founded a Winnipeg-based group called One Nation, One Language Inc. (ONOLI), a kind of Manitoba equivalent to APEC, which circulated petitions calling for a unilingual (English) Canada.[185]

A second exception to the general demise of the fringe parties occurred in the Spirit River–Fairview provincial by-election in Alberta in February 1985. The by-election was called following the untimely death of NDP MLA and leader Grant Notley. The NDP candidate subsequently won the by-election, taking 2511 votes, but four right-wing fringe parties contesting the election (WCC, COR, Social Credit, and the Heritage party) together received 2146 votes.[186]

As a consequence of these election results, Dr Marshall, president of WCC, met the next day with interim Social Credit leader, Martin Hattersley, to discuss a political merger. In October Marshall announced that an amalgamation had occurred and that henceforth WCC and Alberta Social Credit would be called the Alberta Political Alliance (APA). The new party, said leader Jack Ramsay, would abandon separatism in favour of fighting for a Triple-E (equal, elected, and effective) Senate, honesty in government, and free enterprise. In January 1986 Howard Thompson, now interim vice-president of the APA, formally registered the party, stating that it would 'pull the splinter parties together.'[187] But the hoped-for unity never emerged. Instead, the subsequent 1986 Alberta provincial election witnessed a plethora of right-wing parties including wcc, the APA, COR, the Heritage Party of Alberta, and the Representative Party of Alberta, contest eighty-one seats.[188]

In October 1986, in the midst of Alberta's recession and following

WCC's poor showing in the provincial election, Jack Ramsay announced that the party would return to its separatist platform. It was, however, too late. By then, support for WCC had dwindled to between 700 and 1000 members. Said former executive Thompson: 'The WCC had great potential, but personalities got in the way.'[189]

The right-wing fringe parties would continue through several manifestations in the years to come, gradually moving eastward in the process. But they failed, in the main, to reap the full rewards of the discontent evident in western Canada during the early 1980s. Internal organizational factors certainly played a part in this failure. The leadership of Christie, Knutson, and others was often erratic, and their parties' platforms were almost uniformly negative and ill thought out. The result was a failure by the parties' leadership to enunciate a credible vision to the discontented western masses. Even when they were able to tap into the 'system of narration' underlying westerner's grievances, Christie's and Knutson's paranoid extremism and the latter's racial comments soon ripped apart their thin connection to their audience.

In turn, these internal problems seriously reduced tangible outside support for the parties. While many business leaders were sympathetic to at least some of Knutson's and Christie's ideas and sentiments, most were loath to attach themselves to parties that seemed doomed from the start to obscurity. The right-wing fringe parties were thus generally starved of the respect, resources, and prestige that outright support from the business community might have brought them.

Even had the fringe parties received this support, however, the time may not have been propitious for their success. Neither the West, nor any province within it, constitutes a perfectly homogeneous political entity. In the early 1980s, the West was neither a political wasteland for moderate left-wing views, nor a sacrosanct precinct for the kind of extreme right-wing orthodoxy preached by the fringe element. Proof can be found in both the percentages of votes received by the Liberal party and NDP in the West during the 1980s, and the results of polls that showed significant western support for such Liberal policies as the new Constitution, bilingualism, and the NEP.[190] Hence, there was – and remains – a natural, though not impermeable, limit to the growth of any party in the region. The right-wing fringe parties' internal problems and lack of business support simply meant that they fell short even of this limit and did so more quickly than might otherwise have occurred.

Finally, the rise of the right-wing fringe parties also was hampered by the fact that an acceptable political alternative – the federal Tories –

was available and waiting in the wings. To many right-wing elements in the region, it seemed absurd to splinter their electoral strength just when victory seemed at hand. Nonetheless, the fringe parties were a genuine, albeit extreme, reflection of a right-wing resurgence in the West during the early 1980s. To the extent that extremism is succinct and clear, these parties provide a useful analytical prelude to the later emergence of the Reform party.

The rise of populist parties and movements is presaged by a series of political, economic, and ideological crises that delegitimize the dominant hegemony and the existing political parties. By the late 1970s, a series of economic and political crises had resulted in the West as a whole, and its two wealthiest provinces, Alberta and British Columbia, in particular, becoming estranged from the federal Liberal party. While the resultant political gap was filled to some extent by the left-wing NDP and the right-wing fringe parties, the major beneficiary of the Liberal collapse in the West on the federal scene was the federal Progressive Conservative party.

In 1984 a substantial number of Canadians from all areas of the political spectrum were ready for a change. They were tired of the seemingly endless political wrangling of the last few years and the scandals and patronage of the Trudeau Liberals. They were increasingly concerned about the economic situation. Many felt alienated from the political process. Brian Mulroney's Tories – Canada's 'natural government-in-waiting' for much of the century – seemed to offer a positive alternative. Somewhat cautiously, somewhat sceptically, right-wing Tories in the West licked their chops, believing that the political changes occurring elsewhere in the country meant that, perhaps at last, their time had come.

3. The Rise of the Reform Party

What we need is a credible western party.

Ted Byfield, 1986[1]

Neither an organic crisis nor the resultant delegitimation of the dominant hegemony or existing political parties is sufficient to create a populist party. New populist parties do not arise as long as a legitimate political contender exists – one capable of reincorporating the elements 'freed' by the crisis. This inherent conservatism, combined with the possible resolution of the precipitating organic crisis, renders the rise of populist parties an uncommon occurrence. Occasionally, however, the organic crisis continues unabated while the succession of political contenders either fail in their task of reincorporation or succeed in exacerbating the crisis of legitimation. Then the possibility emerges for a new political party, espousing the interests of the alienated social elements.

In 1984, Brian Mulroney's Progressive Conservatives received one of the largest electoral mandates ever obtained in Canada in decisively ending some twenty years of Liberal dominance. Among those voting for the Tories – for the first time – was the estranged Liberal, Francis Winspear. 'I believed the representations of the Conservatives that they would be receptive and prepared to ameliorate the grievances of the West; so I voted Conservative for the first time in my life.'[2] By the spring of 1987, however, a frustrated Winspear sat in his Ardmore Drive home in Victoria, feeling once more betrayed:

Once again, I found that the West had been sold down the river. Admittedly, the controls on petroleum and natural gas have been removed, but in the meantime world prices had declined, so this was not much help. The Meech Lake Agreement was most distasteful. Why should the Quebec French be recognized as a special group[?] A Canadian is a Canadian.[3]

In Vancouver a few weeks later, Winspear, along with Stan Roberts, Preston Manning, and Ted Byfield, took the first step in creating an alternative right-wing party.

This chapter examines, by way of example, the problems facing a 'successor' party during a period of organic crises and hegemonic shifts. In particular, I examine the Tories' winning electoral coalition in 1984; the events that subsequently began the disintegration of this coalition; the people, events, and organizational processes that led to the formation of the Reform Party of Canada in 1987; and the important 'Free Trade' election of 1988.

THE TORIES' WINNING COALITION OF 1984

The Tories won the election of 1984 in a manner rarely achieved by any party in a liberal democracy. The party received 6,278,697 votes (50 per cent) in taking 211 of 282 seats. By contrast, the Liberals received 3,516,486 votes (28 per cent), and the NDP 2,359,915 votes (19 per cent). In the West, a traditionally strong region of Tory support, Mulroney's party took 58 of 77 seats. Astonishingly, the man who led the Tories to their massive victory had first won political office only the year previous – in a Nova Scotian by-election.[4]

Brian Mulroney was born in Baie Comeau, Quebec, in 1939, the son of an electrician. He attended St Francis Xavier University, where he received a BA in political science. He later briefly attended Dalhousie and then Laval, where he gained a law degree.

His university career was generally uneventful; however, Mulroney soon began to make the contacts that would later forge his political career. Mulroney became increasingly active in the Quebec political scene during the early 1960s, reportedly campaigning to dump John Diefenbaker as leader of the Progressive Conservatives in the late 1960s. In the years following Robert Stanfield's succession in 1967 to the leadership, Mulroney continued to strengthen his position within the small Quebec Tory establishment.

His political prominence was raised during 1974–5 as one of three commissioners on Quebec's Cliche Commission inquiry into violence and corruption in the province's construction industry. This enlarged public profile, coupled with his political contacts within the Quebec political establishment, led Mulroney in 1976 to try for the leadership of the federal Progressive Conservative party. The leadership contest was brutal as Quebec delegates divided their support between native sons Mulroney and Claude Wagner. Many delegates were concerned by Mulroney's ties to big business and his lack of real political experience. In the end, Joe Clark, another political unknown, was elected leader.

Mulroney was reportedly devastated by the defeat. Nonetheless, he was soon hired as president of the Iron Ore Company of Canada, a branch plant of an American conglomerate based in Cleveland. He would subsequently oversee the closing down of the company's Shefferville operations. During this time, Mulroney was never far from the political scene. After the Tories' 1980 election defeat, he began to work behind the scenes to undermine Joe Clark's leadership. When Clark narrowly failed to receive two-thirds of membership support at the 1981 Tory general meeting, the door opened for a leadership convention. At that convention in 1983, Mulroney defeated a host of candidates, including Clark and the colourful right-wing businessman, Peter Pocklington. Slightly more than a year later, Mulroney was prime minister.

Although the Tories drew widespread support throughout Canada in 1984, their victory was secured by the backing they received from Quebec nationalists, big business, and conservative elements in Ontario and the West, particularly Alberta. Support from the first two elements of this troika flowed from Mulroney's being both a Quebecer, with strong connections to that province's nationalist élite, and a businessperson with equally strong connections to Canada's corporate élite. Support for the Tories in the West redounded, meanwhile, to long-entrenched ideological predispositions combined with a certain political habit dating to the Diefenbaker sweep of 1958.

Hence, the election of 1984 saw the Tories take fifty-eight of Quebec's seventy-five seats. In order to fully understand the magnitude of this result, consider that in 1980 the Liberals had taken seventy-four of seventy-five seats! The 1984 results were even more astonishing if one considers that the Tory machine in the province was almost non-existent.[5] Yet, despite the party's inadequacies, the Tories achieved success in Quebec in 1984. The reasons for this success in a province historically hostile to the party can be attributed to Mulroney's personal appeal to Quebecers in general and to Quebec nationalists in particular.

Still bitter over their referendum defeat in 1980 and the subsequent Constitution of 1982, Quebec nationalists saw in Mulroney an ally who would promote a greater decentralization of federal powers and the strengthening of the Quebec state. Many supporters of Parti Québécois leader and premier René Lévesque worked actively for Mulroney's Tories. Moreover, many of the Tory candidates in 1984 had actively worked for the 'yes' side in the 1980 referendum. Mulroney even received support from the lukewarm-federalist Quebec Liberal leader, Robert Bourassa, who believed that his provincialist ambitions would be better met by Mulroney than John Turner.

Mulroney's Tories also received massive support from business. From his earliest university days to his time as president of the Iron Ore Company, Mulroney had cultivated contacts in the business community. These contacts allowed Mulroney to spend over $500,000 on his aborted drive for the leadership in 1976, far more than that spent by the other contenders.[6] Much of the money for Mulroney's campaign came from large businesses, such as Power Corporation. Mulroney received similar support in finally gaining the Tory leadership in 1983. This support continued into the 1984 federal election.

That year, contributions to the Progressive Conservative party from the business and commercial sector totalled $11 million. By contrast, the Liberal party received just over $5 million from the private corporate sector and the NDP only $51 thousand. The latter's shortfall in corporate donations, however, was partially made up by about $2 million received from labour.[7]

The Progressive Conservatives indirectly received additional corporate support in 1984. In July of that year, an Alberta court upheld an application by the right-wing National Citizens' Coalition against the federal government's Bill C-169, which prevented political lobbyists from political advertising during elections.[8] The NCC immediately used the court decision to intervene massively in the 1984 election, spending $700,000 fighting the Liberals, in particular the NEP, and $100,000 denouncing the NDP.[9]

The third major element of the Tories' winning coalition included both fiscal and moral conservatives, a group described by one group of authors as 'anti-abortion, anti-metric, pro capital punishment, pro balanced budgets, pro defence spending, and anti-universality in social programs ...'[10] They were – and are – also fiercely opposed to official bilingualism. In Ontario, petit bourgeois supporters, the organizational efficiency of premier William Davis's 'Big Blue Machine,' and big business support resulted in the federal Tories taking sixty-seven of ninety-five seats. Meanwhile, in the West, where the right wing had faithfully supported the Tories since the Diefenbaker sweep of 1958, the party also took all twenty-one seats in Alberta and nineteen of twenty-eight in British Columbia.

Altogether, Mulroney's Tories were able to reconstitute in Tory terms the Liberal alliance first created by Laurier, between French and English (mainly western) Canada and later refurbished by Mackenzie King, via C.D. Howe, through an alliance with big business. A measure of this success is that 53 per cent and 48 per cent of those of British and French origin, respectively, supported the Tories. By contrast, the Tories were supported by only 36 per cent of voters from other ethnic groups.[11]

Perhaps because the Tories had reconstituted the traditional Liberal alliance, few Canadians expected that politics or policies in Canada would substantially change. Indeed, both in his book, *Where I Stand*, and in speeches before and during the election, Mulroney had promised, if anything, a more progressive, workable form of Liberal-style government.[12]

No more would partisanship mar the political landscape. Gone would be federal-provincial conflict, replaced instead by mutual respect and cooperation. The same would be true of labour-management relations. The new Tory Canada, he stated, would be more prosperous. A Tory government would create hundreds of thousands of new jobs during its first year in office. A Tory Canada would also see increased fairness in the treatment of visible minorities and women. Above all, it would be more politically responsive.

At the same time, Mulroney also promised to retain those features that distinguished Canada from the United States. For example, social programs would be protected by any Conservative government; they were 'a sacred trust.'[13] As for free trade with the United States, long a pursuit of certain elements of big business and the Tories' constituency in the West, Mulroney's answer was even more blunt. 'This country could not survive with a policy of unfettered free trade ... It affects Canadian sovereignty and we will have none of it, not during the leadership campaign or at any other time.'[14]

Examining these policy statements and the results of the election, most political observers believed that, despite their margin of victory, the Tories had not won a mandate for radical change. The *Toronto Star*, a liberal newspaper, commented in its editorial of 5 September: 'What

we have witnessed is not so much a change in the basic political thinking of Canadians as a change in the political positioning of our parties.'
Similarly, journalist Robert Miller, writing in *Maclean's* magazine on
17 September, stated: 'the Mulroney majority does not reflect a fundamental shift to the right by Canadians. Instead, it is in the tradition
of Laurier's Liberal alliance ...'

Although many in the Tory leadership agreed, albeit reluctantly, with
these assessments, the core elements of Tory support – Quebec nationalists, big business, liberal free traders, and traditional conservatives – were determined that radical changes should occur in Canada's
economic, political, and ideological structures. The often conflicting expectations of these elements, combined with the predictable problems
of any government newly elected to power, soon resulted in an unravelling of support for the Tory government.

THE BEGINNINGS OF DISILLUSIONMENT

The Tories came into office carrying enormous expectations and political debts. This baggage alone might well have spelled trouble for the
party. Added to this, however, was the low public esteem to which the
party, and Mulroney in particular, soon fell as the result of a series of
patronage scandals.

Patronage was already a politically loaded issue when the Tories
took office in 1984. Indeed, throughout 1983 they had made much of
Liberal patronage. The issue was magnified during Trudeau's last
month in office when he named friends and associates to 225 posts.
Public anger grew when, shortly after taking over as Liberal leader and
prime minister, John Turner appointed eighteen more Liberals to various posts under a secret agreement previously made with Trudeau.[15]
The public's outrage was equalled only by the Tories' glee at having
been given yet another political whip with which to flay the Liberals.

Indeed, the most memorable moment of the ensuing election came
during a televised election debate, when Mulroney, his finger pointing
accusingly at Turner, challenged the then prime minister to apologize
for having made the appointments. Turner offered a lame excuse:
'I had no option.' Mulroney countered: 'You had an option, sir.' The
incident was the telling moment in the election and effectively ended
any hopes that Turner had of winning.[16]

Mulroney was thus well aware of the public's attitude towards patronage. He even made promises to clean up the system of government

appointments. But Mulroney was also aware that one of the frequent criticisms made by Tories of Joe Clark's brief tenure in 1979 was that he had failed to bestow sufficient patronage 'goodies' upon party loyalists.[17] Given the 'option,' Mulroney decided after the election to carry on business as usual.

Within three weeks in late January 1985, the Tories made seventy-one patronage appointments. In March the Tories fired the entire Air Canada board and replaced it with loyal members of the party. Similar treatment was soon accorded the boards of Via Rail, Petro-Canada, Canadian National, and Ports Canada.[18] Favours, and rumours of favours, for friends did not end, however, with public appointments. Soon there were stories of friends and relatives of Tory cabinet ministers being given untendered contracts to do government work.

The effect of this apparent orgy of patronage and indiscriminate spending upon the Canadian public cannot be underestimated. Many Canadians, among them previously loyal Liberals, had voted for the Tories believing that morality, ethics, and fiscal responsibility would be returned to political life. Instead they were treated within months of the Tories' taking office to what many viewed as a continuation of the same cynicism, arrogance, and waste previously displayed by the Liberals.

About this same time, the government was also beset by a series of cabinet resignations. Between 1985 and 1987, fisheries minister John Fraser, defence minister Robert Coates, environment (later junior transport) minister Suzanne Blais-Grenier, Roch LaSalle, André Bissonnette, Marcel Masse, Michel Côté, Sinclair Stevens, and Michel Gravel all resigned from cabinet or parliament for reasons ranging from poor judgment to criminal action.[19]

For much of the Canadian public, these scandals confirmed a growing sense of Tory incompetence and dishonesty. Moreover, the fact that so many of the allegations and resignations involved ministers from Quebec confirmed an unconscious – and often conscious – perception held by many in English Canada that Quebec politicians were a particularly venal and untrustworthy bunch.[20] Finally, the manner in which the allegations were handled by Mulroney did little to inspire public confidence. Rather than admit folly or error, Mulroney repeatedly went on the offensive in defending his ministers, even in the face of incontrovertible evidence of ministerial wrongdoing. The result was increased hostility and partisanship in the House of Commons. The public was not amused.

The public also became increasingly concerned about the Tories' handling of the economy. Shortly after taking office, the Tories produced a paper entitled *A New Direction for Canada: An Agenda for Economic Renewal*. Journalist Linda McQuaig notes that the paper was almost identical to one written by the Business Council of National Issues only weeks before.[21] Both papers raised public debate over Canada's burgeoning gross national debt, then at over $181 billion. More importantly, government figures showed that the gross national debt now constituted 52.3 per cent of Canada's annual gross domestic product.[22] Clearly, something had to be done about the deficit. But what? Over the next few years, the Tories proposed solutions – cutting or reducing government programs, shifting taxes from corporations to individuals, replacing the manufacturers' sales tax (MST) with a goods and services tax (GST) – would erode public support for the government. The increasing fiscal crisis of the Canadian state, brought about by declining revenues and increasing social expenditures, also would exacerbate federal-provincial conflicts, creating additional problems for the Tories' nascent political coalition.

In 1985, however, 'profitable federalism' still remained a tactic available to the Tories. Despite preaching fiscal austerity, the Tories continued the Liberal practice of dispensing financial largesse to those regions and areas that had voted for them, in particular, the politically important province of Quebec.

For years Mulroney had worked at bringing Quebec into the Tory fold, viewing that province as the key to any Tory victory.[23] After the election of 1984, he set about proving to Quebecers that the Tories were as able to dispense public largesse to their region as were the Liberals. By the summer of 1985, millions of dollars were pouring directly from Ottawa into Quebec. A report from the Department of Regional Industrial Expansion (DRIE) showed that between the time the Tories took power and March 1985 Alberta had received $16 million in DRIE money, Saskatchewan $18 million, Manitoba $30 million, and British Columbia $47 million (a total of $111 million). By comparison, the same period saw Quebec, with less population than the western region, receive $430 million,[24] much of this (almost $195 million) going to pay for roads, ports, airports, and a new federal prison (that both federal officials and prisoners' families opposed) in Mulroney's own riding of Manitouwagan.[25] The flow of capital into Quebec was further indirectly influenced by federal policies as occurred in 1985, for example, when

Hyundai, the Korean automaker, decided to situate a $300-million plant in Quebec over the bids of three other provinces owing to federal decisions regarding subsidies and duty remissions.[26]

Not all federal spending, however, carries equal political weight. Hence, despite Mulroney's previous declarations that universality was 'a sacred trust not to be tampered with' and that he would 'preserve social programmes,' the Tories began attacking social programs almost immediately after the election. When Michael Wilson's first budget threatened to de-index old age pensions, however, Mulroney was accosted outside the House of Commons by a sixty-three-year-old woman, Solange Denis, who shouted at him, 'You lied to us!' The scene, captured on national television, embarrassed the government and it backed down.[27] The retreat would be only temporary.

The financial cuts and other changes in Canada's infrastructure did not end, however, with social programs. Over the next few years, the Tories would privatize Air Canada, cut the CBC's budget, and effectively eliminate train travel throughout Canada. Despite continuing widespread public support for Petro-Canada, they would also move to privatize that company. The economic, political, and emotional ties that many viewed as binding Canada – and Canadians – together would be severed in the name of cost-cutting and competitiveness.

The attack on government programs was supplemented by changes in tax laws that increased the wealth and power of Canada's corporations and entrenched élites. Ignoring his own promises to make the tax system fairer and to shift 'more of the tax burden from individuals to corporations,' finance minister Michael Wilson enacted multiple tax breaks for both corporations and rich individuals. Benefits for the latter included increases in the purchasable amount of Registered Retirement Savings Plans (RRSPS), an allowance of indefinite deferment on inheritance taxes, and elimination of capital gains taxes below a set ceiling.[28]

There were, of course, public protests against these Tory policies by labour unions, cultural interests, and women's groups. At the directly political level, the Liberals and NDP also attempted to attack the Tory agenda. For much of the period between the 1984 and 1988 elections, however, the Liberals were in disarray. Unaccustomed to being in opposition, facing a government that in many ways was only a slightly more right-wing version of itself, and saddled with a leader who was neither liberal by inclination nor accepted by many of the party's sup-

porters and MPs, Liberal attacks on the Tory government often dissipated in unfocused, partisan carping and hopes that the Tories would
self-destruct.

The NDP was in better shape. It had survived the 1984 election
with its core support intact. Its leader, Ed Broadbent, was widely liked
and respected by an electorate that viewed the party as credible and
honest, particularly on social issues. The public remained sceptical,
however, of the NDP's economic policies, a critical failing at a time
when the federal deficit was gaining salience as a political concern and
when neo-conservative solutions to the problems of the welfare state
were gaining support. Moreover, the NDP had never been in power
federally; indeed, in 1985 it had governed in only three provinces (BC,
Manitoba, and Saskatchewan). In short, the NDP had not yet entered
general public consciousness as a 'real' contender.

In the end, external political opposition to the Tories was largely
sporadic and ineffectual. More serious to the party were attacks from
within. Some of the party's supporters, including several long-time MPs,
became increasingly disturbed and embarrassed by the seemingly
endless scandals and resignations. Others, although praising the party's economic policies on taxation and investment, believed that the
Tories were not going far or fast enough to the right in attacking the
deficit or reversing liberal policies on such issues as abortion and capital punishment.[29] Some Tory supporters in English Canada, particularly
the West, denounced the continued pouring of federal moneys into
Quebec. Yet others worried that the public's dislike of Mulroney, combined with the government's generally perceived incompetence, was
opening the door for the Liberals or – worse! – the NDP. All in all, a growing sense of disillusionment began to sweep through many Tory supporters. Typical of those feeling disillusioned was a bright, young economist, Stephen Harper.[30]

Harper, who would later become chief policy officer for the Reform
party, was born (in 1958) and raised in Toronto. During the late 1970s
he had moved to Alberta to work in the oil industry. His formative
experiences there coincided with the recession of the early 1980s and
the implementation of the NEP, events that increased his conservative
leanings.

In 1981, while still working for Imperial Oil, Harper enrolled at the
University of Calgary where, in 1985, he completed a bachelor's degree
in economics. By this time, Joe Clark had been defeated as Conservative leader by Brian Mulroney. Harper hated Joe Clark, a man who

Harper had believed, during the 1980 election, would merely appease the Quebec separatists. Hence, the change to Mulroney was applauded by Harper, who subsequently took a job working in the Ottawa office of Calgary Tory MP Jim Hawkes.

In short order, however, Harper came to view the Tories as unable to make the tough economic decisions that he felt were necessary to deal with the federal deficit. Moreover, he was shocked by what he viewed as the Quebec separatist MPs, ideological left-wingers, and policy manipulators within the Tory party. Disillusioned, Harper left Hawkes's office in 1986 to begin his master's program at the University of Calgary, believing that his active involvement in politics was over.

Harper was not alone in his disillusionment. By 1986, many on the right viewed Mulroney as 'not a real Tory.'[31] In that year, these disgruntled elements found a voice in a book written by Peter Brimelow.

PETER BRIMELOW AND THE GHOST OF GOLDWIN SMITH

If Ernest Manning's *Political Realignment* is thoughtful but bland, and J.V. Andrew's *Bilingual Today, French Tomorrow* paranoid and extreme, Peter Brimelow's *The Patriot Game* is the *pièce de résistance* of the right-wing's articulation of Canada's political problems. Brimelow opens the text with the declaration that he is 'a wandering WASP,' a British-born journalist educated at both the University of Sussex in England and the Stanford University Graduate School of Business. He wrote the book as a 'modest attempt at presenting a General Theory of Canada.'[32] This theory can be summarized as follows.

Canada is legally a nation-state, but not a nation. It is made up instead of at least two sub-nations (English and French) and perhaps several others based on regional differences. Of these sub-nations, only 'Quebec is emerging as a genuine nation-state.'[33] English Canada lacks a real identity because it has suppressed its true nature both in trying to pacify the demands of Quebec's francophone population and in a futile attempt to deny its cultural similarity to the United States. In an equally futile effort to make Canada work, a 'large and powerful public class' has developed, associated primarily with the Liberal party, which has attempted to mediate differences between regions and ethnic groups.[34] In typically oligarchic fashion, this public class has, according to Brimelow, acted mainly to enhance its own position through such policies as bilingualism, the National Energy Program, and Canadian nationalism, which Brimelow views as a sham and hypocrisy.

Brimelow ends his book with a series of prognostications:

1. Canada's fundamental contradictions cannot be resolved in the present Confederation. In the long run, Confederation must be reformed or even dissolved...
2. Quebec is emerging as a nation ...
3. English Canada will – sooner or later – recover from its post-Imperial hangover, and will increasingly assert its North American identity ... Eventually, Anglophones will question the value of the Quebec connection. *The Quebec issue in Canadian politics may become not whether Quebec will secede – but whether it should be expelled.* [Italics added.]
4. The sectional divisions within English Canada will be a continuing problem...
5. Brian Mulroney will almost certainly fail to create a Tory electoral coalition. But the Liberals won't find it easy to recreate theirs either ... *New splinter parties may emerge.* [Italics added.]
6. Federal elections are a Canadian version of Russian roulette. One day, Confederation may get shot. In every Canadian election, there is a small but distinct chance ... of ... linguistic polarization ... *A ... quite real danger is that a sectional party, probably from Quebec but possibly from the West, could hold the balance of power in the House and demand radical reforms.*[35] [Italics added.]

In light of subsequent events, Brimelow's observations appear to be remarkably prescient. Certainly, they struck a responsive chord with many on Canada's emerging right wing. Yet Brimelow's thesis is also not particularly new. In fact, it owes a considerable debt – one Brimelow acknowledges in his introduction – to a text written nearly a hundred years earlier.

In 1891, an English journalist and quasi-historian, Goldwin Smith (1823–1910), published *Canada and the Canadian Question*. Smith was the son of a wealthy physician, educated at Eton and Oxford. Cold and aloof, Smith was a typical nineteenth-century English liberal. Opposed to hereditary and aristocratic privileges, yet excessively proud of his Anglo-Saxon heritage, Smith was a firm believer in free enterprise, individualism, and the idea of progress. In the late 1860s, he moved to North America, finally settling in Toronto in 1871.[36] Smith soon became a continentalist, and, through a series of articles published in newspapers, espoused the belief that French and English Canada were incompatible and that the latter should follow its natural bent by joining the United States. *Canada and the Canadian Question* is Smith's magnum opus, elaborating upon and justifying this thesis through a selective reading of history. Like all economic liberals, Smith viewed the question of nationhood as something that can be answered on strictly rational grounds. And this, essentially, is the argument put forward by Brimelow.

It is remarkable to read and compare Smith's text with Brimelow's. The format, subjects discussed, and conclusions drawn are almost identical. The question arises: do the similarities between Smith's and Brimelow's texts reflect the fact that the 'Canada Question' has not fundamentally altered in over a hundred years? Or has Brimelow, like Smith, 'forced' the evidence of divisions within the country to fit a preconceived notion of the 'natural' state?

For Canada's right wing in 1986, the answer was increasingly obvious. The old French-English, core-periphery divisions within the country remained. Liberal – and now Tory – governments had only made the divisions worse. Canada was not working. Nowhere was disillusionment with Canadian politics greater than in the West, a region beset, moreover, by the continuing instability of its staple-based economies.

THE ECONOMICS OF WESTERN DISCONTENT

In 1984, the West was only just recovering from the recession of 1981–2. That recession had seen the final devastation of Saskatchewan's potash industry, the continuing decline of British Columbia's lumber industry, the loss of thousands of jobs in Alberta's oil and gas industry, and the ongoing struggle in general of the West's agricultural sector. Along the way, many of the West's financial institutions had also been devastated, beginning with the collapse of Dial Mortgage Corporation (1981), Fidelity Trust (1983), and Pioneer Trust (1984). Believing that many of their economic problems resulted from the actions of the federal Liberals, and wanting to believe as much in Mulroney's promises to create 200,000 new jobs if elected[37], many people in the West – both former Tories and not – voted for the Progressive Conservatives in 1984.

It is important to emphasize, however, that many of these same voters were not entirely enamoured of Mulroney himself. As we have seen, Quebecers in general voted for Mulroney because he was the 'hometown boy,' nationalists, in particular, because they were swayed by his promises to give Quebec more power and autonomy. Similarly, big business supported Mulroney because of, first, a belief that he was one of them and, secondly, a continuing antipathy toward the Liberals.

By contrast, Mulroney had no immediate connection with westerners.

Indeed, journalists Don Braid and Sydney Sharpe noted that Mulroney's 'personal style and rhetoric are profoundly at odds with western expectations of a prime minister.'[38] What are the elements of Mulroney's style that so grated upon westerners? This is not entirely clear. If asked, many westerners would likely describe Mulroney as verbose, blustering, and arrogant. Yet many – if not all – of these qualities could have been equally attributed to John Diefenbaker, W.A.C. Bennett, Sterling Lyon, and Dave Barrett. Nonetheless, it is not an exaggeration to suggest that many westerners voted for the Progressive Conservatives in 1984 in spite of Mulroney, motivated both by a hatred of the Liberals and a long-standing habit of voting for the Tories.

By 1984, however, many westerners had come to feel that the dynamics of Canada's political system, in particular the overwhelming power of Ontario and Quebec, mitigated against the genuine interests of the hinterland regions. This growing sense of scepticism was voiced by Ted Byfield in a series of *Alberta Report* editorials leading up to the 1984 election. While still favouring the Tories over the despised Liberals and the NDP, Byfield expressed the widely held fear of westerners that, in any case, the electoral system would result in politics as usual – that is, controlled by central Canada. Hence, in an editorial written on 6 August, Byfield referred to the election as 'futile' and 'as irrelevant to the West as the West is to the election.' He followed this on 27 August with an editorial entitled 'The best result for Alberta: 16 Tories, 4 COR & one Liberal.' His reasons behind this formula? 'That way, somebody down there [Ottawa] will hear us.'

The *Alberta Report*'s front page on 17 September, following the Tory win, continued in this vein: 'Who Will Save Us Now?' The same issue's story covering the election referred to 'The West's perilous day: As feared, the Tory caucus is flooded from the East.' In short, the regional alienation felt by many in the West was not diminished – indeed, was exacerbated – by the provincial results underlying the Tory's victory.

That the West's right wing was particularly anxious that policies it favoured should be adopted – and fearful that they would not be – was shown in another *Alberta Report* story shortly after the election:

Alarmed over statist policies of both federal and provincial governments, a group of disaffected Progressive Conservatives in southern Alberta is looking for a new political party of the right to form or join, having taken comfort in neither the election of Brian Mulroney as prime minister, nor in this summer's provincial White Paper on Industrial and Science Strategy.[39]

The article, entitled 'Calgary's new right-wing cabal,' went on to describe how the group, consisting of '50 wealthy high rollers' regularly met at the prestigious Ranchmen's Club in Calgary.[40] One of the leaders of the Ranchmen's group was Marshall Copithorne, a wealthy rancher from Cochrane, Alberta, who (along with several members of his family) would later become a prominent member of the Reform party. The same article stated that the Ranchmen's group was enlisting the support of the National Citizens' Coalition and the Fraser Institute to further its demands for a radical change in Canada's political economy. For such right-wing groups, however, there remained the problem of which political party could (or would) bring about these desired changes. In 1984 there seemed no immediate alternative to the Tories:

None of the current crop of right-wing splinter groups is regarded as a credible vehicle, some because they are too shrill, fractious, and devoted to peripheral issues, and others like the Alternative Government Movement, because they lack a leader ... But [the Ranchmen's group] hope the various groups can coalesce into a credible conservative alternative to the Tories, which can then be bankrolled.[41]

Alberta's right wing was willing to give the Tories a chance. Ominously, however, a spokesperson for the Ranchmen's group, R. Campbell Todd, president of Prairie Pacific Energy Corporation, said that Mulroney had 'just six months to set the course or his mandate will begin to drift.'[42]

The report highlights an increasing rift not only between the corporate sector and any federal government, but also with the provincial Conservatives who, under Lougheed, had been far more interventionist in the economy than the previous Socred government. Indeed, as we have seen in chapter two, many on the right fringe, and in the oil and gas industry, had come to blame Lougheed as much as Trudeau for the debacle of the NEP.[43]

In 1984 the National Energy Program remained a flash point for Albertan discontent. Despite the fact that the guts of the program had been cut out by the agreement of 1981, many Albertans, particularly in the oil and gas industry, continued to view the NEP as having robbed Alberta of its 'place in the sun.' Hence, despite comments from prominent Tory MP Sinclair Stevens, just prior to the election, that a Tory government would continue to control foreign investment in the energy industry,[44] an immediate expectation of westerners was that the NEP and its companion programs would be abolished. As the months went by, however, these programs remained in effect.

The failure of the federal Tories to end the NEP immediately was only one of several actions – or inactions – that bothered the western right wing. In addition, the Tories soon also showed themselves reluctant to sell off the still-popular Petro-Canada. Likewise, some members of the right wing, such as Peter Brimelow, saw the renaming of the Foreign Investment Review Agency into Investment Canada as window-dressing. In short, the western right wing was chagrined that the federal Tories had not taken government shackles off free enterprise. Six months into office – R.C. Todd's deadline – Tory economic policies seemed little different than Liberal policies. At the same time, the political scandals continued to mount.

By the spring of 1985, Alberta's economy was about to enter its second recession in five years. It was signalled, as in 1981, by the collapse of a major financial institution, this time the Canadian Commercial Bank (CCB). For political and economic reasons, the Tories tried at first to bail out the corporation. In April 1985 a conglomerate of the Alberta and British Columbia provincial governments, the federal government, the Royal Bank, Bank of Montreal, CIBC, Bank of Nova Scotia, National Bank of Canada, and Canadian Deposit Insurance Corporation underwrote the bank's debts. Wary investors, however, stung by the previous collapse of financial institutions in the West, continued to withdraw their funds. The haemorrhaging of capital from the CCB continued unabated. Finally, a few weeks after the attempted bail out, the company was allowed to sink into bankruptcy.[45]

The collapse of CCB was only the beginning. Later Calgary's Northlands Bank suffered the same fate. In February 1987 the Alberta government merged the assets of North West Trust and Heritage Savings and Trust in order to save them. In June of the same year, the assets of two subsidiaries of the Principal Group of Companies (First Investors Corporation and Associated Investors of Canada) also were seized by the government. Then, in August, the entire Principal empire collapsed, fuelled by rumours, as well as considerable evidence, of questionable financial transactions by its management.

The failure of many of western Canada's financial institutions was repeated in other sectors of the region's economy. The year 1985 saw the beginning of a subsidy war between European and American grain producers. Combined with increased competition from Third World grain producers, the result was a sudden and drastic decline in the prairie grain industry. By the end of 1986, federal economists were predicting a decline in Alberta's farm income for that year of 60 per cent, with similar severe declines in Manitoba (50 per cent) and Saskatchewan (40 per cent).[46]

Heavily dependent upon its oil and gas industry, the province of Alberta was hardest hit. The situation was not without irony. As we have seen, the Alberta government and the oil and gas industry had long sought the removal of the NEP. The lobbying continued in earnest after the Tories took office in 1984. They were partially rewarded in November 1984 when Michael Wilson's mini-budget brought in cuts in government programs and a reduction in the Petroleum and Gas Revenue Tax (PGRT) paid by oil and gas producers. When the NEP was finally ended, in March 1985, Alberta government officials, Calgary's oil executives, and conservative ideologues in general toasted the event, predicting rapid growth and wealth to come. Oil rigs, they said, soon would be drilling across the province. The oil industry had wanted to be free to compete in the marketplace. Now, it had its wish.

Oscar Wilde wrote that there are only two tragedies: one is not getting what one wants; the other is getting it. In the fall of 1985, the latter tragedy befell Alberta's oil industry. The OPEC cartel failed to agree upon a world oil price. The result was a global free-for-all among producing nations. Canada's oil and gas producers were caught in the middle. Having recently gained freedom from the NEP, Canada's oil and gas industry was also not protected as the price of oil fell from US $27 per barrel in the fall of 1985 to $8 per barrel by August 1986. Many of Alberta's smaller companies (and some of the larger) were wiped out. Forty-five thousand oil workers lost their jobs.[47]

The effects of the recession of 1985–6 upon Alberta are congruent with predictions made by 'relative deprivation theory.' This theory has a long and illustrious pedigree, dating back at least as far as Alexis de Tocqueville and Karl Marx in the last century. Briefly, the theory states that individuals or groups may feel deprived (and may react in a number of ways) when their current economic circumstances compare negatively to the real or imagined situation of others, or their own previous or anticipated future situation.[48] The greater the discrepancy in the comparisons, the greater the likelihood of political unrest.

If relative deprivation theory is correct, we would expect that regions experiencing high volatility in their economies, despite the occasional bounty of boom times, would also experience higher political unrest than places with lower-functioning, but stable, economies.[49] Does relative deprivation theory 'fit' the situation of Alberta and the other western provinces during the 1980s?

One measure of the economic performance of the western provinces is provided by looking at per capita gross domestic product as a percentage of national GDP. During the period 1980–9, Alberta's per capita GDP was higher than that of the other western provinces, averaging 136 per cent of the Canadian average, to British Columbia's 103 per cent, Saskatchewan's 90 per cent, and Manitoba's 87 per cent. Alberta's apparent economic prosperity, however, concealed an otherwise uncertain pattern of productivity.[50] The volatile nature of Alberta's economy, relative to that of the other western provinces, is made apparent by comparing the standard deviations of each province's per capita GDP during the 1980s. While the standard deviations in per capita GDP for British Columbia, Saskatchewan, and Manitoba during this period were relatively low (0.053; 0.09, and 0.016, respectively), Alberta's standard deviation (0.174) indicates far greater economic volatility.[51]

A second measure of economic volatility – unemployment rates during 1980–9 – reveals a similar pattern. Traditionally, British Columbia has had a higher rate of unemployment than the Canadian average, and this pattern continued during this period (11.2 per cent compared to the national average of 9.3 per cent). Both of these average rates were high compared to the mean unemployment rates for Alberta, Saskatchewan, and Manitoba (8.1, 6.9, and 7.6 per cent, respectively) which tend historically to have higher outmigration than British Columbia. Again, however, the unemployment rates for British Columbia and Alberta were much less stable than those of Manitoba and Saskatchewan. While Saskatchewan's and Manitoba's standard deviations for unemployment (1.33 and 1.17, respectively) remained far lower than that of Canada (1.71), British Columbia's (2.89) and Alberta's (2.64) standard deviations show a high degree of instability in the workforce.[52]

In short, during the 1980s both gross domestic product and unemployment rates for Alberta and unemployment rates for British Columbia reveal a high degree of economic volatility.[53] By contrast, Manitoba and Saskatchewan, though less prosperous than their neighbours, had more stable economies. According to relative deprivation theory, we would expect Alberta (followed by British Columbia) to exhibit greater political instability during this period than either Manitoba or Saskatchewan; and indeed that was the case, both in the early 1980s and again after 1985.

As Alberta's economy went into relative decline in the mid-1980s, its social structure also decayed. The result was a proliferation of food banks and labour violence, culminating in 1986 in the infamous Gainers strike in Edmonton, and similar strikes at Fort McMurray (Suncor), Slave Lake (Zeidler Forest Products), and Red Deer (Fletcher's Fine Foods).[54]

Increasingly, the federal Tories were viewed by at least some of their western supporters as oblivious to the West's, particularly Alberta's, plight.[55] Tory supporters, including many of the party's Alberta MPs, were particularly annoyed when Michael Wilson's March 1986 budget withdrew funding for western programs, particularly for agriculture, and failed to guarantee support for either the Husky Oil Upgrader at Lloydminster or the expansion of the Syncrude plant in Fort McMurray.[56] Although a federal bail-out of farmers occurred shortly thereafter – in time for Mulroney to assist fellow-Tory Grant Devine's re-election bid in Saskatchewan – the cuts only highlighted bitterly the stories of federal largesse pouring into Quebec.

Some western Tory MPs began to voice their discontent with the government's economic and other policies. In March 1986 Alex Kindy, an extreme right-wing Tory MP from Calgary East, attacked Justice Minister John Crosbie's proposal to ban discrimination against homosexuals and women.[57] In 1987 Kindy called his own energy minister, Marcel Masse, 'stupid' for his handling of energy negotiations with the Alberta government.[58] During this period, another Alberta Tory MP, David Kilgour, the brother-in-law of Liberal leader John Turner, began also to complain loudly of his party's treatment of the West.

Despite these exceptions and growing public anger, however, Tory MPs in the West and elsewhere by and large remained loyal to the party. In part, this commitment was the result of their loyalty to Mulroney, the man who had brought the Tories out of the political wilderness. Many, no doubt, were also aware that internal dissension during the Diefenbaker years had ripped the Tories apart, resulting in their subsequent opposition status for nearly a quarter century. In any case, the perceived refusal of western Tory MPs to stand up for their constituents against the policies of the party led Tory supporters to begin a search for alternative means of political representation.

Traditionally, provincial governments in Canada have represented the counterbalance to federal authority.[59] During the Trudeau years, normal federal-provincial conflict had been exacerbated by the non-Liberal governments in the four western provinces. With the coming to power of the Tories in Ottawa, however, the conflict did not end. Hence, in the midst of Alberta's recession of 1985–6, for which the provincial Tories did not wish to be blamed, Tory premier Don Getty exclaimed:

I feel in Alberta a frustration that we don't have the kind of policies coming out of Ottawa we hoped we would have. Once we thought it's because we're not supporting the Liberal government. But now we've supported the Conservative government, and there's still this sense of frustration.[60]

As if to put an exclamation point on his frustration, Getty subsequently refused to campaign for the federal Tories in the Pembina by-election in 1986. The seat, won by the Tories in 1984 with a margin of over 34,000 votes, was retained by PC Walter Van De Walle who defeated his nearest rival, the NDP candidate and former mayor of Edmonton, Ivor Dent, by a slim 232 votes.

As in the past, however, westerners' search for a means of ameliorating what they viewed as systematic political injustice did not end at the party or provincial level. Rather, they began to seek out institutional solutions for bringing western influence to bear at the national level. The most proffered solution involved Senate reform.

The idea of Senate reform was not new. Indeed, it had been spoken of, off and on, for several decades. Spurred by the support of the Canada West Foundation, and the constitutional and energy wrangles, the idea of Senate reform had received a major boost in the late 1970s and early 1980s. Support for the idea had peaked in 1983 at 43 per cent, but declined in 1984 to 37 per cent following the election of the federal Tories.[61] Now, however, in the midst of growing political discontent, the idea was once more gaining public favour. In particular, the idea of a 'Triple-E Senate' – equal, elected, and effective – began to gain currency.

As often was the case, Ted Byfield led the charge. In his column in the *Alberta Report* on 18 March 1985, Byfield wrote:

We were satisfied in the past to blame the NEP on the Liberal government. It was, we said, their payoff to Ontario for putting Trudeau back in power in 1980. But now we have had a Tory government in office for six months and the NEP remains fully in effect in every major particular ... We need therefore fundamental constitutional change. We need, in short, the Triple-E Senate.

Byfield's demand was echoed elsewhere. The same month, an Alberta provincial Tory committee further recommended the Triple-E Senate.

The committee's recommendation gained wide provincial support, including from the Western Canada Concept whose president, Dr. Fred
Marshall, had made a brief to the committee in August 1984. In May
1985 the Alberta legislature passed a motion approving the committee's
report.

On 21 April 1986 Byfield again wrote dolefully in the *Alberta Report*
of the Canadian political situation and again of the need for senate
reform:

we must conclude that the conventionality of the present Canadian political
system cannot work for us. If a government with an enormous majority, almost
unanimously elected across the West, cannot shape policies that defend the
West against international conditions we cannot control or contend with, if it
cannot do this in an era when economic conditions in the centre are affluent
and buoyant, if it cannot do this purely because the political price is too high,
then no Canadian government regardless of its political stripe, can ever properly serve us. Hence, what we require is not a change of party, not a change of
government, but a change of constitution ... We need the Triple-E Senate ...

In short, by 1986 Senate reform had come to be viewed by Byfield,
and many others in the West, as a means of solving the recurrent economic and political problems of the region. By this time, however,
many had also come to believe that fundamental change in Canada's
political structures could be achieved only through a new political vehicle. Hence, in his column in the *Alberta Report* of 4 August 1986,
Byfield also began to argue in favour of a new political party:

Elections are won and lost in Ontario and Quebec. Hence, all three parties are
the same ... The system doesn't work ... What we need is a credible western
party. Not separatist. Not dedicated to some strange Balkanization of the whole
estate. Not particularly right wing, not particularly left. Well, what then. It
requires another column to explain.

Byfield followed that column on 25 August with a list of policies that
the new party should stand for. At the head of the list, said Byfield,
was a Triple-E Senate. But other policies included 'changes to the bank
act that would make it possible for regional banks to survive, prosper,
and provide capital to local industry'; 'changes to the tariff structure,
that would reopen the commodity markets' [for the West]; '[s]trong
initiatives by Ottawa to open for ... western commodities an access to

the American west coast markets'; '[r]emoval of the Canadian National head office in Montreal' and of much of the CBC production from Toronto; '[t]ax incentives to industries ... encouraging them to locate in the West'; and '[a]n Ottawa program to offset provincial subsidies on such things as hog production, thereby keeping them in their natural locale in the grain growing areas.'

On 15 September 1986, Ted Byfield's editorial spelled out five additional 'conditions' that a western party should meet:

First, I think, it should consist, as do most populist movements, largely of people of no previous identity ...

Second, it ought to have trouble finding a leader, not because no one is convinced enough, or able enough, to do the job, but because of the humility of the membership ...

Third, when a leader is finally chosen he ought to meet two qualifications. For one, he would best not be an Albertan, since the reputation of Alberta for producing extremism hopelessly prejudices his chances in the other provinces. For the other, he ought to be a member of a minority group. Preferably he would be Jewish ... the fact of a Jewish leader would discourage the weirdo element that seem so inevitably to attach itself to such movements in Alberta. The James Keegstras of the province would not feel impelled to join.

Fourth, this party should not – in its initial stages anyway – run provincially, only federally ...

Finally, I do not conceive of such a party as having permanence. Its mission would be to change the system. When the system was changed, it should fade into history, its work done.

Byfield's call for a new political party came at a time when the polls were saying what everyone was already sensing: Mulroney's Tories were in trouble.

After a brief 'honeymoon period,' the Tory slide had begun in the spring of 1985. Monthly Gallup polls recorded the precipitous decline. In June the PC's garnered 44 per cent national support. By September, however, support for the Tories had slipped to 37 per cent. And although the following March Tory support rebounded to 41 per cent, it fell again quickly to 32 per cent in June. In October Tory support was at 31 per cent. It was at this time that an incident happened that more than anything solidified western opposition to Mulroney's government and led to the formation of the Reform party.

In the fall of 1986 the federal government announced a decision to give a CF-18 contract to Canadair-CAE Ltd of Montreal over Bristol Aerospace Ltd of Winnipeg, despite federal civil service evaluations that recommended acceptance of Winnipeg's lower bid. The politically motivated decision caused an immediate furor. The Manitoba premier, Howard Pawley, denounced the decision. Tory provincial opposition leader, Gary Filmon, in an act of political self-defence, distanced himself from the federal party, while the secretary of the Winnipeg-Assiniboine PC Association quit his post in disgust. Manitoba Tory MPs were more acquiescent, although some mumbled their disagreement with the CF-18 decision.

In the days and weeks that followed, however, anger with the political decision was not confined to Manitoba. Rather, the incident provided a rare symbol of alienation with which all westerners could identify, in the end taking on the same symbolic resonance as had the NEP. (The incident was replayed in early 1987 when a bid for construction of icebreakers went to the Montreal company, Lavalin Inc., over two western Canadian consortia out of Calgary and Vancouver.)

After the CF-18 incident, support for the federal Tories steadily eroded. A December 1986 Gallup poll, conducted shortly after the announcement of the CF-18 decision, showed that Tory support had slumped to 30 per cent. Much of this slide in support had occurred in the West where key elements of Tory support began to break free of their political orbit.

The anti-Quebec, anti-French element, provided with fresh evidence of domination by Quebec, began to search out (or return to) some of the fringe parties, such as Elmer Knutson's Confederation of Regions Party (COR). Similarily, businesspeople, such as James Gray (Canadian Hunter Exploration) and Richard Elenko (Mannville Oil and Gas), also began to withdraw support from the Tories. In their pandering to Quebec and Ontario, said Elenko, Mulroney's Tories were 'just as bad as the Liberals.'[62]

In the midst of a worsening crisis in agriculture, the farm community also began to drift from the Tory fold. In Lethbridge, Alberta, a group formed the Agricultural Stability Action Committee to lobby for more farm aid. The co-chair of the committee, and a former president of the Cardston Progressive Conservative Association, Robert (Bob) Grbavac announced that he would no longer support the Tories financially.[63]

The new year did not bring happier tidings. Throughout 1987, national support for the Tories hovered in the mid-twenties. Particularly worrisome for the right wing in Canada were several national polls giving the NDP the lead – an event previously replicated only by the gains of the CCF during the Second World War.[64]

Nor was the rise of the left curtailed in the West. Indeed, support for the NDP in the West continued to rise into early 1988. The Gallup poll in March of that year gave the NDP 33 per cent nationally, compared with 37 and 28 per cent for the Liberals and PCs, respectively. In the western region, support for the NDP was at 40 per cent, the Liberals 27 per cent, and the Tories 31 per cent.

In summary, by the fall of 1986, a Tory government had been in office in Ottawa for two years, yet things did not seem any better than they had been under the hated Trudeau Liberals. To be sure, Mulroney's Tories generally supported deregulation of business and had finally gotten rid of the NEP and FIRA, but their slowness to eliminate those programs led many in the West to believe that they had been reluctant. Indeed, the Tories appeared, at least for a time, to still be committed to Canadianization. Moreover, many in Alberta blamed the Tories' slowness in dismantling the NEP for the impact, if not the cause, of the recession that hit the province in 1985–6.

Indeed, in many ways the Mulroney Tories seemed perhaps even worse than the Liberals. Many who had supported the Tories in 1984 viewed 'big government' and its deficits as growing ever larger. To many, also, Mulroney's government seemed even more corrupt and partisan than the previous Liberal regime. Moreover, the fact that so many of the government scandals involved members of the Quebec caucus only confirmed the perception of many westerners of the particular venality and corruption of that region's political élite.

For many westerners, however, the CF-18 incident had been the last straw. The incident revived long-standing antagonisms over government spending, regional exploitation, and ethnic divisions within the country. The CF-18 fiasco provided a powerful symbol to westerners of the perceived injustice of the current political system.

Although these feelings cut across party and ideological lines, the West's right wing was particularly angered by all these incidents. Its avowed saviour, the Progressive Conservative party, had displayed feet of clay. To whom could the right wing now turn for redemption? The predicament of the right was only made worse by the fact that the Tories' faltering was accompanied by a real possibility that the left-wing New Democrats might ascend to federal power.[65] What was to be done?

In April 1987 Francis Winspear telephoned Stan Roberts about holding a large conference in Vancouver, similar to the Canada West Foundation conference organized by Roberts in 1980, to discuss western grievances and to consider the creation of a new political party. Since leaving the CWF, Roberts had briefly been president of the Canadian Chamber of Commerce, Canada's largest business group, but had left that position in 1982 under pressure from board members who feared that Roberts's very public attacks on Liberal policies were closing Ottawa's doors to the chamber.[66] Roberts had then returned to British Columbia, where he was president of both Fraser Resources ('a family-owned multi-interest company') and the Roberts Group ('consultants specializing in international marketing and government relations.'[67] But Roberts was never far from politics.

Indeed, Trudeau's resignation in the spring of 1984 rekindled rumours that Roberts might be a possible replacement for Trudeau. Publicly, Roberts scoffed at these reports, but privately he began to ponder the possibilities of his own candidacy. He retained important contacts in the West from his days at Simon Fraser University and the Canada West Foundation, and also had strong connections in Quebec as a result of his recent work with the chamber. Although he likely would not have won the Liberal leadership, Roberts believed that his candidacy might establish him as a regional 'lieutenant' and begin the process of broadening the base of Liberal support.[68]

Turner's candidacy and subsequent elevation to leader ended this speculation. Roberts was disappointed, viewing the choice of Turner as an opportunistic move choreographed by insiders in the Liberal party. Nonetheless, he chose to run for the Liberal party in Lachine, Quebec, during the subsequent election, coming second with 15,156 votes (32 per cent) to Tory candidate Bob Layton (24,301 votes, 52 per cent).

The continued malaise of the post-Trudeau Liberals, combined with disgruntlement over the Mulroney government, had intensified Roberts's political concerns, as they had Winspear's. As early as 1985 Winspear and Roberts spoke of forming a new political party. Gordon Gibson, former leader of the BC Liberal party, remembers attending a meeting in Vancouver that year, attended by Winspear, Roberts, and David Somerville (among others) at which such a possibility was discussed.[69] Winspear's call to Roberts in the spring of 1987 was therefore not unusual.

At about this same time, Winspear and Roberts learned through their connections with the Canada West Foundation that several influential people in Alberta also were pondering the creation of a new political party. During 1986, groups opposed to the Mulroney Tories had sprung up throughout Alberta. In the south of the province, a group headed by Bob Grbavac and Ken Copithorne (of the Copithorne ranching family) had emerged. In Edmonton, another group had formed around Preston Manning and included Cliff Breitkreuz (a municipal councillor from Onoway), Robert Chapman (of Chapman-Weber Motors), John Poole (Poole Construction), Ray Speaker (former Socred and Tory MLA, and long-time friend of Manning), and Dick Shuhany.

Even more than Roberts, Manning in recent years had been on the political periphery. During the constitutional wrangling of 1977–8, Manning had created the 'Movement for National Political Change.' In *The New Canada*, Manning describes the MNPC as a study group, consisting of 'interested friends and acquaintances' who 'met once a month of so' 'to discuss the lessons to be learned from the political reform movements of the past and to discuss the knowledge and skill needed to participate in contemporary federal politics.'[70] In contrast, journalist Murray Dobbin describes it as a 'very private, if not secret, organization' with extensive political and business contacts, particularly within the oil industry.[71] The reality probably lies some place between these two descriptions. The election of the Clark government in 1979, however, undercut any chances that the MNPC might get off the ground. For the next few years, Manning's political forays were limited to making the occasional speech.

Following Kesler's by-election victory in Olds-Didsbury in 1982 (see chapter two), for example, Manning spoke to a small gathering of separatists. But, disagreeing with their 'tactics and avowed objective'[72] – and probably (correctly) viewing their movement as not going anywhere – Manning ended any further dealings with them. In 1984, Manning (along with his father) made a presentation in Calgary to the Marigold Foundation, a charitable organization, discussing 'the possibility of the West producing yet another populist party and the lessons to be learned from its predecessors.'[73] By and large, however, Preston Manning remained on the political margin until 1986. Even in the spring of 1987, Manning remained a small business consultant, quietly living in St Albert, a satellite community of Edmonton.

In Calgary, meanwhile, another group had formed that later would have even greater impact upon Reform's political direction. The Calgary group featured prominent oilman Jack MacKenzie, Bob Muir (a long-time Calgary lawyer for Dome Petroleum), Jim Gray (co-founder and vice-president of Hunter Oil), David Elton, Diane Ablonczy (an oilpatch lawyer), and Cliff Fryers (a Calgary tax lawyer).[74]

Fryers, who would later become 'chief bagman' for the Reform party, was born in Winnipeg in 1947, the son of a brakeman with the CPR. Following a series of moves, the family settled in Moose Jaw where the father's promotion to superintendent placed the family 'in the upper strata of what was then a town of 26,000.' Cliff Fryers later attended the University of Saskatchewan, in Saskatoon. Apparently unimpressed with student radicalism ('I was somewhat turned off by their think-ing'), Fryers graduated with a degree in commerce and law. In 1977, he moved to Calgary where he got a job as general tax counsel to Mobil Oil Canada Ltd. In 1980, Fryers joined a law firm that subsequently became Milner Fenerty.[75]

By 1986 Cliff Fryers was a very successful tax lawyer, living in the expensive Mount Royal district of Calgary, belonging to the prestigious Ranchmen's Club, and acting as governor of the Canadian Tax Founda-tion. He had been a supporter of the Liberal party before switching to Mulroney's Tories, in part because of what he viewed as the discrimi-natory aspects of bilingualism. In 1984 Fryers even helped PC MP Bobbie Sparrow in her campaign. Later, Fryers would say of his change from the Liberals to the Conservatives: 'I switched because, as a Westerner, I thought we would see some real changes, like getting rid of the PGRT [Petroleum and Gas Revenue Tax].'[76] Now, like so many others in the western, particularly Alberta, establishment, Fryers was seeking a new political home.

By the time Winspear and Roberts contacted Fryers and the other discontented individuals in Alberta, the latter already had begun to cohere around the leadership of Manning. On 17 October 1986 a meet-ing took place in Jim Gray's boardroom, attended by David Elton, Bob Muir, Doug Hilland, an oil company executive, and Manning. This meeting was followed on 13 November 1986 with Manning making a presentation to some prominent members of the oilpatch entitled 'Proposal for the Creation of a Western-Based Political Party to Run Candidates in the 1988 Federal Election.'[77]

Nonetheless, in the early spring of 1987 the formation of a new party seemed far off. At that time, therefore, Francis Winspear (and perhaps also John Poole) arranged to bring together the various disenchanted factions for a coordinating meeting. A dozen or so businesspeople, including Winspear, Manning, Muir, Chapman, Roberts, Poole, Shuhany, and Grbavac, held a luncheon meeting in Edmonton.[78] Chapman suggested that Manning and Roberts should head up an association which the group decided to name the Reform Association of Canada. Manning and Roberts accepted. The group then decided to organize a convention to be held almost immediately in Vancouver at which the decision would be made whether or not to form a new political party.[79]

In a letter to *Alberta Report* on 22 July 1991, James Partridge, a longtime friend of Winspear, recounted some particulars of this luncheon meeting as he had heard them from Winspear. Partridge noted that, following the meeting, 'Messrs. Winspear and Roberts travelled to Toronto and endeavoured, unsuccessfully, to interest a society dedicated to influencing the government without formal political action.'

That society was the National Citizens' Coalition. Winspear's firm is a contributor to the NCC and, as we have seen, the meeting was not the first between the various parties. In the spring of 1987, however, Colin Brown, the founder of the NCC, was seriously ill with cancer. As a result, Roberts met with Somerville alone. Recalling the results of this meeting, Winspear later stated that 'ultimately the two groups couldn't agree on methods' (for influencing the political system). 'The NCC wanted us to remain non-political, and we wanted them to join us.'[80] The Vancouver assembly went ahead. A couple of months later, in July 1987, Brown died. David Somerville, whose role within the organization had been ascendent for some time, replaced Brown as head of the NCC.

Meanwhile, Ted Byfield, who had attended some of the formative meetings of the Reform Association, and whose articles had heralded the need for a new political party, agreed to arrange publicity for the Vancouver meeting through his various magazines. For their parts, Manning helped set the assembly's agenda and recruit speakers, while Roberts used $50,000 and a letter of credit for an additional $40,000 – all provided by Winspear – to establish an association office in Vancouver and to reserve the Hyatt Regency Hotel for the 'Western Assembly on Canada's Economic and Political Future' – its formal name – to be held from 29 to 31 May.[81]

In short, the proposed new political organization primarily was the offspring of four men: Winspear, Roberts, Manning, and Byfield. Despite some differences between them – Roberts was a slightly left-of-centre liberal, Byfield an extreme right-wing fiscal and moral conservative – each nonetheless brought something of value to the relationship. Winspear, of course, had money. Roberts was a skilled organizer with previous political experience, as was Manning. Manning, moreover, had the political name, while Byfield possessed the means of disseminating the ideology of the new party. The results of this partnership were evident only a few weeks later.

THE WESTERN ASSEMBLY AND THE ROAD TO WINNIPEG

The Western Assembly attracted nearly 300 delegates. They were treated to an impressive array of speakers, including John Richards, a former NDP member of the Saskatchewan legislature and currently professor of business administration at Simon Fraser University, whose own work on populism I have previously noted. Also attending was Alan Beachell, reeve of a Manitoba municipality, who had run as a provincial Liberal candidate in 1973.[82] Beachell's other claim to fame had come a year earlier when, as president of the Union of Manitoba Municipalities, he had allowed that organization to mail its 160 members a petition, distributed by One Nation, One Language Inc., which called for the elimination of official bilingualism.[83]

Beachell was not the only prominent former Liberal in attendance. Jo Anne Hillier, editor-publisher of a Manitoba newspaper, a former member of the Canada West Council, and a long-time member of the Liberal party, was also a delegate, as was Jane Heffelfinger, a Vancouver marketing consultant who had been a federal Liberal candidate in 1984. A number of prominent Tories also took part in the assembly, including Larry Birkbeck, former Saskatchewan PC MLA (1975–86), Walter Nelson, founder of what is now the Western Canadian Wheat Growers Association and a member of the Tories' Saskatchewan executive, and Bob Grbavac.[84]

There were also many speakers at the assembly who did not have their political affiliations sewn to their chests, including Bert Brown, a prominent Albertan farmer and founder-chairman of the Canadian Committee for a Triple-E Senate; Dr David Elton; Gordon Engblom, a Calgary energy consultant; Dr Gerald Gall, a professor of law at the University of Alberta; Dr Brian Scarfe, professor and chairman of the Economics Department of the University of Alberta; Melvin Smith, QC, director of the Canada West Foundation; Dr Charles Stewart, an agricultural engineer; and Bob Muir.[85] There were also a number of observers, including David Somerville and a young economist from the University of Calgary, Stephen Harper.

After leaving Tory MP Jim Hawkes's office in 1986, Harper had enrolled in the University of Calgary's master's program. At the same time, he had continued to 'network' with some of the conservative think-tanks, such as the National Citizens' Coalition and the Fraser Institute, trying 'to mobilize some of the conservative resources,' and also helped to establish a right-wing organization, the Northern Foundation. Nonetheless, he believed that his days in direct politics were at an end. In the spring of 1987, however, he was asked by his university supervisor, Dr Robert Mansell, to go to the Western Assembly for him.[86] Harper would later recall that he was 'very impressed with Mr. Manning and his ideas, although I didn't think at the time that the party was going to go anywhere [because] it didn't have a clear agenda, and it was very small.'[87]

On the first evening, Harper and the delegates heard Ted Byfield give the keynote address. Then, on Saturday afternoon, Preston Manning delivered his major speech, making clear his preference regarding the decision whether or not to form a new political party:

Let me make clear from the outset that when we refer to the possibility of creating a new political party to represent the West, we are not talking about another splinter party of the strange and extreme. The West has produced too many of these in the past years, and there is no need for another.

Rather ... we should be thinking about the creation of a new vehicle to represent the great political 'reform tradition' which runs like a broad and undulating stream through the length and breadth of Canadian politics but which finds no suitable expression in any of the traditional federal parties.[88]

Why were the existing political parties not appropriate vehicles for resolving the West's economic and political difficulties? The 'Progressive Conservative Party at the federal level has a congenital inability to govern'; 'the professional Liberal politician is still defined as "a politician who puts party and patronage ahead of principles and province"'; and the federal NDP advocates and supports 'the centralization of power in the hands of government,' 'the welfare state,' the redistribution rather than the creation of wealth, and the interests of class over region.[89] Therefore, said Manning, a new political party must be created possessing the following 'general specifications':

1. A new federal political party representing the West should have a positive orientation and vision.
2. A new federal party representing the West should have standards of performance, policy, and people that exceed those of the existing political parties.
3. A new federal political party representing the West should be ideologically balanced. (In order to ... draw support from ... the Liberals and the NDP as well as the Conservatives ...)
4. A new federal political party representing the West should be committed to preserving and strengthening Canada through the institution of needed reforms.
5. A new federal political party representing the West should have 'room to grow' into a truly national party.[90]

In short, Manning made a broad populist appeal for support.[91]

Manning's speech continued on that Saturday until 5:30 p.m. The assembled delegates were duly impressed. They then broke to attend the Saturday reception and dinner, and to hear the guest speaker of the evening – author Peter Brimelow – diagnose Canada's 'problem.' The following day, the assembled delegates held a straw vote on the issue of forming a new party. The result was a foregone conclusion. By a wide margin (76.7 per cent), the delegates voted in favour.

Not everyone, however, would be going to the founding convention to be held in Winnipeg. Despite Manning's call for balance, the ideological mix of the new party had already begun to congeal around certain right-wing principles, in particular the principle of free enterprise. Looking back on his own experiences at the assembly, John Richards would later remark: 'My participation in the founding convention ... says nothing about the ideological direction of the Reform Party.' As for the delegates' response to his speech (an unapologetic defence of social democratic principles, and a warning to the assembly against reverting to conservative solutions to deal with western Canada's problems), Richards later commented: 'I received a smattering of boos but most of the crowd heard me out as a minor off-key player in their orchestra.'[92]

It would be overstating the point to suggest that most of the assembly's delegates were as extreme as June Lenihan, a Vancouver anti-abortion lobbyist, who somewhat imprudently remarked: 'I'm one of the people in this room willing to admit that I'm an evangelical right-wing red-neck, anti-socialist, ultra-conservative, fundamentalist Christian.'[93] Nonetheless, it seems clear that the majority of delegates were committed right-wingers, as several observers noted. John Cruickshank, a reporter with the *Globe and Mail*, wrote: 'While Mr. Manning and Mr. Roberts spoke ceaselessly about creating "a broadly based party," their delegates were almost uniformly social and economic conservatives.'[94] Similarly, reporter Don Wanagas remarked:

In spite of Preston Manning's efforts to present the 'new' organization as something else altogether, it was all too clear that it was dominated by old-time Socreds dying for another kick at the political cat ... [T]he 'Assembly' will be identified as just another Alberta-based 'fringe group.' Which I regret to say, is all it ever was.[95]

Cruickshank's and Wanagas's impressions were shared by Bob Grbavac.

Grbavac, who describes himself as slightly left of centre politically, viewed the delegates to the assembly as primarily a bunch of 'neo-conservatives,' 'right-wingers,' and 'former Social Crediters.' Finally, Grbavac also felt uneasy that the finances of one individual – Winspear – had dominated the meeting. As a result, Grbavac shortly thereafter left the nascent movement to join the Liberal party.[96]

Nonetheless, the Reform Association began preparing for the upcoming Winnipeg convention. As before, Roberts took care of the organizational aspects, while Manning, and his Calgary supporters, were in charge of delegate selection. As well, an interim executive, headed by association president Jo Anne Hillier, a former member of the Canada West Foundation (and later a supporter of Roberts's leadership bid), Roberts, and Manning, set about raising money and forming party organizations in the West's eighty-eight federal ridings.

The following months provided Manning with the opportunity to further his leadership hopes, and to otherwise put his stamp upon the emerging party, through a series of speeches to potential delegates and supporters. One of these speeches occurred on 10 August 1987, at the Marlborough Inn in Calgary. The new federal political party should be built, he said, upon the following foundations:

1. Draw upon our Western conservative tradition with respect to the value of the individual, the energizing and direction of the economy, the proper role of government, and sources of moral and ethical guidance. That means commitment to individual freedom, responsible private enterprise, modest government, and respect for traditional Judeo-Christian values.

2. But I say at the same time, break new ground on broadening the base of the
   private enterprise system, in the area of labour-management relations, in
   relations to the environment and science, in the area of social policy and
   constitutional change.[97]

Manning's speech, an updated version of his father's social conservatism, was long on generalities and short on specifics. The only concrete
proposal was that the Constitution should be amended to provide for
a Triple-E Senate. Regarding the Meech Lake Accord, which had
been formally signed two days after the Western Assembly, Manning's
only criticism was that it made 'meaningful Senate reform a virtual
impossibility.'[98]

In his public speeches, Manning espoused the end of traditional left-
right politics and called for a broad-based party. In private, however,
Manning appears to have reverted to some of the 'scare tactics' used
successfully by his father during his political career[99], as evidenced in a
couple of fundraising letters he wrote during this period: 'the federal
Conservatives already have lost the West and will probably lose Quebec as well. The task now ... is to provide some constructive alternative
for Western Canadians in the absence of which many will decline to
vote, or will vote NDP or even separatist, by default.'[100] And again, to the
same prospective contributor: 'it would be extremely unfortunate if
Canada were handed over to the socialists ... If the PC's cannot be revived, then there is a great danger that up to 50 % of *our people* will not
vote ... In this event, the NDP will elect members by default.'[101] As we
have already seen, Manning's fears were well founded.

Nonetheless, it is important to emphasize that the formation of the
Reform party was from the start as much a defensive reaction to the
perceived gains of the left as it was an attempt to institute a new political regime. The continued de-alignment and disintegration of the Tory
alliance realistically threatened many on the right with the possibility
that their worst nightmare – a social democratic government in Ottawa
– might come true. The creation of a new right-wing party was thus
intended, at least in part, as a solution to a potential problem. In the
days that followed the assembly, some members of the West's political
and business establishment showed that they welcomed the solution,
as the new party was endorsed by two former western premiers, Douglas Campbell (Manitoba) and Ernest Manning, and businessmen James
Richardson, the former Liberal cabinet minister, and Jack Gallagher,
founder of Dome Petroleum.[102]

The Reform Party of Canada was born on the weekend of 30 October–1 November 1987. The event was attended by 306 delegates. Of these, 140 came from Alberta, 91 from British Columbia, 65 from Manitoba, and 10 from Saskatchewan.[103] The delegates faced three tasks as they met that weekend: to decide upon a name for the party, to devise a constitution, and to pick a leader. The delegates chose the party's name – the Reform Party of Canada – the first day. How many Reformers knew at the time of the resonance that name had in Canadian history, we cannot tell. Certainly, however, Preston Manning, who prides himself on his knowledge of history, must have known.

The Reform Party of Upper Canada, led by William Lyon Mackenzie, had fought for popular democracy before, during, and immediately after the Rebellion of 1837. After the Act of Union in 1840, the Reform Party of Canada West formed half of what later became the Liberal party. In subsequent years, as the population of Canada West (formerly Upper Canada) began to increase relative to that of Canada East (formerly Lower Canada), the Reformers, led by George Brown, the legendary anti-Catholic, anti-French editor of the Toronto *Globe*, began to agitate for 'representation by population.' As historian P.B. Waite relates, however, the 'rep. by pop.' issue merely disguised a deeper issue:

the great bulk of the Reform party [of] Canada West wanted an end to French-Canadian influence (or interference) in her internal affairs: nothing less, in fact, than the separation that would be realized in a separate province of Ontario, and yet without the disadvantages of a complete dissolution of the Canadian union.[104]

Despite its reactionary bent, the Reform Party of Canada West became, in the end, one of the major forces behind the constitutional changes that led to Confederation when, in 1864, Brown agreed to an unlikely coalition with Sir John A. Macdonald's Conservatives.[105] Could Preston Manning, or the other Reformers, have intended this symbolism? Manning, himself, makes no claims to this.[106] Perhaps the delegates chose the name meaning solely that they intended to 'reform' Canada's existing political system. But the name also had currency with several notable elements attending the convention. A couple of years earlier, disenchanted Social Credit supporters in British Columbia had formed the Reform Party of British Columbia. Similarly, in 1981 several former Alberta Social Crediters, including Alfred Hooke, a long-time member of Ernest Manning's cabinet, got together to form the MIDAS Reform Party of Canada.[107]

In the end, the delegates chose the name 'Reform Party' by a wide margin over other possible choices. Then the delegates began reviewing a draft constitution put together by a committee headed by Bob Muir. By the time of the Winnipeg convention, the party was already solidly on the right of the political spectrum on economic and social matters. Nonetheless, Preston Manning was acutely aware of the need to attract a wide range of voters if it was to avoid being marginalized. Hence, Manning alone devised ('using materials I had collected for the past twenty years'[108]) a comprehensive preamble to the party's constitution that paid homage to a plethora of political icons, including Joseph Howe, Louis-Hippolyte LaFontaine, Robert Baldwin, Egerton Ryerson, the Fathers of Confederation ('particularly Georges Cartier, John A. Macdonald, and George Brown'), Louis Riel, F.W.G. Haultain and his followers, the Progressive party, the CCF, the Social Credit Movement, and 'the leaders and supporters of the Quiet Revolution in the Province of Quebec.'[109] The fact that some of these recognitions were scarcely credible, given the regionalist and increasingly right-wing tenor of the movement, did not seem to bother Manning or, presumably, anyone else.

Ignored, for example, was the fact that the Fathers of Confederation – hardly populists – had put together the National Policy, a policy with similar philosophical roots to the hated NEP. Similarly disregarded was the fact that Louis Riel had fought for minority rights, in particular recognition of a kind of distinct (French-speaking) society that would soon become controversial with Meech Lake. Nor was it apparently recognized by the delegates that the Progressives, the CCF, and even the Social Credit League of Alberta in the early days of Aberhart believed strongly in government intervention in the marketplace.[110] In this sense, the party's constitution represented, at least in part, an attempt to create a kind of illusory ideological bridge between the past and present.

At the same time, the party also wanted to create, if possible, a bridge between disenchanted Tories and those right-wing fringe elements that had been in free fall for several years. Hence, the preamble to the Reform party's new constitution also paid homage to '[t]he leaders and supporters of such Western protest groups, parties, and interest groups as the Confederation of Regions Party, Canadians for One Canada, the Western Canada Concept, the Canada West Foundation, and the Committee for a Triple E Senate'[111]

An incident at the convention makes clear the political meaning of the latter section of the preamble. In response to a motion to drop mention of wcc, an Alberta delegate said: 'Let's leave it in. We may need them later on.'[112] The motion was subsequently defeated. In short, the party leadership was trying to broaden its right-wing support while not entirely surrendering its attraction to fringe elements, at least some of whom were present at the Winnipeg convention. For example, one working delegate at the Convention was Fred Debrecen, the founder of One Nation, One Language Inc. Another active delegate was Mary Lamont, a founder of REAL Women.[113]

That Reform's leadership was acutely aware that the party's success would lie in culling its natural support within the right wing was further evidenced by a speech given at the convention by Stephen Harper. The speech, which Manning later said was the 'best speech and most influential presentation' at the convention,[114] and which propelled Harper into a central role in making party policy, was entitled *Achieving Economic Justice in Confederation*.[115] In his presentation, Harper recited a litany of western grievances, from Macdonald's National Policy to 'the unlimited appetite of the Welfare State for tax grabs' and 'the special treatment accorded the Province of Quebec' in the form of transfer payments 'paid exclusively by Western Canada.' He then stated his reasons for believing that the existing political parties were incapable of correcting these injustices: 'The Liberal Party ... places a profoundly insecure Central Canadian nationalism ahead of its historic commitment to freer trade. The NDP ... places its socialist ideology ahead of its historic roots in Western protest.'

But Harper's comments regarding the Conservative party were the most telling, revealing implicitly where the new party believed its greatest potential support lay:

the Mulroney government has shown itself far too willing to back down on the issues that matter to its political base. We must serve notice to the Red Tory leadership that we will provide its Western supporters an option they can desert to en masse should they, for any reason, fail to successfully deliver on [free trade] or any other major initiative of importance to Western Canada.

In short, Harper, like many of Reform's leadership, believed that the core of its support would come from disgruntled right-wing Tories.

It would take a very special leader, however, to hold together the disparate elements of the fragmented right wing and otherwise to bathe the party in the kind of respectability that might broaden its appeal. On the second day, the party began the process of choosing a leader. Since Vancouver, the issue had settled down to a choice between Manning, Roberts, and Byfield. Byfield, however, wanted to stick to his newspaper business.[116] Roberts, too, was reluctant to enter the race. Hence, in the months leading up to the Winnipeg convention, the only person actively running for the leadership was Manning.

During this time, Roberts apparently became more and more concerned at the direction that he saw the new party taking. A man with pan-Canadian views, he saw the new party as becoming increasingly controlled by a regional and provincial clique operating out of Calgary. He also saw the new party as harbouring the kind of anti-French sentiment that he had long disliked and feared. Finally, Roberts viewed the movement's lean towards free market solutions alone as excessive.[117] Albeit reluctantly, Roberts decided to enter the leadership race one week before the convention.

The popular myth growing out of the convention suggests that the leadership contest pitted Roberts's old political style and money against Manning's grass-roots populism.[118] Certainly, Roberts's campaign featured many of the traditional political accoutrements: buttons, embossed scarves, posters, daily newsletters – even a hospitality suite for beleaguered delegates – provided at a reputed cost of about $25,000, mostly supplied by Winspear. By contrast, Manning is said to have spent as little as $2000.[119] Still, Manning was hardly the ill-equipped underdog. By then, he had surrounded himself with a cadre of capable political advisers, such as Muir. Manning also had spent several months recruiting delegates, mostly from Alberta, whose allegiance to him was unquestioned.

As the crucial vote neared, tensions between the two camps increased. Fearing that the Roberts camp was about to bus in a number of 'instant delegates,' Manning supporters closed delegate registration on the Friday evening. (It was supposed to have continued until Saturday.) Winspear, who was supporting Roberts, stood up before the delegates and denounced the decision to suspend registration. This incident was followed by further accusations from Roberts that association moneys were unaccounted for. With animosities rising, Jo Anne Hillier called a meeting between the two sides on Saturday night to attempt to resolve the disputes. The attempt at reconciliation failed.

The next morning, following another effort at reconciliation, Roberts made a brief, emotional statement to the delegates, announcing that he was withdrawing from the race. 'It is with deep regret,' he said, 'that

I have taken this step ... This party was founded on the principles of honesty and integrity – those principles appear to have been compromised during this convention.'[120] Declaring Manning's supporters 'fanatical Albertans' and 'small-minded evangelical cranks,' Roberts then stormed out of the convention.[121]

Winspear, who had been so involved in creating the party, had mixed feelings about the result of the leadership convention. He openly had supported Roberts because he did not want the party to be labelled an Alberta affair. He also was afraid that the party might become just another Social Credit party. But Winspear had been disappointed with Roberts's performance at the convention, finding him 'erratic' in comparison with the Banff conference of 1978.[122]

As for Manning, his only reaction to the events was to tell reporters that, while he would look into his opponent's complaints, the convention would not miss Roberts to any great degree and that the latter had made a mistake in bringing the old political 'baggage' to the convention. Some of Manning's supporters were more blunt. '[I]t was ideal,' said one Manning supporter from Calgary, calling Roberts's leaving an 'absolutely clear-cut exorcism.'[123]

Roberts – one of the founding fathers of the party – was gone. Later, he would fail in an attempt to gain the Reform party's nomination in Saanich–Gulf Islands before the 1988 election. The loss effectively ended his involvement with the party. In late August 1990 he was stricken with a brain tumour, and died on 30 August. He was sixty-three years of age.

What would the Reform party have been like had Roberts won the leadership and survived to shepherd it through its formative years? The evidence suggests that a party headed by Roberts might have been somewhat less anti-government and more constrained in its attitudes on bilingualism and Quebec. At the same time, it would no doubt have remained supportive of free enterprise.

Would the party have been as successful? Probably not, at least in the short term. As we shall see, the Reform party under Manning generally has been successful in bringing together many of the disenchanted elements of the extreme right wing. These elements would likely have viewed Roberts as too 'liberal' in some respects. At the same time, the party would have been less open to charges of being a haven of Christian fundamentalism, as suggested by some[124] and therefore might have been more acceptable, in the long run, to moderate voters.

This potential outcome, however, was not to be. In Winnipeg, Preston Manning became, at least for the moment, the undisputed leader of the new party. But who is he? 'Off stage,' Preston Manning is affable, but quiet and almost shy. A devout Christian (First Alliance Church) and a solid family man (wife Sandra and five children), Manning possesses a record of helping various community causes and individuals in need. By all accounts, he is a decent man.

As noted early on in his political career, Preston Manning also is something of a scholar.[125] He is said to read a lot of history and is genuinely interested in ideas. Indeed, in this regard, Manning constitutes something of an anomaly among recent Canadian politicians – Pierre Trudeau being another exception.

Manning draws strength from crowds. In front of them, much of his frail awkwardness disappears. And while a kind of shy nervousness sometimes surfaces, it usually succumbs to a calm certitude reflected in Manning's slow, almost rasping drawl. His speeches are well crafted, often strewn with historical images and a kind of folksy humour. His family background, particularly his political and business connections, are never mentioned. He is simply 'one of the people.' Taken together, these qualities give Manning the appearance of a kind of Jimmy Stewart–cum–Will Rogers–cum–country preacher.

Behind this folksy demeanour, however, Manning is an astute and able politician. His speeches carefully wrap issues in historical symbols that appeal to his audiences. He does not tell the people what they should do about an issue. But he always makes it clear what he thinks they should do. For Manning has very firm ideas about Canada's problems and their solutions. There is little casualness or genuine spontaneity in Manning's presentations. Even his humorous anecdotes appear to have been carefully pretested.[126] In short, Manning is a person of firm – some would say rigid – ideas and principles.

Indeed, as he stood before the crowd in Winnipeg, Manning seemed to display just how little his political beliefs had evolved since assisting his father in writing *Political Realignment* in 1967. Despite drawing upon a modern analogy to give his speech the appearance of currency, the doctrine he espoused that night was traditional social conservatism. 'We need efficient solutions to social problems in a welfare state,' said Manning. 'So, Rambo, meet Mother Teresa.'[127]

The party came away from the convention with a name, a leader, and a constitutional set of principles. The delegates also had given some direction over certain policy initiatives. Over the next few months, the party leadership began hammering out the finer details of these policies. When, in August 1988, 250 delegates met in Calgary to go over a draft platform of policies drawn up by Stephen Harper,[128] it was obvious that Rambo had got the better of Mother Teresa. The party's policies adopted at that time, and largely unchanged since, married pure populism to free enterprise and traditional conservatism, along with aspects of regional and political alienation, thereby consecrating the party's emergence as a right-wing populist party.

Under a policy section dealing with constitutional reform, for example, the party called for a Triple-E Senate, regional fairness tests, popular ratification of constitutional change, the entrenchment of property rights, and the rejection of the Meech Lake Accord. Concerning political reforms, the Reform party called for more free votes and less party discipline in the House of Commons and party caucuses, greater accountability by members of parliament, fixed election dates, policies of direct democracy (that is, referenda and citizens' initiatives), less government bureaucracy, and the end of tax credits for political lobbying. Economically, the party called for a greater reliance on the market, free trade (both with the United States and within Canada), an end to all government agricultural subsidies, changes to monetary and banking policy, tax reform (since translated to mean a flat tax), balanced budgets, privatization of government agencies, tighter control of government spending, and right-to-work (that is, anti-union) legislation.[129] Finally, on social policy, the party called for an end to the social welfare state; a rejection of proposals for state-run day care; an end to government financial involvement in the unemployment insurance system; an end to federal encroachments on provincial jurisdictions in the areas of medicine (through the Canada Health Act which underpins the medicare system), education, and the like; an end to official bilingualism, immigration policies based on primarily economic reasons and subject to public opinion; a 'justice system which places the punishment of crime and the protection of law-abiding citizens and their property ahead of all other objectives;' and reform of the RCMP designed to 're-store the RCMP to its former stature.'[130]

As the 1988 federal election approached, social conservatism, rechristened Reform, at last had a vehicle by which it could enter into Canada's political discourse. In the meantime, the party's fortunes were buoyed by the continuing political problems of the ruling Tories.

REFORM AND THE NORTHERN FOUNDATION

Beset by scandals, unpopular policies, and a deep-seated hatred directed at the party's leadership, the Progressive Conservatives languished in public estimation throughout 1986–7. Indeed, as late as May 1988, the federal Tories were still in third place in national polls. At 28 per cent, Mulroney's party trailed both the Liberals (39 per cent) and NDP (31 per cent).[131]

A number of organizations continued to arise, moreover, which threatened to splinter the Tory's right-wing support in the belief that Mulroney's government was not going far enough or fast enough in reversing the policies of the previous Liberal regime. One of these organizations – a kind of umbrella organization for many of the other single-issue, right-wing groups – deserves particular mention because of its links to the Reform party: the Northern Foundation.

The foundation's own literature describes its history and purpose:

The Northern Foundation was started in 1988 by individuals who were concerned and angered by the continuing deterioration of their country. In Canada, common sense had been drowned out while unprincipled politicians, arrogant bureaucrats, and leftist media elites did all the talking – and thinking – on behalf of everybody ... [T]here was no party, movement or organization to fight for the needs and aspirations of the majority of Canadians who were common-sense, small-'c' conservatives in both the social and economic sense.[132]

In short, the Northern Foundation portrays itself as a kind of 'radical vanguard' for the dissemination of social and economic conservative ideas.

Complaining of socialist/progressive thinking, and a media/political system controlled by 'lib/left' elites, who had been 'able to impose their agenda on the Canadian people because small-"c" conservatives' had been divided, the Northern Foundation was the creation of a number of generally extreme right-wing conservatives, including Anne Hartmann (a director of REAL Women), Geoffrey Wasteneys (a long-standing member of APEC), George Potter (also a member of APEC), author Peter Brimelow, Link Byfield (son of Ted Byfield and himself publisher/president of *Alberta Report*), and Stephen Harper.

The roster of conservative adherents speaking at foundation conferences in 1989, 1990, and 1992 is equally instructive. Among speakers were Dr Walter Block (the Fraser Institute), Ed Vanwoudenberg (leader of the Christian Heritage party), Lubor Zink (an extreme right-wing columnist with the *Sun* chain), Dr John Whitehall (of the Canadian Christian Anti-Communist Crusade), Ron Leitch (president of APEC), Gwen Landolt (founder of REAL Women), Ken Campbell (founder of

Renaissance Canada), Paul Fromm (former member of the Western Guard, a neo-fascist group, and later founder of CFAR), and author William Gairdner.[133] The foundation's quarterly tract, *The Northern Voice*, regularly provides advertising space for these same individuals, their ideas, and their organizations.[134]

Ostensibly, therefore, the Northern Foundation is a vehicle for bringing together several disparate right-wing groups and otherwise disseminating an extreme conservative ideology. Significantly, it also has substantial connections to the Reform party. Brimelow's and Harper's connections to Reform were discussed previously. Link Byfield's father, Ted, was a founder of Reform. But the ties go even deeper than this. At the 1989 Edmonton convention, a policy resolution was made with the description that it was 'proposed by Link Byfield.'[135] At times, Link's columns in the *Alberta Report* appear not to be commentaries so much as policy memoranda.[136] George Potter also is a member of the Reform party.[137] And William Gairdner has been a frequent speaker at Reform party functions, including the party's 1991 Saskatoon convention.

Despite these connections, however, there is no evidence that the foundation is a 'front' for the Reform party. Indeed, it is worth noting that the foundation later banished Harper from the movement because he was not right-wing enough; for his part, Harper now calls the foundation 'quasi-Fascist.'[138] In the end, the Northern Foundation appears to represent yet another example of the right wing's 'spinning-off' from political control by either the Tories or Liberals.

REBUILDING THE TORY ALLIANCE

Despite centrifugal forces pulling at his political coalition, Mulroney believed that he could hold on to power if he retained the support of Quebec nationalists and of big and small business interests in the rest of the country. To achieve this support, Mulroney entered upon two fundamental policies, one political, the other economic: Meech Lake and free trade.[139]

If Trudeau's central objective in the constitutional hearings of 1981 had been to bury Quebec nationalism within a strengthened federal state, Mulroney's objective was to bury the Liberal party in Quebec through granting that province greater autonomy. As we have seen, Mulroney garnered the support of Quebec nationalists in 1984 through promises to reopen constitutional discussions, implicitly suggesting that in doing so he was willing to delegate greater provincial powers to that province. Discussions towards this end began shortly after the Tories took power in the fall of 1984.

Throughout 1985 and 1986 discussion papers flowed between the various capitals. Then, in late April 1987, Mulroney and the premiers of all ten provinces met at Meech Lake, just outside Ottawa. The meeting was to be part of a series of meetings designed to deal with a set of five points proposed by the Quebec Liberal government the previous May as its conditions for signing the constitution. These five points were a role for Quebec in selecting Supreme Court justices; greater powers over immigration; return of the constitutional veto lost by Lévesque in 1981 or full compensation for opting out of federal programs; a limitation on federal spending power in areas of provincial jurisdiction; and recognition of Quebec as a 'distinct society.'

Much to everyone's surprise, except perhaps Mulroney's, the meeting arrived at a consensus. The consensus was made possible by the fact that everyone got something. Mulroney got the deal that he had promised Quebec nationalists in exchange for their support. Bourassa got all five of his demands, a fact that would solidify his position with Quebec's electorate. Newfoundland's Brian Peckford and Alberta's Don Getty received vague commitments from Mulroney and Bourassa to look at the former's concerns over fishing rights and the latter's desire for Senate reform. All of the provinces received additional powers. Mulroney and the premiers left Meech Lake with what Mulroney would later repeatedly call a 'done deal.' The agreement had to be ratified by all of the provincial legislatures within the next three years, but that seemed a formality.

Few Canadians paid much attention to the announcement of the deal, the debate on the accord in the House of Commons on 11 May, or the Quebec hearings which wrapped up on 25 May. On 27 May, however, Pierre Trudeau re-entered the constitutional process with a blistering attack in the media upon the accord's provisions. From then on, criticisms of the accord would accelerate. Even as the accord was formally signed on 2 June 1987, storm clouds could be seen rising on the political horizon.

Although, for the most part, dissension within the Tory party was kept under wraps, confined to the backrooms and silent thoughts of its members, there were early signs of internal disagreement. Mark Yakabuski, a senior aide to federal Tory MP Monique Vézina, resigned shortly before the accord's signing to protest its hasty creation and its failure to address multiculturalism. Similarly, Pat Nowlan, a long-time Tory backbencher, began to vocalize his opposition to the accord.

Signs of internal opposition to the accord existed also within the NDP. Although the accord appeared to point the way towards a more decentralized federation – something the NDP traditionally had fought against – the party's executive, particularly the leader, Ed Broadbent, supported the Meech Lake Accord, believing that doing so would enhance the NDP's chances of making an electoral breakthrough in Quebec. Still, the party's decision to support the accord was opposed by some, notably British Columbia MP Ian Waddell.

The Liberal party was also divided by the accord. The party had long fought for a centralized, bilingual country where all the provinces were treated equally. Now, John Turner's support of the accord seemed to many in the party to be a dangerous reversal of policy. Trudeau's criticisms of the accord, which gained approval from several key Ontario Liberals, as well as federalists within the party such as Don Johnston and Charles Caccia, ex-Trudeau aides Dennis Mills and James Coutts, and former finance minister Donald Macdonald, therefore served to spur opposition not only to the agreement but also to undercut Turner's leadership.

For the most part, however, opponents of the accord within the major parties remained silent. In the end, this silence had a political cost. Feeling that their concerns regarding the accord were not being given a proper, formal hearing within the existing political institutions, the accord's critics began to use extra-parliamentary means of expression, chiefly the various communications media. Gradually, the existing polity lost control of the issue.

At first, opposition came mainly from Quebec's anglophone population who wanted, at the least, a postponement of the accord's signing until further study of its effects upon minority rights could be completed. In the months and years that followed the accord's signing, however, opposition also was heard from other groups. Women and some ethnic groups, particularly native Canadians, began to suggest that the accord might abrogate gains won under the Charter of Rights and Freedoms. And while some academics warned – and some politicians and ordinary people outside Quebec feared – that the accord gave unprecedented, or at least unspecified, powers to Quebec, the PQ denounced the accord as a hollow document that did not go far enough in protecting Quebec's distinctiveness.

Having at first tried to bury discussion of the accord, and thereby losing control of the debate, the federal government thenceforth tried to familiarize people with the accord's provisions. Significantly, however, these attempts only increased the polarization between Quebecers and people in the rest of Canada, in large measure because the accord's supporters interpreted the meaning of the accord's provisions differently to each group.

A Gallup poll conducted a year after the accord was signed showed that 63 per cent of the people in Quebec and 67 per cent of the people in the rest of Canada were still not familiar with the content of the agreement. More importantly, while Quebecers who claimed to be familiar with the accord were slightly more likely to view it as good for Canada than unfamiliar Quebecers (69 to 64 per cent, respectively), familiar respondents in the rest of Canada were more inclined than unfamiliar respondents to view it as *not* a good thing (55 to 51 per cent). Similarly, familiar respondents outside of Quebec were more likely than unfamiliar respondents to view the agreement as giving too much power to the provinces (54 to 51 per cent).[140]

The most telling difference between Quebec and the rest of Canada, however, concerned the accord's 'distinct society' provision. While over 70 per cent of either familiar or unfamiliar Quebecers approved of the provision, over 60 per cent of familiar or unfamiliar respondents outside Quebec disapproved of it.[141] 'Distinct society' already was taking on two very different symbolic meanings and visions of Canada for francophone residents inside Quebec and anglophones inside and outside the province.

Two Goldfarb polls conducted in Ontario in June and July 1988 obtained similar results. A majority of those polled wanted amendments to the accord. Many of the accord's opponents viewed it as giving too much power to Quebec. They also objected to the clause that defined Quebec as a distinct society.[142]

As it turned out, however, the Meech Lake Accord would not be the central issue of the 1988 campaign. Because all three federal parties had agreed to support the deal, it was not a point of difference between them. It was, as Mulroney said, 'a done deal,' an estimation perhaps grumpily agreed with by the electorate. A Gallup poll released in October 1988, just prior to the election, showed that only 1 per cent of the electorate viewed Meech Lake as the main issue of the campaign. The overwhelming issue, said 59 per cent of those polled, was free trade.[143]

Next to French-English relations, free trade with the United States historically has been one of the most divisive issues facing Canada. The roots of this discord go back to the mid-point of the nineteenth century. Between 1854 and 1866, Canada and the United States actually had a Reciprocity Treaty, but it was abrogated by the Americans following their civil war in response to Britain's support for the South. Confederation in 1867 came about, in part, as a response to the ending of reciprocity. Similarly, the Conservative party's National Policy of 1879 arose out of the failure during the subsequent years to reach free trade agreements with the United States as well as Great Britain. Thereafter, the policy took on a political life of its own, with the Tories becoming identified as 'protectionists' or 'nationalists,' the Liberals as 'free traders' or 'continentalists.' The issue of which economic policies to pursue figured prominently in the election of 1891 and, even more, in what became known as the Reciprocity election of 1911. In both cases, Laurier's Liberal party lost to the Conservatives. Thereafter, although the idea of pursuing free – or at least freer – trade with the United States would occasionally reappear, the issue became viewed as a kind of political albatross, good for dinner table theorizing among corporate executives, liberal economists, and government bureaucrats, but otherwise unsaleable to the Canadian public.[144]

It is important to note, however, that even in 1911 the concept of free trade was not rejected uniformly throughout the country. In the years preceding and immediately following the 1911 election, many eastern farmers favoured protectionism as a means of strengthening their home-based markets, while the more export-dependent farmers of western Canada, particularly those in Alberta and Saskatchewan, tended to favour free trade with the United States.

In later years, central Canada's, particularly Ontario's, development of its manufacturing base enhanced the inclination of people in that region to support protectionist policies. Conversely, after the boom of the late 1940s, Alberta's perceived need for outside capital to develop its oil and gas industry strengthened support for free trade in that province. Along the way, the idea of free trade took on a kind of mythic quality among many in western Canada's business and political élite. Particularly in Alberta, many viewed free trade as an antidote to the perceived injustices of an eastern-dominated economic and political system that skewed the costs of exchange with central Canada while hindering the development of the West's 'natural' trade links to the south. Throughout the decades, however, Alberta's appeal for free trade fell on deaf ears. When at last the idea did begin to receive support, it was because of a reconfiguration of business, regional, political, institutional, and ideological interests throughout Canada.

During and before the 1984 election, Mulroney had denied strongly any interest in pursuing free trade.[145] Yet, within a year of taking office, he met with US president Ronald Reagan at what became known as the 'Shamrock Summit,' and they signed a trade declaration signalling the intent of their respective administrations to examine ways of reducing and eliminating trade barriers between the two countries. How did this change come about?[146]

Ironically, the Conservative government's decision to pursue free trade was something of a bequest from the previous Liberal administration. In general, Liberal economic policies since the Second World War had moved towards greater continental integration with the United States. In the wake, however, of the Liberal's halting attempts at economic nationalism during the 1970s and early 1980s, the vehement response of the Reagan administration, and the disastrous recession of 1981–2, the Liberal administration began in the fall of 1981 a full review of trade policy. As part of this review, Trudeau's government established the Royal Commission on the Economic Union and Development Prospects for Canada, headed by Donald Macdonald, 'a strongly partisan Liberal and a member of the nationalist wing of his party.'[147] The report of the Macdonald Commission, as it came to be called, would later be central both to the Tories' subsequent economic decision to pursue free trade and to the politics of the 1988 election.

During this period, however, the Liberal administration's review of trade policy gave few hints of the comprehensive trade agreement that would eventually emerge. Canadian officials, and even business leaders, were interested primarily in the possibility of enacting sectoral trade arrangements similar to the Auto-Pact. By contrast, although Ronald Reagan mentioned free trade with Canada in his inaugural address in 1981, American officials in general seemed only casually interested in trade issues with Canada. This lack of interest changed, however, with the election of the Mulroney Tories in 1984.

The Reagan administration had intensely disliked and mistrusted the Trudeau administration, but it believed it could do business with Mulroney's government. Many of the Tories, particular Mulroney and finance minister Michael Wilson, in turn believed that the structural problems of the Canadian economy could only be addressed by policies that reduced public and business reliance on government and returned sovereignty to the market. In the end, although free trade did not lead the Tories' policy agenda, it was congruent with the Tory government's general economic strategy.

In his first budget, shortly after taking office, Wilson tabled a policy agenda that included an intent to secure market access for Canadian exports, particularly to the United States. The issue was becoming critical as, throughout 1984 and into 1985, American investigations into Canadian export practices and U.S. protectionism both increased. In March 1985 Mulroney and Reagan held the Shamrock Summit. The events that would lead to the signing of the Canada–U.S. Free Trade Agreement (FTA) had been set in motion.

During the following months, Canadian trade minister James Kelleher carried on cross-country consultations on attitudes towards a comprehensive free trade agreement. By and large, business was supportive and labour was not. During this same period, the C.D. Howe Institute produced a report in favour of free trade. In August the majority report of a House of Commons–Senate committee cautiously supported pursuit of an agreement. It was opposed by the New Democratic members of the committee who offered their own dissenting report. Then, a couple of weeks later, the report of the Macdonald Commission came out recommending free trade with the United States.

Bruce Doern and Brian Tomlin note the political, as well as economic, importance of that Report:

[Mulroney] saw immediately the opportunity it presented for a bold policy initiative with ready-made bipartisan support. And Mulroney relished the prospect of using a former Liberal cabinet minister to give bipartisan legitimacy to the initiative. The volumes of the report arranged on his desk, Mulroney spread his hands over them and told officials present in his office that summer day that he would use the report to beat John Turner in the next election.[148]

Mulroney's belief in the political advantages of a free trade agreement was furthered by the support that the prospect of such an agreement began to receive from big business and the regions of western Canada and Quebec – three core elements of the Tories' 1984 political coalition.

Big business support for free trade resulted from more than just a fear of American reprisals. Rather, it was the product of increased confidence among many in Canada's business community that they could compete successfully in the emerging global marketplace. This increased confidence had its roots in changes in Canada's economic structure that began in the wake of the economic crisis of the early 1970s.

Following that crisis, a massive consolidation of capital and industry occurred in eastern Canada through a series of mergers and take-overs. During the 1970s, an average of 380 mergers occurred per year; in 1986 this figure rose to 938; in 1987, 1082. Moreover, the number of large transactions and total value of transactions had increased signifi-cantly.[149] In short, the number, value, and scope of corporate concentra-tion in Canada increased dramatically during the 1980s, particularly during the early years of the Tories' regime. As much as these large corporations wanted ensured access for goods they were already ex-porting, many also desired opportunities to expand into new markets.

If big business support for free trade was relatively recent, western Canada's support, as we have seen, was historic. In the election of 1911, Laurier's 'continentalist' Liberal party won fifteen of seventeen seats in the grain-growing areas of Saskatchewan and Alberta.[150] Although the region's support for free trade was more restrained by the 1980s – a report by the Canada West Foundation in 1986 found that support for the deal varied according to the type of business, with 25 per cent of businesses supportive, 68 per cent indifferent, and 7 per cent opposed – political support for free trade, particularly in the wealthy conservative provinces of Alberta and British Columbia, remained strong.[151] Indeed, the 5 May 1986 issue of *Alberta Report* was headlined: 'Free Trade: New Hope for the West.'

Big business and western Canadian support for free trade surpris-ingly was matched in Quebec. There, the miracle of 'Quebec Inc.' had given confidence to government officials and businesspeople that they could compete in outside markets. Their support for free trade was augmented by that of nationalists eager to reduce Quebec's economic dependence upon the Canadian federal state. Hence, as negotiations began in June 1986, the three major elements of the Conservatives' 1984 electoral coalition were 'on side.' Even before negotiations began, how-ever, the trade agreement was arousing passionate debate in Canada.

Supporters of the agreement argued that it opened the way for ex-pansion into the United States' market and for protection against puni-tive American actions of both the tariff and non-tariff variety. Business leaders and economists in particular further argued that free trade was justified by comparative advantage, economies of scale, and consumer sovereignty. In practice, free trade would lower the price of consumer goods, thereby increasing purchases, and hence leading to a further expansion of Canadian plants and equipment and a second bout of consumer and investment spending. Some Canadians, particularly in business, also hoped that free trade would reduce, if not eliminate, the state's 'interference' in the marketplace through such policies as FIRA and the NEP, and the welfare state in general. Finally, Canadian finance capital hoped that free trade would enhance its ability to invest in the United States without fear of American reprisal.[152]

By contrast, opponents argued that the FTA would eventually result in the reduction or elimination of social programs as businesses tried to compete with the American market. Such a deal also would make the Canadian economy even more dependent upon the United States at a time when that country's economic dominance in the world was on the wane. Finally, Canada's political, economic, and cultural sovereignty also would be lessened. In the end, the role of the Canadian state would be diminished, resulting in the fragmentation of the country and its eventual absorption into the United States.[153]

There has perhaps never been a political debate in Canada where the two sides have been more clear-cut, the key proponents of both sides so identifiable, as the ensuing free trade election. The pro–free trade side formed around the Canadian Alliance for Trade and Job Opportunities (CATJO). The alliance was heavily weighted towards big business, led by the Business Council on National Issues and the Canadian Manufacturers' Association. But small businesspeople, in selected sectors and regions of the country, also joined the alliance, led by the Canadian Federation of Small Business. Along the way, most of Canada's major economic think-tanks also lent support to the FTA. Similarly supportive were the right-leaning Tory governments of Grant Devine in Saskatchewan and Don Getty in Alberta, and Socred premier Bill Vander Zalm in British Columbia, as well as Robert Bourassa's Liberal government in Quebec.[154]

The opponents of the FTA were equally identifiable, if more diverse. Opposing it was a broad-based coalition, collectively known as the Pro-Canada Network (PCN), consisting of feminists, economic nationalists, organized labour, some farmers (particularly in the fruit and dairy industries), aboriginals, church groups, the cultural community, some small and large businesses in particular sectors (for example, textiles) and regions (notably Ontario). The NDP government in Manitoba also expressed concerned opposition, as did the recently elected Liberal premier of Ontario, David Peterson, and several of the Maritime premiers.[155]

By the time the election was held in 1988, a clear line also had been drawn politically between the federal Tories and the Liberals and NDP. As Mulroney had predicted, the deal presented particular problems for

John Turner and the Liberal party. As we have seen, the Liberal party historically had been the party of continentalism. During and after the Second World War, under Mackenzie King and his minister of finance, C.D. Howe, the Liberal party had pursued avidly a gradualist policy of economic integration with the United States. Only briefly, under Pierre Trudeau, had the party attempted to reverse this trend – much to the chagrin of Turner who resigned from the cabinet at least in part because of the party's increasingly nationalist stand. Now the same John Turner was prepared to fight against free trade. For many traditional Liberal supporters, Turner's conversion to economic nationalism was too much to bear, a combination, they felt, of opportunism and poor judgment. When free trade became *the* issue in the 1988 election, these pro–free trade Liberals, including many Quebec Liberal MNAs and at least some Liberal MPs, felt compelled to support the deal. As a result, the Liberal party, which had been in the process of unravelling since the 1970s, entered the 1988 election as a party deeply divided, not only over the Meech Lake Accord, but also over the free trade agreement.

THE ELECTION OF 1988

The free trade election of 1988, as it came to be called, signalled a revolution in the manner in which politics was carried on in Canada. Long after the election was over, the level of party financial contributions and third-party involvements, and the use of the communications media and polling, would raise serious questions about how the election had been conducted.

As we have seen, business had gradually been moving away from the Liberal party and towards the Conservative party since the mid-1970s. Nonetheless, in most elections, business has tended to 'hedge its bets' by supporting, more or less equally, both the Liberals and the Conservatives. In 1988, however, business had a clear choice between the Tories, who favoured free trade, or the Liberals, who opposed it. Given its own overwhelming support for the FTA, big business turned disproportionately to the Tories. Moreover, the total amount of money received, and subsequently spent or overspent, by all political parties continued to increase.

In 1988, financial contributions to the Tories exceeded $24.5 million, $14.3 million of which came from corporations, the rest primarily from individuals. By contrast, the Liberals took in $13.2 million, only $8.4 million of which was from business, the rest again mainly from individuals. For its part, the NDP received $17.8 million, counting both federal and provincial contributions. This total consisted of $7.8 million from individuals and $9.7 million from other sources, including $2.7 million from unions.[156]

But the continued increase in direct funding to political parties was only one issue coming out of the 1988 election. Making full use of the 1984 judicial ruling that had allowed third-party involvement in elections, proponents and antagonists of the FTA entered wholeheartedly into the fray. An estimated $4 million dollars was spent by various extra-political organizations in the course of the 1988 campaign, including $750,000 by the Pro-Canada Network, which opposed free trade, and $1.5 million by the Canadian Alliance for Free Trade and Job Opportunities.[157] Additionally, the National Citizens' Coalition spent $840,000 'exposing' the 'frightening agenda' of the NDP, which opposed the deal. (The NCC was on the rise. By 1991, it would claim a membership of 39,000 and had an annual budget reported to be $2.4 million.)[158]

The various parties in the debate spent millions of dollars on glossy pamphlets designed to win converts to their side. Unfortunately, in many cases these pamphlets neither informed nor seriously discussed the important issues. On the one hand, the anti–free trade coalition failed to address the real concerns of businesspeople that Canada's economy was threatened by increased global competitiveness and American protectionism. On the other hand, the Tories and their supporters failed to calm the fears of opponents that the agreement would result in massive restructuring and a loss of hundreds of thousands of jobs, the levelling or abandonment of national social programs, and a reduction in Canadian sovereignty.[159]

The massive intrusion of money from special interest groups alone, however, did not make the 1988 election unique. More than ever, polling became an integral part of political strategy.[160] Despite a massive and unprecedented attempt by capital to reorganize popular opinion, many people remained unconvinced of the necessity of free trade, a fact shown by the volatility of public opinion polls throughout the months leading to the election.[161]

As in 1984, the quintessential moment of the campaign occurred during a public debate held in English between the three main party leaders. In 1984 Brian Mulroney had secured victory with his savage attack on John Turner's credibility. In 1988 Turner replied in kind. On 25 October, in an exchange that lasted little more than two minutes, Turner and Mulroney engaged in what many perceived to be an embarrass-

ingly theatrical and pompous – albeit memorable – display of flag wav-
ing. Turner's unexpectedly strident performance electrified many voters and won back many votes to the Liberals and cut into Mulroney's
margin of victory.[162] Perhaps more importantly, Turner's performance
during the debate – and the election as a whole – preserved the position of the Liberals as the official opposition, much to the chagrin of the
NDP and Ed Broadbent who, earlier in the campaign, had predicted that
his party was about to supplant the Liberals.

As the election day approached, Canadians remained both volatile
and uneasy about free trade. A Gallup poll conducted in late October,
just prior to the election, revealed that there remained strong opposition to the agreement. While 34 per cent favoured the deal, 42 per cent
opposed it. Moreover, 61 per cent of those polled nationally believed
that the United States would gain more from the deal than would Canada.
This ranged from 53 per cent in the Atlantic provinces to 66 per cent in
Ontario. At the same time, 42 per cent believed that Canada would be
better off if tariffs between the countries were eliminated, while 33 per
cent believed Canada would be worse off. In short, evidence suggests
that the public was in favour of free trade *in the abstract* but was opposed to the particular deal.[163]

In the end, many Canadians felt compelled to make a choice between
the still-hated and floundering Liberals and the slightly less disliked
Conservatives who, far more than either opposition party, possessed
the reputation of being sound fiscal managers.[164] The Tories won the
election, taking 169 seats (43 per cent of the vote), including 63 (of 75)
seats in Quebec, 46 (of 99) seats in Ontario, and 25 (of 26) seats in
Alberta. By contrast, the Liberals took 83 seats (32 per cent of the vote),
43 in Ontario, while the NDP took 43 seats (20 per cent), mainly in the
West. No other party won a seat.

As in the free trade debate itself, voters for the two sides were somewhat distinguishable by income and, to a degree, by gender. Gallup
polls, conducted prior to the election, showed that males and older
voters were more likely to be Tory supporters than females and younger
voters. Although Tory support in the lower-income groups was not
negligible, support for the party generally correlated positively with
income.[165] The latter finding was corroborated by a *Globe and Mail* report of 24 November 1988, showing that the seven wealthiest ridings in
the country voted Tory while the seven poorest ridings voted either
Liberal or NDP.

Another Gallup poll, conducted after the election, indicated a significant split between the two 'founding nations.' Tory support was higher among those whose mother tongue was French than among those whose mother tongue was English (60 to 46 per cent, respectively).[166] Indeed, as political scientist Philip Resnick noted, with no little chagrin, the Tories had received barely 40 per cent of the popular vote and a minority of seats outside Quebec, but the 53 per cent of the vote which the party received in that province had carried the day.[167]

Owing to the polarizing of the election around free trade and the vagaries of a 'first-past-the-post' electoral system, Mulroney had succeeded in gaining electoral victory. His winning alliance of 1984 had been cobbled together one more time. Beneath the victory hoopla, however, there remained deep divisions within Canada's right wing, as made obvious by the Reform party's performance in its inaugural election.

THE REFORM PARTY AND THE ELECTION OF 1988

The 1988 election witnessed the continuation of the drift towards, and simultaneous fragmentation of, right-wing politics that had been occurring in Canada throughout the 1980s. In 1988, the Confederation of Regions party took 41,342 votes. Another right-wing party, the Party for the Commonwealth of Canada, a shadowy organization that endorsed the conspiracy theories of now-discredited American entrepreneur and erstwhile presidential candidate, Lyndon LaRouche, captured 7497 votes. And the Christian Heritage party ran sixty-three candidates and took 102,533 votes (64,707 in the province of Ontario).[168]

By any standard, however, the Reform party did the best of any of these right-wing parties. Only one year old and running in only 72 western ridings – (30 in British Columbia, 26 in Alberta, 4 in Saskatchewan, and 12 in Manitoba) – Reform nonetheless took 275,767 votes, or slightly more than 2 per cent of the total national votes cast (13,281,191). Computed as a percentage of total votes cast in the western provinces (3,776,373), the Reform party's share was a not-negligible 7.3 per cent. This figure rises to 8.5 per cent if calculated as a percentage of the total votes cast in the contested ridings (3,240,236).[169]

Reform party strength was particularly pronounced in its founding provinces of British Columbia and Alberta. In British Columbia, the party garnered 4.9 per cent of all votes, while in Alberta Reform votes accounted for 15.3 per cent of all votes cast. By contrast, the party received only 3.3 per cent of Manitoba's and 0.7 per cent of Saskatchewan's total votes cast.[170]

Although Reform gained the majority of its votes in urban ridings, it received proportionately greater support from rural than urban residents in each of the four Prairie provinces. This was particularly evident in Alberta, where the party received over 21 per cent of all votes cast at rural polling stations against 13 per cent of those cast at urban polling stations.[171] Does this mean that the success of the Reform party in 1988 represented a return to agrarian populism alone? Hardly. Although many farmers no doubt supported Reform, it is also likely that many rural supporters were employed in other (service or professional) occupations. The strength of the Reform party in several urban areas, particularly Calgary, further argues against any description of the party as being simply an agrarian phenomenon.

In 1988 the seven Calgary ridings returned percentages of Reform party vote ranging from a low of 12 per cent in Calgary-Centre, a low-income riding, to 17 per cent in Calgary West, a high-income riding.[172] These results suggest that the anger of people in the oil and gas industries may have translated itself into support for the Reform party. Such support would further be natural for a party that has its head office in the city and whose founding or current executives feature several Calgary residents, including Bob Muir, Diane Ablonczy, Cliff Fryers, and Stephen Harper – all of whom also have extensive connections to the oil and gas sector. Nonetheless, it must be remembered that most people in Calgary do not work directly in the oil and gas industry, though their own economic conditions are no doubt influenced by it. Hence, the results at best support the notion that the presence of a strong, single industry – one that is heavily foreign (American) owned – has resulted in the creation in that city of a unique micro-political culture.[173]

But Reform also made a credible showing outside Calgary, mainly in the south and central districts. In the Alberta riding of Crowfoot, the Reform party candidate, Jack Ramsay, former head of Western Canada Concept, received 32 per cent of the vote. Reform captured more than 30 per cent of the vote also in the ridings of Wild Rose and MacLeod and 28 per cent in Yellowhead, where Preston Manning ran against former prime minister Joe Clark. The Alberta Reform vote also was high in Elk Island, Red Deer, Wetaskiwin, and Edmonton Strathcona.[174] Finally, Reform also garnered respectable vote totals in some areas of British Columbia, notably Okanagan Centre, where Reform's candidate was former Alberta Socred leader Werner Schmidt, as well as Prince George–Peace River and Saanich.[175]

What factors allowed the Reform party to garner the relative amount of success that it did in the 1988 election? Several factors appear to have been at work. First, as we have seen, the party rode an unprecedented wave of anger towards the federal Progressive Conservatives over such issues as patronage and perceived favouritism towards Quebec. In Alberta, this anger was fuelled by the province's second major recession in less than ten years.

Secondly, in positively detailing its own policies, the Reform party implicitly appealed to traditional conservative voters by placing on its policy agenda such moral or normative issues as immigration, bilingualism, capital punishment, and abortion. These policies may in turn have gained some appeal through their vagueness, a vagueness further obfuscated by populist calls to 'let the people decide.' Nonetheless, the majority of Reform supporters no doubt perceived the party's stand on these policies as essentially conservative and moreover, that its appeal to a popular democratic policy of majority rule would ensure the implementation of such a regime.

Thirdly, unlike its more radical right-wing predecessors of the early 1980s, the Reform party in 1988 possessed several important attributes, notably a qualified and able executive, a degree of financial resources, and a credible and recognizable leader. The latter factor in particular should not be underestimated. Although Preston Manning himself was largely unknown, his name resonated with many older voters, particularly in rural Alberta, a fact no doubt reflected in the pattern of electoral support for Reform.

We should not, of course, overstate Reform's success in 1988. After all, the party did not win any seats. At best, the 1988 election was a testing ground, setting the stage for the party's major breakthrough five years later. Still, it is probably also true that the 1988 results masked growing support for Reform, and that the party would likely have garnered more support had it not been for the election's focus on the issue of free trade. As a western right-wing party, one of Reform's major planks was the support of free trade. But it had several other policies up its sleeve, including free parliamentary votes, referenda on major issues, Senate reform, a simplified tax system, balanced budgets, an end to indirect taxes and tariffs on farm inputs, an end to discriminatory freight rates, an end to official bilingualism, tighter immigration laws, and targeted financial assistance to the needy.

When free trade became *the* issue of the campaign, however, the Reform party found itself in a bind. Because Reform supported the

Tories' Free Trade Agreement, it could only score political points against the PCs by claiming that the latter had only been 'converted to the free trade position when Quebec demanded it. The West,' the party's official organ, *The Reformer*, went on to say, 'needs MPs in the next Parliament who are committed to freer trade on the basis of principle and fairness, not political expediency.'[176]

Despite its substantial efforts to grab the free trade vote, the Reform party fell victim to the Tories' strategy of polarization. Many western voters, particularly in Alberta, supported the agreement. While they did not like Brian Mulroney's Tories, they feared that a vote for the Reform party would split the free trade vote, opening the door for an FTA opponent (either a Liberal or an NDP candidate) to win a seat. Hence, many potential Reform supporters likely 'held their noses' and voted for the Tories. The size of the Tories' victory, however, served only to mask the growing support for Reform.

The factors that facilitate the rise of a populist party are not entirely planned. More often, they are fortuitous, the result of failures originating in existing institutions and leaderships. Often, the essential quality of leaders of would-be populist parties is a readiness to seize the moment.

On election night, 1988, Brian Mulroney also attempted to seize the moment:

Canadians ... have spoken with a loud and clear voice of their desire for unity ... And that's what the election was about ... The Free Trade Agreement and the Meech Lake Accord are the chief instruments of our prosperity and unity. They constitute a brilliant affirmation of the new spirit of national reconciliation and economic renewal that benefits us all.[177]

But Mulroney's words of unity were a sham. He had tried to recreate the Liberal coalition in Tory terms but had failed. The country, already deeply divided before Mulroney took power, was rapidly sundering along class, regional, and ethnic lines.

The Reform party already had camped on the outskirts of Canada's crumbling polity, ready to offer to the fleeing masses a cup of populist rhetoric and a dish of right-wing policies. Formed in 1987 by disenchanted western, former Liberal and Conservative businesspeople and politicians, the party from the start had inclined towards pro–free enterprise solutions, while simultaneously appealing to traditional conservative values. Despite its populist appeal, the Reform party's range of latitude, ideologically, had since become even more constrained, its policies shaped and moulded by Preston Manning and an in-group of the largely Calgary-based western political and economic establishment. How far could the party go, however, riding the wave of political discontent? Could it broaden its appeal and become a national force, without losing its western right-wing base? Could it, in short, create a broadbased political coalition? These were but some of the questions facing Preston Manning and the Reform party as 1988 drew to a close.

4. The Legitimation of Reform

'Old Canada' ... is dying ... Can we define a New Canada to replace the Old Canada ...?'

Preston Manning, speech to the Saskatoon Assembly, 1991[1]

The appeal of populist parties and movements is to a socially constructed notion of the 'people' whose survival is viewed as threatened by 'outside' forces – a 'power bloc.' Being socially constructed, both the 'people' and the 'power bloc' are thus contested concepts. But they are not entirely arbitrary. Rather, each concept has deep historical, cultural, and ideological roots that, in turn, infuse and shape the debates about the nature and causes of the current organic crisis.

In the two years following the 1988 election a series of events not only shattered the Tory coalition but also seemed to threaten Canada's existence. Shortly after the election, Quebec premier Robert Bourassa brought in Bill 178, overriding a decision of the Supreme Court that had ruled unconstitutional the province's law prohibiting the use of English on outdoor signs. Bourassa's action reawakened animosities among many in English-speaking Canada who felt that French-speaking Quebecers were imposing unilingualism in Quebec while demanding bilingualism elsewhere. Thus began a series of events, played out against the backdrop of history, which would culminate in the failure of the Meech Lake Accord in 1990.

The failure of the accord, however, was not the only incident to plague the Canadian body politic during this period. In the spring of 1990, a recession began which further eroded the legitimacy of the

Canadian state and of the existing polity, leading many Canadians to believe that – in Preston Manning's words – 'Old Canada was dying.'

In the midst of the resultant legitimation crisis, the Reform party gained in political stature by offering people outside Quebec a vision of a 'New Canada.' This chapter examines the events that led many to question Canada's survival. It examines also Manning's explanation for the failure of the 'Canadian experiment,' linking this explanation, and the Reform party in general, to a uniquely Anglo-Canadian brand of nativism. The chapter begins with a brief discussion of two elections that, in the immediate aftermath of the 1988 election, elevated the Reform party to a place of prominence in the eyes of the Canadian electorate.

GREY AND WATERS: GAINING A PLATFORM

The mood of Canadians as 1989 began was already uneasy. The Tories had won the free trade election, but polls showed that a majority of Canadians still wanted the policy put to a referendum. Other Tory policies, such as the proposed implementation of a goods and services tax (GST) and the Meech Lake constitutional agreement, were increasingly coming under intense criticism. There also remained intense anger and mistrust directed at Brian Mulroney, affecting his capacity to form necessary political coalitions. These intense feelings soon translated themselves in the West into two significant political victories for the Reform party.

The first occurred in the northeastern Alberta riding of Beaver River. Five days after the 1988 election, the newly elected Tory MP, John Dahmer, died of cancer. Dahmer had won the election handily. The Reform party candidate, Deborah Grey, a thirty-six-year-old, straight-talking, gospel-singing schoolteacher with strong anti-abortionist views and a political pedigree that included a great-uncle who shared British Columbia's coalition leadership from 1947 to 1952 and a great-grand-father who was a former BC Liberal MP, had finished fourth with 4150 votes.[2]

By-elections, however, are different from regular elections. By-elections allow voters to protest a government's policies without (usually) bringing it down. Just as the election of WCC's Gordon Kesler in the Olds-Didsbury by-election of 1982 allowed voters to register a protest against federal and provincial policies, the Beaver River by-election allowed voters in that riding the chance to protest against Mulroney's Tories. With free trade assured, voters looked to the candidate whose election would most 'shock' the current polity. That candidate was Grey.

Campaigning, in particular, against the proposed goods and services tax and the Meech Lake Accord and in favour of the Triple-E Senate, Grey rapidly gained the support of voters in the riding. When the byelection was held on 13 March 1989, Grey took 11,154 votes. By contrast, the second-place Tory candidate took 6912 votes, while the Liberals and NDP received 2756 and 2085 votes, respectively.

A short while after Grey's victory, the issue of Senate reform gave the Reform party another boost. As we have seen, the idea of Senate reform had grown steadily in the West over the years. Despite the Tories' victory in 1988, discontent with Mulroney's government remained high. This discontent was based in large part on the perception that the Tories, like the Liberals before them, were captive to the interests of central Canada. By 1989, many westerners had come to believe that the powers of an unresponsive and largely eastern-based polity could only be curbed by a reformed Senate.

When one of Alberta's constitutionally allotted Senate seats became vacant, premier Don Getty announced that it would be filled through an election to be held on 16 October 1989. Traditionally, Senate seats have been filled through often highly partisan appointments made by the federal government. With the signing of the Meech Lake Accord in the spring of 1987, the federal Tories had committed themselves to making selections from a list of names of candidates provided by the provincial governments. Never previously, however, had a Canadian senator been elected.

Getty's decision to elect Alberta's Senate candidate was heralded by democrats everywhere. It particularly won him accolades in Alberta where, since taking over leadership of the governing Tories from Peter Lougheed in 1985, support for the party had noticeably declined. Despite winning an election in March 1989, taking fifty-nine of eighty-three seats, the party had received only 44 per cent of the popular vote. Moreover, Getty himself had been defeated and only re-entered the legislation following a by-election victory in the safe rural riding of Stettler. Ominously, the Tories were also gradually being shunted off to Alberta's rural hinterland – the same fate that had befallen Social Credit before its defeat in 1971. Getty's decision to hold a Senate election, therefore, appears, at least in part, to have been an attempt to bolster his party's sagging political fortunes by laying claim to a popular political issue.

Be that as it may, the ensuing election provided a further opportunity for voters 'to send a message' to Ottawa. The election drew an impressive group of candidates, including the Reform party candidate, Stanley Waters.[3]

A man of strong conservative convictions regarding fiscal and law and order matters, but of somewhat more liberal moral opinions – unlike Grey, he was pro-choice on abortion – Waters was born in Winnipeg on 14 June 1920. Raised and educated in Edmonton, he later joined the Canadian army and had a distinguished military career, eventually rising to the position of lieutenant-general before his retirement in 1975. Waters subsequently returned to Calgary where he became a senior executive of Fred Mannix's business empire. Befitting his military background, Waters was a straightforward man of action who rapidly achieved a prominent status in the business world. By 1980 Waters was president of the Calgary Chamber of Commerce. Like so many others in the Reform party, he was also a member of the National Citizens' Coalition and the Fraser Institute. The business connections he made during these years proved useful during the Senate election as vast sums of money flowed into his campaign from the corporate establishment, including such people as A.J. Child and Francis Winspear.

By the time the Senate election was held, the Reform party was already seen in Alberta as a legitimate vehicle for political reform. Moreover, the election occurred during a period of increasing public anger over the federal Tories proposal to implement the GST. Although generally favouring the tax, the Reform party quickly got in front of popular opinion on the issue, and even subsequently gave token leadership to public protests against the tax measure.[4] In the end, Reform's ability to turn public discontent over the GST into political support for its candidate resulted in Waters handily winning Canada's first Senate election.[5] Waters received nearly 260,000 votes compared with the 140,000 votes received by the second-place finisher, Liberal Bill Code.

The impact of Waters's election to the Senate was magnified during the following months by Brian Mulroney's delay in appointing him to the upper chamber. Mulroney viewed the election as a high-handed attempt by the Alberta government to force Senate reform upon the federal government and the members of the House of Commons. His refusal to respect the will of the people, however, was widely viewed as undemocratic. The non-appointment of Waters was a public relations gift to Reform, as noted by Stephen Harper:

I remember Stan Waters calling me the night he won and saying, 'Do you think Mulroney will appoint me?' And I said 'no.' He said, 'Well, what can we do to get him to appoint me.' And I said, 'Nothing. You're more valuable to us as a martyr.' And I was right. It became a fundamental question of democracy, and a colossal blunder on Mulroney's part.[6]

Waters became, in effect, a living symbol of Canada's apparently failing democracy. Over the next two years, before his death in the fall of 1991, Waters became a key part of the Reform party's team. Waters and Grey became complementary bookends for Preston Manning as his entourage moved from town to town across the country.

The elections of both Grey and Waters were entirely fortuitous – the former resulting from the death of a Tory MP, necessitating a by-election, the latter resulting from the political machinations of Don Getty who had hoped to use the Senate election as a means of boosting his own increasingly unpopular government. Nonetheless, Reform's victories provided the party with a degree of instant respectability and, perhaps more importantly, a federal platform from which to observe and comment on the national crisis which would soon destroy Mulroney's fragile political alliance and engulf the country in a mood of national despair.

REFORM, MEECH LAKE, AND THE RECESSION

As we have seen, Brian Mulroney and the Tories had won re-election in 1988 in large measure because of the Meech Lake Accord and the free trade agreement. These twin policies had won the support of the core elements of the Tory coalition of 1984 – Quebec nationalists, big business, and the western, particularly Albertan, petite bourgeoisie – while simultaneously polarizing and fragmenting the opposition Liberals and New Democrats. Despite the Tories' margin of victory in 1988, however, support for the party was shallow. Moreover, they forgot, or ignored, the fact that political legitimacy requires constant reinforcement; that legitimacy is not something won, once and for all, at election time, but must be reconstructed on a frequent basis if it is to be possessed at all.

Instead, the years that followed saw Mulroney's Tories often pursue policies for which there was no clear popular mandate and to which, indeed, there was often substantial opposition. In the spring of 1990, the public perception that the Mulroney government was autocratic, arrogant, and manipulative fuelled long-simmering ethnic, regional, economic, and political grievances to bring about the collapse of the Meech Lake Accord. As I will show, the public vitriol surrounding the accord's provisions and its demise provided the seed-bed for Reform's immediate rise to national prominence.

Concerns regarding the Meech Lake Accord were present from the beginning. Opposition to the accord became even more pronounced, however, as the three-year deadline approached for provincial ratification. A remarkable aspect of this opposition – and one which Mulroney's Tories in Ottawa and Bourassa's Liberals in Quebec ignored at their peril – was its disparate nature.

Indeed, Canada's diversity, which supporters of the accord viewed as making its compromise provisions necessary, was a hallmark of the accord's detractors. For example, federalists and many on the left in English-speaking Canada viewed the accord as overly decentralizing a system already dangerously balkanized. Conversely, 'provincialists' in English Canada, bent on using the agreement's treatment of Quebec as a means of prying further powers from Ottawa, complained that the accord didn't respect the equality of the provinces. The territories, meanwhile, complained that the accord would be used by the existing provinces to perpetuate the north's second-class status within Confederation. While anti-French bigots in English-speaking Canada viewed the accord as a 'sell out' by Ottawa to Quebec, nationalists in that province condemned it as a 'sell-out' by Bourassa's government of the French historical 'fact.' And minority groups, particularly natives and women, viewed it as neglecting their concerns and entrenching inequalities.

The Reform party – whose Vancouver assembly in 1987 was held, ironically, at virtually the same time as the accord was formally signed – both grew out of and tapped into this discontent. As the 1988 election approached, Reform had concentrated on free trade. Nonetheless, opposition to the Meech Lake Accord remained a consistent part of Reform's agenda, differentiating it from the three major political parties. 'The Reform Party is the only party that calls for the withdrawal of the deeply flawed Meech Lake Accord and an end to granting "special status" for Quebec.'[7] It is important to understand Manning's, and Reformers' in general, opposition to the accord.

According to Preston Manning, the accord's 'flaws' involved 'the top-down, closed-door approach to constitution making,' 'the rigid amending formula,' and the 'lack of substantial assurances that real progress would be made' regarding Senate reform.[8] There is some substance to Manning's charges. It is unlikely, however, that any or all of these issues alone would have led to substantial opposition to the accord and, ultimately, its failure. Rather, at the heart of much of the

opposition to the accord in English-speaking Canada, and among Reform supporters in particular, was the agreement's clause recognizing
Quebec as a 'distinct society.' In Manning's words:

Behind ... the distinct society clause was a fundamental question, not fully
explored during the Meech Lake debate, which will be at the heart of any
future attempt to rewrite the Canadian constitution: will we achieve constitutional unity by insisting upon the *equality* of all Canadians and provinces in
the constitution and in federal law, or by guaranteeing *special status* to racial,
linguistic, cultural, or other groups?[9]

In the end, Manning and his followers believed that the accord threatened the principle of *absolute* individual and provincial equality, elevating Quebec to a status above that of other provinces and potentially hindering the rights of others.

This belief was festering throughout English-speaking Canada as
1989 began. It grew when the federal Tories, Liberals, and New Democrats, and the various provincial governments, failed to deal with the
issue head-on. Concerns over the exact meaning of 'distinct society'
were only heightened by official statements that, alternatively, told
Quebecers that the accord gave them real powers, and then told people
in the rest of the country that it was purely symbolic.

This obfuscation soon led to the perception among many English-
speaking Canadians that they had not been told the whole truth about
the impact of the accord. Some reactionary elements in English-speaking Canada used this official ambiguity as proof that 'the French' were
'once more' being given special privileges. Bigotry and fear went searching for an old enemy – bilingualism.

Throughout the fall and winter of 1989–90, under the guise of 'fiscal
restraint,' forty municipalities in Ontario, and several in Manitoba,
declared themselves unilingual English. In the fall of 1989, also, a hand-
ful of APEC supporters in Brockville, Ontario, wiped their feet on a
Quebec flag. Captured on film, the incident was repeatedly broadcast
on Quebec television throughout the spring of 1990, resulting in the
expected and also filmed stomping of the Canadian flag by young Quebec nationalists. This symbolic 'tit for tat' could not have come at a
worse time: the Meech Lake Accord was already in danger of failing
and, no matter the rational arguments for why it should or should not
have failed, the incidents added an unnecessary emotional content to
the already explosive situation.

Sensing the increasing hostility to the accord throughout English-speaking Canada, Preston Manning and the Reform party stepped up their campaign against the accord, in particular its granting of 'special status' to Quebec. At the party's third assembly, held in Edmonton in October 1989, Manning's keynote speech stated what has remained the party's stance on Quebec ever since. Drawing on an analogy previously used by both Jesus Christ and Abraham Lincoln, Manning's speech, entitled 'Leadership for a House Divided,' stated:

Either all Canadians, including the people of Quebec, make a clear commitment to Canada as one nation, or Quebec and the rest of Canada should explore whether there exists a better but more separate relationship, between the two ... Our clear preference is for a united Canada in which Quebec is prosperous and culturally secure ... If, however, we continue to make unacceptable constitutional, economic and linguistic concessions to Quebec, at the expense of the rest of Canada, it is those concessions themselves which will tear the country apart.[10]

Manning's phraseology is ambiguous. What does 'more separate' mean? Does it mean 'totally separate'? Or does it suggest a kind of 'asymmetrical federalism'? For many in English-speaking Canada, however, Manning's conditions were clear: Quebec would either have to accept a status of absolute equality with the remaining provinces or it would have to leave the federation.

By January 1990 the accord clearly was in trouble. Manning stepped up his attacks, demanding that the Alberta legislature withdraw its support for the agreement as a means of pressuring the federal Tories to appoint Stan Waters to the Senate.[11] Despite growing opposition, however, the accord could only be overridden legally by a failure of provincial ratification. By early 1990 only three provinces – New Brunswick, Manitoba, and Newfoundland – remained to ratify the accord, but the political circumstances of each had changed dramatically since the agreement's signing in 1987.[12]

In New Brunswick, on 13 October 1987, Richard Hatfield's Conservatives lost every seat in going down to defeat to Frank McKenna's Liberal party. McKenna, who had opposed the accord before the election, immediately began to press for changes to the agreement which would ensure protection of minority language rights and the removal of the notwithstanding clause. While this was occurring, events were also transpiring elsewhere.

In March 1988 the minority NDP government in Manitoba went

down to defeat on a motion of non-confidence. The subsequent election saw the Tories under Tuxedo MLA Gary Filmon win a minority government. The rejuvenated Liberals, led by Sharon Carstairs, became the official opposition while the NDP, under new leader Gary Doer, came third with only twelve seats. The election of Filmon was even more significant than the election of McKenna. Filmon had vigorously opposed the extension of French language rights in the province in the early 1980s, an opposition that had won him many votes in the 1986 election. He was, thus, beholden to the anti-French vote in the province. Moreover, although he initially supported the Meech Lake Accord, Filmon's support was lukewarm; he had hoped that his support might curry favour with his federal cousins. Hence, when the accord ran into real problems, Filmon lacked either the electoral base or the principled will to continue the fight.

The accord's real opponent in Manitoba, however, was Carstairs. A friend and confidante of Jean Chrétien, who had become the favourite in the race to replace John Turner as Liberal leader and who himself strongly opposed the accord, Carstairs viewed the agreement as involving a significant devolution of federal powers. Following the federal election in November 1988, Doer took a similar position. Although his predecessor as leader of the NDP, Howard Pawley, had signed the accord in 1987, Doer felt that the now-certain passage of the Canada–U.S. Free Trade Agreement would combine with the accord to threaten doubly Canada's national social programs.

Hence, when Filmon rose in the Manitoba legislature on 16 December 1988 to speak to the introduction of the bill ratifying the Meech Lake Accord, his political support was precarious. Nonetheless, his speech that day was unqualified in its support for the accord. By coincidence, the day prior to Filmon's speech had seen the Supreme Court of Canada rule as unconstitutional Quebec's Bill 101, which prohibited the use of English on outdoor signs. Two days later, on 18 December, pressed by Quebec nationalists, premier Bourassa announced that he would invoke the 'notwithstanding clause' in the Charter of Rights and Freedoms to override the Supreme Court decision.

Bourassa's decision was immediately condemned outside Quebec and threw a monkey wrench into the difficult Manitoba debate. Faced with insurmountable opposition, both inside and outside the legislature, Filmon withdrew Manitoba's ratification bill the next day. Thereafter, he would join with Carstairs and Doer in opposing the accord and demanding changes.

In Newfoundland, the Conservatives had already ratified the accord when they were defeated on 20 April 1989 by the Liberals led by Clyde Wells. Like Carstairs, Wells was a staunch Trudeau Liberal and opposed the accord as a threat to national unity. On 6 April 1990 Wells's government rescinded Newfoundland's approval for the accord, demanding that it be reopened for negotiation. The accord was in real jeopardy with only weeks to go before the ratification deadline.

For months, Mulroney had refused to hold a first ministers' conference to deal with the problems with the accord. The accord, said Mulroney, could not be reopened. Those who opposed it were threatening the breakup of the country. Failure to ratify the accord would be, in Mulroney's words, a rejection of Quebec, leading to that province's secession from Canada. In this hyperbolic vein, Mulroney made constant speeches warning the accord's chief opponents – Wells, McKenna, and the Filmon/Doer/Carstairs triumvirate – of the dire consequences that would befall the country should they fail to ratify the agreement. It was a high-risk strategy that ultimately backfired. Mulroney's interpretation of motives and events, including repeatedly insisting that Quebec had been 'rejected' during the constitutional negotiations of 1981, fanned the flames of separatism in Quebec, while enraging people outside Quebec who felt that they were being bullied and their legitimate concerns ignored.[13]

As the deadline for the accord's ratification approached, Mulroney at last called for a meeting of the first ministers. The meeting was, as he later admitted, a 'roll of the dice' designed to add further pressure to the dissenting premiers. The ensuing meeting was viewed by many as a sordid display of political brinkmanship, and ultimately brought into further disrepute the accord and Mulroney's Tories, in particular, and Canadian politics, in general.

Between 3 and 10 June 1990, Mulroney and the ten provincial premiers met privately in Ottawa, appearing only infrequently to describe for the television cameras set up outside their progress in deciding the future of Canada. Excluded from the process, many Canadians watched with growing anger and apprehension as day by day, hour by hour, fatigued and overwrought ministers emerged to give their side of the events transpiring.

Inside, the dissenting premiers were under relentless pressure to reach an agreement. As Mulroney had anticipated, the sheer weight of numbers, the importance of the issue – 'the fate of Canada' – and fatigue started to wear on the intransigent minority. Before the meeting, McKenna's opposition to the accord had already begun to wilt in the face of political pressure from the Acadian population within his province. Filmon's opposition, as we have seen, was lukewarm in any case. In consultation with Doer and Carstairs, however, Filmon finally agreed to bring the accord forward for public hearings and a vote in the Manitoba legislature. Wells, whose opposition to the accord was perhaps the most principled of any of its opponents, was the toughest nut to crack, but in the end he too agreed to put it to either a provincial referendum or a vote of the legislature. The accord appeared to be saved.

It was clear, however, that the mood of many Canadians had been soured by the entire affair. An Angus Reid–Southam News poll conducted shortly after the Ottawa meeting found that only 18 per cent of Quebecers and 9 per cent of non-Quebecers thought that the accord was a good deal. Still, for reasons of both fatigue and fear of the consequences of rejecting it, the majority of Canadians (55 per cent) wanted it passed.[14] In the days following the Ottawa meeting, however, support mounted in English-speaking Canada for rejection. Preston Manning and the Reform party joined in calling for the accord's rejection. Speaking in Brandon, Manitoba, Manning stated:

the people of Manitoba and Newfoundland ... have got [a] real opportunity to pass judgement on the Meech Lake accord now ... Our hope would be that Manitobans would feel free to reject the accord and the top down pressures that were used to pressure your politicians over the last week.[15]

In the end, Manning got his wish.

As the deadline for ratification approached, Wells believed increasingly that the accord would not pass a vote in the Newfoundland legislature, and that he and the province were being manipulated by the federal Tories into being held accountable for its defeat. Still, it seemed that Wells had no choice: the vote must proceed. At this point, however, fate intervened in the person of Elijah Harper, a previously little known native Manitoba NDP MLA. Believing that the accord dealt insufficiently with native concerns, Harper withheld crucial agreement to proceed immediately with legislative debate on the accord. His refusal delayed a vote on the accord, making impossible its ratification before the appointed deadline. The accord thus died on the order paper. In turn, Manitoba's failure to ratify it provided Wells with sufficient justification to adjourn the Newfoundland legislature without holding a vote.

The day following the death of the Meech Lake Accord – 24 June – was Quebec's national holiday, Saint-Jean-Baptiste day. As one might expect, the recent events added renewed fervour to that year's nationalist celebrations. While the rest of Canada looked on, Quebecers turned out en masse to declare their intentions to pursue independence. The cameras, of course, captured the requisite scene of a Canadian flag in flames. That same day, Jean Chrétien was named the new Liberal leader, replacing John Turner. The choice of Chrétien was filled with typical Canadian irony. In choosing him as their leader, Liberals picked a francophone Quebecer who was overwhelmingly disliked in his home province but supported in English-speaking Canada, while Brian Mulroney – an anglophone Quebecer – might well have been the most despised man in all of English-speaking Canada, even as he still retained enormous support among Quebec's francophone population.

For their part, people in English-speaking Canada were consumed by a range of emotions. Mostly, however, the events of Meech Lake had left them numb. With trepidation and some fear, they asked: What would happen now? What political leader or party could they turn to at this time of apparent crisis? Underlying all of these questions was an even more fundamental one: Would Canada survive?

The answers were not immediately forthcoming, certainly not from Mulroney's Tories or the other elements of Canada's political establishment. Bourassa announced that Quebec would no longer attend interprovincial meetings. Some of the other premiers, perhaps believing like many Canadians that the country was dying, declared their intentions to have first dibs at the carcass.

As other politicians dove for cover, only Preston Manning (and the separatists in Quebec) stood up, unscathed. Uninvolved directly during the growing carnage, Manning was in a good position now to say 'I told you so!'

Meech Lake was dead for a long time. The deal, its supporters and the way it was done were all totally discredited. The question was, would it die now or have to be revealed as unworkable a few months from now.[16]

But the resultant sense of crisis was also exploited by Preston Manning and the Reform party during the months that followed to delegitimate further the traditional political parties. With the rise in strength of the separatist Bloc Québécois, the Reform party especially began to play upon the fears of English-speaking Canadians that the traditional parties were about to sell out to Quebec in order to buy constitutional peace. Of Mulroney and the Tories, for example, Manning stated:

Mulroney is hopelessly compromised. He is in the most blatant conflict of interest anyone could find himself in. If he presumes to negotiate Quebec's separation on Canada's behalf, it will be like Quebec negotiating with itself. This is totally unacceptable.[17]

And again (regarding Mulroney and Chrétien): 'They're seen as having a profound conflict of interest on this issue. As long as you're playing for votes on both sides ... you can't be trusted by the rest of Canada to articulate its interests.'[18] As for the NDP: 'They're going to have to choose. Either you represent the rest of Canada in this, or you represent Quebec. But you can't represent both.'[19] In short, Manning and Reform exploited the Meech Lake crisis to further discredit the existing political parties.

What effect did the Meech Lake controversy have on Reform party success? We may use Preston Manning's 'House Divided' speech to the Edmonton assembly in October 1989 as a benchmark for measuring the effects of opposition to Meech Lake upon the party's support. A Gallup poll taken in November, following the Edmonton assembly, showed that opposition to the accord nationally stood at 31 per cent, up from 18 per cent the previous January. The November poll showed that opposition was particularly high in the Prairies (45 per cent) and in British Columbia (46 per cent).[20] Significantly, a Gallup electoral poll, taken that same month, showed that Reform support stood at 16 per cent support in the Prairies and 14 per cent in British Columbia.[21]

In January 1990 Reform support stood at 4 per cent nationally, the majority of this support being centred on the Prairies and in British Columbia.[22] During the next few months, however, as the deadline approached for the ratification of the accord and as opposition to it grew, Reform began a slow rise in the polls.

Between February and May 1990 Reform support nationally rose by one percentage point each month. The rise was particularly dramatic in the prairies where, in May, 26 per cent of respondents announced their support for Reform.[23] That same month saw opposition to the accord nationally reach its highest recorded level (42 per cent). Opposition remained particularly high in the Prairies (52 per cent) and in British Columbia (46 per cent).[24]

It is likely, of course, that general hostility towards both the Tories and the other traditional parties, arising from other, cumulative issues, also underpinned much of Reform's rise in support during this period. Nonetheless, the Meech Lake controversy was the salient political event in Canada during the first six months of 1990. Reform's consistent opposition to the constitutional agreement, while probably not swaying public opposition to the accord – it remained at a high level throughout this period – no doubt won the party support from many in English-speaking Canada who saw themselves, and their vision of Canada, as betrayed by the traditional parties.

Over the next two years, there would be meetings, hearings, reports – the Spicer Commission, the Bélanger-Campeau Committee, the Allaire Report, the Beaudoin-Dobbie Commission, various provincial hearings – all designed to address complaints arising out of Meech Lake process that 'the people' had not been informed or consulted on the constitution. Despite these actions, however, there remained a sense that a constitutional solution would not be found, that this time Canada's historic scars, reopened by Meech Lake, could not be healed. Whereas in June 1990 only 20 per cent of Canadians believed that the country was in danger of breaking up, less than a year later this number had risen to 80 per cent.[25]

Moreover, English-speaking Canada appeared to be growing less willing to accommodate Quebec's differences. An Angus Reid poll, conducted in September 1991, found that opposition to distinct society status for Quebec had risen to 63 per cent, up from 56 per cent in May 1991.[26] Likewise, support for official bilingualism began to drop throughout Canada. In 1986, three-quarters of Canadians supported official bilingualism.[27] The failure of the accord, however, led many Canadians outside Quebec to believe that the country was breaking up and that the policy of bilingualism had failed to hold the country together. Between 1990 and 1991, the percentage of Canadians believing that bilingualism was a failure rose from 59 to 63 per cent, while those believing the policy was a success dropped from 31 to 22 per cent.[28] Canada's 'two solitudes' seemed to be drifting inexorably apart.

The failure of Meech Lake in June 1990 was only the first in a series of crises, however, to afflict Canada's political system that summer. Soon, a conflict between the Mohawk community in Oka, Quebec, and its neighbouring white municipality over the proposed use of disputed land to make a golf course resulted in an armed stand-off that lasted for nearly two months. The sight of federal soldiers being sent in to

disarm heavily fortified native warriors shocked, angered, and sad-
dened Canadians from coast to coast. Coming on the heels of Meech
Lake, the incident reinforced the feelings of many Canadians that the
country was coming apart, riven by ethnic, regional, and linguistic
differences. The incident also smugly comforted some elements in
English-speaking Canada who simultaneously gloated over Quebec's
'problem' with its own 'distinct society.' The hopelessness felt by many
Canadians was reinforced by the perception that the Tory government
in Ottawa, stunned by the defeat of Meech Lake, had lost its direction.

By September the Oka crisis was competing for public attention with
events in the Middle East following Iraq's invasion of Kuwait, while in
the House of Commons a critical debate on the government's proposed
goods and services tax got under way. But, of all the crises that Canada
faced after the Meech Lake debacle, none was more damaging to the
country's collective psyche, and to the legitimacy of the Tories, than the
recession that followed. In the end, the effects of the recession upon
Canadians' confidence in the Tories, and the failure of the other existing parties to replace Mulroney's government in the hearts and minds
of some members of the electorate, paved the way for another surge in
Reform support.

The material effects on Canada of the recession that began in 1990
can be measured in various ways. The unemployment rate, 7.5 per cent
in 1989, rose to 8.1 per cent in 1990. In 1991 it hovered around 10.5 per
cent (about 1.4 million people), and then rose again in 1992 to 11.7 per
cent, or 1.6 million workers. Despite some signs of economic growth,
unemployment remained obdurately at 11.2 per cent in 1993.[29] But
even these figures disguised the true nature of what was occurring. As
unemployment benefits ran out, more and more people dropped from
official recognition, turning instead to provincial welfare roles.[30] By the
end of 1992, perhaps as many as 2.6 million Canadians were on welfare. The following year, as welfare rolls continued to rise, provincial
governments throughout Canada, notably Alberta, reduced benefits and
otherwise began well-publicized attempts to force clients off the dole.

As unemployment, wage rollbacks, and general austerity became increasingly the order of the day, a kind of siege mentality began to grip
Canadians. Lacking disposable income, or simply fearful for their future, consumers spent less. In turn, small and large business began to
suffer. In 1989, prior to the recession, 38,436 individual and corporate
bankruptcies (and proposals) occurred in Canada. Beginning in 1990,
however, the total number of bankruptcies began to rise precipitously,

to 55,424 in 1990, 75,773 in 1991, and 76,139 in 1992, before finally falling to a still unhealthy total of 66,983 in 1993.[31]

The recession also negatively, and perhaps permanently, affected the overall shape of the Canadian labour market. Over the course of the recession, more than 500,000 full-time jobs were lost, most of them in the manufacturing sector. At the same time part-time jobs increased to 2,287,000 by December 1993, an increase of more than 260,000 since 1990.[32] Many of the latter jobs were in the service sector, fuelling concerns that a structural shift was taking place away from full-time, high-wage, skilled positions towards part-time, low-wage, unskilled and semi-skilled employment.

Throughout the recession, repeated government predictions that the economy was on the rebound were belied by economic statistics, which showed that the recovery was, at best, shaky.[33] Canada's gross domestic product (GDP) during this period revealed the tentativeness of any recovery. Over the four quarters of 1990, Canada's GDP went from +2.2 to -0.6 to -1.1 to, finally, -4.9. It started 1991 at -4.7, then rebounded to +5.7, then fell again to +0.9 before ending the year at an even zero.[34] And, although Canada's GDP grew in 1992 by 0.7 per cent, allowing textbook economists to declare that the recession was officially over, the recovery was shallow and uneven. Exports increased but, as predicted by free trade's opponents, these were primarily staples (oil and gas, mining, forestry, and agriculture).[35] Meanwhile, Canada's domestic economy remained in limbo.

Unlike previous recessions, this one was not confined to one geographic area of Canada. Rather, it equally devastated the industrial heartland of Ontario, the agricultural lands of the Prairies, and the oilfields of Alberta, while bringing even more hardship to the 'have-not' areas of the country left reeling in the wake of federal cutbacks in transfer payments. These cuts, in turn, further strained Canada's east-west links at a time when free trade was binding the provinces ever more tightly into a system of north-south exchanges.

In short, the recession that began in 1990 was both severe and widespread. What was the effect of the recession upon the Canadian political scene, in particular, upon support for the Reform party? Like most voters, Canadians are generally more apt to blame than to praise governments for changes in national and personal economic circumstances.[36] The recession devastated the public image of the Tories as sound fiscal managers and otherwise undercut support for specific party policies such as the FTA and the GST. But how much blame did the Tories – or these policies – deserve for the recession?

In truth, some of the public's blame of the Tories was unfair. Canada did not experience an economic downturn alone during the period after 1990. The United States, much of Europe, and later Japan also had recessions during this period, part of a worldwide restructuring viewed with almost benign indifference by some economic theorists.[37] Moreover, the reasons underlying the recession's particularly adverse impact upon Canada were complex, involving historic, geographic, political, economic, and ideological factors.[38] The more immediate failure of the Liberals in the 1970s and early 1980s to develop a truly *national* economic policy, combined with a heavy debt-load from the recession of 1981–2, which the same government had failed to tackle, had left the Canadian economy in particularly precarious shape when the Tories came to power in 1984.

Nonetheless, the Tories can be criticized justifiably on several counts. They had first won election in 1984 in large part because they were able to convince voters that they were better fiscal managers than the discredited Liberals. And, indeed, the first two years of Tory reign had been relatively buoyant for the Canadian economy as Canada rode the coat-tails of a recovery spurred by American government military expenditures – what political economist Reg Whitaker once accurately described as 'Keynes-in-khaki.'[39]

Arguably, however, these first two years were also the period during which the Tories sowed the seeds for much of the country's later fiscal problems. Following the 1984 election, Mulroney's Tories possessed a massive majority in the House of Commons. They also had widespread public support. Moreover, the prosperity that had preceded them into office, and continued throughout 1984–6, provided the opportunity for the Tories to begin to control and otherwise pay down the gross federal debt (GFD), which stood at $181 billion (in constant dollars) in 1984, or 52.3 per cent of the GDP.[40]

But, like the Liberals before them, the Tories avoided fiscal restraint.[41] Certainly, the government made a tentative bow in the direction of the kind of trickle-down economic policies implemented by neo-conservative governments elsewhere.[42] These policies included the giving of enormous tax breaks to corporations and wealthy Canadians, while shifting the burden of taxation to lower-income, primarily middle-class, wage-earners.[43] But, to the consternation of some supporters, the Tories also retained much of the welfare state infrastructure established by the Liberals. Similarly, the Tories were criticized by some for increasing public spending in some non-essential areas (building roads, prisons, etc.) purely to curry public favour.[44] The combination of tax cuts and increased government spending were precisely the wrong prescription for the still-ailing economy.

In effect, the Tories ignored John Maynard Keynes's dictum that governments should spend during lean times, thereby stimulating the stagnant economy, and exercise tight money policies during boom times, thereby controlling inflation while using the appropriated money to pay down the previously accumulated debt.[45] Instead, they increased expenditures and overstimulated the economy during a period of economic plenty, while leaving untouched the gross federal debt (GFD).

By the end of 1986, the GFD, in constant dollars, stood at $224 billion, or 59.7 per cent of the GDP. By the election year, 1988, the GFD, in constant dollars, had risen to $254 billion, or 63.7 per cent of GDP.[46] By then, the window of opportunity for dealing with the debt was closing, and, in any case, no sitting government attacks a deficit during an election year. Indeed, few of the parties mentioned the federal deficit during the free trade election. Undoubtedly, the most outspoken party regarding the GFD was the Reform party, which called for a reduction in federal government spending.[47]

When Canada subsequently was hit by the recession, the Tories' room for fiscal manoeuvring was genuinely constrained by the federal debt. Moreover, as they slipped in public opinion polls, the Tories also lost political manoeuvrability. The 1988 election had badly polarized Canadian society, cementing the Tories' relationship with big business even as it isolated the government from some other sectors of the public. The Meech Lake Accord had only furthered the government's isolation, resulting in many of its traditional small 'c' conservatives going over to the Reform party. In an effort to regain the support of this element, Mulroney's government brought in a series of conservative economic initiatives, including tight-money policies, hiring and wage freezes in the public service, the slashing of government programs and spending, the privatization of crown corporations, and the deregulation of business.[48]

Arguably, these economic policies, designed to reduce the federal debt and win back public approval, ultimately strangled the economy, prolonged the recession, and further damaged the reputation of the Tory government, while having little or no effect upon the deficit itself. Moreover, in pursuing their policies, the Tories also undercut the positive effects from, and support for, their most important achievement: the Canada–U.S. Free Trade Agreement.[49]

The timing of the recession, coming little more than a year after the

Free Trade Agreement's implementation, was enough to bring the agreement into disrepute, particularly in the hard-hit manufacturing region of Ontario. But support for the agreement and the Tory government was also severely damaged by the Tories' overselling of the economic benefits of the trade pact during the 1988 election. People easily forgot promises kept, but not those stridently proclaimed and broken. As the recession wore on and unemployment rose, Tory claims that the FTA would create 120,000 new jobs within five years, while protecting existing jobs, came back to haunt the government.[50] Similarly damaging were Mulroney's unfulfilled promises, also made during the election, of 'generous' unemployment and retraining programs to offset the deal's negative effects. Instead, Canadians saw unemployment insurance payments cut, premiums for workers and employers increased, and the conditions for obtaining benefits made more onerous.[51]

Yet, despite these notable political imperfections, and ignoring broader issues of cultural and political sovereignty, the FTA might theoretically still have been economically advantageous to Canada, allowing Canadian companies to increase exports to the United States during this period. Critics argued, however, that, in order for this to occur, three conditions needed to be present. First, sufficient low-interest capital had to be made available to Canadian manufacturers with which to retool. Secondly, the value of the Canadian dollar had to be low enough to keep exports cheaper than American domestic products. And thirdly, Canadian and U.S. tax regimes had to be similar.[52] But these conditions were not met, nor perhaps could they be. To have brought in similar tax regimes would likely have required the downward harmonization of social programs in Canada that opponents of free trade had warned would happen. At the same time, increasing world economic interdependence placed limits on the Tories' use of monetary policies to shape Canada's economy. In short, Mulroney's government was constrained both by political realities at home and by the dynamics of economic realities abroad. In the end, the federal Tories, in conjunction with the head of the Bank of Canada, John Crow, and perhaps fulfilling a secret side-deal to the FTA, opted to keep interest rates above 10 per cent and the Canadian dollar around 89 cents U.S. for much of 1990–1.[53] While the high rates retained capital in the country, they also had the disastrous and counterproductive side-effect of increasing the government's cost of servicing the GFD. Finally, the Tories also introduced the GST, a tax that raised consumer prices, thereby changing the level playing-field created by the FTA into one tilted in favour of the American states.

This being said, the logic behind implementation of the GST was reasonable. The GST was meant to replace the existing manufacturers sales tax of 13 per cent, thereby allowing Canadian exporters to compete more effectively with American companies in the post–free trade environment. The GST also was designed to increase government revenues by broadening the base of taxation and lessening the opportunities for tax evasion. At the same time, the government hoped that a consumption tax would create an incentive for taxpayers to save and invest in the economy. Finally, the Tories viewed a consumption tax as a means of levelling the tax treatment between domestic and imported goods, while not increasing the cost of exports.[54]

Coming in the midst of the recession, however, the tax only further constrained the circulation of money in the economy, while politically the manner of the tax's implementation proved a further blow to the credibility of the Tories. Already viewing themselves as unfairly burdened by personal tax increases, Canadian voters became more and more restive as the GST moved closer to enactment. The loudest GST protests occurred in Alberta where opponents of the tax attempted (successfully in one case) to take over the riding associations of several Tory MPs.[55] The New Democrats and Liberals pounced on this growing popular discontent. Both political parties knew that public opinion polls showed the tax to be widely unpopular, a fact also noted by policy makers within the Reform party who soon appropriated popular opposition to the GST and even led several anti-GST rallies, including one in Winnipeg that attracted a thousand people.[56] Seemingly inexorable, however, legislative passage of the GST moved forward. Armed with a massive majority comprised of cowed and compliant MPs, Mulroney's government easily passed the motions necessary through the House of Commons. Soon, the GST required only Senate approval.

In May, however, a Gallup poll revealed that 68 per cent of Canadians wanted the Senate to block implementation of the tax.[57] Faced with two despised alternatives – a hated, regressive tax versus a hated, undemocratic Senate – the public came down on the side of the Senate. Buoyed by this and similar results, the Liberal-controlled Senate made it increasingly obvious that it intended to stall, if not stop, passage of the GST. The Liberals knew a good political issue when they had one and, led by Jean Chrétien, who had only recently replaced John Turner as leader, were spoiling for a fight. The fight was joined readily by Reform's Stan Waters, who had recently been appointed to the Senate.

Mulroney's government was in desperate straits. With the Meech

Lake Accord having recently collapsed, and trailing badly in popular opinion polls – 20 per cent in the August Gallup poll – the party now seemed to be in danger of losing control of its economic agenda. Faced with this situation, Mulroney took an unprecedented action. Relying on a never-before-used legal technicality, in September he expanded the Senate by eight seats and filled them with loyal Tory/GST supporters. The hated tax was soon passed into law, but not before the Senate descended into a farce of shouts and pompous posturing by both sides.

The GST incident further soiled the Senate's reputation and increased demands for either its reform or its abolition. Insofar as the Reform party had clearly staked its claim as the chief proponent of Senate reform, the GST squabble served to legitimize further the party while simultaneously adding to the discredit of Reform's chief rival, the Conservatives. In September 1990 the Tories slumped to 15 per cent in Gallup's national opinion poll where the party hovered well into the next year. Their popularity would not again climb out of the teens until July 1992. The country was still in recession, unemployment remained in double digits, and bankruptcies were occurring in record numbers.

Moreover, the federal debt continued to grow. In 1991 it stood at 66 per cent of the gross domestic product.[58] Certainly, the Tories could legitimately claim some headway in reducing both the real size of annual deficits (8 per cent of GDP in 1984, 4.5 per cent in 1992) and the rate of inflation (virtually zero in 1992 and 1993). But these reductions were also somewhat illusory. Deficit reduction had been largely financed by off-loading program costs to the provinces.[59] Thus Canada's total debts continued to increase, but with the additional straining of national ties. Moreover, Canada's debts continued to grow even as the Tories sold off public assets, such as Petro-Canada and Air Canada, and many long-cherished social programs were either eliminated (family allowance), downgraded (unemployment insurance), or threatened (medicare).[60] As for inflation, the more important real rate of inflation (the difference between the inflation rate and the interest rate) declined only slightly during the period of 1984 to 1992 from 6.9 per cent to 4.4 per cent.[61]

A study by political scientists Harold Clarke and Allan Kornberg suggests that the recession, and the Tories' perceived handling of it, was the major factor resulting in the party's loss of public support during this period.[62] Given that the majority of Reform supporters are former Tories, we can infer that the recession probably was also a major factor in Reform's gains over the following two years as party support moved into double digits.[63] Of equal importance to Reform's success, however, was the failure of either of the Liberals or NDP to take advantage of the crisis of legitimation suffered by the Mulroney Tories to increase or deepen their own support.

The Liberals had not recovered yet from its devastating defeats in 1984 and 1988. Divisions within the party between those who supported unbridled free enterprise and those who continued to support the welfare state were becoming more evident, as was continued friction between former federalist supporters of Trudeau and those who believed in more provincial power or special status for Quebec. The party's fortunes were particularly desperate in its traditional fortress of Quebec where many viewed Jean Chrétien as a lap-dog to English-speaking Canada who had long ago betrayed that province's birthright. But much of the West also viewed the Liberals with suspicion. This was particularly the case in Alberta where both the memory and the myth of the National Energy Program had only grown over time, and where, moreover, the Liberals still lacked an effective party organization. Added to these problems was the fact that the party still possessed numerous debts incurred during the previous election.

For its part, the NDP remained a largely untested quantity. In the fall of 1989, the widely popular Ed Broadbent stepped down as leader and was succeeded by Audrey McLaughlin. A year later, following the collapse of Meech Lake, the NDP was in first place in the national polls.[64] But this support was soft. Voters tended to view the NDP as well-meaning but untrustworthy in its economic policies. Moreover, in many ways, it was not even truly a national party, since it lacked a genuine presence in either Quebec or the Maritimes. Then, in September 1990, the party's Ontario provincial wing, under Bob Rae, gained a surprise election victory.

At first, supporters had high hopes that the Ontario victory might provide a springboard for the federal NDP. But these hopes were dashed during the three years that followed. Beset by political inexperience, a heavy debt-load left by David Peterson's defeated Liberals, the negative effects of the recession and free trade, and subjected to unrelenting attack by business, Bob Rae's government steadily lost support, even among its traditional allies.[65] Although the NDP won impressive provincial victories in Saskatchewan and British Columbia in 1991, these governments soon fell also into disfavour as they struggled to deal with deficits and the recession. In the end, the problems of its provincial counterparts, particularly in Ontario, dragged the fortunes of the federal NDP under. In early 1991 McLaughlin's party began a slide in national public opinion polls that would continue unabated throughout the following two years and see the party devastated in the election of 1993.

In summary, the recession, following in the wake of the Meech Lake fiasco, added further to the sense of crisis felt by many Canadians. When this sense of crisis went unrelieved by the traditional political parties, some elements of the electorate took a second look at the policies, proposals, and personalities of the Reform party, coming to believe that Canada, as they had known it, was, in the words of Preston Manning, 'dying.'

PRESTON MANNING'S 'OLD CANADA'

Political scientist David Laycock has suggested that 'any populist project ... must be integrated into a structure of meanings and connotative associations existing in "the people's" historical experience.'[66] The chief architect of this structure for the Reform party is Preston Manning. Manning, who prides himself on being a student of history, has spent years devising the historical underpinnings for an explanation of why 'Old Canada' has failed and why a 'New Canada' must arise. The gist of his analysis follows.[67]

The British North America (BNA) Act of 1867 was both an act of union and an act of separation, meant simultaneously to lay the basis for a new country from sea to sea and to sever the provinces of English Upper and French Lower Canada. Issues of language and culture were provincialized to end ongoing disputes between the French and English nations. More importantly, in Manning's view, the BNA Act was meant to replace the old 'two nations' concept of Canada with the notion of a confederation of equal provinces. Contends Manning:

If subsequent generations of politicians had left the problem of French-English tension within the provincial confines to which the Fathers of Confederation had relegated it and expanded and built on the new foundation of Canada as a federation of provinces rather than a federation of founding peoples, Canada might not be in the dilemma it is today. But unfortunately this was not to be.

As each new western province after British Columbia was added – Manitoba, Saskatchewan, and Alberta – there was a controversy as to whether the constitutions of those provinces should provide special status for the French minority in the areas of education and language. These provisions were promoted by federal politicians of the old two-nation school and provincial politicians from Quebec, and generally resisted by western politicians, who fully embraced the new vision of one nation from sea to sea.

Then, nearly a hundred years later, after the disintegration of the British Empire and the emergence of the Quiet Revolution in Quebec, Lester Pearson established the Royal Commission on Bilingualism and Biculturalism and revived the concept of Canada as an equal partnership between two founding races, languages, and cultures – the English and the French ... Pearson 'nationalized' the very issue which the fathers of Confederation had 'provincialized' in 1867.

This vision was pursued with vigour by Prime Minister Trudeau, and it continues to shape the thinking of the current prime minister [Mulroney] ...[68]

Manning's version of Canadian history is not flawless. For example, readers lacking knowledge of Canadian history would conclude from his remarks that Confederation resulted solely from English-French tensions. It is true that ethnic-based sectional squabbles led to the collapse of several Canadian governments before 1867. But economic and military considerations were at least as important as political factors in the forging of Confederation.[69]

Perhaps even more flawed is Manning's implicit depiction of the cultural history of Canada outside Quebec. Again, reading Manning's account, some readers would conclude that only French-English relations in Canada ever resulted in conflict, that Canada outside Quebec was settled with a high degree of harmony. In fact, this 'harmony' was in the main the product of cultural, legislative, and sometimes military pressures exerted by the dominant English majority upon minorities to make them assimilate. The military conquest of aboriginal and Métis peoples in the Red River and North-West rebellions of 1870 and 1885, and illegal abrogation of the rights of the French and Catholic minorities in Manitoba and the North-West Territories (later Saskatchewan and Alberta) during the years 1890–2 provide only the most striking examples.[70]

One might easily find other flaws in Manning's arguments.[71] His use of the term 'race' to describe the English and French ethnic groups might have a basis in historical discourse but has no current value; indeed, it seems needlessly inflammatory. Similarly, Manning's constant use of the term 'nation' (French nation, English nation, Canadian nation), to the detriment of other terms (society, country, state) is more than imprecise. Rather, it both adds to, and is an index of, the terminological confusion that underpins much of Quebec-Canada and French-English debate.[72]

Practically, one might oppose Manning's stance on official bilingualism. The program's benefits are certainly debatable, particularly when weighed against the economic and political costs of its implementation.[73] But neither Manning's, nor the Reform party's, territorial solution to language and culture adequately addresses the problem of Canada's 'two solitudes.'[74] In particular, it does not appear to deal effectively with the role of language policy in federal jurisdictions.

In short, there are several grounds on which to argue Manning's depiction of Canadian history. Ultimately, however, such arguments miss the point. For Manning is not so much presenting Canadian history as providing a narrative structure that will illuminate Canada's problems and mobilize the discontented masses towards their solution. For Manning, Old Canada's political problems lie in the 'excess' demands increasingly made by various minority groups:

Reformers believe that going down the special status road has led to the creation of two full-blown separatist movements in Quebec and to the proposal of the Quebec Liberals to emasculate the federal government as the price of keeping Quebec in a non-confederation. It has led to desires and claims for 'nation status' on the part of hundreds of aboriginal groups, claims which, if based on racial, linguistic, and cultural distinctiveness, are just as valid as those of the Québécois, if not more so. It has led to a hyphenated Canadianism that emphasizes our differences and downplays our common ground, by labelling us English-Canadians, French-Canadians, aboriginal-Canadians, or ethnic-Canadians – but never Canadians, period.

In other words, this road leads to an unbalanced federation of racial and ethnic groups distinguished by constitutional wrangling and deadlock, regional imbalance, and a fixation with unworkable linguistic and cultural policies to the neglect of weightier matters such as the environment, the economy, and international competitiveness.[75]

In the wake of the recession and the failure of the Meech Lake Accord, some in English-speaking Canada began looking for an explanation of the crisis. Manning's explanation, glittering with the broken shards of a fragmented popular history, reflected back to many people, particularly those within the once dominant Anglo-Saxon culture, their unconscious interpretation of the source of the problem: that Canada was in trouble because 'special interests,' particularly Quebecers and other minority groups (natives, Asian immigrants) were demanding their individual or group 'rights' at the expense of the majority. Differences were being accentuated instead of similarities, leading to a lack of social cohesion.

Manning's analysis of Canada's 'problem,' and his resultant 'solutions,' are not new; they mirror similar explanations given in the past when the country has been in crisis. Moreover, they lie at the heart of a peculiarly Anglo-Canadian nativism that has frequently arisen during similar periods of crisis in the country's history.

THE PECULIARITY OF ANGLO-CANADIAN NATIVISM

Nativism is a conjunction of nationalism with prejudicial attitudes based on ethnicity, religion, or race.[76] Nativist attitudes generally arise among previously dominant social elements during times of social, political, and economic crisis, suggesting a possible link to relative deprivation. The demand of nativist groups is for increased conformity to the historically based traditions and customs common to the territory.[77]

American historians first coined the term to describe the attitudes of such groups as the 'Know-Nothings' in the mid-nineteenth century and the various 'America First' movements that arose during the same century.[78] Nativism also lies, at least implicitly, at the heart of Richard Hofstadter's critique of populism.[79] Indeed, nativism is a particular aspect or form of the more general phenomena of populism. Unfortunately, few attempts have been made to apply the concept of nativism to Canadian history. Among notable exceptions are Carl Berger's examination of Canadian imperialism in the late nineteenth century, Howard Palmer's study of nativism in Alberta's history, and Martin Robin's recent examination of right-wing nativism in Canada during the years prior to the Second World War.[80]

As in the United States, nativism in Canada has revealed itself historically in the majority's 'opposition to an internal minority on the grounds that it posed a threat to Canadian national life.'[81] In particular, visible minorities, such as the Chinese and Japanese on the west coast, Catholics and the French in the Prairies, and Jews in central Canada, at various times have been deemed 'threats.' Historically, however, the nationalist content in Canadian nativism has been different from that of its American counterpart. Whereas American nationalism traditionally has attached itself to the territorial, and often imperial, ambitions of the state, Canadian nativism has more often involved a transnational appeal to the commonality of people of Anglo heritage.

The reasons for this difference are, initially, historical. The United States was born of revolution, which allowed Americans, despite their common heritage with Britain, to separate psychologically from the parent country. Although Americans often have carried on a love-hate relationship with Britain, their identity has attached itself to the national, territorial goals of the United States – an attachment made easier by the fact of that nation's enormous economic, military, and political power.[82]

By contrast, Canada had no such formative event, although segments of the population can point to certain defining moments in their history. French-speaking Quebecers, for example, can point to the battle of the Plains of Abraham as the time when their 'nation,' in the sociological sense, was born. And a similar sense of 'nationhood' appears to be re-emerging among Canada's indigenous peoples.

English-speaking Canada, however, experienced no such event. Far from breaking with the mother-country, its ties to Britain were strengthened after the American Revolution by the arrival of the United Empire Loyalists. The result was the stillbirth of any unifying vision of a territorially based and distinctive nationalism in the English-speaking colonies.

With the retreat or eviction of the French culture to its provincial citadel, British North America succumbed to a peculiar form of nationalism that Carl Berger has termed 'Canadian imperialism.'[83] This imperial nationalism came in two varieties. The first, nurtured by the loyalists in Ontario and found in writers such as Stephen Leacock, viewed Canada as a corner of the British empire; the second, fertilized, particularly in western Canada, by an open border for goods, people, and ideas, was continentalist, viewing Canada as a cultural extension of the American republic. The former viewed the British connection as the only hope against annexation to the United States; the latter viewed annexation as inevitable and perhaps even desirable. In the nineteenth century, the idea that a third alternative – full independence – was achievable was either rarely discussed or quickly dismissed.

The debate as to Canada's future gained renewed vigour every time the British colony faced a crisis. The Confederation debates of 1864–7 revolved around the two 'imperialisms.'[84] The same debate over whether Canada was – or could become – a genuine nation state defined by a coherent and distinctive cultural identity also underlay the reciprocity election of 1891, prompting Goldwin Smith to write *Canada and the Canadian Question*.

A typical upper-class product of mid-century England, Smith viewed with pride his Anglo-Saxon heritage. In particular, he lauded this heritage as having given birth to liberal democracy. But he viewed the United States as his culture's future. Smith's conviction that America was, in Frank Underhill's words, 'the hope of the English-speaking race' was reinforced following a trip to that country in 1864.[85] In Smith's eyes, English-speaking Canada stood intermediate to its British past and its American future, lacking any distinctive identity of its own. Especially after immigrating to Canada in 1871, Smith espoused his belief that the French-speaking nation eventually would assert its independence while English-speaking Canada would recognize its affinity with the broader Anglo-Saxon world and would join the United States.

The debate as to whether British or American imperialism would frame Canadian identity occasionally arose thereafter. With the collapse of the British empire at the end of the Second World War, however, the matter was all but settled. Few people willingly would hitch their sense of identity to a falling star. By contrast, America was ascendant. Moreover, the war had solidified economic ties between Canada and the United States. Under Mackenzie King and subsequent Liberal governments, economic and political ties with the United States only grew stronger. In a sense, the flag debate of 1965 represented the final symbolic act in Canada's escape from British colonial status.

The debate over Canada's identity, however, did not end there. By the 1960s, a new territorial nationalism was arising in English-speaking Canada. Spurred by the Vietnam War and scenes of racial unrest and urban decay in the United States, many Canadians came to believe that their country had to carve out a distinctive identity. The road to the new Canadian nationalism necessarily involved both economic independence and a willingness to forego traditional French-English divisions. Hence, the widespread support for such policies as bilingualism and economic nationalism.

Opposing the new nationalists were the imperial nationalists, both remnants of the British type and continentalists of the American variety, whose allegiance to Anglo-Saxon cultural institutions, including a belief in liberal democracy and free enterprise, was deeply entrenched. These imperial nationalists are the bearers of a tradition of 'peculiar' nativism in English-speaking Canadian history. While nativism elsewhere involved prejudicial attitudes and actions directed towards minorities perceived as threatening the national territory or nation state, *nativism in English-speaking Canada has tended instead to fasten its loyalty to the wider Anglo-culture rather than to the territorial notion of Canada.*

It is important to emphasize that Anglo-Canadian nativism is not solely, or even largely, a response to the francophone presence in Canada. During the nineteenth century, immigration came primarily from the British Isles, hence posing little threat to English-speaking Canada's predominantly Anglo-Saxon culture.[86] But the early years of this century saw changes to this pattern of immigration. Moreover, these changes accelerated following the Second World War.

By 1958, the trend away from British immigration to Canada was evident. That year, 124,851 immigrants arrived in Canada. Of these, 24,777 (20 per cent) came from the British Isles, 75,598 (60 per cent) from other European countries, and 24,476 (20 per cent) from assorted other countries.[87] But changes in the origin of immigrants were accelerated, beginning in the 1960s, by a series of administrative changes including the removal of national origin restrictions in 1962, the introduction of a point system in the Immigration Act of 1967, and a closer alignment of immigration to labour market needs during these and subsequent years.[88]

In 1978, for example, 14 per cent of immigrants came from the British Isles, 21 per cent from other European countries, and 65 per cent from other countries. Thirty-two per cent of all these immigrants settled in western Canada, mainly in Alberta and British Columbia.[89] In response to criticism from some Canadians regarding the arrival of a large number and percentage of 'non-traditional' immigrants, and to the recession of the late 1970s, the Liberals gradually reduced immigration during the years following 1974. In that year, 218,465 immigrants came to Canada, but only 88,302 arrived in 1984 when the Liberals left office.[90]

Despite this, many Canadians criticized the Liberals as a party changing the cultural make-up the country.[91] Indeed, as previously shown, anti-immigrant feeling and outright racism constituted at least some of the appeal of the right-wing fringe groups that arose in the early 1980s. Both these extreme elements and more moderate Canadians threatened by the increased cultural and ethnic heterogeneity of Canadian society looked to Mulroney's Tories, when they came to power in 1984, to reverse what they perceived to be, in William Gairdner's words, 'the silent destruction of English Canada.'[92]

Instead, beginning in 1986, the Tories began to increase immigration levels. That year, 99,219 immigrants entered Canada. In 1987, this total increased to 152,098; in 1988, 161,929; in 1989, 191,886.[93] Perhaps more alarming for many Canadians was the accelerated rate of non-traditional immigrants entering the country. In 1989, 50 per cent of immigrants to Canada originated in Asia (primarily Hong Kong, the Philippines, India, China, and Lebanon), 26 per cent in Europe (including the British Isles), 13 per cent in the Caribbean and Central and South America, 7 per cent in Africa, 3 per cent in the United States, and 1 per cent in Oceania. Fifteen and 11 per cent of all immigrants settled in British Columbia and Alberta, respectively. The percentage of Asian immigrants settling in British Columbia was slightly higher than elsewhere, with fully 65 per cent of immigrants in Vancouver coming from that continent.[94]

The changed pattern of Canadian immigration following the 1960s, and the perception held by some Tory supporters that the party had 'betrayed' them in accelerating immigration, particularly from 'non-traditional' countries, provides a necessary backdrop to an examination of the nativist leanings of Reform supporters. If the Reform party is a reflection of traditional English-speaking Canadian nativism – if, indeed, the party is impelled, at least in part, by perceived changes in Canada's cultural 'heritage' – then we would expect that Reform's leadership, members, and supporters should, by contrast, be predominantly Anglo-Saxon or Celtic and perhaps also Protestant.

Anecdotal evidence has suggested previously that this is the case.[95] Consider also the overwhelmingly 'Anglo' names of key people who have influenced the party's formation: Brimelow, Brown, Burns, Byfield, Chapman, Copithorne, Fryers, Gray, Grey, Harper, Manning, Muir, Roberts, Somerville, Waters, Winspear. The names read like a collection of Fleet Street barristers. But is there any empirical evidence identifying the ethnic and religious backgrounds of Reform members and supporters?

The 1991 Alberta Survey conducted by the University of Alberta Population Research Laboratory – of Alberta residents only – provides a partial answer to this question.[96] The question asked was, 'What is the religious and ethnic background of Reform Party supporters?' In response 63 per cent were found to be Protestants, while 29 per cent identified themselves as being of Anglo-Saxon or Celtic background and a further 32 per cent of European ethnic background. Another 34 per cent of Reform supporters identified themselves as 'Canadian.'

In a further examination of the same data, the question was reversed: 'What is the preferred party of people who come from Protestant or Anglo-Saxon-Celtic or "Canadian" backgrounds?' The sample displayed a very high level of voter uncertainty, with 40 per cent stating that they did not know for whom they would vote, were ineligible to vote, or would vote for a party other than the Tories, Liberals, New Democrats, or Reform. Nonetheless, among decided voters, 36 per cent of voters who identified themselves as Protestants said they would vote for Reform, compared with only 23 per cent who said they would vote for the Tories, the party with the next highest support among this group. By contrast, Reform had the least support of the four major parties among Catholic identifiers, obtaining only 19 per cent support, compared with 34 per cent for the Liberals.

A similar story was found among ethnic identifiers. Fully 32 per cent of decided Anglo-Saxon-Celtic identifiers and 34 per cent of decided 'Canadians' declared their intention to vote for Reform. Interestingly, the NDP obtained the next highest declared support among each of these groups, at 27 and 25 per cent, respectively. Reform also received considerable support among European identifiers, with 29 per cent support compared with 25 per cent for the Liberals. Among decided voters in the remaining ('other') category, however, only nine respondents (16 per cent) declared their support for Reform, compared with 28 per cent for the Liberals.

Before leaving Reformers' ethnic affiliations, it is worth asking a supplemental question: 'Who are these "Canadians"?' We cannot know for certain what secondary or even unconscious identifications this group may possess. Nonetheless, it is worth noting that, far from being amorphous, this group is actually fairly distinctive. Ninety-six per cent of those self-identified as Canadians were born in Canada. Seventy-two per cent stated that their father had been born in Canada, 12 per cent said the United Kingdom or Ireland, 5 per cent the United States, while most of the rest mentioned some other European country. Almost identical results were found for mothers' place of birth. Finally, 91 per cent also stated English as their first language.

In short, the ethno-cultural backgrounds of Canadian identifiers seems very similar to those who identify themselves as Anglo-Saxon or Celtic. Why the difference in ethnic identification? Again, we cannot be certain. It seems, however, that many Anglo-Canadians may be making a political statement in identifying themselves as Canadian. In turn, the Reform party, at least in Alberta, is perhaps viewed as the best political vehicle for expressing the unease of many in this group with the kind of 'hyphenated Canadianism' which they perceive as fragmenting Canadian society.

Is the making of such a political statement a sign of nativism? We cannot say with any certainty. To answer the question, we would have to know something of each respondent's notion of who is a 'true' Canadian, and of what actions, ideas, and beliefs he or she views as constituting 'Canadianness.' Moreover, what are we to make of the almost equal level of support within this group for the NDP, a party with a presumably strong but nonetheless different notion of Canada and Canadians?

Still, although the statistical evidence is not overwhelming, the overall *pattern* of Reform party support among Protestants and Anglo-Saxon-Celtics is precisely the historically specific pattern of support, in Alberta at least, that one would expect if Reform were appealing on some level to nativist tendencies. But the notion that some Reform members may have strong Anglo-Saxon nativist inclinations is supported by more than merely the background profiles of its leaders, members, and supporters. It is supported also by the words of many of its ideological mentors who depict Canada as not only historically an Anglo-Saxon country but also as part of a wider Anglo-Saxon culture that is in need of recognizing and re-establishing its heritage.

Read, for example, Peter Brimelow's words bemoaning the eclipse of Anglo-Saxon hegemony:

At the end of the nineteenth century, belief in the superiority of 'Anglo-Saxon' values ... [was] the social norm in every English-speaking country ... For WASP supremacists everywhere, however, the twentieth century has been a most distressing experience.[97]

Or again:

The twentieth century has proved bitter. The values that are common to the English-speaking peoples are in a minority in the world, and on the defensive. Future historians might well be surprised that at this late date the English-speaking countries remain so self-absorbed, and despite their common heritage, show so little conscious awareness of their common interests.[98]

Voiced by some prominent Reform supporters, the notion of a 'common heritage' seems to encompass the white settler colonies of the former empire, including white South Africa. Consider, for example, Stan Waters's reluctance to criticize the slow pace of ending apartheid in South Africa:

If history has any parallelism [*sic*], you might find a very serious problem emerging in South Africa which may dwarf the objectionable features of the current administration ... I always ask Mr. [External Affairs Minister Joe] Clark, if South Africa's going to change, what black nation do you want it to imitate? Most of them are despotic, president for life in almost every case. They don't have a democratic system. Mr. [Winston] Churchill said it best, he said when the freedom was spreading in Africa, he said it will be 'one man, one vote – once.'[99]

Waters's musings are not singular. Murray Dobbin has chronicled extensively the pro–white South Africa actions and sympathies of numerous people connected with the party, including Ted Byfield and Arthur Child.[100] This support for white South Africa, a country whose political system was based on racial group affiliation, by many within the Reform party, a party that otherwise espouses the principle of individual rights over group rights, cannot be explained adequately unless one accepts the notion that many Reformers strongly identify with 'Anglo' culture. This identification is nowhere more strongly enunciated than in William D. Gairdner's *Trouble with Canada*.

Gairdner, child of a wealthy family, a former Olympic athlete, holder of a PhD in English, and member of the Northern Foundation, is a frequent speaker at Reform party meetings in Ontario. In 1991 he was a featured speaker at the party's Saskatoon convention in 1991. His book, a fast-paced, unrelenting denunciation of such things as bilingualism, multiculturalism, immigration, welfare, feminism, and criminal justice, counterposes two simple models of human organization:

all societies must choose between two radically different methods for organizing society: either (1) they must insist on the same rules for everyone and let all social outcomes evolve according to natural and freely expressed individual differences, or (2) they must impose an equality of outcome that can be achieved only by creating different rules for different social groups.[101]

Gairdner terms the first method of organizing 'English,' the second 'French.' His attempt to suggest that these are merely 'convenient labels,' and that other terms could have been used seems scarcely credible. Gairdner makes clear in his book that he believes in the natural superiority of traditional Anglo-Saxon culture and fears that heterogeneous cultural, and normative or moral, intrusions are eroding this 'ideal.' Hence, the concern he evinces in chapter fifteen of his tome entitled, 'The Silent Destruction of English Canada.' For Gairdner, Canada's 'core heritage and culture ... is [and must remain] Judeo-Christian, Greco-Roman, and Anglo-European.'[102]

Like Brimelow, Gairdner contends that the superiority of Anglo-Saxon culture lies in its historical discovery/creation of the values of individualism, free enterprise, and liberal democracy. These values lie also at the core of most Reformers' world-view. For many Reformers, the values of individualism, free enterprise, and liberal democracy have been 'naturally selected,' in a very Darwinian sense, over other belief systems, particularly 'socialism,' in any of its forms. The proof of this test, for Reformers, is the United States. This belief brings me back to the central aspect of Reform's nativism to which I alluded earlier: its incipient pro-Americanism.

Idolatry of 'things American,' even as he mourns the loss of 'things British,' moves gently, if inexorably, through Goldwin Smith.[103] The same idolatry runs even more rampantly through Peter Brimelow, who now lives and works in the United States as editor of *Forbes*' magazine, and William Gairdner.[104] But one can also detect it in Byfield who, by and large, views the United States as a benign friend and who frequently extols the virtues of the American political system, while heaping scorn on those who would define Canadian identity in terms of difference from the United States.[105] And – although few are as articulate as these spokespeople – such idolatry also can be found among many Reformers.

This is not to say that many Reformers would desire outright political union with the United States. Indeed, a study of the attitudes of Reform party delegates to the 1992 Winnipeg assembly found considerable ambiguity on questions bearing on support for continentalism. Significantly, however, this ambiguity occurred along east-west lines, with pro-continentalism highest in Reform's heartland provinces of Alberta and British Columbia, while lowest support was found in Ontario, the residual heartland of loyalist sentiment.[106]

To be sure, not all, or even many, Reformers like every aspect of American society. Like many Canadians, Reformers view with smug disdain the homelessness, poverty, and crime that mark many American cities, pointing instead to the apparently greater civility and gentleness still to be found in most Canadian cities. At the same time, however, Reformers generally disparage those aspects of Canadian society, particularly the relatively greater role of government in economic, cultural, and social policy, as well as efforts to seek a different balance in protecting *both* collective and individual interests, that have historically distinguished Canada's development from that of the United States. In the end, Canada *in its present form* constitutes for many Reformers a kind of 'failed experiment' relative to that of the United States.

Undoubtedly, however, the most openly 'Americanized' Reformer is Preston Manning, a man whose political ethos is fundamentally republican and who, indeed, frequently quotes from American heroes. Of more than passing interest is that Manning drew inspiration from Abraham Lincoln in making his own 'House Divided' speech at the Edmonton convention in 1989. His inspiration by an American president appears symbolic of Manning's vision of 'the good society' – and of New Canada.

Manning's New Canada would be modelled on the American 'melting pot.' Individual, rather than collective, rights would be upheld. Canada also would be, on the whole, 'a better U.S. ally.'[107] Above all, Canada would be much more supportive of free enterprise capitalism, a belief he stated most openly at the Saskatoon convention in 1991:

The proponents of New Canada can safely argue that the constitution of New Canada should entrench a commitment to freedom, federalism, and democracy, but any attempt to go much beyond that – to entrench the concepts of a Swedish-style welfare state (as Audrey McLaughlin suggests) *or an American-style market economy (as some of us might prefer)* cannot, in my judgment, be sold to the Canadian public at this time.[108]

In short, at least in economic matters, Manning's intentions would seem to be to make Canada into a country very similar, if not indistinguishable, from the United States.

Of course, not all Reformers are nativists. Neither would the reverse be true. Moreover, nativism, where it does exist, varies both in form and degree. If some Reform party members have nativist inclinations, is the party also racist, as some have suggested and others, particularly in the ethnic communities, fear?[109] The simple answer is no. Certainly, it is difficult to attach the label to Manning himself. Regarding Quebec, for example, he has repeatedly stated in the past that 'There is no room in the Reform Party for people whose sole motivation is anti-French, or anti-Quebec.'[110]

To their credit, some Reformers also seem to be somewhat aware that the statements of other followers (such as Gairdner's referral to 'natural differences' and warnings against 'demographic capture, or ... passive racial or cultural take-over') may appeal to exclusionary, xenophobic, and racist instincts.[111] Hence, the party moved at the Saskatoon convention of 1991 to moderate a controversial section of its multiculturalism policy that stated: 'The Reform Party supports the responsibility of the state to promote, preserve, and enhance the *national culture*. The state may assist, and should encourage, ethnic cultures to integrate into the *national culture*.'[112] The key section now reads: 'The Reform Party stands for the acceptance and integration of immigrants to Canada into the mainstream of Canadian life.'[113]

Nonetheless, one does not have to go far to find expressions of intolerance, xenophobia, and bigotry made by some Reform supporters. The hysterical reaction of party delegates in 1989 to the decision to allow Sikhs in the RCMP to wear turbans and the draft proposal made by some members in 1991 that newly arrived immigrants and refugees be denied Charter protections for five years provide two examples.[114] (The executive removed the proposal from policy discussion before it made it to the convention floor.) Similarly, delegates to the 1991 Saskatoon convention gave William Gairdner enormous applause, even more than Manning later received, for his vitriolic speech denouncing feminists, bilingualism, and multiculturalism, among other things.[115]

Consider, also, the following quotes, made in anger and consternation, by John Williams, who was later elected in 1993 as the MP for the Alberta riding of Pembina: 'We must tolerate people regardless of their sexual orientation. We cannot take pride in our race for fear of putting someone else down.' And later, from the same individual: '[W]e have to tolerate everyone's point of view in everything, Canadians stand for nothing.[116]

Examine, also, the remarks made in a letter to Liberal MP Sheila Copps by a self-described Reform supporter: 'Canadians are at 80 per cent saying no to more Third World immigrants. As our governments let them (sic), the minority immigrants force their will on the majority. Now we have mop heads in the RCMP ... It's the end of Canadian ways.'[117] Or the comments of John Beck, a Reform candidate for York Centre in 1993, regarding immigration. 'You have a $150,000 guy there coming to buy a citizenship into Canada to create a job, fine, he's bringing something to Canada. But what is he bringing? Death and destruction to the people.' When asked to clarify his remarks by the *Financial Post*, Beck stated that he felt like a minority because he speaks English, adding that 'I feel it's time some white Anglo-Saxons get involved' in politics. Later interviewed by the CBC television, Beck repeated his earlier remarks concerning immigration: 'I feel if an immigrant comes into Canada and gets a job for $150,000, he is taking jobs away from us, the gentile people.'[118]

Beck subsequently withdrew from the election under pressure from an embarrassed Reform executive. Nonetheless, it is clear that at least some – perhaps many – Reformers view the party's policies, and even Manning's public utterances, as possessing an inner code, the meaning of which signals an intent to return to a predominantly Anglicized, white nation. Certainly, many extremists appear to view Reform as a comfortable haven. In late 1991 the party was embarrassed when it was reported that Gordon LeGrand, one of the Brockville group who had stomped the Quebec flag in 1989, was a member of the party.[119] This embarrassment was intensified a short while later with the revelation that several neo-Nazis, including Wolfgang Droege, head of the extremist Heritage Front had also joined the Reform party.[120] Though all of these individuals were later expelled from Reform, the fact remains that some extremists are attracted to what they see as covert anti-racial/anti-ethnic overtones and appeals in Reform's message.[121] And although it is certainly true that recent years have seen some other party members, especially Tories, make intolerant remarks, Reform appears to have recruited more than its statistical share of extremists.[122] It is ultimately insufficient to explain this attraction, as Manning does, with the glib rebuttal that, 'A bright light attracts bugs,' or that, because populist parties are bottom-up organizations, they are more subject to extremist elements entering them than are top-down parties.[123] Rather, the explanation lies in Reform's particular discursive use of the concept of 'people,' a use that, in the minds of at least some party supporters, is code for the exclusion of certain groups and individuals.

Finally, there is another aspect of nativism that appears to underlie the Reform party's appeal: its sense of a calling. Max Weber referred to a calling as the 'sense of a life task.'[124] This quasi-religious sense of mission is frequently found in nativist and populist (both right- and left-wing) movements. It is a byproduct of the perception by movement members of their historical dominance within a given domain. Power always comes with certain responsibilities, one of which is duty – the calling – felt by movement members to save a territory, a country, or indeed the world, during times of crisis. This sense of mission seems very much to be a part of Reform's message and appeal.

Take, for example, William Gairdner's statement 'we have a new moral obligation to ensure that the principles from which [the tools of freedom and wealth creation] are derived are spread as far afield as possible.'[125] Anyone who witnessed the Reformers' emotional rendition of 'O Canada' at the Saskatoon convention, or heard Manning's 'charge' to the delegates at the same convention to go out and find the best candidates, cannot doubt the religious sense of mission with which party members are infused. The naming of the Reform party as beneficiaries in their wills by some party members in early 1992 similarly evidences the zeal of what political philosopher Eric Hoffer termed 'true believers.'[126] No one can question that Manning and his followers are doing what they sincerely believe to be the best for Canada. But what kind of Canada?

On this count, Reformers have little allegiance to the present notion of Canada. Instead entranced by the 'two imperialisms,' many Reformers fasten their allegiance to the wider Anglo-American culture and its 'mission' here on earth. Hence, the peculiar strains of a populist party which seeks to defend what it perceives as Canada's national interests against internal elements while simultaneously advocating policies such as free trade that, some would contend, integrate Canada even more tightly into the American orbit.

A group's sense of 'peoplehood' may be imaginary, but it is not entirely arbitrary.[127] Rather, it is built upon a reservoir of symbols, based in history, that may be summoned upon by adept leaderships during times of apparent crisis. The failure of the Meech Lake Accord, and the beginning of the recession in 1990, coming on the heels of integrationist pressures released by the implementation of the free trade agreement, made many Canadians question the continued viability of the Canadian state. In the midst of the resultant crisis, both Canada's traditional political parties and its political system became delegitimated.

Into the void stepped the Reform party. By playing upon the fears of people outside Quebec that the country was about to end or that they were about to become the victims of a conspiracy hatched by Quebec and the three traditional political parties, Reform gained a legitimacy among certain elements in English-speaking Canada. To these people, Manning held out a vision. 'New Canada,' he said,

should be a balanced, democratic federation of provinces, distinguished by the conservation of its magnificent environment, the viability of its economy, the acceptance of its social responsibilities, and the recognition of the equality and uniqueness of all its citizens and provinces.[128]

As visions go, it is rather prosaic. No matter, though. The people that Reform was gathering had enough poetry from Trudeau, enough pompous bluster from Mulroney. They wanted simplicity, and Manning gave it to them. A year and a half after Meech Lake, the Reform party would have 100,000 members, a substantial war chest, and 12 per cent of popular support.[129] Moreover, it would no longer be confined to the West. It would be a national party – *sans* Quebec.

From Canada's increasingly tattered social, political, and economic fabric, the Reform party was weaving its success. To many observers, reason and understanding seemed in retreat, replaced by passionate intensity. But what did the rapid growth mean for Reform? Who was now joining the party? What would happen to Reform's avowed populist roots? These are but some of the questions that I examine in the chapter that follows.

5. The Transformation of Reform

The perversion of populism ... or the disintegration of a populist party ... occurs from within rather than from without.'

Preston Manning, *The New Canada*, 1992[1]

Even given fortuitous historical, economic, and political circumstances, the success of a populist party is not necessarily ordained. Successful populist parties require a capable organization, material and human resources, a coherent ideology, and a credible leadership. Impacting upon all of these attributes is the nature of people drawn to the party.

By early 1992, the Reform party stood at a crossroads. The party had enlisted its 100,000th member – a 16-year-old, female, Scarborough high-school student. The previous month, a Gallup poll suggested that Reform would garner 12 per cent of national support if a federal election were held. Moreover, Reform was gaining a substantial 'war chest' with which to fight the next federal election. Finally, it was becoming more evident that, despite lacking any formal power, the Reform party was influencing in a profound way the policies of several parties on both the federal and provincial political scenes.

Countering these harbingers of increasing legitimacy for the party were signs of increasing internal discord. The party's rapid growth since 1987 had precipitated changes that revealed contradictions and tensions within the party and, in turn, challenged the party's profession of grass-roots democracy. By early 1992, Reform was being shaken almost daily by membership scandals, expulsions, and resignations, and some supporters were raising accusations that the party had abandoned its populist roots.

This chapter examines the continued growth of the Reform party during 1991–2 as the party expanded eastwards, the political effects of Reform's increased influence during this period, and the problems that accompanied the party's rise in stature. Along the way, the party's executive, members, and supporters, the core principles of Reform party ideology, and Reform's financing and organizational structure are profiled. Finally, the notion of popular democracy espoused by Preston Manning is examined. The chapter begins with a look at the Saskatoon convention of 1991 that ostensibly transformed the Reform party into the ostensibly 'national party' of English-speaking Canada.

ROADS CHOSEN AND ABANDONED: THE SASKATOON CONVENTION

From the inception of the party in 1987, Reform party members knew that one day they would have to decide on two critical issues: whether to form provincial affiliates, and whether to expand beyond the party's western base to become a truly 'national' party. By the time Reform held its semi-annual convention in Saskatoon in April 1991, feelings on both issues were mixed and heated.

Particularly strong feelings in Alberta and British Columbia favoured forming provincial Reform parties. The ruling parties in each province (Don Getty's Tories and Bill Vander Zalm's Socreds) were increasingly disliked and mistrusted, perhaps as much by Reform's right-wing elements, who viewed these parties as having abandoned their constituencies, as by the non-Reform left, who disliked the Tories and Socreds in any case.

The case of provincial advocates was strengthened by an internal survey conducted prior to the party's 1989 Edmonton convention which revealed that 62 per cent of party members were in favour of Reform forming provincial parties.[2] Moreover, nascent Reform organizations had already been formed in several of the provinces, including British Columbia, where an affiliated namesake, the Reform Party of BC, was headed by a former member of the federal Reform party's executive council, Ron Gamble. Similarly, the COR party in Manitoba, which from the beginning has had numerous connections to the federal Reform party, had appropriated the name Reform with the intent of running provincially.[3] In Alberta, meanwhile, the Alberta Political Alliance (APA), a party formed in the early 1980s out of the wreckage of Western Canada Concept, hankered to use the name or, barring this, to otherwise make known its ideological and organizational affiliation with Reform.[4]

The opponents of provincial expansion also were strong. Headed by

Manning, who pointed out that the party originally had been formed to address problems in the federal political arena, opponents contended that a premature turn to provincial politics would squander Reform's resources and energies, resulting in abortive gains at both levels of government. They further pointed to a survey conducted at the 1989 convention which indicated that over 75 per cent of delegates opposed contesting provincial elections.[5]

Just as opinion on the provincial question was divided, so too was it on the question of whether Reform should become a national, rather than a purely regional, party. Many in the party, including Stan Waters, believed that Reform should concentrate first on winning western Canada, that expansion would spread the party resources too thin, that the party would be swallowed up by the large ridings of central Canada, and that the party might have more influence as a regional party than as a national one.

Some, such as Stephen Harper, also feared that expansion risked the party's being swamped by fringe elements. 'We're at a stage now where we're attractive to a lot of people on the fringes ... who are anxious to jump in and swing the party to the right.'[6] Harper's fears were not unfounded, given the past record of extremism in Ontario.[7]

But the arguments in favour of expansion were equally compelling: that the party would not be taken seriously if it did not obtain a national platform; that its policies on regional fairness would have appeal elsewhere; that Canada outside Quebec was looking for a party to champion its interests in the constitutional negotiations which were likely to follow; and that the election of the NDP in Ontario had provided a window of opportunity for the right-wing Reformers.[8] Furthermore, the party's executive, fuelled by some initial contacts, believed that expansion would bring Reform the kind of corporate funding enjoyed by the Tories and Liberals.

As with the question of provincial parties, Preston Manning had long made his own preference known regarding eastern expansion. As early as the 1987 Vancouver assembly, Manning had stated that the new party should have '"room to grow" into a truly national party.'[9] Before the 1991 convention vote, Manning and several other party officials had stated even more insistently that he had no interest in leading the party if the members voted against expansion.[10]

By that time, Manning's importance to – and power within – the party had increased in geometric proportion to the party's rise in support. Few delegates were therefore willing to go against Manning's wishes on the issues of provincial parties and eastern expansion. In the end the votes were a foregone conclusion. The motion to allow provincial Reform parties was defeated by 61 per cent of the delegates (448 to 291).[11] Similarly, nearly 97 per cent (762 to 27) voted in favour of expansion.

The general membership then voted on expansion by mail-in ballot. At a Vancouver rally in June, Preston Manning announced the results of the vote. They virtually mirrored the convention decision, with 92 per cent of the 24,042 ballots cast voting in favour of expansion.[12] Reform had recast itself as a national party.

The move, however, was far from spontaneous. Indeed, the party executive had been planning expansion for some time. Spearheaded by Gordon Shaw, a retired oilfield executive, the party had made initial contacts in the East beginning in late 1989. In March 1990 Manning made a two-week 'exploratory tour' to Ontario and Atlantic Canada.[13] Following this tour, six individuals in Ontario, including Brian Hay, a long-time friend of Manning, volunteered their services to the party.[14] That same month, Reg Gosse, a certified public accountant and owner of a Kitchener printing and publishing house, contacted Shaw about starting up an expansion committee. These individuals got together in July to form the committee.[15] The following month, they created the party's first Ontario riding association in Brampton.[16]

In September, Manning made another trip to Ontario. By then, the party's membership in that province had risen from 200 to 1600.[17] During that extended trip, Manning was greeted by large crowds in Hamilton, Ottawa, Thunder Bay, Brampton, and Sudbury and was the guest of media magnate Conrad Black and Hal Jackman, an influential lawyer, current Ontario lieutenant governor, and prominent former Tory bagman, at a private function held at Toronto's prestigious Toronto Club.[18]

Throughout the remainder of 1990 and into 1991, the party continued to lay the groundwork for expansion into eastern Canada, excluding Quebec. By the time the party held its April convention – a convention attended by Reg Gosse and a host of unofficial Ontario delegates – the mechanics of expansion were in place awaiting the now largely perfunctory delegate vote.

The organizational preparation for expansion paid Reform immediate dividends. At the time of the convention vote (April 1991), Reform had 65,467 members, located as follows: Alberta, 28,376 (43 per cent); British Columbia, 20,265 (31 per cent); Saskatchewan, 5127 (8 per cent);

and Manitoba, 4068 (6 per cent). The remaining 7631 (12 per cent) members resided elsewhere (NWT, Yukon, eastern Canada, and unassigned or unknown addresses). In May, overall membership rose to 71,249; in June, to 77,170. Most of these new members were recruited in Ontario. By the end of May 1991, the party reported having 9947 members in that province. By the end of June, this figure had risen to 13,687 – nearly 18 per cent of Reform's overall membership at the time![19]

The spillover effects of the party's nationally broadcast assembly and its decision to go east also had immediate impact in polls taken at the time. The Gallup poll for March 1991 gave Reform 7 per cent support nationally. Gallup's April poll, however, conducted after the convention, showed that national support for Reform had jumped to 16 per cent. Particularly significant was the rise of Reform support in the Prairie region. At 21 per cent the previous month, Reform support rose to 43 per cent in April.

Reform's national support would only reach this lofty height once more during the coming year. Nonetheless, polls would continue to show national support for the party in the low teens. Moreover, Reform's decision to go national, combined with increased support for the party, had raised the status and legitimacy of the party and its policies. As a result, Reform's role on Canada's political stage began undergoing a subtle transformation from silent walk-on to that 'fifth business.'[20] Over the next two years, as Canada's economic and political crises drew towards a climax, Reform increasingly would influence the direction of policies followed by the traditional parties, both federally and, to some extent, provincially. For Reform, no one could have written a better script.

THE TIME OF INFLUENCE

As long as Reform remained at 3 or 4 per cent in the polls, confined to the West, its influence upon Canadian politics could easily be dismissed. And, indeed, for the first few years, the other major parties scarcely acknowledged the existence of the brawling neophyte, believing that Reform soon would fade from view. As time went on, however, they were increasingly forced to reckon with Reform's critique of the existing political system, its proposed policies, and (more importantly) its growing electoral support. At the provincial level, Reform's impact was particularly pronounced in those provinces – Alberta and British

Columbia, and to a lesser extent, Saskatchewan – out of which the party had sprung and where its support remained highest.

In British Columbia, a polarized political climate had given rise to nearly four decades of Social Credit rule, which continued in 1986 with Bill Vander Zalm's surprise victory over the opposition NDP. During the ensuing years, however, Vander Zalm's government was rocked by a series of scandals and resignations that cut away at the party's electoral support. Finally, in the spring of 1991, Vander Zalm himself resigned in disgrace after a provincial inquiry found that he had mixed private business with his public office. Rita Johnston, a long-time cabinet minister and supporter of Vander Zalm, replaced the latter as Socred leader and provincial premier. At the time, polls showed the ruling Socreds trailing badly to the NDP with time running out on the party's electoral mandate. Deciding to ride the coat-tails of Reform's evident popularity in British Columbia – the party had over 22,000 members in the province – Johnston announced in September that her government would be designing plebiscites asking provincial voters whether they wanted the right to initiate their own plebiscites or to recall MLAS between elections, policies found in Reform's *Blue Book*.[21] The attempt to regain the support of its former ultra-conservative supporters, many of whom now appeared to be Reform adherents federally, was both too late and likely too transparent. The ensuing election, held on 17 October, saw the NDP take fifty seats, the rejuvenated Liberal party seventeen seats, and Johnston's Socred's seven seats. The right-wing coalition that W.A.C. Bennett had constructed in the early 1950s had, at least temporarily, come unglued.

A similar attempt to co-opt Reform support occurred during this same period in Saskatchewan. Premier Grant Devine's Tories had won in 1986, owing in large measure to the timely intervention of Mulroney's federal government, which provided agricultural assistance to the Tories' rural constituency just prior to the election. The years since, however, had not been kind to either the province's economy or the ruling Tories. Consistently down in the polls to the opposition New Democrats, Devine postponed an election call well into the fifth year of the government's mandate, attempting to improve the Tories' electoral chances through gerrymandering electoral boundaries, buying the votes of farmers, and launching an assault on the largely urban and NDP-supporting public service unions.[22] When these tactics failed to increase their support, the Tories (like the Socreds in BC) announced that they had been – as some wags were apt to say – 'Divine-ly inspired' to hold plebiscites on the issues of balanced budgets, constitutional amendments, and whether the provincial medicare plan should pay for abortions.[23] As in British Columbia, the issues selected for plebiscitarian democracy had been lifted from Reform's stated policies.[24] Again, however, the effort to co-opt Reform's positions and supporters failed, in part because Reform's support in Saskatchewan was less substantial than in British Columbia. The subsequent provincial vote of 21 October hence saw the NDP under Roy Romanow gain power, taking fifty-five seats to the Tories' ten and the Liberals' one.

Reform's indirect influence upon the provincial political scene in western Canada, however, was perhaps greatest in Alberta. The reasons are obvious. Much of the early impetus for creating the Reform party came from Alberta. Since then, the province has supplied Reform with the bulk of its membership. The party's headquarters are in Calgary and the most influential members of the party's executive (Harper, Ablonczy, Waters, Fryers) are long-time Alberta residents. And, of course, Preston Manning himself is the son of Alberta's longest-serving premier.

When Alberta suffered through its second major recession of the 1980s (1985–6), the ruling Tories under premier Don Getty began to find themselves caught between the province's traditional small 'c' conservative political culture, of which Reform would later be an adherent, and new political forces, which had risen in the province during the boom years and which underscored and solidified the rise of the moderately left-wing NDP in the provincial elections of 1986 and again in 1989. During the recession, and subsequent to Reform's rise, Getty attempted to ride the crest of political opinion, giving voice to western alienation and presenting himself as a staunch ally of the new party on such issues as the Triple-E Senate. But many of the Tories' former (right-wing) supporters remained unimpressed by Getty, a lackluster leader who too often seemed unsure of his position, and by a government that preached free enterprise but too often intervened in the economy.

In the months following the 1989 election, support for Getty's Tories declined while the opposition NDP, Liberals, and provincially uncommitted Reform party gained, the latter noticeably in Calgary.[25] A year after the election, an Angus Reid poll indicated that the Reform party would get 43 per cent support if it ran provincially, compared with 20 per cent for the Liberals, 19 per cent for the New Democrats, and 18 per cent for the Tories. Another poll, conducted by the Dunvegan Group, showed that 20 percent of decided voters would vote for Reform, despite the fact that the party was not named on the questionnaire. These results prompted Getty to remark at the time: 'The Reform Party is strange ... in that they've pretty well picked up on everything that we have stood for in this province except for one and that is Meech Lake.'[26]

To many, it seemed a rather facile attempt to quell disenchantment with his government by tying the Tories to Reform's ascendant star. But the statement also highlights once again the centrality of the Meech Lake Accord to the fortunes of the federal Reformers and – in this case – also to Alberta's provincial Tories. From the time of its signing, Getty had been a strong supporter of the accord. His continued support of it during the fall of 1989 and spring of 1990 further alienated many provincial Tory supporters, many of whom already held dual memberships in the federal Reform party, which opposed the agreement. For many more, however, Getty's performance at the critical first ministers' meeting in the spring of 1990 was the final straw, particularly when reports began to leak out that, at one point, he had physically blocked Clyde Wells, viewed by many in English-speaking Canada as a hero, from leaving the meeting.[27]

When the accord failed in any case, Getty's Tories found themselves in a particularly precarious situation. They had been on the losing end of a widely discredited political agreement. On top of this, the party was denounced as not conservative enough by right-wing supporters, too aligned to big business by the left, and corrupt and incompetent by voters of nearly all political stripes. Support for Getty and the Tories continued to slide over the next year, as shown by an Angus Reid poll, conducted in February 1991, which found that Reform would get 48 per cent of the vote if it ran provincially in Alberta, compared with the Tories 12 per cent.[28]

In the face of these pressures, the Alberta Tories made a dramatic move to the right in an effort to co-opt Reform support. The party's annual assembly in April 1991 saw the provincial Tories sever ranks with their federal namesakes, a decision that provincial cabinet minister Ken Kowalski admitted would make Reform party members in his constituency more comfortable.[29] (Reportedly, a third of Kowalski's own riding executive held Reform memberships.)[30]

The same assembly saw the normally placid Getty, who previously had been a strong supporter of the federal system, revert to provincialist sentiments in stating what would be Alberta's stance in the constitutional negotiations soon to begin. 'Here in Alberta we have been generous – not just to Quebec but to all of Canada. But if all we get for our generosity is people turning their backs on us, then the generosity will diminish.' As for the threat of Quebec's separation, Getty had a warning. 'We don't like the idea of a huge gaping hole in the middle. But if the hole is created in the map of Canada, we too will remember. *"Je me souviens"* has its own equivalents in English.'[31] Getty's position was widely applauded by Tory delegates to the assembly. But there were even stronger signs of the growing influence of Reform party policies upon the Alberta government.

During the ongoing constitutional hearings that followed the failure of the Meech Lake Accord, Alberta's provincial Tories increasingly took a hard line in parroting the opposition of Reformers to such things as the Charter of Rights and Freedoms, official bilingualism, and multiculturalism, while favouring increased provincial rights and the establishment of a Triple-E Senate.[32] When taking these positions did not greatly improve the Tories' electoral appeal, Getty and some of his colleagues (particularly those in the rural areas) moved even further to the right. This finally culminated, in early 1992, with Getty's strident, if confused, attack on official bilingualism and multiculturalism designed to win back disenchanted supporters from Reform.[33]

In the fall of 1992, Getty surprised everyone by resigning in the midst of the Charlottetown referendum campaign. He was replaced as Tory leader by former Calgary mayor Ralph Klein who led the party to an impressive election victory in June 1993. The victory was very much a testament to the popularity of Klein, whose populist image allowed the Tory party to distance itself from the fiscal ineptness of the previous Getty regime. Nonetheless, the months leading up to the election also showed how far the party had moved to the right in order to capture and maintain rural and Reform party support, as numerous backbenchers made intolerant remarks about gays and immigrants while supporting such traditional conservative themes as law and order and the patriarchal family.

The move of Alberta's Tories to the right does not mean that the province has altogether moved with them. Indeed, there remain indications that Alberta's previously one-dimensional political culture is today rather fragmented.[34] Nonetheless, it does show once again Reform's influence upon the political culture of a particular province. Reform's shadowy presence on Alberta's political scene, combined with lingering public memories of such fiscal disasters as Principal and Novatel, discredited government intervention in the province's economy, leading to a kind of renaissance for the traditional laissez-faire sentiments that impelled Reform's predecessor, Social Credit. Similarly, in the area of moral values, Reform's perceived threat has encouraged verbal support for a return to traditional notions of family values, sexual roles, and law and order among some elements of the provincial Tories' rural constituency.

Reform's considerable, though indirect, influence upon the West's provincial political scene pales, however, in comparison with its influence upon federal politics. As with the various provincial governments, the other federal parties largely ignored Reform during the early days of its existence. Following the failure of the Meech Lake Accord, however, and as it became increasingly apparent that Reform was reaping the whirlwind of resentment swirling around the traditional parties, each began to launch verbal attacks against Reform's policies.[35] The chief agent of these attacks were the Tories, in large measure because the evidence suggested that Reform was, by and large, 'stealing' Tory supporters. The level and frequency of these attacks only increased in April 1991 when a Gallup poll revealed that the Tories had slipped into fourth place, with 12 per cent support compared with Reform's 14 per cent. 'How does one define fringe? Does one define it as someone with less than 14 per cent in the polls?' quipped an obviously ecstatic Preston Manning.[36]

Simultaneously with these attacks on Reform, however, the ruling Tories also began to adopt some of Reform's policies in an effort to win back its right-wing constituency. Political strategy motivated the decision. The Tories had won re-election in 1988 through a coalition of Quebec nationalists, small and big business, westerners (particularly Albertans), and assorted small 'c' conservatives everywhere. Although this coalition had since unravelled, Mulroney's Tories still believed they could bring together the essential elements of this electoral alliance before the next election. Their belief was not entirely illusory. For one thing, although the failure of Meech Lake had damaged severely the party's credibility in Quebec, the Liberal party and Jean Chrétien, in particular, remained strongly disliked there. Similarly, Mulroney's Tories continued to believe that Canada's economy, tied more than ever to the United States, would soon turn around, thus limiting the damage caused by the recession and winning back much of the business support, which had been almost solely theirs in recent years. There remained, then, only the problem of how to win back the West, and small 'c' conservatives in general, from the surging Reform party. In the end, the stick attack on Reform began also to be supplemented by the Tories' carrot approach to Reform's membership.

In April 1991 Mulroney shuffled his cabinet, making Joe Clark minister for constitutional affairs. In a move even more deliberately designed to win back Alberta support, popular Vegreville MP Don Mazankowski became finance minister – the first time in sixty years that a westerner had held that position. Later that same month, Mulroney gave a speech in Calgary where he simultaneously attacked the Reform party for its policies on Quebec while making a Reform-like appeal to western history and regionalism, fiscal responsibility, and parliamentary and Senate reform.[37]

But Mulroney's token efforts at appeasing the right wing were largely unsuccessful. Hence, during the following months, as the Tories prepared for their August convention, there rose among them voices of many of the same extreme right-wing elements from which some of Reform's supporters had been cut, and who previously had been held silent by years of victory or hopes of victory. Down in the polls, perceiving Reform's recent success as having blazoned the trail that the Tories should now follow, these elements submitted a series of resolutions so extreme in some cases as to make one journalist remark that they made 'Reformers look like closet Liberals.'[38] Among the more extreme of these resolutions were ones that would restrict where new immigrants could live, force other immigrants who had 'temporarily left their homeland during difficult times' to return when times improved, and make the stetson the sole headgear of the Mounties.

The Tories, however, are not a homogeneous entity, nor, despite their loss of support, had the party been totally taken over by the lunatic fringe. As a result, these resolutions were defeated at the August convention. Moreover, though no doubt for political reasons, the Tory delegates also grudgingly passed a resolution that recognized the right of Quebec to decide its own political future, a move the Reform party would surely have eschewed.[39] But the Tory delegates also made an implicit appeal to their alienated right wing in passing resolutions calling for the restoration of the death penalty, the privatization of the CBC, and the dismantling of the department of multiculturalism – resolutions that seemed to show, as Stephen Harper noted at the time, that 'the views of the rank-and-file members of the Conservative party are embarrassingly close to the policies of the Reform party.'[40] Indeed, extreme right-wing Tory MPs, such as Garth Turner and fellow Ontarian Bill Domm, proudly declared that the Tories had already implemented or were pushing through much of Reform's agenda.[41]

But these moves had limited success in reconstituting the Tory alliance. Rather, the party continued to languish in the polls throughout late 1991. Equally important to note, however, is that voter dissatisfaction was no longer swelling the ranks of Reform alone. Former Tory supporters also were shifting to the Liberals and the NDP.

Despite the fact that voters were perhaps not moving to the right as quickly as either the Tories or Reform, the next year saw the Tories continue their shift to the right. The clearest indication was on economic issues. Lacking genuine political support and otherwise beset by continued pressures to deal with the deficit, the Tories proved politically – some would say viscerally – unable to take the steps necessary to deal with the ongoing recession. Despite growing criticism, not only from the left, but also from chambers of commerce, municipalities, various provincial governments, and even small business, the Tories continued to adhere to Reform's narrow focus on the deficit alone, thereby strangling the economy. In the end, the Tories' failure to deal effectively with the recession did immeasurable harm both to Canada's economy and to the party's own electoral chances.[42] Similarly, the Tories also followed Reform's social agenda in capping medicare expenditures and killing plans for a national day-care program.[43]

Meanwhile, during this same period, the moral conservatives within the Tory caucus, emboldened by their relative success at the convention and similarly pressed by Reform's growing support, continued to flex their muscles. In December 1991 reports suggested that a number of Tory MPs, such as John Reimer of Kitchener, were prepared to make 'a last stand' in fighting against proposals to grant gays and lesbians protection against discrimination under the Canadian Human Rights Act.[44] The proposed amendment to the act dragged on in committee well into the next summer before being dropped.

Lest anyone think, however, that Reform's presence on the Canadian political scene (in consort with pressures emerging from other economic and political precincts) had moved the Tories alone, it is worthwhile noting that similar pressures were also moving the Liberal party to the right during this period. A three-day thinkers' conference held in Aylmer, Quebec, in November 1991 revealed divisions within the Liberal party between those who still believed in economic nationalism and the liberal welfare state and those committed to the big business agenda concealed in such terms as 'globalization' and 'competitiveness.' In the end, the renewed right wing of the Liberal party seemed to win out, a victory signalled by MP (and free-trade advocate) Roy MacLaren's gloating remark, 'Eat your heart out, Lloyd Axworthy,' a reference to the Liberal party's leading left-wing critic and an outspoken critic of the FTA.[45]

That both the Tories and the Liberals were tripping over each other in moving to the right to undercut Reform support seemed even more apparent the following spring when MPs from both parties overwhelmingly supported a private member's bill, put forward by Tory MP Bill Hicks, that would make it a criminal offence to burn or deface the Canadian flag. 'Somebody who defaces the Canadian flag should be put in jail for life,' said Liberal MP Mac Harb from Ottawa, a sentiment shared by fellow Liberal MP Dan Boudria, who wanted the bill extended to cover provincial flags, and Tory MP Felix Holtsmann, who wanted it extended to make it illegal to burn the flag of any country.[46]

Finally, the NDP also tacitly acknowledged during 1991–2 the shifts in Canada's political culture brought about, at least in part, by Reform's presence. This was particularly the case on the provincial scene where, heeding both the economic realities of the recession and the well-orchestrated attacks by business upon the party in Ontario following its victory in 1990, the NDP in Saskatchewan and British Columbia promoted an image of fiscal conservatism during the lead-up to the elections held in those provinces in 1991. In the end, both parties easily won election, in large measure owing to voter displeasure with the governments they replaced. Even afterwards, however, the NDP remained cautious, aware that fiscal and political considerations had shifted Canada's political spectrum to the right. One indication of this is that the NDP in Saskatchewan and British Columbia, like the federal Tories, also capped medicare expenditures.

In summary, the period following the failure of the Meech Lake Accord saw the Reform party gain not only in members and electoral support but also, perhaps more importantly, in influence. In the following two years, Reform was able to transform significantly the political landscape of Canada, shifting debates as to the nature of the country's problems and the solutions available to their resolution. How did Preston Manning and the Reform party – a party formed less than five years earlier – so rapidly achieve such a level of political influence? In order to understand this achievement, it is necessary to take a look at Reform's organizational structure, including its finances.

REFORM'S ORGANIZATION AND FINANCES

The Reform party was formed in 1987 by several people with extensive backgrounds in business and politics. The practical experience of these individuals should not be overlooked in studying the rise of the party, since it greatly reduced the learning curve of the party and made possible its impressive performance in the federal election of 1988.

As a student of history, Manning in particular is acutely aware of the importance of organization. He frequently refers to the experience of the Progressives in the 1920s, whom Manning rather obviously has used as a kind of 'negative model' in shaping Reform.[47] Without organization, the Progressives soon degenerated into incoherence, making the party's MPs easy pickings for Mackenzie King's machinations.

But there is another reason why Manning views organization as vitally important. While Manning views populism as the most 'potent political force on the face of the earth,' he is not unaware that there is a 'dark side of populism.' Hence, the role of political organization is to 'tap into ... and harness [the] power [of populism] to the formulation and implementation of public policy.'[48] The fate of the party that fails to do this is, for Manning, clear: 'The perversion of populism, as in the case of Peronism in Argentina, or the disintegration of a populist party, as in the case of the Progressives in Canada, occurs from within rather than from without.'[49]

I will return to a discussion of the meaning of populism within the Reform party towards the end of this chapter. For now, however, it is sufficient to suggest that much of Reform's organizational structure appears designed to allow the party executive to harness these populist impulses. To this end, the party possesses a simple, rationalized, and centralized organizational structure, comprised of the Calgary head office and the riding constituencies. Observers both inside and outside the party describe the heart of this formal power structure as consisting of a 'clique' of Manning confidants, mainly Harper, Ablonzcy, Shaw, Fryers, and, until his death, Waters.[50] At the start, head office maintained a tight control over policy, strategy, and communications, while leaving the constituencies the task of signing new members and soliciting funds. In recent years, however, this latter function seems also to have fallen increasingly under the direction of headquarters, with some success.[51]

In 1987, the Reform party collected approximately $250,000, mainly from farmers or small and independent business people. In December of that year, Francis Winspear donated a further $100,000. It is likely that some other prominent business people also gave money to the party. In any case, Reform closed out 1987 with a deficit of $30,700.[52]

Reform's funding for 1988 is more contentious. William Stanbury, who has studied party funding, contends that the Reform party in 1988

had total revenues of $799,134 ($688,419 from memberships and donations; $108,402 from sales of merchandise, such as signs, buttons; and
$2313 from 'other' sources). He notes, however, that Reform party can-
didates themselves raised $1,001,600 in 1988 – more than the total of
revenues stated above – and that they spent $995,695 on 'election ex-
penses' and $57,696 on 'personal expenses.'[53] Meanwhile, *The Reformer*
of May 1989 reports 1988 revenues of $804,521, made up of $737,848
from memberships and donations, $113,793 from sales and merchan-
dise, and $11,945 from 'other.'

Worth noting are the names of some of Reform's contributors in
1988. Winspear provided $15,000 and Canadian Occidental Petroleum
Ltd. $10,000. Other notable Reform contributors that year included Bob
Matheson, a lawyer and former supporter of wcc ($1000), Beaver River
Ranch Ltd. ($1000), Maraval Resources Ltd. ($1000), and Truco Resources
($1000).[54] In the main, however, the Reform party seems to have re-
mained supported by moderately wealthy individuals and small businesses, mainly Alberta-based, and primarily connected with the oil and
gas industry.

In 1988, the party still relied on Byfield's magazines to disseminate
Reform's 'message.' In April of that year, however, the party also started
its own internal newspaper, *The Reformer*. It is a measure of how small
the party remained at this time that its first editor was a nineteen-year-
old University of Alberta student.[55]

The election of that year similarly reflected the party's newness, combining a kind of fresh enthusiasm and inventiveness with surprising
competence. The party organization's electoral strategy was simple and
effective, appealing to anti-government, anti-establishment sentiments
and focusing on a few basic issues (fairness, honesty in government).

The simplicity of Reform's style, however, belied its organizational
sophistication. Simplicity is not something achieved simply. Manning
and his executive worked extra hard to maintain the party's down-to-
earth image and were suitably rewarded. By and large, the electoral
strategy went off without a hitch. The other parties contemptuously
dismissed Reform as unsophisticated and Manning as a kind of gawky
country bumpkin. They thought that Reform would be only a temporary blip on the electoral landscape. They were wrong.

The only real difficulty faced by Reform in 1988 was, as Manning
might have predicted, internal. Even then, however, Manning's refusal
to sign Doug Collins's nomination papers for the bc riding of Capilano-
Howe Sound was not without benefits. Although the incident perhaps

cost the party some initial support in the province, Manning's actions undoubtedly garnered the party support from more moderate voters. By the end of 1988 the Reform party already was a substantial force. It gained further legitimacy the following year through the elections of Deborah Grey to the House of Commons and Stan Waters as Alberta's nominee to the Senate. In 1989 it held its first assembly since 1987.

That the party was gaining in legitimacy is shown by the fact that, by the time of the Edmonton assembly, Reform had more than 26,000 members, 1000 of whom attended the assembly.[56] The convention attracted widespread attention, increasing Reform's profile. It also launched Manning's entry into the debate over the Meech Lake Accord, which was soon to consume the country and, as we have seen, propel the party into a second stage of major growth. This phase would see its membership increase from nearly 33,000 by the end of 1990 to 100,000 by the end of 1991![57]

Reform's increased legitimacy is demonstrated further by its revenues in 1989 and subsequently. In 1989, Reform Fund Canada reported total revenues from memberships and donations, merchandise, and interest of $1.1 million.[58] At the same time, the party declared total contributions of $1.3 million. Eighty-nine per cent of this funding came from individuals, the bulk of the remainder from businesses.[59] Francis Winspear again gave $15,000. Among the party's other notable contributors that year were two numbered companies, Alberta Ltd. #280955 and #125482 Canada Inc., which gave $1000 and $15,000, respectively. The largest single contribution came from Jack Mackenzie, an oil business executive and founder of the Marigold Foundation who gave $16,000.[60] Again, a number of other oil and gas companies provided money to the Reform party, including Numac Oil and Gas ($1000), Gasland Oil Ltd. ($1000), and Permez Petroleum Ltd. ($1000). Construction magnate John Poole also gave $3000.[61]

In 1990 Reform party contributions rose to $2.2 million, 94 per cent of which again came from individuals.[62] The size of some individual and business contributions rose markedly during this period. Major business contributors to Reform were Van Naren Construction ($10,000), Vycom Electronics ($5000), and Winspear Securities ($5000). (Francis Winspear also personally donated $5700.) Reform also received $3445 from the Pirie family and its oil-based company, Pirie Resource Management.[63] Major individual contributors to the party included John Poole ($1,200), popular author W.P. Kinsella ($3000), and several party insiders, notably Cliff Fryers ($1560), Lloyd and Helen Kirkham ($3221), and George Van Den Bosch ($1150).[64] (Ironically, the latter two contributors left or were later expelled from the party.)

Despite its increased funding and popular support, by the fall of 1990 some party insiders had become concerned that organizational weaknesses also might hinder Reform's success. A story in the *Alberta Report* of 12 November 1990 starkly detailed these problems. The article specifically noted that Reform was 'almost a one-man show,' that the 'party hierarchy, with disproportionate representation from the Calgary legal community' had not produced anyone 'to share the role of chief public spokesman with Mr. Manning,' that '[t]he Calgary headquarters has reportedly gone through four office managers in three years,' that 'Reform's upper echelon is conspicuously short of professional political experience,' and that '[i]t has been operating without first-rate polling, public relations and fund-raising services.'

Not everyone within the party apparently believed that Reform needed to adopt more sophisticated methods and techniques in order to compete with the traditional parties. Stephen Harper, in particular, expressed doubt about where strategic polling and public relations material had gotten the Tories. Nonetheless, in May 1991 the Reform party underwent a massive reorganization. Diane Ablonczy became special council to Preston Manning, while Tom Flanagan, a well-known (and somewhat controversial) professor of political science at the University of Calgary replaced Harper as the party's new director of policy.[65] That spring also saw the party's head office in Calgary moved to larger premises.

Other major organizational changes soon followed. In September the party commissioned a Canadian polling firm and hired a Calgary-based advertising organization, Hayhurst Communications. During this same period, the party hired Frank Luntz, an American pollster and campaign strategist, who had previously worked in the Reagan White House and who had written a text on political campaigning.[66]

The most important change, however, saw the appointment in May 1991 of Cliff Fryers as the party's chief operating officer and chair of its executive council. The appointment of Fryers, a lawyer with extensive corporate contacts, particularly with the oil and gas sector, signalled that the party hierarchy was about to make a renewed effort to gain corporate financial support.

Since its inception, Reform has relied almost entirely upon individual donations. The previous September, however, Manning had actively primed the corporate pump at a much publicized private dinner held at Toronto's prestigious Toronto Club hosted by Conrad Black and Hal Jackman. Afterwards, Black not only gave a favourable review of Manning's economic policies, but also contributed $5000 through one of his companies, Sterling Newspapers.[67] Throughout the remainder of 1990, as the party executive prepared for Reform's expansion, overtures continued to be made to central Canada's business community. Nonetheless, by the summer of 1991, Reform remained largely unknown to business outside Alberta. It was a situation Cliff Fryers hoped to remedy quickly.

Thus, Fryers announced in June 1991 that the party would soon be embarking on a major corporate drive for funding. 'Corporations are part of our constituency,' said Fryers, a remark echoed several months later by Gordon Wusyk, Reform's chief executive in Edmonton: 'What we have to offer corporate Canada is significant.'[68] Based in part on the anticipated success of the campaign, the party revised upwards to $20 million its estimates of the money it anticipated having in the bank by the time of the next election.[69]

Manning kicked off the campaign for corporate funds the following month with another trip to Bay Street. While there, he gave a talk to 450 members of the Financial Services Institute, an organization described by journalist Norm Ovenden as 'an elite organization made up of bank, trust company and insurance executives, top corporate lawyers, accountants, stock brokers and pension-fund managers.' Ovenden reported that the trip also saw Manning hold several informal discussions with 'investment dealers, the Canadian Bankers' Association (CBA), and company presidents, as well as one meeting at the exclusive Toronto Club attended by at least three chief executive officers of Canada's big banks.' While not overly impressing the corporate chiefs, Manning apparently did gain some support. According to Ovenden, Helen Sinclair, president of the CBA, later told Manning: 'We want to have you with us, as much as you want to have us with you.'[70]

October saw the beginning of a different kind of financial campaign, the 'Save Canada Campaign.' Directed at the party's 90,000 members, and operating within the period 6 November 1991 to 6 February 1992, the campaign was designed to collect $12 million. The campaign proved less successful than the corporate offensive, however, a victim (according to Reform officials) of bad weather and the recession, and was mothballed at the end of 1991. Nonetheless, during its brief period of existence the campaign apparently solicited $2 million.[71]

Altogether, Reform's political contributions in 1991 amounted to $5.2

million. Of this, $4.7 million (91 per cent) continued to come from individuals, the rest from businesses. Prominent individual contributors included Francis Winspear ($10,000) and Preston Manning ($1500). But Reform also received large business contributions from some prominent sources, including Canadian Pacific Ltd. ($25,000), Scotiabank ($20,000), Prowest Professional Partition People ($14,755), Canadian Occidental Petroleum ($10,000), and Jim Pattison Industries Ltd. ($5000).[72] The following year Reform's political contributions totalled $6.25 million. But the majority of this funding (90 per cent) continued to come from individuals.[73]

To place the Reform party's funding in context, it is useful to compare its sources of funding with that of the other major parties. In 1992, for example, the federal Tories received $11.5 million dollars in contributions, only 41 per cent of this from individuals, the rest from business and commercial sources. That same year, the Liberals received $7.6 million, 53 per cent from individuals, the bulk of the rest from business. Meanwhile, the NDP obtained $13.5 million, 41 per cent from individuals, 9 per cent from unions, 1 per cent from business, and the rest from other social organizations, including provincial affiliates.[74]

Reform's general lack of big business support, despite the party's efforts to elicit funding, resulted from two factors. First, Reform was not yet perceived by the business community at large as a legitimate contender for power. Secondly, the party was still largely confined to the western region – not the heartland of large corporate donors. Therefore the bulk of Reform's meagre corporate support continued to come from small- to medium-sized Alberta companies, primarily within the oil and gas sector, a sector beset by economic uncertainty.

In summary, by mid-1993 the Reform party was a highly centralized, professional, and tightly controlled organization. The party had a full-time pollster, a campaign manager, and an advertising agency working full time on the next federal campaign. The party organization was assisted further by enthusiastic members, numbering over 133,000.[75] Finally, the party was pulling in an increasing amount of money, primarily from individuals, but with hopes of corporate donations to come. Within a scant five years of existence, the Reform party had developed into a remarkably efficient political organization. And it is to the efficiency of this machine – its capacity to mobilize and utilize resources of both money and people, and to churn out a set of coherent and saleable policies – that we must attribute much of the political success of the party.

Despite this, the Reform party is far from infallible. Indeed, the organization suffered some rather well-publicized embarrassments along the way. On the financial end, the failure of the Save Canada Campaign and the party's continued difficulties in selling itself to the corporate sector have already been noted. To these failures may be added the dubious efforts of some zealots in Reform's organization to convince party members that they should take out insurance policies listing Reform as the chief beneficiary.[76]

In January 1992 the party's political image took a further blow when the press got hold of an internal memo, sent out by Tom Flanagan, that seemed to smack of political dirty tricks. Specifically, the memo asked constituency associations:

Study the careers of the incumbent and of all other candidates. Search to see if they have violated legality, morality or propriety in their public lives. Keep a current newspaper clipping file on these people; look also for material in old newspapers, magazines and books. Study their public statements to see what causes they have supported and what promises they have made in the past.[77]

The publication of such a memo would have hurt any party, but to one like Reform, which has built its reputation in opposition to the unethical practices of the old-line parties, the stories were a particular embarrassment.

Throughout 1991 and early 1992, long-time party members increasingly complained about what they perceived as the authoritarian manner in which the party was being run. The result was a series of resignations and expulsions in each of the western provinces, particularly in Alberta and British Columbia.[78] Some Reformers again complained in early 1992 when Tory MLA Ray Speaker, a twenty-eight-year member of the Alberta legislature, former Socred, and personal friend of Manning, resigned his seat to run for Reform's federal nomination in the Alberta riding of Little Bow. Other candidates for the Reform nomination were highly critical of Speaker's sudden entry into the race, seeing him as symbolic of everything the new party was supposed to be against. Some party members were also very critical of Manning's obvious welcome of his personal friend to the party, viewing this as blatant interference with the independence of the constituency.[79] In the end, Speaker won the nomination, but hard feelings remained.

The party's organizational problems, however, were not confined to headquarters alone. Some party members in Ontario accused the party's regional coordinator, Reg Gosse, of being autocratic and secretive. These accusations went back to December 1990 when Gosse apparently dismissed Ontario's expansion committee in favour of a parallel committee that he had secretly created the previous September.[80]

As the party prepared for the 1993 election, Reform suffered also from a number of scandals at the constituency level. Specifically, the party was hit by accusations of dirty tricks and voting irregularities at nomination meetings held in Medicine Hat and Edmonton South, with the result that several long-time Reform party members resigned in disgust.[81] As Stephen Harper feared, expansion seemed also to result in some local constituencies being taken over by right-wing extremists. This appeared to be particularly the case in Ontario, a province with a long history of right-wing extremism.[82] Murray Dobbin, for example, documented evidence suggesting that COR had succeeded in taking over the executive of at least one Ontario constituency (Peterborough).[83]

But a series of even more politically damaging stories became public in late 1991. In December a news report stated that Gordon LeGrand, one of the Brockville protesters who became famous in 1989 for stomping on the Quebec flag, was the secretary of Reform's Leeds-Grenville riding association. To make matters worse, the party at first expressed no plans to get rid of LeGrand. 'For something someone has done before they joined the party, it has to be pretty significant before the Reform party will expel them,' stated Virgil Anderson, Reform's national director of constituent development and a party policy officer.[84] It was a singularly naive statement considering Reform's public image in some quarters as having policies that catered to racists and extremists. In January, under intense political pressure from the other political parties and from the media, Manning reversed this decision, announcing that LeGrand would either have to resign from the party or be expelled under a clause in the party's constitution.

The Reform Party advocates mutual respect among Canadians – we don't tolerate the deliberate insulting of one Canadian group or another. It's the symbolic nature that's the concern – particularly when we're getting into a very tense discussion of relations between Quebec and the rest of the country.[85]

A short while later, while declaring his continued support for the party, LeGrand resigned.

Even more embarrassing, however, was the discovery in late February 1992 that several neo-Nazis, including Wolfgang Droege, head of the extremist Heritage Front, had joined the party and that the Front had been encouraging other members to join Reform in hopes that Manning's party might provide a vehicle for bringing about the racial 'purification' of Canada.[86] A few days later, Cliff Fryers announced that Droege, three other Heritage Front members, and an executive of the Beaches-Woodbine Reform constituency who had signed up the neo-Nazis, had been expelled from the party. Fryers announced at the same time that a committee had been set up to weed out 'unacceptable' membership applications. The expulsions brought to seventeen the number of members who had recently been cast out of the party.[87] Even so, the taint of neo-Nazi affiliation continued to dog Reform into the following year.

These incidents rekindled questions about Reform's members and supporters. If not neo-Nazis and assorted rednecks, who were the people joining the party? To whom did Reform's anti–government, anti–welfare state, pro–free enterprise message appeal?

WHO ARE THE REFORMERS?

Previous, largely journalistic, descriptions of Reform party supporters generally have focused on its leadership, including the executive. These accounts describe the party's executive and membership as consisting of white, middle-aged or elderly males, of upper-class or upper-middle class, professional, business, or agrarian backgrounds. Reports also suggest that members are predominantly discontented former supporters of the Progressive Conservative party, with significant connections also to the Social Credit party, particularly in Alberta and British Columbia, and more extreme right-wing fringe parties (Western Canada Concept, the Confederation of Regions Party).[88]

Such descriptions are problematic on several counts. First, they tend to view party supporters in general as synonymous with certain of the party's high-profile members. Yet, significant differences may exist between supporters, activists, and leaders.[89] Secondly, particularly in the case of new movements and parties, the profile of each of these elements may be quite volatile. Any description of a party's adherents must therefore be sensitive to changes occurring over time. Thirdly, it is necessary also to compare party adherents with similar elements in other parties.

It is possible to describe fairly accurately four distinct elements within the Reform party: executives, assembly delegates, general members, and general supporters. Reform's executive councils tend to be heavily, and perhaps increasingly, male-dominated.[90] The average age of councillors has dropped somewhat since the first executive. Today, the average councillor is in his late forties. Occupationally, executive council members have traditionally been small businesspeople, self-employed professionals, or retired. The proportion of professionals, however, particularly with connections to the financial service sector, seems to be increasing. On each of these factors – gender, age, and occupation – Reform's executive seems not dramatically different from, for example, previous Liberal and Conservative cabinets.[91] Compared with each of these parties, Reform's executive may be somewhat more representative of small business and somewhat less so of the legal profession, but the differences are small.

Studies of Reform assemblies held in 1989 and 1992 indicate that party delegates tend to be somewhat older than executive members, although the percentage of delegates fifty years and older dropped slightly between 1989 and 1992.[92] Delegates are predominantly male. Indeed, the percentage of female delegates actually dropped from 32 per cent in 1989 to 29 per cent in 1992. Delegates are overwhelmingly English speaking (99.7 per cent in 1992) and well educated, certainly above the Canadian average. Many are retired (23 per cent in 1989; 25 per cent in 1992). But a large percentage in 1992 also declared their occupation as business owner (20 per cent), self-employed (13 per cent) or employed (13 per cent) professional, or farmer (8 per cent). In keeping with these high-status occupations, delegates tend, perhaps increasingly, to possess relatively high incomes. While 42 per cent of delegates to the 1989 assembly reported an annual total family income of over $50,000 (less than 18 per cent over $80,000), nearly 52 per cent of delegates to the 1992 assembly claimed an annual family income of over $60,000 (nearly 35 per cent over $80,000).

The political background of Reform party delegates is instructive. Far from being career politicos, involvement in Reform for most delegates seems to represent the end point of a gradual process of politicization which saw them move from passive political interest to active commitment. Certainly, many Reform delegates have previous political affiliations. For example, Reform's 1989 assembly survey found that nearly 64 per cent had previously been members of another federal party. But the study of delegates to the 1992 assembly suggests that such affiliations, in most cases, stopped short of direct political involvement. Only about 10 per cent of party delegates in 1992 had previous direct political experience.

Among both passive or active party delegates, which party or parties had been the previous political vehicles of choice? The data support the widespread contention that Reformers are, in general, disgruntled Tories or previous supporters of other right-wing parties. The party's 1989 delegate survey found that 78 per cent of the delegates identified themselves as previous Tories, 5 per cent Socreds, 5 per cent Liberals, and just over 1 per cent COR members.[93] Similarly, the 1992 delegate survey found that over 79 per cent had voted Tory in 1984, while 46 per cent did so again in 1988, compared with 36 per cent who shifted to Reform. For each of these electoral years, the remaining delegates reported either distributing their votes among other parties, or simply not voting.

How do Reform delegates compare to those in other parties? Strict comparisons are made difficult by the fact that each party has somewhat different policies governing delegate selection. Thus, for example, the Liberals, New Democrats, and Tories have all instituted policies – each with different results – specifically designed to attract women and younger delegates. By contrast, Reform has no youth wing with special delegate status. Neither has the party made a concerted effort to recruit women.[94] Thus, for institutional reasons, Reform delegates tend to be predominantly older and male particularly compared with the Liberals and Tories. In general, however, the profile of Reform delegates (older, retired, relatively well-off) is consistent with previous studies showing that party activists tend to be drawn from those segments of society with time, resources, and motivation to become involved in politics.[95]

Reform party delegates are a distinct subset of party members in general. Two studies of the party's general membership, conducted in 1989 and 1991, describe the latter.[96] Like delegates, Reform party members tend to be overwhelmingly male (nearly 67 per cent in 1991), but somewhat less well educated, somewhat older (mean of fifty-six years in 1991), and even more likely to be retired (38 per cent in 1989, 35 per cent in 1991). Even more strongly than delegates, Reform's general membership draws people from the farming sector. In 1991, nearly 15 per cent of party members reported their engagement in agriculture. By way of comparison, less than 2 per cent of Canada's entire workforce is engaged in farming, and only 4 per cent if those engaged in horticulture or animal husbandry are included. Moreover, this high level of

Reform support among farmers is not explained by regional variations. Even in the Reform's western heartland, farmers make up only slightly more than 3 per cent of the labour force, and only 7 per cent if those employed in horticulture and animal husbandry are included.[97] This finding of high Reform support among farmers coincides with other information in the 1991 survey indicating that the party draws a significant proportion of its members (49 per cent versus the Canadian average of 37 per cent) from rural rather than urban areas.

Socio-economically, Reform members appear very similar to Tories and, to a somewhat lesser extent, Liberals.[98] Like these parties, Reform draws its membership disproportionately from autonomous professionals (particularly in the legal and financial service sectors), independent businesspeople, and managers. This occupational profile is consistent with the fact that less than 18 per cent of Reformers in non-agricultural occupations are union members, compared with the Canadian average of 36 per cent union members among non-agricultural paid workers.[99] The occupational status of Reformers corresponds with moderately high incomes reported by most members. In 1991, 43 per cent reported family incomes of $50,000 or more (mean of $44,340). To quote columnist Jeffrey Simpson: 'Many [Reformers] have nest eggs; few have yachts.'[100]

Like party delegates, Reform's general membership is heavily made up of former Tory supporters. In 1989, 73 per cent of Reform's members stated that they had previously supported the Tories. But, also of note, another 22 per cent had previously supported Social Credit. No doubt, this reflected Reform's strong roots in the Socred provinces of Alberta and British Columbia. With Reform's growth and expansion, the percentage of former Socred supporters has decreased sharply in recent years. For example, Reform's 1991 membership survey found only 7 per cent of former Socred supporters. But the percentage of former Tory supporters remained high: 73 per cent, compared to 10 per cent Liberal, 4 per cent NDP, and 6 per cent other (or multiple). Despite Reform's success in the 1993 federal election, it is probable that the party continues to draw most of its membership from former Tories. Indeed, the precipitous decline in the latter party's fortunes will likely add to Reform's dominant profile.

If Reform members are somewhat distinguishable, what of the party's supporters? How do Reform Party supporters compare with supporters of other political parties and with Canadians at large? Surveys conducted by Environics Research in May 1991 and July-August 1991, as well as at the University of Alberta that same year, shed some light on this question.[101] Compared to average Canadians and to supporters of other parties, Reform supporters were found to be disproportionately well educated, male, older, and retired. They were more likely than other party supporters to be non-unionized and home-owners. Compared with both Canadians in general and other party supporters, Reform supporters were also disproportionately and predominantly English-speaking, Protestant, and Anglo-European.[102] Reform tended to draw somewhat greater support than the other traditional parties from technical and semi-professional occupations and owners of small businesses, and somewhat less from unskilled workers. Reform also tended to draw support from slightly higher household income groups than the other parties. Overall, however, the occupational and income differences between Reformers and other party supporters were not significant. The University of Alberta survey found that, at least in that province, Calgary and small town or rural residents tended to be attracted to the Reform Party more than other voters, a finding congruent with the pattern of votes obtained by the Reform party in the 1988 election.

In a specific test of theory, Harvey Krahn and I used data from the 1991 Alberta Survey to examine the class backgrounds of party supporters. We were particularly interested in testing C.B. Macpherson's well-known theory regarding petit bourgeois support for populist parties.[103] On the surface, the theory appeared applicable to the Reform party given previous descriptions of so many of the party's members and supporters as farmers, small businesspeople, and self-employed professionals.

The results indicated only partial support for Macpherson's grand theory.[104] As a whole, only 29 per cent of the petite bourgeoisie supported the Reform party, compared with 14 per cent the Tories, 13 per cent the NDP, 7 per cent the Liberals, and 37 per cent who were undecided. Significantly, however, just over 41 per cent of Alberta's agrarian petite bourgeoisie stated that the Reform party was their electoral preference, compared with nearly 15 per cent who said the Tories, 8 per cent the NDP, 3 per cent the Liberals, and 33 per cent undecided. It should be noted that this was one of the few instances in which decided voters for *any* party actually outnumbered those in the 'undecided' category, and that, if only *committed* voters are considered, Reform support among farmers actually rose to 62 per cent! By contrast, neither small business owners (the non-agrarian petite bourgeoisie) nor members of any other class were significantly more likely to support

Reform than any other party. Finally, it should be noted that this finding of disproportionate Reform support among farmers was replicated in other studies conducted of the three Prairie provinces.[105]

Do the results mean that Reform support in Alberta in 1991 was a reflection of traditional agrarian populism? No. In the University of Alberta sample, farmers made up only 13 per cènt of Reform's overall Alberta supporters. The results suggested simply that, if one was a farmer, then he or she was likely to be a Reform supporter. The party, however, also appeared to be drawing reasonably well in 1991 from other social classes in Alberta, a fact later reinforced by the party's overwhelming success in that province in the 1993 election.

In summary, Reformers in general tend to be English-speaking, older, well-educated males, with moderately high incomes. A statistically significant number of Reform delegates, general members, and supporters are farmers, while many others occupy technical or professional occupations, or own small businesses. Class position, however, does not strongly describe Reformers. Congruent with the finding of definite farm support, the party has tended since its inception to attract a disproportionate number of rural dwellers. But, again, it would be an exaggeration to label the party as simply a rural phenomenon. The predominant ethno-cultural background of Reformers has tended in the past, and seems to remain, Anglo-European and Protestant. The vast majority of Reformers are former Tory supporters, with a significant number of former Socreds in Reform's strongholds of Alberta and British Columbia. While some of these characteristics may be changing over time, particularly regarding age, location, occupation, and perhaps also gender, it is clear that the profile of Reformers is somewhat distinctive, though certainly not peculiar. Finally, this profile is most similar to that of Tories and, to a lesser degree, Liberals.

But if Reformers tend to possess certain social characteristics in common, what beliefs might tie them together? Is it possible to decipher a coherent ideology driving Reform? Moreover, can such an ideology, if found, be tied to its members' concrete circumstances? To answer these questions, I turn now to an examination of the ideology of Reformers.

WHAT DO REFORMERS BELIEVE?

Despite Preston Manning's frequent insistence that the Reform party is non-ideological, it is hard to imagine a more ideologically driven party or leadership. Indeed, Manning himself was heavily involved in the writing of *Political Realignment*, a text that called for political parties to return to pure ideology. This same insistence on ideological purity, or non-pragmatism, is found in William Gairdner's division of the world into two philosophical camps, and in the Byfields' frequent derisive labelling of non-ideologues as 'muddlegrounders.'

It is clear, moreover, that most Reform party members view themselves from an ideological perspective. The party's own 1989 convention survey found that on a seven-point scale defining left-right ideology (left=1, right=7), Reformers placed themselves at 5.08, compared to the perceived positioning of the Canadian electorate at 3.74, and the Reform party at 5.09, compared to the federal Conservatives at 3.5, the Liberals at 2.63, and the NDP at 1.85. It is interesting to note that the convention delegates tended to view the provincial wings of each of these parties, especially the Tories, as being somewhat more right wing (PCS 4.26, Liberals 3.25, and NDP 1.97), while Reform delegates from British Columbia gave the Socreds in that province a rating of 4.96.[106] In short, delegates to Reform's 1989 convention tended to view themselves and their party as far to the ideological right of both the Canadian electorate and most of the existing parties, either federally or provincially.

The finding that Reformers exhibit a strong ideological commitment is not surprising. Only those with pronounced ideological beliefs would be willing to expend the energy and resources necessary to start up a new party or to sustain one with a commitment to ideas over power alone. In this sense, the motivations of Reform members appear more similar to that of NDP members, another ideologically driven party, than either Liberals or Conservatives, whose motivations for joining those parties tend to be more social or practical.[107]

What beliefs and opinions do Reformers hold? Sophisticated analyses of party supporters in Alberta, drawn from the 1991 Alberta survey, and conducted by Harvey Krahn and myself, and of data from the survey of delegates to Reform's 1992 assembly, conducted by Keith Archer and Faron Ellis, provide some answers.[108]

Archer and Ellis's study found that Reform party delegates tend to be strongly, distinctively, and unanimously anti-government (re: big government, the deficit, and government ownership), anti–social welfare (re: the welfare state and assorted policies), and anti-Quebec (re: bilingualism in the federal government, a constitutional veto for Quebec, and distinct society status for Quebec). The vast majority of delegates also are in agreement as to the causes of today's social ills: family and community disintegration, and excessive leniency towards criminals. On other issues, however, there is somewhat less unanimity. While most Reformers appear to support assimilation and to oppose multiculturalism, this agreement is positively correlated with age. Similarly, delegates agree somewhat on issues of institutional reform. Again, however, a split is evident, this time along predominantly east-west lines. An especially contentious single item involves the importance of the monarchy to Canada. Finally, on at least two issue indexes – civil liberties and continentalism – the party appears to be significantly fragmented. Regarding the former, Reformers (like many supporters of other parties) appear to be torn by notions of community versus individual rights. This is particularly evident on the issues of abortion rights and the right of homosexuals to teach school, with male delegates being significantly more 'anti' than female delegates. Regarding the latter, Reform support for continentalist policies is significantly enhanced by wealth, gender (male), and region of residence (Alberta and British Columbia).

The results of Harvey Krahn's and my analysis of party supporters in Alberta in 1991 are generally congruent with these findings.[109] Reform party supporters were somewhat distinct from other party supporters in their ambivalence towards government support for women's equality (50 per cent) and hostility to the notion of 'distinct society status' for Quebec (13 per cent), although it should be noted that support for the latter was minimal in all parties. On no other single items, however, were Reformer's 'outliers.' They tended to mirror Tory supporters in believing that society has become too lenient in dealing with criminals and opposing Canada's continued acceptance of large numbers of immigrants. But Reformers were less supportive than the Tories and closer to the Liberals on the need for more laws to limit the power of unions. Similarly, 66 per cent of both Reform and Liberal supporters agreed that large corporations were too powerful in Canada, compared with 55 per cent of Tory supporters and 79 per cent of NDP supporters. Reformers, Tories, and Liberals alike tended to agree that abortion should be a matter of a woman's personal choice. Perhaps surprisingly, Reformers were somewhat less in agreement than either Tory or Liberal supporters with the notion that aboriginal people should be treated the same as other groups in Canada, although there was substantial agreement by all party supporters with this notion.[110] Finally, to complete a somewhat confusing picture, Reformers were similar to both the Liberals and NDP in their dislike of the GST and seemed to share with NDP supporters a high level of political alienation.

A subsequent factor analysis of this same data set suggests, however, that people drawn to Reform do share a constellation of attitudes on certain broad issues.[111] Consistent with the results of Archer and Ellis's examination of Reform party delegates, reported above, Reform was found to attract the most politically alienated elements of the Alberta electorate, to have strong assimilationist and anti-pluralist views regarding immigration, to believe that society is too lenient with criminals, and to be strongly opposed to the notion of 'distinct society status' for Quebec. The analysis suggested also that people drawn to Reform were less likely to agree with statements about gender equality.

Taken together, the findings of these studies suggest that Reformers may possess a unique and coherent configuration of attitudes, while remaining similar to other party supporters regarding certain issues. Is it possible to tie together this pattern of attitudes with the structural characteristics of Reform party members?

Yes. The roots of the Reform party go back much before the Vancouver assembly of 1987. Indeed, Reform's roots can be found in a series of structural and ideological changes that have occurred in Canada, and all of western society, over at least the past thirty years. In many case, these changes have been revolutionary, and like all revolutions they have had negative consequences for people in certain circumstances. Over time, these negative consequences resulted in casting adrift from the influence of the dominant political parties many of the people residing within these structural locations, making them potentially vulnerable to any legitimate political alternative promising to restore the traditional order.

We have seen that, among decided voters of Anglo and Protestant backgrounds, a large number would vote for the Reform party. In terms of status and power, has any ethnic or religious group lost more than Anglo-Saxons and Protestants since the 1960s?[112] Moreover, have not anglophone powers been challenged most directly by francophone Quebecers and visible minorities – two groups towards whom many Reformers tend to harbour particularly negative attitudes? While it seems true that francophone Quebecers and visible minorities also may not be particularly well liked by other party supporters, Reform seems to have provided a legitimate vehicle for the expression of anger towards them and, more generally, over changes in Canada's traditional hierarchies.

The data also have shown that an overwhelming number of farmers, and rural voters in general, are Reform supporters. Has any occupation and class in Canada lost more income and status than farmers in the past twenty-five years? Have not rural dwellers, in general, seen their way of life slipping under the wheels of seemingly irresistible modernity? Similarly, the statistical evidence presented here shows that males tend to be overrepresented among Reformers, and that Reformers are less supportive of gender equality issues than other party supporters. Has not the traditional occupational and social status of males been gradually eroded by the gains of women over this same period?

Of course, attitudes and ideas are not reducible to material circumstances alone. But even in circumstances where their concrete circumstances are not directly affected, people may feel a sense of alienation resulting from changes in their normative order. This sense of social dislocation explains much of what Reformers feel. In the face of the numerous changes – economic, political, demographic, and ideological – that have occurred in Canada, many Reformers would simply like the world, if it cannot be stopped, to at least slow down for a while. Taken even further, however, can Reformers attitudes and beliefs be raised to a different level of abstraction? Is it possible to define what might be termed Reform's 'ideology'?

Yes. Two major ideological elements have coalesced within Reform party thought. The first of these elements is pure populism, dealing with primarily political issues: power to 'the people,' greater accountability by elected officials, an end to political patronage, and a curtailment of the power of the 'big interests.'[113] In its basic form, populism provides the Reform party with a potential bridge to those many Canadians of various ideological persuasions who have grown disillusioned with government bureaucracy, scandal, insensitivity, and arrogance.

Contiguous and, in some cases, overlapping with this populist element in Reform is a second element: neo-conservatism. Neo-conservatism, in North America at least, combines classical liberal economic and political theory with traditional conservative social and moral doctrine. In practical terms, neo-conservatism has proven particularly useful as an ideological umbrella for the creation of political alliances in opposition to the dominance of postwar, or welfare state, liberalism. In the case of Reform and similar parties, neo-conservative discourse has substituted for the 'big interests,' opposed by traditional populists, the term 'special interests,' meaning groups such as women, gays, environmentalists, and visible minorities, who have benefited from state or judicial intervention.[114]

In truth, however, few Reformers – except perhaps Preston Manning himself – literally embrace all the tenets of neo-conservatism. Moreover, within Reform's corridors of power, the forces of economic liberalism – even libertarianism – appear to dominate both traditional conservatism and the impulses of populism.

Economic liberalism dominated even at the party's inception. As I have shown, the party was formed with generous financial and administrative support from the western business community and has made repeated efforts to increase its corporate support elsewhere. As well, most of Reform's executives have strong ties to the corporate community, particularly the oil and gas sector, a sector whose espousal of strict laissez-faire economics – even as it benefits from all kinds of government intervention and support – is notorious.[115] The party's chief ideological mentors – Brimelow, Gairdner, Manning, and Byfield – also express an extreme faith in unbridled capitalism, individualism, and the workings of the marketplace, a stance found in the party's strong support of free trade in 1988. Finally, Reform from the beginning has had numerous links with the National Citizens' Coalition, an organization with strong ties to Canada's business community.[116]

But Reform's radical pro-market stance is not confined to the party's hierarchy alone. Although the survey results reported above showed that Reform party members and supporters, in general, are somewhat wary of large corporate power, there remains a rather uncritical – some would say 'naive' – faith in the business sector as a whole. The results of a Gallup poll of 14 November 1991 reveal this uncritical attitude. In response to the question, 'In general, who do you believe are more honest and trustworthy, political leaders or business leaders?' 74 per cent of Reformers selected the latter. By contrast, 57 per cent of Tory, 60 per cent of Liberal, and 54 per cent of New Democrat supporters said that they viewed business leaders as more honest and trustworthy.

Reform's current policies on privatization, property rights, social programs, flat taxes, agricultural subsidies, and labour relations similarly reflect this unquestioning support of business and the private accumulation of capital. For many Reformers, the central problem of modern life is 'big government,' and the solution lies in turning Canada into the kind of *ideal* 'free market' economy described by Adam Smith and David Ricardo roughly two centuries ago. Consistent with this ideal, the Reform party has among its policies one that calls for the 'elimination of subsidies and tax concessions to business.'[117] True to its erstwhile ideological roots, the party proposes 'letting the market decide,' even if this presumably means allowing large corporations to fold as a result of economic downturns.

Even ideology, however, has its limits. In time, the Reform party will likely abandon this policy. Manning, and the rest of Reform's executive, are too close, psychologically and politically, to big business to ever cut loose the corporations.[118] In the end, the laissez-faire liberal ideology that currently dominates Reform polices likely will evolve into the kind of right-wing, pro-business conservatism practised by Preston Manning's father in the 1950s and 1960s when he was premier of Alberta.

As this occurs, the economic liberal elements within Reform increasingly will move to curtail the party's populist drives, since these drives, if left unchecked, ultimately might challenge the leadership's rather restricted notion of political democracy. Indeed, the populist elements of Reform ideology already are being restrained and re-channelled.

What of Reform's traditional small 'c' conservative element? There is no doubt that conservatism has a strong voice within the party. For example, Preston Manning and Deborah Grey are staunch and outspoken anti-abortionists. Similarly, such issues as immigration, multiculturalism, and 'feminism,' which disturb Reformers' sense of 'normative order,' rankle many in the party. In general, however, the degree of support for traditional conservative values is not as pronounced as the support for economic liberalism and demands for less government. I have already noted, for example, the ambivalence of both Reform delegates and supporters regarding abortion and homosexuality.[119] Except for Manning and Grey, the values of moral conservatism are not readily found in the highest echelons of the party.

Perhaps for this reason, Manning studiously avoids discussing moral questions. But while Manning's avoidance seems based on a wish to avoid controversy, a number of influential people connected with the party appear genuinely uninterested in the conservative moral agenda. Stephen Harper is one. So is Peter Brimelow whose writings are strongly libertarian. Stan Waters was pro-choice on abortion and once remarked, 'Why do middle-aged men in Parliament want to decide what a woman should do?'[120] If the economic liberals within the party are opposed to programs or policies that might change the normative order, their opposition stems less from a moral imperative and more from a desire to reduce the power of 'special interest groups' and the size of government expenditures.

But this marriage of economic liberalism and traditional conservatism is an uneasy one. Neo-conservatism is a Janus-headed ideology. While one of neo-conservatism's faces looks to the past, longing for the sense of community, stability, and permanence, its other, more classically liberal face looks to the future, denigrating – or worse, ignoring – the past, scoffing at the very notion of community and embracing the notion of perpetual change. The first preaches limits; the second bridles at the fetters that history and tradition place upon its personal freedom.[121]

C.B. Macpherson defined the essential 'ethos' of classical economic liberalism as 'possessive individualism.'[122] Possessive individualism is based on the assumption that people are free and human by virtue of their sole proprietorship of their own persons and capacities, a proprietorship for which they possess no intrinsic obligation to society (past or present), such society being defined as essentially a series of market relations between atomistic individuals solely motivated by economic considerations.[123] That Reform ideology carries within it this element of classical liberal thought is aptly displayed by party mentor William Gairdner:

I will argue ... that a key factor in the moral and economic success of democratic capitalism is ... its very *impersonality*, and that this impersonality is not cruel, but humane ... it is precisely the vast network of impersonal, economic actors, each serving the whole in a self-interested, but necessarily other-regarding way, that breeds success, and greater wealth for all.[124]

Such a notion of society and social obligations clearly would be anathema to many traditional conservatives, although it is worth noting that Gairdner received repeated, thunderous ovations from Reform delegates who heard his speech at the Saskatoon convention. Moreover, it is not uncommon to hear Reformers express the same atomistic view that they should not have to pay for such things as health care ('I'm never sick') or school tax ('I don't have children'). What is most worth noting, however, is Gairdner's rather tortured efforts to retain some basis of social obligation. Why, for example, are economic actors *necessarily other-regarding*?

Manning attempts to overcome the conflict between possessive individualism and social responsibility through a resort to religious notions of reward and punishment meted out in the hereafter. Those who give in to excessive self-indulgence and fail to meet their social obligations 'will be held accountable to God for their actions.'[125] But how are people to learn of their obligations towards self and others? For Manning and other Reform mentors, such as Byfield and Gairdner, the family is ultimately the chief social agent charged with this task:

If the first building block of democratic capitalism is the individual and his person-hood, the second is the family, which nurtures and creates this reality. Practically speaking, however, we could reverse this order, and say that the family is first, for it is in the bosom of the family that the crucial values, disciplines, and standards of individual behaviour are formed, and transmitted from generation to generation.[126]

The importance of the family and marriage for Reformers is mirrored in their personal lives and attitudes. Environics, for example, found that the Reform party was the only federal party, including the Bloc Québécois, whose percentage of support among married voters was greater than the percentage of support among unmarried voters.[127] Reform's own research indicates that 82 per cent of its members are married, a much higher percentage than found in the general Canadian population.[128] And Archer and Ellis's study of delegates to Reform's 1992 convention found that the vast majority (94 per cent) believed that family and community disintegration were responsible for many social ills.[129] Reformers clearly place a high value upon the role that marriage and the family should play in society. More fundamentally, many Reformers view societal problems as resulting from the state's usurpation of traditional family functions which now must be returned to the family.[130]

On the surface, it is hard to disagree with this analysis. Clearly, the state has taken over many functions formerly done by families. Arguably, however, this has occurred in response to broad societal changes. The family since the Second World War has been subject to numerous centrifugal forces, most of which originate in the dynamics – and ideology – of capitalism. As a collectivity, the emotional and psychological structure of which is the reverse of possessive individualism, the family is caught within the internal logic of modern consumer capitalism. This logic demands the intrusion into, and revolutionizing of, not only the narrowly defined instruments of production, but all social formations, including the family.[131] On this basis, Reformers' blame of the state for the problems of the family seems overly determined. Some Reformers are no doubt aware of this. But none seem willing to deal with the systemic pressures unleased by market forces to which they otherwise subscribe.

What lies ahead for an ideology whose separate elements, in many ways, are in fundamental contradiction with each other? In the United States, under Ronald Reagan, neo-conservatism provided a convenient umbrella for the creation of a coalition of interests during much of the 1980s. But, under George Bush, the coalition fragmented, particularly over the emotional issue of abortion. Will a similar fragmentation occur within Reform? Occasionally, the party's traditional conservative elements show signs of taking a more pronounced role. In November 1990 Reform assembled a 'women's work group' to examine such issues as employment and pay equity, family violence, and women's health care. Shortly thereafter, however, a number of party supporters, including several with strong ties to REAL Women, declared their objection to both study materials being used for discussion and what they viewed as a typically feminist construction of specifically 'women's problems.' Stated Mary Lamont, a founding member of both REAL Women and the Reform party:

I've been involved in the Reform party from the start and I've always thought of it as a strong conservative party. I thought it stood for a different approach. I expected it would do more on these family issues than give us feminist slogans, attitudes and agendas. The feminists get enough attention from the other parties.[132]

Under pressure, the controversial women's group folded. But the potential internal conflicts extend to other moral issues, in particular the abortion question. Ted Byfield believes that abortion has the greatest potential to split the Reform party. A reader's letter to the *Alberta Report* of 17 December 1990, regarding Stan Waters's defence of abortion rights, captures this conflict exactly:

Waters states he is personally supportive of the right of women to have an abortion and that the issue should [be] resolved through a referendum. He follows the pathetic populist Reform party line of succumbing to the tyranny of the majority ... [T]hese power-mad 'Reformers' would decide whether the preborn child lives or dies by the sentiment of a mob ...

Similarly, some of the party's traditional, small 'c' conservatives show occasional discontent with Manning's insistence upon strict liberal economic initiatives. The issue of farm subsidies is particularly divisive. So controversial was an executive proposal to end subsidies that Saskatchewan delegates to the Saskatoon Assembly in 1991 had the issue tabled, insisting that they could not sell their local memberships, or the voters, on such an idea. In response, Manning and Reform's executive oversaw a watering down of the proposal, stating that the party would not advocate Canada's unilateral abandonment of farm subsidies.

At a meeting in November 1991, however, Manning returned to the question of strict free market principles, suggesting that Canada would have to move to a market-driven system, that this would mean fewer farmers, and that those who remained would have to become accustomed to 'living with less.'[133] In apparent response to this statement, George Visser, a well-known Reform party member, suggested at a meeting of Christian Farmers of Alberta that Reform reverse its policies and guarantee to grain farmers floor prices but 'not call them subsidies.'[134]

The conflict between Manning and the farming community over solutions to Canada's agricultural problems escalated in August 1992 following a speech in which Manning stated: 'The brute truth is that the Prairie provinces can't support, with a high standard of living, the number of farmers they have been supporting.' The next day, both Charlie Swanson, president of Manitoba Pool Elevators, and Hartmann Nagel, president of the Alberta farm group Unifarm, condemned the speech, insinuating that Manning does not understand the problems of farmers.[135]

The controversy was still brewing when the party held its 1992 convention in Winnipeg. After much discussion, the party upheld a resolution backing – in the abstract – the removal of agricultural subsidies but otherwise supporting their continuance as long as other countries employed them. Moreover, the resolution also tied the party to reforming supply management at home in the interests of both consumers and domestic producers.[136] At least for a time, the motion seemed to heal the growing rift between the party's ideologues and its agrarian elements.

A similar potential split in Reform ranks appears to be arising around the issue of the universality of old age pensions. Reform's policy regarding income security and income support programs reads, in part, as follows:

The Reform Party supports the development of a family or household-oriented comprehensive, social security system administered through the income-tax system. This could replace many forms of social policy, such as the Family Allowance, Child Tax Credit, Spousal Exemption, Child Exemption, federal contributions to social assistance payments, retirement plans, federal social housing programs, day-care deductions, and minimum wage laws.[137]

In simple terms, Reform advocates non-universal social policies, including programs for the elderly, that are based on means tests. Perceiving such a proposal as a threat to their pensions, a number of seniors have withdrawn support for the party, urging others to beware of Reform's agenda.[138] Given the concerted anger which greeted Tory attempts to de-index old age pensions in 1985, and the fact that Reform supporters tend to be older than other party supporters, this controversy suggests the potential for yet another fracture in Reform support.

Perhaps the growing clash between the two ideological halves of the party was made most evident, however, by an incident at the Saskatoon convention. A guest speaker at the convention was Ruben Nelson, a 'futurologist.'[139] Nelson described in flowery and optimistic terms a new high-tech world where change was infinite and desirable. The better educated, younger, urban members of the party were highly impressed. They had seen the future, and it looked worth entering. By contrast, the older members seemed rather scornful of Nelson, viewing him as a purveyor of space-age bafflegab. Said one older woman: 'How has the party strayed so far from its original path?'

The potential for disputes within Reform raises questions of power, control, and decision-making within a populist party. As we have seen, Reform's growth has been accompanied by problems as well as benefits. On the one hand, in a few instances, the voice of the people has appeared as a shrill injunction to racism and bigotry. On the other hand, the voice has often seemed to be that of Preston Manning alone, uttering the same views on moral, economic, and political matters that he held twenty-five years ago when assisting his father in writing *Political Realignment*. What is the nature of this relationship between party and leader? How are potential conflicts resolved? How does the party leadership legitimate its policies and actions? In short, what is the nature and place of democratic populism within the Reform party?

REFORM AND THE POPULIST 'IDEAL'

Late 1991 and early 1992 saw the Reform party shaken by a series of expulsions and resignations. Some of these expulsions, such as those of

Gordon LeGrand and Wolfgang Droege, were understandable and acceptable to the membership at large. More damaging, however, were a number of incidents that seemed to call into question Preston Manning's, and the party's, commitment to genuine populist politics. Typical of the complaints heard were those of Sylvia Rehwald, a Reform party riding director in North Vancouver:

The party is functioning in a top-down manner – some say more so than the three major parties – and appears to be giving 'lip service' only to the ideals of direct democracy ... Head office insists the business of constituency executives is to build membership and warchests, period! I didn't join a political party to be a cheerleader–fund raiser only.[140]

In Reform's influential Wild Rose (Alberta) constituency, Dal Brown (the party's candidate in 1988), party secretary Vic Weibe, Jim McRae, and director Norm Gaskarth raised similar complaints. Said Gaskarth: 'A lot of people are frustrated – we're seeing the inevitable erosion of grass-roots politics into a smaller, more dominating group at the top.'[141]

In the wake of Manning's active recruitment of Ray Speaker to the party, Manning's earlier insistence that prospective party candidates be required to complete an apparently intrusive questionnaire, and later reports that Manning was actively seeking other high-profile candidates to run for the party, some party members complained that head office was attempting to manipulate the nomination process.[142] This feeling was made explicit in a letter to the *Edmonton Journal* by Charles Cripps, a Reform party candidate in the 1988 election:

It would appear that an organization akin to that of the Social Credit party under the direction of E.C. Manning is emerging, a strong and tightly-controlled nucleus equal or superior to any of the 'old boy' networks in the mainline parties ... I now have serious misgivings regarding the veracity and purpose of [Reform's] policy-makers (the national executive) as they steer the party into the future. After a great deal of soul-searching, I am obliged to relinquish my party membership.[143]

In short, many long-time party insiders complained throughout 1991 and 1992 that Reform had abandoned its populist roots, that Reform had become a tightly controlled organization manipulating its members into pursuing the aims of Manning and his Calgary clique.

There is considerable truth to these allegations. Reform's tightly controlled and centralized organizational structure reflects both Manning's deep reservations about populism and his own view of the role of leadership. Ted Byfield, one of Reform's most ardent supporters, describes Manning's ambivalence about populism in the following way:

It always seems to me that he [Manning] is always advocating something [populism] that is absolutely incompatible with his own instincts. Nevertheless, I think he is quite sincere in saying that he believes in populism. And I think that will likely get him into trouble before he's finished, too, because it isn't his [first] instinct. [Preston] is an authoritarian of the first order, [just] as his father was ...[144]

And again: 'It is not that [Preston Manning or other populist leaders] say things [about popular democracy] that they don't believe. They do believe it. It's just that [popular democracy] is not compatible with their own inclinations.' Concerned with the possible excesses of popular democracy, Manning thus places his faith in organizational and technocratic mechanisms that can 'tap and harness' the energy of populism. What are these mechanisms?

One of these is surely Manning's relationship to the membership. As Sydney Sharpe and Don Braid note: 'His bond with the party runs so deep that members accept inconsistencies from him that they simply would not tolerate in another politician.'[145] But what is the basis of this bond? At least initially, I would suggest that this bond is a by-product of the general homogeneity of Reformers' backgrounds and ideology. But Manning clearly also understands his supporters' world-view. Understanding their world-view, and possessing a knowledge of the narrative symbols necessary to enter into a dialogue with them, Manning is able to constrain the questions and, hence, the responses of Reform members to specific proposals. The GST provides a useful example.

Originally, the Reform party opposed the tax and gained a lot of support by doing so. Indeed, Stan Waters's Senate election in 1989 was in large measure attributable to Reform's opposition to the GST. Shortly after the GST's implementation, however, Manning reversed his promise to scrap the tax. His reason for deciding to support a tax which shifts the tax burden from business to consumers is understandable given Manning's emotional affinity and close relationship to the business community. Rather than admit this affinity, however, Manning's defence of his apparent 'flip-flop' has since taken a different and more saleable tact: the government needs money to pay the deficit. The deficit, defined by Manning as *the* critical issue hence becomes the means of defending the tax, while he ignores the general question of tax policy.

With the terrain of discussion delimited in this fashion – who, after all, is not concerned about the deficit? – Reform members accepted Manning's change of position.

In a similar manner, Manning and Reform's executive regularly limit the terms of debate. These constraints are not obviously coercive. Indeed, members are left believing that they have made the decisions. They in turn also presumably experience an enhanced sense of self-efficacy. The party is they, and they are the party. Thus, the party is legitimated in the eyes of the membership at the very instance of their ostensible control by the leadership. The party's populist image – 'control by the people' – is strengthened.

The GST incident is not the only example of this method of executive control. Perhaps the most glaring example occurred in Manitoba in early 1992. Despite possessing apparently favourable conditions for Reform – the CF-18 controversy still rankles and a large segment of the province is staunchly anti-bilingual – Manitoba is not yet a hotbed of Reform support. Nor have its few members been pliant to the dictates of Reform's Calgary executive. The autonomy of Manitoba members was made particularly apparent at the Saskatoon convention in 1991 when Winnipeg tax consultant George Van Den Bosch, who was later elected to the executive council, stood up and asked that the party declare its support for universality of health care. An obviously uncomfortable Manning immediately suggested that universality was 'implied' under Reform's policy of 'ensuring that adequate health-care insurance and services are available to every Canadian.'[146] Van Den Bosch's motion never got to the floor.

The growing dissent in Manitoba came to a head in late 1991 when discontented party insiders released a year-old memo to the press. The memo recommended replacing policy task forces with a member of the party policy committee headed by Manning. Confronted with the memo, Stephen Harper suggested that it was meant to protect the grass-roots members and head office from the 'unorthodox and most times extreme policy opinions' of members of the task forces.[147] Harper's explanation was plausible. Still, his comments did not address how the grass-roots were to be protected from an increasingly centralized head office.

The leaked memo provided Manning and Reform's head office with the excuse to silence an increasingly independent and vocally critical branch of the party. Claiming that Van Den Bosch was the source of the leak, and that other members of his St James riding were otherwise 'guilty' of arguing over who should pay for telephone bills, trying to set up their own provincial organization, and failing to put their efforts towards obtaining new members and money, Manning sent a letter to Manitoba's 5268 members asking them to vote on whether or not the four dissident members – Van Den Bosch, Lloyd Kirkham, Gary Cummings, and Herb Shulz – should be expelled from the party. In his letter, Manning revealed something of how he views the issues of power and control in populist parties.

The difference between a traditional party and a democratic populist party like the Reform Party is the manner in which internal discipline is exercised.

In a traditional party, internal discipline is exercised almost exclusively from the top down ... In a democratic populist party, internal discipline must be exercised 'from the bottom up' by the rank and file membership itself, in co-operation with the party leadership, caucus and national office.[148]

But the case of the 'Manitoba four' revealed even more. In particular, the incident suggests that Manning advocates direct or popular democracy not as a value in itself *but rather as a means of legitimating the actions taken by a leadership and therefore pre-empting dissent.*

Indeed, despite his frequent populist musings, Manning seems far more at home with the traditional idea of representative democracy than that of direct democracy. This is hinted at in Manning's own statements regarding what he perceives to have been the problem posed by dissidents in Manitoba and elsewhere: 'In each case, a small group of individuals claimed that their position on the issue in dispute was more legitimately representative of majority opinion within the party than the position of the executive council and leadership, which the membership itself had chosen through a party assembly.[149] In short, when faced with opposition, Manning falls back upon the argument that, during the period of his tenure, the leader's position on issues cannot be challenged seriously. Manning appears to view referendas as instruments used only under certain circumstances to support, and therefore legitimate, the actions that the leadership already wishes to pursue. The nature of these 'certain circumstances' is specific, that is, those occasions when no clear consensus is apparent or when the leadership would suffer a loss of legitimacy from acting unilaterally.

The Manitoba incident supports this conclusion. Why was a vote not required in the case of other expulsions from the party, as discussed above? The answer is self-evident. Unlike other expulsions from Reform, the members expelled in Manitoba were not demonstrably without support. They were well-respected members of the Manitoba community and had held lofty positions within the Reform party. They even were major financial contributors to the party. In short, the dissidents were credible. For this reason, Manning could not unilaterally expel them. *He needed the appearance of popular support to proceed with the expulsions.* But what if the Manitoba members had voted not to expel the dissidents? To pre-empt this possibility, Manning wrote to the members in such a way as to 'weight' the vote in the direction of his own preference. The letter stated the dissidents' 'crimes' (but no possibility of defences). Stated also was Manning's recommended 'sentence.' The membership, confused by accusations presented only through the media, were left with no formal or actual means of resolving the impasse except to accept Manning's recommendation.

The Manitoba incident suggests some of the pitfalls of plebiscitarian democracy, a mode of democratic practice that John Richards has suggested is a defining quality of right-wing populist parties.[150] Populism as more than just a style of leadership must involve the direct participation of all citizens or, in this case, members of a party, in a political discourse occurring within an 'ideal speech situation' designed to arrive at a rational decision based on the force of better arguments.[151] By contrast, plebiscitarianism too easily devolves into political manipulation by a governing party or a well-financed private élite or prestigious group of 'experts.' Under such circumstances, issues and solutions are distorted readily, leaving people with the semblance but not the substance of genuine democratic participation.

In stating the evidence that Reform's leadership manipulates its member's decisions, I hasten to refute any suggestion that Reform party members are dupes. Indeed, as we have seen, many are well-educated and capable people. It would also be wrong to suggest that Reform's 'masses' do not, in some sense, support Manning's positions and policies. The idea of populism, however, is its own form of intoxicant. Delivered by Manning, a man whose utterances Reformers appear too readily to accept at face value, the elixir is especially potent. In the politically unwise words of Stephen Harper: 'It's amazing what you can persuade [the membership] to do once you convince them that it's the leader who is telling them.'[152] The result is that many Reformers appear to latch on to Manning's particular diagnosis of Canada's problems and solutions without due consideration of the long-term consequences.

Having said this, it is unclear whether the practice of populism within

Reform differs significantly from that of previous populist parties, either right-wing or left-wing. Leaders are, by nature, people with strong views and a desire to persuade others as to the correctness of their views. Certainly, this was the case with both Tommy Douglas of the left-wing CCF/NDP and Ernest Manning of the right-wing Social Credit. The extent to which a populist party remains true to its democratic ideals ultimately depends upon its mechanisms for grass-roots involvement and the regular replacement of executive members, including the leadership. On this count, Reform's form of populism and perhaps the limitations of popular democracy within the party reflect the primacy of Preston Manning to the party. As one member is reported to have commented, concerning Reform's rise: 'It wasn't a group [Reformers] picking a leader; it was a leader [Manning] picking a group.'[153]

In the end, Reform's version of populism is not without substance. But it is also very much what Laycock has referred to as a style of leadership.[154] Even more important, in a political sense, the *idea of populism* is employed by Reform's leadership as a kind of organizational resource for the mobilization of other resources towards goals and policies long espoused by Manning and a small party élite.

The 'success' of a populist party is measured as much by its influence upon the given political culture of the day as by its electoral wins. On this basis, the Reform party has been markedly successful since its founding in 1987. By the summer of 1992, however, the Reform party stood at a crossroads. On the one hand, polls showed that Reform continued to have significant popular support, particularly in Alberta and British Columbia. On the other hand, this support had for some time shown signs of levelling off. Moreover, internal dissension over party policy and recurrent accusations of an authoritarian head office had begun to erode party morale and support even among Reform's most staunch supporters. Events, however, were about to present Reform with the opportunity to reverse its recent fortunes.

6. The Great Realignment

... a populist party is like sailing a ship: it makes headway only when the winds are blowing in its direction.

Preston Manning, July 1993[1]

Rarely do populist parties actually replace a member of the existing polity. More usually, when faced with a crisis of legitimacy, the dominant parties incorporate sufficiently some of the ideas and policies of the populist movement so as to reconstitute their ruling coalition. In rare cases, however, the underlying organic crisis might be so severe, the existing political parties so delegitimated, and the winds of fate so fortuitous that a populist party can rise to a position of real political power.

This chapter examines the critical events of 1992–3 that led to the final break-up of the Tory coalition put together by Brian Mulroney in 1984, and the party's replacement in much of English-speaking Canada by the Reform party in the federal election of 1993. Along the way, I detail the Charlottetown referendum of 1992 and the Reform party's part in that process. I look also at the subsequent resignation of Brian Mulroney, the rise of Kim Campbell to the office of prime minister, and the remarkable election of 1993 that saw Reform take 52 seats. Finally, I examine the Reform party's future prospects.

REFORM AND THE CHARLOTTETOWN ACCORD

On 26 October 1992 nearly 13.5 million Canadians voted in the largest referendum ever held in Canada. The Charlottetown referendum was the culmination of a process of hearings and meetings that had been going on since the failure of the Meech Lake Accord two years before.

In response to that failure, the Mulroney government brought forward in September 1991 its own proposals for constitutional reform. An all-party committee of the House of Commons and the Senate was then created to receive submissions. Despite internal problems, including the resignation in November of one of its initial co-chairs, the Beaudoin-Dobbie Committee, as it became known, was up and running by December and delivered a final report in February 1992. Meanwhile, throughout January and February a series of constitutional conferences, hosted by five regionally based research organizations, held meetings in Halifax, Calgary, Montreal, Toronto, and Vancouver. The reports coming out of the 'Renewal of Canada' conferences were completed in March and reflected the considerable public unease with the federal government's proposals.

At times, this unease bordered on extreme cynicism. The Meech Lake Accord had foundered, at least in part, on a lack of public input. And, although the Charlottetown proposals had come at the end of numerous hearings, such as those held by the Spicer Commission, there remained a widespread public belief that these hearings and conferences had been more show than substance. There was particular scepticism that the federal Tories were manipulating the public hearing process so as to sell such controversial concepts as 'asymmetrical federalism' and Quebec's 'distinctiveness.'[2] To the Tories' lack of credibility was added the problem that any proposal to change the constitution required provincial consent. Given Quebec's refusal since the Meech Lake débâcle to participate in constitutional meetings or even in intergovernmental conferences, the hopes for a constitutional deal were at best uncertain.

Informally, of course, meetings and discussions had gone on among the various capitals during this time. The federal government met separately with both the Quebec government and the other provincial premiers, acting as an intermediary. But this process, known to many, only increased public scepticism and hostility. Inside and outside Quebec, the view arose that a shell game was being conducted in which interests and ideals were being surreptitiously traded without public input.

It also was a time of a kind of 'phoney war.' While Ottawa bluffed that it would proceed unilaterally with amending the constitution, the provinces outside Quebec blustered. For its part, Quebec kept up a front of intransigent indifference to the interests and powers of its provincial counterparts.

But all the governments were also operating under a time restraint. In January 1991 the Quebec government had tabled its own response to Canada's constitutional crisis. The Allaire Report, named after Liberal MP Jean Allaire who chaired the committee that produced the document, called for a sweeping decentralization of powers to Quebec. It also set a deadline for English-speaking Canada's response: eighteen months. Quebec was committed to holding a referendum on a new constitutional deal or on Quebec sovereignty by the fall of 1992.[3] By May 1992 time was running out. Spring had come to most of Canada, but in the various capitals the governments were wilting.

In Quebec, premier Robert Bourassa was increasingly desperate for a constitutional offer that would preclude a sovereignty vote. To placate the mood of Quebec nationalists, including many in his own party, Bourassa believed that the offer would have to include at least the symbolism of the Meech Lake Accord's recognition of Quebec as a distinct society. It also would have to involve the substance of a distribution of powers to Quebec. But Bourassa – a lukewarm federalist with an aversion to outright sovereignty – was increasingly willing to settle for somewhat less, as long as he had an offer. Finally, in May 1992, Bourassa broke Quebec's self-imposed isolation and came west to talk to the premiers of the four western provinces, although ostensibly not about the constitution.[4]

Meanwhile, Mulroney continued his threats to place the federal government's constitutional proposals to a national referendum. For their part, the premiers of Canada's English-speaking provinces were increasingly frustrated with Quebec's absence from the table. The talks seemed to be going nowhere. Nonetheless, they agreed to begin holding multilateral meetings on the Constitution in April. Over the next few months, the constitutional train stopped and started. Sometimes it seemed as though it would crash altogether. Slowly, however, it made progress.

On 3 July the premiers of Canada's English-speaking provinces got together with the federal government's minister of constitutional affairs, Joe Clark, to try to resolve the latest constitutional impasse. By now, the premiers had decided more or less to ignore Quebec and fashion their own deal. Still, hopes were not high for success as talks began at the Pearson Building in Ottawa.

To perhaps everyone's surprise, however, the premiers announced on 7 July that a deal was in place. The deal provided for some redistribution of powers to the provinces and agreed to further discussions on trade barriers. But its most illustrious plank was agreement on the creation of a Triple-E Senate. The deal was immediately heralded, particularly in western Canada, as a major breakthrough.

Within days, however, the Pearson Accord was in trouble, attacked by various members of the federal cabinet. Finance minister Don Mazankowski and trade minister Michael Wilson, for example, disliked the agreement's failure to dismantle interprovincial trade barriers. But more important for the ruling Tories were the criticisms of its Quebec MPs who stated that the Triple-E Senate proposal was totally unacceptable to their province. Faced with a cabinet revolt, Mulroney declared following a cabinet meeting on 15 July that: 'Nothing is settled until everything is settled.' Everything, including the proposed changes to the Senate, was still on the table.[5]

It was an undoubtedly embarrassing moment for Clark whose authority – and acumen – as minister of constitutional affairs was openly questioned.[6] But it was an even more critical time for the Tory party, as the Quebec caucus, led by defence minister Marcel Masse and health minister Benoit Bouchard, demanded changes to the Senate, while western Tories, such as Alberta MPs Al Johnson and Louise Feltham, and BC MP David Worthy, insisted that the Senate deal was untouchable.[7] Already down in the polls, Mulroney's historic coalition between Quebec and Alberta was in imminent danger of collapse.

Amid growing tension, Brian Mulroney announced a few days later that the premiers, including the premier of Quebec, and the leaders of the two territories, would get together in Ottawa on 18 August to try to carve out a constitutional deal. From the start, the meeting seemed destined to repeat the grueling and secretive ordeal that had led to the failure of the Meech Lake Accord in 1990. Over five days, often filled with high tension and emotion, Mulroney and the premiers talked, denounced, and cajoled. Mulroney was at first adamant in his refusal to accept the Senate proposal. 'You should all have to deal with a Triple-E Senate,' he declared.[8] The federal government also wanted changes on interprovincial trade. Quebec needed 'distinct society,' while the other premiers needed senate reform. The Territories and native peoples had certain demands. Gradually, however, the sides began to compromise.

Finally, on the night of 22 August, Canada's political leaders emerged to announce that a deal had been struck. The proposed deal included specific sections on parliamentary reform, native rights, federal spending powers, interprovincial trade barriers, the creation of a Canada clause in the Constitution, and the future creation of new provinces.[9]

In particular response to western and Newfoundland demands for a Triple-E Senate, the deal called for a new Senate. It would be equal, with each province having six senators and the territories one. It would also have more effective powers than the old Senate, at least in some areas. Notably, the Senate would have an absolute veto on new taxes on natural resources. On questions of French language or culture, a double majority of total senators and of francophone senators would be required. On other Commons' bills, a simple majority of Senate votes would force a joint sitting of the Senate and House of Commons to resolve the impasse. The method of election to the Senate, however, whether by legislative appointment or direct popular election, remained unsettled. Moreover, some provinces, such as Nova Scotia and British Columbia, suggested that at least some seats in the new Senate should be set aside for women and natives. Finally, the deal called for an increase in House of Commons seats, 18 more to Ontario and Quebec to offset their Senate losses and 4 more for British Columbia and Alberta, bringing the total number of seats to 337 from the current 295. Quebec was also guaranteed a minimum of 25 per cent of Commons' seats.

The deal recognized the inherent right of native people, including those off reserves, to self-government. The meaning of self-government, however, was left undefined. Other related issues, such as land claims and how self-government would be financed, were left to future negotiations.

The deal significantly decentralized powers to the provinces. For example, federal money spent on housing, recreation, forestry, mining, tourism, urban affairs, and manpower training would be turned over to any province that so desired. Provinces could also seek more control over immigration and regional development, and could opt to run new cost-sharing programs using federal money. Culture was similarly provincialized, although the federal government retained control over national institutions. Federal financing of programs in such areas as highways and education was set over for future negotiations.

The deal included an agreement in principle to eliminate interprovincial trade barriers between provinces and on a long list of exemptions. No timetable or mechanism for elimination, however, was determined.

The deal also proposed a preamble to the Constitution, known as the 'Canada clause.' The clause expressed the fundamental values and characteristics of the country, including parliamentary democracy, respect for human rights, racial and sexual equality, equality of the provinces, and recognition of the native right to self-government. It also contained a clause recognizing Quebec as a 'distinct society.' The Canada clause also committed the federal government to the development of the English minority in Quebec and the francophone minority outside of that province.

Finally, the deal stated that the Yukon and Northwest Territories would be able to negotiate one-on-one with the federal government for provincial status. The existing provinces, however, would need to approve the amending of the Constitution to admit them as provinces and the granting of a full complement of senators.

On 28 August Canada's leaders met in Charlottetown, PEI – where the Fathers of Confederation had met 125 years before – to sign the Charlottetown Accord. In truth, the patchwork agreement did not fully meet anyone's demands. Quebec did not get all the powers it wanted. The federal government did not achieve its desired goal of creating interprovincial free trade. The desires of the hinterland provinces for a Triple-E Senate similarly were not met. But could any deal have been struck that would have unequivocally met the demands of the participants and the Canadian public at large? This seems doubtful. In the end, the deal was a typical Canadian compromise among significantly disparate interests.

There remained the question of how the accord would be ratified. A legislative vote? This would have been legal, but since Meech Lake people had become more adamant about having a say in political decisions, and politicians were increasingly willing to defer to this demand. Moreover, Quebec, British Columbia, and Alberta were bound by legislation to hold a referendum on the constitutional agreement. This opened the possibility that a different question might be asked in different parts of the country. A clear response by Canadians to the agreement was needed. Thus, for the third time in history, Canadians went to the polls to vote in a nation-wide referendum.

In the days immediately following the agreement's signing, the Canadian public seemed strongly to support it. An Angus Reid poll conducted on 31 August showed that the newly signed agreement had 58 per cent support nationally, distributed evenly across the country. As Canada's various cultural, political, and economic leaders began to line up in support of the deal, YES supporters had every reason to believe that the agreement would be ratified by Canadians.[10]

Yet, within a couple of weeks, the Charlottetown Accord was in trouble. A subsequent poll conducted by Angus Reid on 22 September showed that national support for the deal had fallen to 42 per cent, with a particularly sharp drop in the West. In British Columbia and Alberta, support had fallen to 34 per cent, levels from which the YES side never recovered. In Quebec, support had similarly fallen to 38 per cent.

Another Angus Reid poll conducted on 15 October, eleven days before the referendum, confirmed that the deal was in significant trouble. National support had fallen to 40 per cent and defeat was likely in several provinces.

What happened to the accord's support? There is no easy answer. After all, it seemed to have everything going for it. Besides its initial public support, fuelled by a not insubstantial constitutional ennui, the accord was also backed by much of Canada's political, economic, and cultural élite. All of Canada's elected political leaders, including Ovide Mercredi, the grand chief of the Assembly of First Nations, supported the deal, as did the federal Liberals and NDP, and most provincial opposition parties. Influential former politicians, such as Peter Lougheed and William Davis, spoke in support of the agreement. Much of Canada's business and financial establishment, led notably by the Business Council on National Issues and the Royal Bank, also came on side. The YES side also received support from some environmentalists (for example, the Green party), some non-native ethnic groups, and various leaders in the cultural community, such as June Callwood and Pierre Berton.[11]

If these endorsements were not enough, the YES side also benefited from enormous financial support. The federal government spent an estimated $10 million to $12 million dollars in directly promoting the accord. It spent perhaps another $10 million on defence department, Canada 125, and Buy Canada commercials which, though not directly linked to the referendum, nonetheless invoked patriotic themes.[12]

By contrast, the NO side presented a more variegated group. As expected, Parti Québécois leader Jacques Parizeau and Bloc Québécois leader Lucien Bouchard opposed the accord. They were joined, albeit for different reasons, by former prime minister Pierre Trudeau, Manitoba Liberal leader Sharon Carstairs, and her counterpart in British Columbia, Gordon Wilson. Similarly, Ted Byfield, Ruben Nelson, former Liberal cabinet minister Eric Kierans, and Elijah Harper opposed the accord, as did, somewhat unexpectedly, the National Action Committee on the Status of Women. They were joined by several left-wing intellectuals, such as Philip Resnick, as well as numerous right-wing organizations, such as the Northern Foundation and the National Citizens' Coalition, the COR party in New Brunswick, the Christian Heritage party, and, of course, the Reform party. The accord was also opposed by numerous fringe elements, including former BC premier Bill Vander Zalm, his former numerologist, Judd Cyllorn, former WCC leader Doug Christie, and an expelled member of Reform, Roger Rocan. In short, although the NO forces were not an unimpressive group, they certainly lacked the heft of the YES side.[13] Why, then, was the accord rejected?[14]

First, the initial support for the accord found in the Angus Reid polls was 'soft.' A secret poll conducted for the federal government a week after the referendum was announced, but only released to the public after the vote, showed that the NO side had already taken the lead in Quebec, and that Canadians elsewhere did not trust the first ministers who had negotiated the deal and did not believe claims that the accord would end the constitutional crisis.[15]

Secondly, the accord was too large and complex. As such, it was open to many divergent views and interpretations. For people in Quebec, for example, the deal did not go far enough in granting the province new powers. There was also concern over the accord's provisions for native self-government. In the abstract, Quebecers' support for native rights is generally higher than Canadians living elsewhere.[16] But Quebecers were concerned that the accord might lead to a sizeable area of the province being turned over to aboriginal control. Finally, many in Quebec believed that inserting the 'distinct society' clause into the Canada clause rendered the former ineffective in protecting Quebec culture.

By contrast, many Canadians outside of Quebec voted NO in the belief that the accord granted too many concessions to Quebec. The guarantee of 25 per cent of the House of Commons seats in perpetuity was denounced as infringing on the principle of representative democracy. The guarantee was particularly disliked in those provinces experiencing rapid population growth, such as British Columbia, whose distribution of seats lagged behind its population.

After their initial euphoria, many supporters of the Triple-E Senate, such as Bert Brown, decided that the accord did not go far enough on Senate reform. In particular, the legal text seemed to suggest that the proposed Senate might not have the opportunity to block a future National Energy Program.

There were other criticisms. Right-wing elements disliked the proposed social charter, believing it would give the courts the power to enforce social programs and their expenditures. Left-wing groups contended the accord did not go far enough in protecting womens' and minority rights. Opponents, in general, denounced it as incomplete and complained that they were being asked to sign a blank cheque. This criticism was given support by the failure of the YES side to produce a legal draft of the accord until 9 October. The legal draft was altered in some respects from the 28 August agreement.[17] Perhaps more importantly, however, the slowness in providing a final document allowed the NO side to argue that there was, in fact, no actual 'deal,' in the contractual sense, but rather a loosely conceived document, bound together by bailing wire and hope.

In short, the accord was too many things to too many people, and not enough to others. While some viewed the document as dangerously decentralizing, others viewed it as too centralizing. It either threatened individual rights or did not go far enough in protecting collective rights. It gave too much to Quebec and too little. In the end, the Charlottetown Accord was simultaneously both too explicit for a constitutional document and too vague.

Thirdly, the accord was defeated because the YES side was not entirely unified, credible, or coherent in presenting its case. In many instances, political leaders faced internal party divisions over the accord which they had signed. This internal dissension was most noticeable in Quebec where Jean Allaire and much of the Liberal party's youth wing broke publicly with Robert Bourassa. Bourassa's influence was also sabotaged from within in mid-September when the leaked tape of a telephone conversation between one of his constitutional ministers, Diane Wilhelmy, and an unnamed bureaucrat revealed that some Quebec government officials felt that Bourassa had 'caved in' to the English premiers in making the deal. The 'Wilhelmy affair,' as it was coined, no doubt influenced many Quebecers, already lukewarm on the accord, to vote against it.

In Alberta, similar internal discord within the ruling Tory party, combined with sinking support in the polls, led to Don Getty's resignation as premier midway through the campaign. Even where dissension was absent, however, the accord's promoters were ineffectual. In British Columbia, Mike Harcourt's defence of the accord was confused and haphazard. In Ontario, Bob Rae's support was staunch but lacklustre. Only in Newfoundland did a provincial leader substantially sway voters towards acceptance of the accord. But Clyde Wells's unfettered support was late in coming and did not greatly influence voters beyond the confines of the island. The other provincial leaders took a generally low profile during the campaign.

Among federal leaders, the performance of Liberal leader Jean Chrétien and NDP leader Audrey McLaughlin provided modest support for the accord. But, in the main, neither leader was prominent in the campaign. Such was not the case, however, with Brian Mulroney. By the fall of 1992, much of Canada's political establishment had lost considerable legitimacy in the eyes of the public. But no one had lost more credibility than Canada's prime minister. Mulroney's partisanship, combined with an excess of rhetorical flourish, had long ago soured many voters. Yet, in typically hyperbolic fashion, he declared at the start of the referendum campaign that he expected the 'enemies of Canada' to attack the deal.[18] Later in the campaign, in Sherbrooke, Quebec, Mulroney theatrically ripped up the accord as if to symbolize what would happen to Canada if it were rejected. The Canadian public, inured by years of Mulroney's crisis politics, gave a collective snort of derision. An Angus Reid poll conducted during the referendum campaign showed that Mulroney's performance was massively influential, but in a negative fashion. While he had won 16 per cent of voters to his YES side by his performance, Mulroney had also driven fully 34 per cent into the NO camp.[19]

By comparison, Pierre Trudeau was a major positive force for his 'side' in the referendum campaign. While not specifically mentioning the accord, a Trudeau essay attacking Quebec nationalism was published in *Maclean's* and *L'actualité* magazines on 28 September. Quebec's nationalist élite would never be satisfied, said Trudeau. Instead, he called for Canada's leaders to show 'a bit of courage' and stand up to Quebec's blackmailers.[20]

Trudeau followed this up on 2 October with a much-publicized speech at Maison Egg Roll, a Chinese restaurant in Montreal. In typical scorched-earth fashion, Trudeau took apart the accord clause by clause, excoriating its signators and sympathizers. The accord was an attack on individual rights, he declared. Moreover, it would never satisfy Quebec's nationalist elements. YES side supporters were both livid at, and dismissive of, Trudeau's remarks, but the damage had been done. The same Angus Reid poll that measured Brian Mulroney's negative impact during the referendum showed that, by contrast, Trudeau's performance had influenced 40 per cent of voters to vote NO while only 13 per cent were contrarily persuaded to vote YES. Particularly striking was Trudeau's influence in English-speaking Canada, notably the West.[21] Despite the anger directed at Trudeau's Liberal governments by westerners during his tenure in office, his tough stand against Quebec's nationalist aspirations had always won him support in that region and continued to do so throughout the referendum campaign.

In the end, the problems of a patchwork agreement, cobbled together in haste by a discredited federal government and its leader, combined with general public disenchantment were too much baggage for the accord to carry. The Charlottetown Accord went down to defeat in Nova Scotia, Quebec, and all of the western provinces, as well as the Yukon. Nationally, 54 per cent of Canadians voted against it.[22]

What was the Reform party's role during the referendum campaign? And how did the campaign affect Reform's overall political support?

The announcement of a constitutional referendum in August 1992 could not have come at a better time for Reform. Since 1990, the party had steadily lost support in the national polls. Although a July Gallup poll showed that 39 per cent of Canadians viewed Reform as a serious contender to win the next federal election, this belief was not being translated into political stock.[23] In August, as the referendum deal was struck, Reform support stood at only 11 per cent nationally. Even in British Columbia and Alberta, the party trailed behind the Liberals and NDP.[24] Thus, as the referendum debate got under way, some party supporters wondered if Meech Lake II – as they quickly dubbed the Charlottetown Accord – could rekindle the party's sagging fortunes.

No sooner had the referendum campaign begun, however, than rifts appeared in the party. Reform's YES side was led by Richard Anderson, a member of the party's national executive.[25] Anderson and others contended that the party should support the accord because (a) it would probably pass, at least in English-speaking Canada; and (b) it wasn't altogether demonstrably a bad deal. Indeed, the agreement did contain provisions for a substantially reformed – if not Triple E – Senate.

On Reform's NO side stood party officials such as Stephen Harper, who stated shortly after the accord was announced that it was 'entirely unacceptable' and 'a tragic mistake.' Said Harper: 'All our members are opposed to it and Albertans will defeat it [in a referendum].'[26] The NO side urged Manning to attack the accord immediately and aggressively because (a) most Reform supporters opposed it; (b) it might not pass in any case; (c) opposing it, no matter the referendum outcome, would solidify Reform's right-wing constituency; and (d) the deal was not demonstrably good enough.[27]

In the midst of this internal conflict, a third option emerged, proposed by research director Tom Flanagan. The strategy called for Reform to take the high road in the referendum. 'We will ... point out the deal's bad and good points,' said Flanagan, adding that the bad outnumbered the good. 'But we will not be drawn into name-calling sessions about who is and who isn't an enemy of Canada.'[28]

Within days, however, this strategy was abandoned. On 10 September Manning announced the party's decision: Reform was strongly opposed to the Charlottetown Accord. The deal was badly flawed, said Manning. Indeed, it was not a final constitutional agreement but rather a 'consensus report' laced with 'vague statements of principle' requiring additional 'political accords' to be negotiated between the various levels of government.[29]

Manning would later state precisely four more reasons for Reform's opposition. First, the accord did not, in the party's view, resolve the sovereigntist threat in Quebec. Secondly, it further divided Canadians 'into such categories as French-Canadians, English-Canadians, aboriginal-Canadians, and other Canadians, rather than advancing equality of all Canadians.' Thirdly, the agreement weakened 'a reformed Senate by allowing it to be overridden by an enlarged House of Commons on all subjects other than French language and culture, and perhaps natural resource taxation.' And fourthly, because it gave every province a veto over future institutional changes, it made future reform of the Senate, House of Commons, and Supreme Court 'virtually impossible.'[30]

Manning's criticisms of the accord were legitimate. But another, more political, reason undoubtedly played a part in Reform's change of strategy: the party had become aware that the accord was increasingly in trouble throughout Canada. Early on, Manning himself apparently considered supporting the deal, but changed his mind as time went by and after receiving advice from the party's American pollster.[31] By 10 September party officials seem to have been in a hurry to get on side with the public's imminent rejection of the accord, an observation supported by Manning's hasty announcement of the party's decision even before receiving the results of its own membership referendum on the accord.[32]

Thereafter, Reform's performance digressed more and more from the 'high road.' In his speeches, Manning urged his followers not to attack personalities or any part of the country in opposing the deal.[33] But midway through the referendum campaign, Reform launched a series of television ads and speeches in which the Charlottetown Accord was referred to as 'the Mulroney deal.' This rather transparent attempt to

234 Of Passionate Intensity

render the agreement guilty by association with an unpopular leader was condemned by many people, even within the party.[34] Resorting to the same inflammatory threats made by the accord's supporters, Manning also suggested that the accord, if passed, would hurt the Canadian economy.[35]

By mid-October, it was apparent that the Charlottetown Accord would be defeated. Despite, however, the predictions from both inside and outside the party that the accord's defeat would translate into support for Reform, this did not happen. In September a Gallup poll showed Reform with 8 per cent national support, down from August. The party rebounded marginally to 9 per cent in October and, after the referendum vote, to 11 per cent in November.[36] In general, however, Reform had not received the expected 'bounce' in popular support. What went wrong?

First, unlike the vastly more disliked Meech Lake Accord of two years previous, public opinion on the Charlottetown Accord was mixed. And Reform mirrored this general uncertainty. A survey conducted by the party during the early days of the campaign showed that, while 40 per cent of Reform's supporters opposed the accord, 37 per cent supported it, while the remaining 23 per cent were uncommitted.[37] Moreover, as we have seen, the party's executive was itself riven with conflict over the party's position on the agreement. In short, the referendum divided Reform nearly as much as it did the country, making it difficult for Reform to stake out an unambiguously 'winning' position.

Secondly, these divisions were exacerbated by Reform's performance during the referendum. Since the party's inception, Reform had attempted to run as the consummate outsider, the 'non-political' political party. This was the essence of the inverted logic that Manning conveyed to voters during the referendum when he said: 'If you vote YES, you are following the politicians. If you vote NO, you will be leading them.' He thus implied that he was not a politician.[38]

But the referendum damaged this image. Long-time supporters like Elmer Brooker, chair of EBA Engineering Consultants Ltd., and Jim Gray, president of Canadian Hunter Exploration Ltd., noted the change in Reform. 'They're turning into a political machine and I don't like political machines,' said Brooker.[39] Said Gray: 'One of the Reform party's great strengths was they were going to be a breath of fresh air. They were going to do things differently. They were going to rise above the thrust of partisan politics. Canadians were ready for that. And then here comes this Mulroney Deal.'[40]

Brooker and Gray were not alone in their criticisms. An Angus Reid poll conducted after the referendum showed that Manning's disapproval rating among voters had risen from 34 to 44 per cent.[41] Given that Preston Manning's credibility has always been the Reform's greatest asset, this was a particularly unwelcome result, reinforced by one perhaps portentous footnote: although the Charlottetown agreement was passed in only one Alberta riding, that riding was the one in which Preston Manning was running in the next federal election.[42]

Days after the referendum vote, and apparently linked to divisions in the party, Reform's head office was purged. Several key party insiders, including communications manager Laurie Watson and speech-writer George Koch were fired, while Tom Flanagan stepped down from his position as policy director, although he remained an adviser to the party.[43] Rick Anderson had earlier left the party's advisory committee because of his support of the YES side.[44]

Ironically, the Reform party, which had risen to prominence at least in part as a result of discontent with the Meech Lake Accord, seemingly had fallen at the hands of its successor. The referendum vote, for which Reform itself had so long lobbied, had opened wounds within the party and damaged its leader's credibility. The party had also expended considerable scarce financial and other resources in waging the NO campaign, even while alienating some in the business community whom Reform had hoped to win to its side.[45]

Even more ironic, however, the mere holding of the referendum, combined with general public fatigue, sidelined the Constitution as a major plank in Reform's political platform.[46] For Canadians, the referendum seemed cathartic, cleansing them of their anger at politicians, pundits, and assorted experts. No doubt, constitutional issues would again rise to the fore one day. But in the weeks and months following the referendum, all talk of constitutional matters disappeared, replaced by concern over the economy, the forthcoming general election, and the Stanley Cup playoffs. Canadians would no longer abide talk about the Constitution.

Over the following months, Reform's fortunes continued to slide. In December national support fell to 7 per cent.[47] A confidential internal report produced during this period showed that Reform might win as few as eleven seats in the West and none in Ontario.[48] Gone seemed to be the hopes of only a year previous that the party was on the verge of a major electoral breakthrough. With the referendum off the political table, and the Tories and Liberals now adopting much of Reform's rhetoric and policies, party support seemed increasingly dependent once more on people's visceral dislike for Brian Mulroney. And, then, suddenly, that playing card also disappeared.

REFORM AND THE CAMPBELL INTERREGNUM

'I've done my very best for my country and my party, and I look forward to the enthusiasm and renewal only new leadership brings.'[49] With those words, Brian Mulroney announced his resignation as prime minister of Canada in February 1993.

His resignation had been expected for weeks. In the aftermath of the referendum vote, a Gallup poll revealed that 54 per cent of Canadians wanted Mulroney to quit.[50] Rumours that Mulroney would soon be leaving office were fuelled by other polls suggesting that support for the Tories would rise under almost anyone else.[51] Buffeted both within and outside his party, Brian Mulroney bowed out of Canadian political life.

Mulroney's resignation seemed to offer the Tories the possibility of political resurrection. His too easy charm, his too obvious desire to be liked by the powerful, his inflammatory rhetoric and blatant partisanship had long since made him an untrustworthy, even comic, figure to much of the Canadian public.[52] By early 1993, the social base of Tory support had narrowed almost entirely to the corporate sector.[53] With his departure, the Tories' brain trust hoped that under a new leader a coalition of centre right-wing forces might again be persuaded to support the party.

By contrast, Mulroney's resignation could not have happened at a worse time for Reform. By early 1993, the sun appeared to be rapidly setting on the party's electoral hopes. Eastern expansion had brought Reform few benefits and, indeed, some embarrassing moments as right-wing extremists joined the party. Dissension was still rife in Manitoba over Manning's expulsions the previous year. Support was down even in Reform's heartland provinces of Alberta and British Columbia. Moreover, the party had gained no bounce from the referendum decision. Reform also was finding it increasingly difficult to distinguish itself from the Tories who had already stolen much of its platform, Reform's only argument being that it could be trusted more than the Tories to enact conservative policies. And now Mulroney, the source of so much of Canadian's venom (and Reform support) had left the scene.

In the immediate wake of Mulroney's resignation, a number of leadership candidates seemed likely.[54] But one name quickly moved to the forefront in the search for a new Tory leader and prime minister: defence minister Avril Phaedra 'Kim' Campbell.[55] Born in Port Alberni, BC, in March 1947, Campbell is a lawyer with training in economics and Russian affairs. Witty, intelligent – she is a member of MENSA – and sophisticated, but with a reputation for arrogance, Campbell was elected to the BC legislature in 1985. In 1986, she ran for the leadership of the Socreds but lost to Bill Vander Zalm. She subsequently quit her position as an MLA in Vander Zalm's cabinet over the latter's decision to cut funding to abortion clinics. In 1988, she entered federal politics and won election in the riding of Vancouver Centre. Known as a 'red Tory,' Campbell soon became justice minister where she oversaw controversial legislation dealing with the abortion issue and gun control. Then, in 1992, Campbell moved to the defence ministry.

Many Canadians were initially intrigued, if not altogether impressed, with Campbell. Her popularity soared throughout the country. Indeed, within days of announcing her candidacy, reports suggested Campbell had already locked up sufficient delegate support to ensure a leadership victory. Talk quickly turned to a Campbell 'coronation.'

Of course, not all Tories wanted Campbell as leader. Her status as divorcee and her lack of children were both openly frowned upon by some traditional conservatives within the party. In comments that seemed aimed particularly at her gender, Campbell was also labelled by some as 'unstable.' Finally, her competent but uneasy French and lack of roots in Quebec made some delegates fear that a Campbell victory would spell Tory defeat in that province.

But Campbell seemed to have the 'right stuff' to make voters forget Mulroney and go on to beat the Liberals. Moreover, there seemed no one to challenge her seriously. Three of the leadership candidates opposing her – Patrick Boyer, Garth Turner, and Jim Edwards – were backbenchers simply positioning themselves for what they hoped would be a later cabinet post. A fourth candidate, John Long, was not even an MP and dropped out before the June convention. Only Jean Charest, the remaining candidate, was a worthy opponent for her. Only thirty-four and already a proven cabinet minister, the personable Charest added the only real excitement to the leadership campaign. Indeed, in the days and weeks immediately leading up to the convention, it was Charest and not Campbell who had the momentum, a fact reinforced by polls showing that a Tory party led by Charest – but perhaps not one led by Campbell – had a good chance of defeating the Liberals in a federal election.

Campbell's rapid fall in the public's estimation and Charest's climb were fuelled by several factors. Certainly, Charest performed very well in the run-up to the convention. Articulate and bilingual, he was clearly the favourite of most Quebec Tories for whom Campbell was a relative unknown. By contrast, Campbell's own performance during the leadership campaign was decidedly uneven. Occasionally too clever by half, Campbell also displayed a ready penchant for putting her foot in her mouth.[56] Finally, Campbell's personal and political record did not sit well with many in the former Tory heartland of the West, as indicated by Ted Byfield's editorial in the *Alberta Report* of 22 March 1993. In the article, written before the leadership convention, Byfield listed four reasons why Reform hoped the Tories would choose Kim Campbell as leader:

First: The whole Tory establishment backed her, proving she represents the Same Old Crowd, still in charge.
Second: She has already served notice she will put Quebec first ...
Third: She's promoting a radical feminist agenda ... And two divorces won't endear her to people trying to make marriages work and raise children.
Finally, she is recognized as a red Tory, meaning soft on spending cuts.[57]

In the end, Byfield and Reform got their wish. Campbell's delegates held firm, providing her with a close victory over Charest on the second ballot.

In the immediate aftermath of the convention, however, it seemed that Campbell's victory would not be the kind of boon to Reform that Byfield had predicted. Indeed, initial polls seemed to suggest just the opposite. Gallup's 24 June poll found that the Tories had risen to 36 per cent, trailing the Liberals at 41 per cent. By contrast, the NDP stood at 10 per cent, and both Reform and the Bloc Québécois at 6 per cent. After three years of political free fall, the Tories at last had something to build on. Reform, meanwhile, continued to look like a spent force.

In the spring, rumours abounded that a shortage of funds had resulted in staff lay-offs and poor morale. Staff director Gordon Shaw denied the rumours, but did admit that eighteen of fifty-seven staff had been let go.[58] The party's internal problems escalated in July with news that Rick Anderson had been appointed campaign manager. Anderson, who had left the party's advisory committee the previous fall over his endorsement of the Charlottetown Agreement, was viewed as 'too centrist' by many in the party, including Tom Flanagan.[59] In August, Flanagan was fired as policy adviser. Now outside the party, Flanagan began complaining that Reform had abandoned its conservative roots in order to attract Ontario voters. Termed 'ridiculous' by Reform's election campaign chair, Cliff Fryers, Flanagan's comments were nonetheless supported by many Reformers, including Ted Byfield.[60] In his *Alberta Report* editorial of 23 August 1993, Byfield advised Reform to return to certain hard-line conservative positions, such as ending official bilingualism and grants to 'special interest' groups, and removing the right to strike of federal workers providing essential services. Byfield contended that such a platform would polarize the Canadian electorate, resulting in the right-wing vote flocking to Reform and ensuring the party's victory.

In the summer of 1993, however, such a prediction seemed more wish than genuine hope. The Tories' selling of Kim Campbell was under way. Night after night, Canadians were treated to an endless 'photo op' as Campbell flew from one side of the country to the other, kissing babies, lighting barbecues, and pre-testing election promises. In speeches throughout July and August, Campbell announced a series of policies, including a new 'get tough' policy on crime, increased protection for the Canadian publishing industry against foreign publishers, an end to patronage appointments, and a more streamlined cabinet and parliament.[61] This was followed in August by Campbell's announcement of cuts in a controversial helicopter contract.[62] The series of policy announcements were meant to appeal to various interests – fiscal and moral conservatives, socially concerned liberals, cultural nationalists – but its packaging was based heavily on Reform-style politics, and its roots lay in Reform's backyard, Alberta.

Less than a year before, Don Getty's Alberta Tories had been given last rights by many political observers. But, when Getty resigned in the fall of 1992, the party renewed itself, picking Ralph Klein as leader. The popular Klein, a former news reporter and mayor of Calgary, quickly moved the Tories to the right to capture the province's Reform supporters. But Klein's most politically astute action, coming in the face of much public anger at politicians, was to eliminate MLAs' pensions. It was probably the decisive act ensuring that the Tories won the election in June.

In part, Campbell's Tories copied policy from Klein's government.

More fundamentally, however, the federal Tories attempted to focus the upcoming federal campaign upon Campbell, whom polls indicated was the most popular of the federal party leaders, in much the same fashion that the Alberta Tory campaign had revolved around Klein.[63] In Alberta, the large election posters had said 'Ralph's Team'; soon, across the country, campaign posters arose with the name 'Kim' writ large.

As the summer went on, however, the law of diminishing returns began to affect the phoney campaign. In particular, criticisms increased of the cost to taxpayers, estimated by the Liberals at $1.5 million, of this unofficial campaign.[64] Still, the road show had fulfilled its mission. It had showcased Campbell, allowing the Tories to put some distance between the party and Mulroney. A 16 August Gallup poll found that Campbell herself had the highest recorded approval rating (51 per cent) since the days of Lester Pearson. Gallup's monthly voting poll, released on 19 August, showed that the Tories had closed to within four percentage points of the leading Liberals (36 to 40 per cent). The Tories were ready – or so they thought – for what would turn out to be perhaps the most remarkable election in Canadian history.

THE ELECTION OF 1993

The Tories entered the 1993 election in a mood of optimism. Over the following weeks, however, the party's hopes dropped like a stone, while the steady if plodding Liberals consolidated their lead. In the end, the Tories suffered the worst electoral defeat ever handed a federal government in Canada, taking only 2 seats (16 per cent of the vote), and were replaced on the right wing of Canadian politics by the Reform party, which took 52 seats (18 per cent of the national vote, 26 per cent outside Quebec). Likewise, the left-wing NDP won only 9 seats (7 per cent of the vote), not enough to retain official party status in the House of Commons, while a separatist party, the Bloc Québécois, took 54 seats (13 per cent of the national vote, 48 per cent within Quebec) in becoming somewhat incongruously Her Majesty's Loyal Opposition. Only the return to power of the Liberals, who captured 177 seats (41 per cent of the vote), suggested a certain continuity with the past. It was a result that, only weeks earlier, few pundits would have predicted. What happened?

It is often said that opposition parties do not win elections, but that governments lose them. In part, the 1993 election bears this out. The Tories' defeat was a long time in coming. Since 1990 polls had repeatedly shown the party to be in serious trouble. That year, the collapse of the Meech Lake Accord and the onset of the recession had rent severe holes in Brian Mulroney's electoral coalition. The holes had only grown larger since, filled in Quebec by the Bloc Québécois and in the West by the Reform party. When Mulroney stepped down in early 1993, Tory support rose slightly but remained low. It rose again under Campbell, who offered Canadians something that she termed 'new politics.' But party support remained shallow. In the end, Campbell's inability or refusal to repudiate past Tory policies, her own disastrous performance throughout the campaign, the party's lack of a solid base of support in any region, and the organizational breakdown of the fabled Tory 'machine' combined with Canadians' economic concerns to ensure that the Tories would suffer not just defeat, but virtual annihilation. In turn, the magnitude of the Tory collapse allowed for the kind of fundamental realignment of Canadian politics that had been in the offing for nearly two decades and that the Mannings, père et fils, had for so long promoted.

Election campaigns are about hope. The major concerns of Canadians entering the 1993 election were unemployment, the preservation of social programs, and the growing deficit and debt.[65] But on the first day of the campaign, Campbell announced that Canadians could not expect any respite from unemployment until at least the year 2000.[66] The next day, Campbell compounded the felony by seeming to suggest that social programs would be cut.[67] A week later, Campbell declared that she could not give details on how she would cut the deficit because of inconsistencies in her own government's bookkeeping.[68] By the end of the first two weeks, the Tory campaign was already headed downhill.

The third week only greased the Tory slide. On 23 September Campbell stated that the election was the 'worst possible time to have [a] ... dialogue' on her government's plans for changes in social programs. 'This is not the time, I don't think, to get involved in a debate on very, very serious issues.'[69] The remark was a double-edged sword, cutting into Tory support in either way it struck. Either Campbell was being evasive, hiding, as the NDP put it, a 'secret agenda,' or she was insulting the intelligence of Canadians.[70]

Increasingly pressed by critics demanding to know how she planned to deal with the deficit without cutting social programs, Campbell finally revealed her plan. But the budget, hastily put together 'on the back of an envelope' as Jean Chrétien remarked, did not slow the Tories' slide into political oblivion. A Gallup poll released on 25 September showed that the Tories had dropped to 30 per cent support, down from 36 per cent the previous month. The main beneficiaries of this drop, however, were not the Liberals, who themselves had dropped to 37 per cent from 40 per cent in August. The real story was the Bloc Québécois, which had more than doubled its support in Quebec to 10 per cent since the beginning of the election, and the Reform party, which had risen from 7 per cent nationally to 13 per cent during the same period. The latter was gaining support particularly rapidly in the Prairies and in British Columbia, where it registered 26 and 27 per cent support, respectively.

The poll's results, released just before the televised debates in early October, shook the Tories. Alarmed at the trend, Campbell's policy advisers apparently urged her to go on the offensive against Chrétien.[71] But the ensuing debates merely highlighted in stark fashion the Tories' central dilemma. Surrounded by the other party leaders, Campbell found herself under constant attack, not from the Liberals, but from the leaders of the two breakaway elements of the former Tory coalition, Lucien Bouchard and Preston Manning. By contrast, Jean Chrétien stood back from the fray looking calm and statesmanlike. The debates, like every other element of the Tory campaign, were a disaster. More importantly, they hurried a decline in public perceptions of Kim Campbell. Until the debates, Campbell's popularity had continued to 'prop up' Tory support. But an Angus Reid/Southam poll conducted shortly after the debates found that public perceptions of Kim Campbell's leadership had declined markedly, while perceptions of Jean Chrétien's leadership had risen.[72]

By the fifth week, the election was all but over. A *Globe* poll conducted between 11 and 14 October showed Liberal support had risen nationally to 40 per cent, while Tory support had slipped to 22 per cent. Reform, meanwhile, had risen to 16 per cent, and the Bloc Québécois to 13 per cent. But the Tory humiliation was not over.

Indeed, week six of the campaign was perhaps the worst for the Tories. Beset by internal dissension, desperate in the extreme, Tory headquarters okayed the use of television advertisements featuring contorted pictures of Jean Chrétien's face, palsied as a result of a childhood illness. Accompanying the pictures were voices asking such questions as: 'Does this look like a prime minister?' The ads offended virtually everyone, even several Tory candidates, who quickly and publicly denounced them. After a rather perfunctory and ineffectual attempt to defend the ads, Campbell had them withdrawn from circulation.[73] But the damage was done.

The next day was no better. In an interview published in *La Presse*, Campbell criticized both Brian Mulroney and former finance minister Don Mazankowski. She also seemed to attack her former chief rival for the leadership, Jean Charest, upon whose profile the party was dependent for success in Quebec. In response, transport minister Jean Corbeil angrily demanded a public apology. A few days later, Isabel Bassett, a Tory candidate in the Toronto riding of St Paul and wife of TV magnate John Bassett, openly called upon Kim Campbell to drop her 'contrived strategies' and 'speak from the heart.' Private infighting was now public. The remaining days of the campaign were marked by bickering and the beginnings of a process of laying blame for the political defeat.[74]

By the seventh week of the campaign, Tory candidates began to admit openly what the polls were showing: the Tories were going to lose, perhaps badly. Campbell's own popularity – all that had propped up the Tories before the election – had plummetted to 17 per cent, a drop of 25 per cent since August. The fight was now to retain official opposition party status.[75] Some extreme right-wing Tories, such as Don Blenkarn, began openly to suggest a coalition with the Reform party.[76]

The Tories had self-destructed. In consequence, Jean Chrétien's Liberals won the election almost by default. Aided by lowered expectations, Chrétien proved to be a better campaigner than many pundits anticipated. His self-deprecating humour, combined with the repeated message of his love for Canada, a country of 'generosity, sharing and tolerance,' touched the hearts of Canadians seeking something deeper and more respectful than the insincere and empty platitudes of the Mulroney years. As a party, the Liberals pursued a minimalist campaign. Stung by the repeated epithet of 'tax-and-spend liberals,' Chrétien's party made few promises. And where there were potential controversies or contradictions, these simply slid away in the face of Chrétien's calm assurances that a Liberal government would restore 'the good old days.'

The Liberal victory was aided by the collapse of the NDP. The unpopularity of NDP governments in Ontario and British Columbia weighed heavily on the federal party. But the federal NDP suffered also from long-simmering organizational problems, the inability of Audrey McLaughlin to attract political converts, and an election strategy that did not address the immediate concerns of voters. Like generals preparing to fight the last war, the NDP fought the 1993 election, as in 1988, on the issue of free trade. While most Canadians viewed negatively both the Canada–U.S. Free Trade Agreement and the impending North American Free Trade Agreement, they were equally leery of the NDP's proposals to pull out of the deals.[77] Finally, the NDP fell victim to the same fate suffered by many third parties when elections polarize. Early on, many Canadian voters decided to throw out the Tories. But, faced with the possibility that the first-past-the-post electoral system might allow the Tories to garner some seats, many traditional NDP voters chose to vote Liberal. The NDP were squeezed out.

In the end, residual discontent with the Liberals, combined with the collapse of the Tories and NDP, provided the opportunity in the West and Ontario for Reform's stunning success in the 1993 election. Reform's success was not immediately ensured as the election began. Indeed, as we have seen, the months leading up to the election saw Reform divided by months of internal dissent, falling donations, and slumping morale. Moreover, the move to the right of both the Tories and Liberals left Manning as the campaign began with only the lame hope that voters would distinguish between his party and 'burned-out reformers' (the NDP), 'reluctant reformers' (the Tories), and 'phoney reformers' (the Liberals).

Like the Liberals, however, Reform was able to ride previous discontent with the Mulroney government and current disbelief in the Campbell administration to success. Throughout the election, Reform stuck to its key conservative issues: the debt and deficit, law and order, immigration, and government accountability. Manning's personal performance during the campaign was low key but solid. Unlike the other major parties, Reform ran a stripped-down campaign. Manning took commercial flights, sitting in the economy section of the plane, or travelled by charter bus. He spoke quietly, making no extravagant claims. He was approachable. In the words of columnist Norm Ovenden, it was a 'just folks' campaign style, and it worked.[78]

In an election dominated in part by 'debt hysteria,' Reform received a particular electoral boost in late September when the *Globe and Mail* announced its unqualified support for Reform's deficit elimination plan.[79] 'Quite simply,' said the *Globe and Mail* in its editorial of 23 September, 'Reform is the only party that has yet shown a credible commitment to getting control of the national debt: a commitment made credible by its detailed 'zero-in-three' plan to halt the growth of public debt.' Reform hurriedly printed off thousands of copies of the editorial.

As Reform's political fortunes rose, so too did its finances. Midway through the campaign, newspaper reports stated that the party was hauling in nearly $1 million per week. The party suddenly had enough money to open a national office and to put extra money into radio ads.[80] By the end of the campaign, business leaders in Alberta who had previously supported the Tories were firmly behind Reform.[81]

Gradually, too, Reform began to expand its electoral base. While Reform's core support remains right-wing, disenchanted Tories it seems clear that the party was able to make inroads among previous Liberal and even NDP supporters.[82] Similarly, the party seems to have drawn reasonably well from all classes and groups. During the course of the campaign, even the long-established gender and age differences that previously marked Reform support were lessened.[83]

Still, Reform's campaign was not flawless. Manning's repeated statements that a Reform government would allow the provinces to introduce private health care, extra-billing by doctors, and user fees cost the party votes.[84] While Reform no doubt garnered support from fiscal conservatives with its stand on the deficit and debt, the party also probably lost support from those whose major concern was unemployment. Manning's monetarist rhetoric that elimination of the deficit – in three years – would eventually have a stimulative effect seemed particularly thin gruel to Canada's 1.6 million unemployed.[85] Finally, in the last weeks of the campaign, Reform was hurt by the statements of John Beck, its candidate for York Centre. Beck's remarks about the need for 'Anglo-Saxons' to get involved in politics and statements contending that immigrants were taking jobs from 'the gentile people' reinforced the public image that Reform was a haven for bigotry and intolerance.[86] Under pressure, Beck withdrew from the election race and was later suspended by the party. Nonetheless, the incident harmed Reform's image, particularly among ethnic minorities in the Toronto area, no doubt costing the party some votes.

All in all, however, Reform ran a smooth and effective campaign, allowing the Tories to self-destruct while simply placing itself in position to pick up the pieces. When the House of Commons reopened to a new session of parliament in early 1994, Deborah Grey was no longer alone.

PROBLEMS AND PROSPECTS: THE FUTURE OF REFORM

The election results of 1993 signal, at least in the short term, the collapse of a hegemonic consensus in Canada. The type of Canada that will eventually emerge, however, is unclear. The only certainty is that the shape of this 'new Canada' and the future of Reform are inextricably linked.

The Reform party has come a long way since its formation in 1987. In its brief history, it already has had a great deal of influence in shaping Canada's political landscape, placing into debate such previously taboo subjects as bilingualism, multiculturalism, and the universality of social programs and bringing into common political usage such phrases as 'the Triple-E Senate,' 'referendums,' 'recall,' and 'initiatives.' Reform can also take much of the credit for increased public concern about Canada's national debt. Today the Reform party has fifty-two seats in the House of Commons, a large and active membership, and considerable support among the general public. The party is financially solvent and is likely to get increased financial support in future, particularly from the business community. In short, Reform shows every sign of being a force to be reckoned with for years to come.

But the Reform party also has changed in the years since the Vancouver assembly. Though still on the right of the political spectrum, the party has shifted closer to the middle. Along the way, it has lost, or at least subsumed, many of the fringe elements upon whom the party relied in the early days.[87] In particular, western regional issues no longer dominate the party's agenda.[88]

What are Reform's future prospects? The first session of the new parliament saw Reform disappoint many of its followers. As Manning promised, Reform brought a certain level of civility to the House. In part, however, this civility seemed reflective of the inexperience and uncertainty of its rookie MPs. The party scored well initially in its symbolic efforts to cut the perks and privileges of public office. But even this victory was soon tarnished when it was revealed that Manning himself, unbeknownst to many in the party, had secretly been receiving a fairly large annual expense account since at least 1989.[89] More importantly, Reform faces several critical obstacles in its efforts to solidify and enhance its position in the Canadian political system.

Many of these obstacles are internal to the party. First, Reform remains somewhat torn by its two ideological halves, traditional small 'c' conservatism and classical liberalism. The resultant conflict continues on occasion to strain Reform's relationship with certain of its core constituencies, notably farmers and the elderly.[90] Secondly, the party is heavily influenced and supported by pro–big business elements, such as the National Citizens' Coalition.[91] This influence is likely to increase as corporate money seeks out a new champion to replace the Tories, placing further strains upon Reform's espousal of populist ideals.[92] Thirdly, despite executive efforts to curtail extremist elements within the party, Reform is still viewed by many as providing a haven for intolerance.[93] Fourthly, despite the broadening of Reform's demographic base during the election, many of the party's policies remain controversial and unlikely to attract support from certain groups, such as ethnic minorities and women.[94] Thus, there may be a limit to Reform's potential for support. Fifthly, although it made substantial inroads into central and eastern Canada during the election, Reform's base remains largely western. Indeed, Reform's support base is even more circumscribed, with forty-six of its fifty-two MPs coming from Alberta and British Columbia.[95] Without a significant breakthrough elsewhere, Reform may experience the same fate as previous western regional parties. Finally, there is Manning himself. It is true that Manning is the primary reason for Reform's success. Ironically, however, Manning's leadership also may limit Reform's future growth. Manning's folksy persona plays better on the hustings than it does in the House of Commons. Moreover, some party members have begun to bridle at the tight leash on which Manning has thus far kept the party. In June 1994, growing dissent within the caucus led to the naming of a shadow cabinet, effectively reducing Manning's power and elevating the status of some Reform MPs. It was a significant victory for the dissenters over Manning and his core supporters. but how the new relationship between Manning and his caucus members will evolve remains to be seen.[96]

A far greater limitation to Reform's prospects, however, is its lack of control over future events. Governing parties fall either as a result of their own mistakes or because of economic or political events largely beyond their control, but for which they are nonetheless held responsible. Reform's future electoral chances appear to depend on one of three possible scenarios. The first is that the Liberals replicate the excesses of the Mulroney and Trudeau governments. This scenario seems unlikely to occur. Immediately after taking office, the Liberals made good on several symbolic election promises, including cancelling the controversial helicopter deal and a perhaps even more controversial privatization of Pearson International Airport in Toronto. In other ways, Jean Chrétien has signalled a different style of government: smaller, less presidential, less ostentatious, less arrogant. The adoption of a few of Reform's other policies – more free votes, for example – would further blunt Reform's appeal.

The second scenario – economic misfortune – is slightly more possible. The Canadian economy is slowly showing signs of recovery. Nonetheless, the recovery is at best bumpy. Unemployment remains high, and the debt and deficit continue to drag on the economy. Reform's future is tied to an ideological debate over what is the best way to deal with Canada's economic problems. On one side of the debate are the Liberals who, in their first budget after coming to power, moved to the right, proposing a revamping of social programs and emphasizing training.[97] Opposed to this 'go slow' approach are the even more radical right-wing policies of Reform's erstwhile provincial counterpart, Ralph Klein's Alberta Conservatives. Klein's policies of privatization and deregulation, among other things, amount to the most concerted effort made since the Bennett regime in British Columbia in the early 1980s to institute neo-conservatism in Canada.[98] They also mirror what a federal Reform party government would do in Ottawa. How well the Klein government is perceived by Canadians elsewhere will greatly determine Reform's chances of future success at the federal level.

The third scenario – political misfortune – perhaps offers Reform its greatest potential for success. The election of the Parti Québécois in September 1994 has set the stage for a potentially divisive referendum on Quebec sovereignty. The outcome of such a referendum vote is uncertain, its uncertainty complicated by the life-threatening illness, in December 1994, of popular Bloc Québécois leader Lucien Bouchard. In the months leading up to the referendum, emotions are likely to run high both in Quebec and elsewhere, fuelled by provocations from the Parti Québécois in the province and the Bloc Québécois in Ottawa. If Canadians outside Quebec respond to these provocations with disrespect and intolerance for the Quebec people, as occurred at the flag burning in Brockville in 1989, Quebecers may be driven, albeit reluctantly, to vote YES in the referendum. In the constitutional crisis that would follow, Reform would once again be able to stake out its territory as the defender of English Canada's interests.

In the long run, Reform appears to be in a good position to supplant the Tories as Canada's major conservative party. Certainly, the Tories are in tough straits. Jean Charest, who took over as leader when Kim Campbell resigned, has evident appeal. But lacking official party status, the Tories receive little political coverage. Moreover, the party is heavily in debt. By contrast, Reform provides a credible, vocal, and visible home for discontented Tories. The next election will tell whether the Tories can rebound or whether Reform will emerge as the new champion of the right wing in Canada.

The 1993 election is now history. In the years that follow, there will be much speculation about what this past decade has meant to Canada. Some will suggest that Canada is now embarking on uncharted and dangerous waters. Yet others, following in the footsteps of Goldwin Smith, will see in recent events the final stage of English-speaking Canada's destined marriage to the United States. Still others will note that the current conflicts threatening Canada are not new, that, in Canada, history does repeat itself, if not as farce, at least with a great persistence. There is not now, nor has there ever been, any certainty of Canada's future. Rather, Canada always has been a matter of will over sense – or cents. Canadians in every generation have always had to redefine themselves and their country, knowing that a failure to do so means a final surrender and absorption into the American empire. This is especially true today.

As for the Reform party, it is now safely ensconced in Canadian history. The party arose out of the general crisis of welfare state liberalism and out of specific disenchantment with the Mulroney Conservatives. In its train, the Reform party gathered up fringe elements, traditional conservatives, and laissez-faire liberals until it was of sufficient mass to shatter the cosmological certainty of Canadian politics.

7. The 'Problem' of Populism Revisited

*A populism for the twenty-first century would bear little resem-
blance to the new right or to populist movements in the past ...*

Social philosopher Christopher Lasch[1]

This book has addressed two fundamental questions: Why do populist
parties arise? What factors influence the ideological orientation of such
parties? In this chapter I examine insights garnered from the case of the
Reform party and how these insights, in turn, help answer these questions. In doing so, I return to the populist debates discussed in chapter
one. Finally, I also go beyond these debates to examine briefly the state
of populism in the late twentieth century, particularly the limitations of
its right-wing variant.

REFORM AND THE POPULIST DEBATES

One easily can recognize the place of the Reform party in several classification schemes proffered by theorists of populism. Reform fits
rather comfortably into Margaret Canovan's subspecies of political
populism known as 'politicians' populism,' defined as a manipulative
appeal to 'the people' used by politicians to integrate and legitimate
political support.[2] The Reform party is even more recognizable in John
Richards's and David Laycock's respective categories of 'right-wing'
and 'plebiscitarian' populism.[3]

   According to Richards, right-wing Prairie populism in Canada tended
(1) to mobilize along regional rather than class lines in its fight against

outside ('eastern') interests; (2) to limit its critique of capitalism to the banking system; (3) to view 'big government' as the central problem; and (4) to eschew participatory democracy in favour of plebiscitarianism. Reform conforms to the last two criteria. It also fits the first criterion, if we substitute 'Quebec' for 'eastern' interests. To the extent, however, that Reform lacks even a limited critique of capitalism, the party seems to diverge (perhaps significantly) from Richards's depiction of past populist movements.[4]

Reform is fairly congruent also with Laycock's description of a 'plebiscitarian' populist party. Like Richards's 'right-wing populism,' Laycock's plebiscitarian variety tended (1) to mobilize along regional lines in opposition to central Canadian interests, and (2) to espouse a limited view of democracy, often confined to such practices as plebiscites and referendas. But Laycock's 'type' includes also two slightly different characteristics: (3) a tendency for rule by a technical élite; and (4) a tendency to present its critique of society as radical and even morally justified. The contours of the Reform party are recognizable in each of these characteristics.[5]

To paraphrase Marx, however, the theorists have categorized populism, in various ways; the point is to explain it. Particularly, how does this study of Reform, and the historical-sociological framework used to analyse the party, help us to explain the rise of populist parties? The theory employed here to examine the rise of the Reform party possessed six basic elements. These elements may be summarized as follows:

1 Social and political stability, in the final instance, results from the capacity of a dominant class (or classes) to form hegemonic alliances with otherwise subordinate social elements or fragments of these elements.
2 Political parties are both the practical embodiment of these hegemonic alliances and the major instrument for their construction.
3 Over time, significant changes occurring in the ideological, economic, and political spheres of society may result in an 'organic crisis,' in the course of which the previous system of political alliances begins to unravel.
4 During this period of unravelling, the existing political order is delegitimated among certain historically specific social elements.
5 If the existing political parties are unable and/or unwilling to reincorporate these latter ('vulnerable') elements, within an unspecified period of time, thus setting them free; and if these elements

share sufficient historical, ideological, territorial, and demographic commonalties and characteristics by which to identify themselves as 'a people'; and if further, there exist within this group actors with sufficient organizational resources and leadership skills to articulate to the freed social elements a new vision of the social and political order: then a populist party may arise.

6 The type of populist party that emerges (that is, either right-wing or left-wing) is contingent on the interplay of several factors, both endogenous and exogenous to the territory in which the movement arises, the primacy and directional influence of any particular factor being, moreover, historically specific. Endogenous factors include the region's historically existing political culture which informs the party's definitions of the crisis, including the nature of the people/power bloc antagonism; the class configuration of elements lacking a current political allegiance; the fortuitous timing of economic crises; and the degree of legitimacy of organizations and potential leaders capable of constructing a counter-hegemony. Exogenous factors include the world-historical dominance of either right-wing or left-wing ideology at a given moment.

The logic of this theory directed my researching of this book in certain ways, in particular: to examine recent economic, political, and ideological crises affecting Canada's dominant hegemony; to determine, specifically, the impact of these crises upon existing political alliances in western Canada; and, where fragmentation of these alliances occurred, to determine the structural, ideological, organizational, and historical factors shaping the potential for a reconfiguration of alliances, either within the existing polity or through a new political alternative. The value of this theory, and the research agenda arising from it, can be measured if set against other theories of populism, beginning with C.B. Macpherson's theory of the petite bourgeoisie.[6]

Based on traditional Marxist theory, Macpherson contended that Social Credit in Alberta was the product of a homogeneous petit bourgeois class structure. Although his particular arguments regarding Social Credit support have now been refuted, Macpherson's general theory of petit bourgeois support for populist parties still possesses a powerful charm.[7] This book specifically examined the applicability of Macpherson's theory to the case of Reform.

As a whole, the petite bourgeoisie was found no more likely to support Reform than any other party. But a careful reading of Macpherson's original work suggests a slightly more nuanced theory. In short, Macpherson seems to suggest that a fundamental split exists within the petite bourgeoisie between its agrarian and non-agrarian elements based on organizational factors, and that these might in turn result in differential mobilization into populist movements.[8] Since Reform's incarnation, farmers have been significantly overrepresented within the party. By contrast, the non-agrarian petite bourgeoisie is no more likely to support Reform than any other party. Still, since farmers make up only slightly more than 13 per cent of Reform supporters, class position alone provides only a partial explanation of Reform support.

Based on assumptions gleaned from Richard Hofstadter's characterization of populist movements as reactionary and nativist, the ethnic and religious backgrounds of Reform's executive, members, and supporters also were examined.[9] The results showed that Anglo-Saxon Protestants are more likely to support Reform than any other party, a fact that may be linked to what I have termed a 'peculiar' type of Anglo-Canadian nativism. Again, however, ethnic and religious variables did not fully account for the rise of Reform.

Indeed, a number of socio-demographic characteristics were found to vie for importance with class, ethnicity, or religion in explaining Reform party support. Age (older), gender (male), location (rural), and income and education (higher than average) were also found to somewhat describe Reform party supporters. The evidence is thus congruent with Ernesto Laclau's observation that '[i]ndividuals are the bearers and points of intersection of an accumulation of contradictions, not all of which are class contradictions.'[10]

Nonetheless, structural factors alone proved insufficient to explain the Reform phenomenon. Rather, this study reveals significant independent effects for certain attitudinal and ideological values. In particular, Reformers tend to reflect significantly strong and negative attitudes towards multiculturalism, gender equality, and distinct status for Quebec. They also tend to be highly politically alienated.

The relationship between structure and ideology is, of course, complex. Few theorists would now support a theory of populism that reduces political phenomena to class alone.[11] Nor would a simple inclusion of other structural variables seem sufficient to flesh out such a theory. At the same time, it is hardly satisfying to surrender to the anarchy of ideas ungrounded in daily experience.[12] I would argue, in-

stead, for a theory that recognizes a certain, though never total, independence of ideology from structure; that recognizes, moreover, that
the distance between them is contextually and historically contingent.

The same indeterminacy must be applied to economic factors. Specifically examined in this book was the adequacy of relative-deprivation theory in explaining the rise of Reform.[13] The evidence generally
supported the theory. Reform initially rose and has continued to be
strongest in Alberta and British Columbia, the two western provinces
whose economic situations were most volatile during the 1980s. By
contrast, the party has had much less success in Manitoba and Saskatchewan whose economies are significantly poorer but less volatile
than their western neighbours. As an aside, this link of economic and
political fortunes may bode well for Reform's future chances in Ontario, should that province's economic decline continue.

But people must still evaluate the causes of economic events and,
although relative-deprivation theory is embedded with social psychological assumptions, it seems insufficient to explain the nature of these
evaluations, the pattern of political expressions arising out of this formulation, or why populist parties – if they arise – might take on a
particular political orientation. In short, relative-deprivation theory alone
does not provide an adequate theory of populist mobilization.

This study also provides support for resource mobilization theorists.[14] As I have shown, many of Reform's policies are almost indistinguishable from those of the right-wing fringe parties of the early 1980s
that failed. Indeed, numerous members of these parties support Reform. Unlike these earlier parties, however, Reform is blessed with an able
and respected leader, Preston Manning, who possesses immediate name
recognition, particularly in western Canada. Secondly, the party has a
highly functional organizational structure defined by centralized control over policy. This organizational structure provides Reform with a
public profile that generally is coherent, while allowing it also to exercise some control over those fringe elements that might otherwise damage the party's reputation among moderate voters. It has also enabled
Reform to mobilize, swiftly and efficiently, more financial and human
resources than its erstwhile right-wing predecessors.

Yet political organizations do not just arise out of thin air. Organizational theory can provide us with insights into the differences between
successful and unsuccessful political movements and parties – the
dynamics of mobilizing discontent. It cannot tell us, however, the causes
of this discontent, why it was not channelled into other, existing politi-

cal parties, or the possible parameters of mobilization open to the new party.

If this study has pointed to the incompleteness of previous theories of populist mobilization in general, it also has pointed to the inadequacy of previous examinations of the Reform party in particular. Murray Dobbin's account, for example, alternates between factual analysis and murky accusations of right-wing intrigue.[15] Likewise, although Sydney Sharpe and Don Braid's depiction of Reform is less strident than Dobbin's in tone, and better in dealing with the party's historical and ideological context, it too falls short of an adequate account of its origins.[16] In particular, because both of these accounts are atheoretical they cannot tell us anything about the populist phenomenon. By contrast, I have attempted in this book to weave a dialectic between a general theory of populism and the specific circumstances of Reform. The result has been a number of insights into Reform that, in turn, bear upon populist parties in general.

Previous theories of populist parties have tended to depict populist parties as discrete entities, arising on the fringes of political life. Both my theory and the evidence presented here refute this assertion. Far from being products of the 'strange and extreme,' my study of Reform supports the notion that populist parties are, by and large, made up of elements at the core of social and political life. This is not to say that some members of the political fringe do not support Reform. But Reform's strength and legitimacy are products of broad-based support, particularly within the West's political and economic establishment.

The results of my study also differ somewhat from depictions of Reform as merely a group of recalcitrant Tories. To be sure, the majority of Reformers were, in their immediate past political life, members of the Conservative party. But my study suggests that, at least in part, Reform also provides a home for some discontented former Liberals. Many of Reform's business supporters, in particular, were lapsed Liberals before they were Tories. One conclusion deriving from this finding is that political support, once dislodged, might enter a prolonged period of volatility.[17]

In a broader sense, the study has justified my general theory that populist parties are a natural result of the fragmentation of political coalitions and their subsequent reconfiguration. But the study also points to the importance of illusion at the heart of political coalitions. All social formations of a non-primary type, whether organizations, religious groups, or nations, are, to some extent, what Benedict Anderson has termed 'imagined communities.'[18] This is no less the situation for political parties, which are coalitions of interests founded, in large measure, on the illusion that those interests are compatible. For both the leadership and the various fractions within a party, the problem always exists of pursuing conflicting interests, even while preserving the appearance of internal solidarity. Increasingly, Reform – like Canadian society as a whole – exhibits the strain produced by this conflict.

On the one hand, Preston Manning and the party have attempted to draw, as in the party's constitution, a line around a fairly broad definition of 'a people' united in opposition to the other 'mere' political parties and the 'special interests' that would harm Canada. On the other hand, variances in power among different fractions within Reform, have increasingly resulted in some interests being advocated either by the leadership or through party policy to the detriment of other segments of the party (for example, free enterprise versus agricultural subsidies).

Ironically, the strain of maintaining the illusion of a commonality of interest is increased when, as in the case of Reform, a party is led by a principled ideologue such as Manning. While ideological purity clarifies, it also tears at a party's imagined sense of political solidarity. In this sense, one of the chief mechanisms working against the continued sense of mission, of quasi-religious fervour, that often infuses nascent populist parties may be their own success. For, as they gain support, or at least have hopes of future success, a populist party must choose between becoming a political party, much like the others, or retaining a voice of political purity.

Concerning the trajectory of political parties, I would like briefly to address the question: 'Was Reform destined to be right-wing?' To a large degree, the answer is yes. Given the party's lack of organic development, its rapid move from protest group to organized party, one might agree with the statement: 'It wasn't a group picking a leader; it was a leader picking a group.'[19] Manning, and many others with influence and power within the party hierarchy, appear to have bided their time, waiting for the moment when they could call upon the residual political culture of Alberta and British Columbia in forming a true 'social conservative' party, as Manning's father had envisioned so many years before.

Political events of the last few years, including the rise of the Reform Party, however, also raise questions concerning the role of ideology on party support. While I agree with those who contend that people are motivated by a fusion of ideas and emotions, I remain unsure how many of Reform's supporters are necessarily right wing. For example, many Reformers appear to be no more enamoured of big business than of big government. Their limited concentration, however, upon a few perceived 'problems' (the deficit, immigration, bilingualism), and their adoption of right-wing solutions to address them, may be more a testament to the persuasive capacities of Preston Manning, Reform's organizational apparatus, and the failure of the left wing to articulate a politically saleable alternative, than to any necessary and unshakable world-view. In short, it seems plausible that, as one theorist has suggested, 'populism can be wedded to any ideological program.'[20] Ultimately, the many manifestations of populism, including that of Reform, are the product of an ideological struggle, albeit one that takes place under real historical, political, and economic circumstances.

Finally, this examination of Reform raises some additional questions about the nature of populism at this stage of the twentieth century. In particular, I would like to conclude with some comments on current differences between left-wing and right-wing populism.

RIGHT-WING AND LEFT-WING POPULISM

Historically, populist movements have arisen in response to a perceived threat to 'the people' and their social order. In practice, however, the definition of 'the people' and the ultimate source of the threat have been open to ideological interpretation; hence, the wide variations in the populist experience, sometimes constrained under the terms 'left' and 'right' populism.[21] Ideologies always edify and illuminate; they also ignore and obscure. I am interested here in the latter, or what I would term the blind spots in traditional left- and right-wing populist movements.

For those on the left, the blind spot has been an unreasonable faith in the state and government as bulwarks against the illegitimate powers of the capitalist economy. For those on the right, in contrast, the blindness traditionally has taken the form of an irrational separation of politics and economics into separate spheres, circumscribing and delimiting the meaning of democracy while placing undue faith in the supposedly 'natural' workings of the market.

Ideologies die hard. The last hundred years have been sobering for the left. In the face of an obdurate reality marked by Stalinism, in all its forms, not to mention recurrent recessions, countless wars, poverty, overpopulation, environmental catastrophes, continued racism and sex-

258   Of Passionate Intensity

ism, the left has undergone a series of sometimes excruciating ideological debates. Some of these debates resulted in mere rationalizations and justifications, a kind of re-establishment of a faith that Marxism was correct and that, eventually, reality would catch up with theory.

By the 1960s, however, many on the left had begun to question sincerely their suppositions and beliefs. This questioning resulted in the New Left. In contrast to the Old Left, an important element of the New Left was its radical rejection of the state in general, and 'big government' in particular, as a mechanism for change. Contrary to their oft-made assertions, neo-conservatives are not alone in recognizing the limitations of state control and intervention. Many on the left have long concurred with criticisms of the type made by Reform supporters that the state is too large, too bureaucratic, and frequently inefficient. In short, the scales have fallen from the eyes of most left-wing supporters.

But if the left wing has – sometimes reluctantly – come to see its own ideological limitations, the same cannot be said of the right wing. No doubt this continued blindness redounds in large measure to the intoxication of apparent victory. For these are indeed heady days for the right-wing. Communism, the zenith of left-wing totalitarianism, the arch-enemy of individualism, private property, Christianity, and the marketplace, lies prostrate and bloodied. The victory of right-wing forces under the umbrella of 'neo-conservatism' is, at first sight, convincing.

Behind the scenes, however, in the opposing dressing-room, a different reality is apparent. Although the right wing has managed to stay on its feet long enough to raise its gloves in triumph, it too is now severely bruised, a victim in large measure of self-inflicted blows. The worst blows have come from an unrelenting recession that has brought massive unemployment and increasing disparities of wealth to many western industrialized nations, particularly those countries – Britain, the United States, and, to a lesser extent, Canada – that have adopted most fervently the neo-conservative economic agenda.[22]

For over two decades, neo-conservative icons, from Hayek to Friedman to Gilder, have reified and deified private property and 'the market' as the basis of freedom, democracy, and justice. Now that the neo-conservative heaven has arrived in the aforementioned countries, why do they look, metaphorically, like bombed-out suburbs, their landscapes pitted by massive unemployment, rising bankruptcies, and increasing poverty? Why do more and more police guard the pearly gates, more and more bars cover the holy windows? Economists, politicians, journalists – and sociologists – may give different, complex answers to these questions, but they all come down to one thing: when freedom and justice themselves are commodities, a few people will 'own' disproportionately more than the rest.

One of the profound ironies of right-wing populism is that its supporters espouse popular democracy while clinging to a naive belief in the so-called 'free market' that can only result in the destruction of community and ultimately democracy. With one breath right-wing populists declare the sovereignty of people over the state; yet with the next they defend the sovereignty of the market over people. They intone the divine right of people to determine their lives, but then raise the impersonal flag of capital over community, morality, ethics, or even consciousness. Similarly, they decry what they term 'social engineering' by the state, schools, or media, but raise not a hint of condemnation over the freedom of capital to mould, shape, and even enslave people's values, morals, tastes, and actions through advertising.

Above all else, the populism of the New Right calls for and defends an illusory separation of economics from politics that can only lead to the destruction of political democracy itself. For, to paraphrase Clausewitz, the marketplace is just politics carried on by different means. Giving control over to the market simply removes economic decisions from discussion within the directly political arena, placing power instead inside the shadowy boardrooms of multinationals, several of which are already economically larger than most nations.[23] Today, there are predictions that these behemoths will soon begin to form their own high-tech armies.[24] What we are witnessing, in effect, is a redefinition of political boundaries, with the resultant removal, in real time and space, of democratic control and responsibility from people affected by corporate decisions. Put another way, globalization, in the form that it is currently being carried out, does not separate politics from economics; it simply renders Adam Smith's 'invisible hand' more invisible than ever.

Right-wing populism, however, offers no solution to the problems of the globalized economy or of political representation in the twenty-first century. As Christopher Lasch states: 'Its advocates call for small-scale production and political decentralization, but they do not explain how those objectives can be achieved.'[25] Right-wing populists have overdetermined the source of threat, focusing aptly upon 'big government' while ignoring the unconstrained power of monopoly capital.

Thus they have fallen prey to the siren sounds of neo-conservatism, a doctrine that is neither new nor particularly conservative.[26] They remain blind.

The title of this book is taken from a poem by William Butler Yeats. One might take issue with Yeats's assertion that 'the worst are full of passionate intensity': apathy in the face of genuine discord seems at least equally a fault. But in many respects, the poet's words seem to reflect accurately a reality of our time. For much of this century, the tension of conflict between the right and the left held the shape of our world in balance. In the wake, however, of the Pyrrhic victory of capitalism, the core of social life has been replaced by a vacuous and endless pursuit of individual ends by any means, powered by excesses of wealth, increasingly isolated in walled enclaves, and protected by private arms. Under these conditions, the sense of a loss of community, for people on both the left and the right, is palpable. Each senses that the world, as they have known it, is falling apart; that the centre no longer holds; that moral and political anarchy have been loosed upon the land. While the left, however, wanders in the wilderness, the right marches confidently and passionately into the hallowed future, watching the sky, believing that at any moment the lost falcon will return.

A Comment on Methods and Sources

An historical sociological approach was used in this study. Diverse and eclectic, historical sociology merges history's concentration on detail with sociology's concern for theoretical generalization. Particular characteristics of the method include a deliberate use of time as a variable in itself; the explicit use of a narrative structure; a tendency to deal, often simultaneously, with events and processes at different levels; and the use of comparisons, either of distinct cases or between elements of a single case.[1]

Historical sociology is both an old and a new way of conducting research, with many excellent examples accessible to the reader. For those interested in studying older works employing an historical sociological approach, I recommend the writings of Alexis de Tocqueville, Karl Marx and Friedrich Engels, and Max Weber.[2] For those interested in examining more recent works, I would recommend E.P. Thompson, Barrington Moore, Theda Skocpol, Daniel Chirot, and Gordon Laxer.[3]

Subsumed under this approach in this particular study are several distinct methodologies. Whenever possible, primary sources, such as party documents, personal diaries, and personal interviews, were used. This information was augmented by secondary historical sources, survey results, and polls. The analysis is further informed by my own unstructured observations of the party membership, obtained at Reform's 1991 convention and other Reform gatherings.

One original source of survey data is also employed – the 1991 Alberta Survey conducted by the University of Alberta Population Research Laboratory. Each year, the laboratory conducts an extensive survey of randomly selected Alberta residents over the age of eighteen. In

1991, 1345 residents were randomly selected and interviewed. A subset of this data was subsequently analysed by Dr Harvey Krahn and myself and is referred to in chapters four and five.

Notes

PREFACE

1 *Alberta Report*, 8 June 1987, 6.
2 See, for example, M. Dobbin, *Preston Manning and the Reform Party* (Toronto: Lorimer and Company 1991); S. Sharpe and D. Braid, *Storming Babylon: Preston Manning and the Rise of the Reform Party* (Toronto: Key Porter Books 1992); and P. Manning, *The New Canada* (Toronto: Macmillan Canada 1992).
3 See, however, P. McCormick, 'The Reform Party of Canada: New Beginning or Dead End?' in H. Thorburn, ed., *Party Politics in Canada* (Scarborough, Ont.: Prentice-Hall Canada 1991).

CHAPTER 1   The 'Problem' of Populism

1 A. Gramsci, 'Prison Writings,' in D. Forgacs, ed., *An Antonio Gramsci Reader: Selected Writings, 1916–1935* (New York: Schocken Books 1988), 217–18.
2 M. Canovan, *Populism* (New York: Harcourt Brace Jovanovich 1981).
3 D. Laycock, *Populism and Democratic Thought in the Canadian Prairies, 1910 to 1945* (Toronto: University of Toronto Press 1990), 15.
4 See H.C. Boyte, 'Beyond Politics as Usual,' in H.C. Boyte and F. Riessman, eds., *The New Populism: The Politics of Empowerment* (Philadelphia: Temple University Press 1986).
5 P.R. Sinclair, 'Class Structure and Populist Protest: The Case of Western Canada,' in C. Caldarola, ed., *Society and Politics in Alberta: Research Papers* (Toronto: Methuen Publications 1979), 74–5.
6 Ernesto Laclau refers to this as the 'people'/'power bloc' antagonism (E. Laclau, *Politics and Ideology in Marxist Theory: Capitalism – Fascism –*

Populism (London: NLB 1977). See also J. Richards, 'Populism: A Qualified Defence,' *Studies in Political Economy*, 5 (1981): 5–27, especially 5–6; A. Finkel, *The Social Credit Phenomenon in Alberta* (Toronto: University of Toronto Press 1989), 202–3; D. Laycock, *Populism and Democratic Thought*, 19; P. McCormick, 'Reform Party,' 350.

7   See J.F. Conway, 'Populism in the United States, Russia, and Canada: Explaining the Roots of Canada's Third Parties,' *Canadian Journal of Political Science*, 11, 1 (1978): 99–124; also J. Richards, 'Populism'; M. Canovan, *Populism*; A. Finkel, *Social Credit Phenomenon*; D. Laycock, *Populism and Democratic Thought*.

8   See F.J. Turner, 'The Problem of the West' [originally published 1896], in R.J. Cunningham, ed., *The Populists in Historical Perspective* (Boston: D.C. Heath and Company 1968); S. Buck, *The Granger Movement: A Study of Agricultural Organization and Its Political, Economic and Social Manifestations* (1913; Lincoln: University of Nebraska Press 1965); S. Buck, *The Agrarian Crusade: A Chronicle of the Farmer in Politics* (Toronto: Brook and Company 1920); and J.D. Hicks, *The Populist Revolt: A History of the Farmers' Alliance and the People's Party* (Minneapolis: University of Minnesota Press 1931).

9   Ibid., 405.

10 W.L. Morton, *The Progressive Party in Canada* (1950; Toronto: University of Toronto Press 1978); S.M. Lipset, *Agrarian Socialism: The Cooperative Commonwealth Federation in Saskatchewan: A Study in Political Sociology* (1950; expanded ed., Garden City, N.Y.: Doubleday Company 1968).

11 R. Hofstadter, *The Age of Reform: From Bryan to F.D.R.* (New York: Alfred A. Knopf 1955), 61.

12 R. Hofstadter, *Anti-Intellectualism in American Life* (New York: Alfred A. Knopf 1963); and *The Paranoid Style in American Politics and Other Essays* (New York: Alfred A. Knopf 1964).

13 I.M. Leonard and R.D. Parmet, *American Nativism, 1830–1860* (Toronto: Van Nostrand Reinhold Company 1971); E.P. Crapol, *America for Americans: Economic Nationalism and Anglophobia in the Late Nineteenth Century* (Westport, Conn.: Greenwood Press 1973).

14 H. Palmer, *Patterns of Prejudice: A History of Nativism in Alberta* (Toronto: McClelland and Stewart 1982).

15 H.D. Graham and T.R. Gurr, eds., *Violence in America: Historical and Comparative Perspectives* (New York: Praeger 1969); R.A. McGuire, 'Economic Causes of Late-Nineteenth Century Agrarian Unrest: New Evidence,' *Journal of Economic History*, 61, 4 (1981): 835–52.

16 The notion of a 'calling' is borrowed, of course, from Max Weber,

The Protestant Ethic and the Spirit of Capitalism (originally written 1904–5, trans. 1930; London: Unwin Paperbacks 1987), 79. Although, to my knowledge, the term has never been specifically applied to the sense of responsibility felt by nativists to their country or region, I think it is quite implicit in, for example, I.M. Leonard and R.D. Parmet's discussion in *American Nativism.*

17 C. Berger, *The Sense of Power: Studies in the Ideas of Canadian Imperialism, 1867–1914* (Toronto: University of Toronto Press 1976); H. Palmer, *Patterns of Prejudice;* M. Robin, *Shades of Right: Nativist and Fascist Politics in Canada, 1920–1940* (Toronto: University of Toronto Press 1991).

18 C.B. Macpherson, *Democracy in Alberta: Social Credit and the Party System* (Toronto: University of Toronto Press 1953).

19 K. Marx and F. Engels, 'The Communist Manifesto,' in D. McLellan ed., *Karl Marx: Selected Writings* (Oxford: Oxford University Press 1977).

20 Ibid., 229.

21 V.I. Lenin, 'The Economic Content of Narodism and the Criticism of It in Mr. Struve's Book,' in *Collected Works* (Moscow: Foreign Languages Publishing House 1960); and 'The Heritage We Renounce,' in *Selected Works* (Moscow: Progress Publishers 1970).

22 See J. Conway, 'Populism.'

23 Lenin, 'The Heritage We Renounce,' 98–9.

24 Lenin, 'The Economic Content of Narodism,' 503.

25 E.O. Wright, 'Class Boundaries and Contradictory Class Locations,' in A. Giddens and D. Held, eds., *Classes, Power, and Conflict* (Los Angeles: University of California Press 1982).

26 See G. Laxer, ed., *Perspectives on Canadian Economic Development* (Oxford: Oxford University Press 1991).

27 M. Pinard, *The Rise of a Third Party: A Study in Crisis Politics* (1971; expanded ed., Montreal and Kingston: McGill-Queen's University Press 1975).

28 N. Pollack, 'Hofstadter on Populism: A Critique of "The Age of Reform,"' *Journal of Southern History,* 26 (1960): 478–500; N. Pollack, *The Populist Mind* (New York: Bobbs-Merrill Co. 1967); L. Goodwyn, *Democratic Promise: The Populist Moment in America* (New York: Oxford University Press 1976).

29 Regarding Social Credit's radicalism, see M. Johnson, 'The Failure of the CCF in Alberta: An Accident of History,' in C. Caldarola, ed., *Society and Politics in Alberta: Research Papers* (Toronto: Methuen Publications 1979); and A. Finkel, *Social Credit Phenomenon.* For a convincing refutation of Macpherson's theory of petit bourgeois support for Social Credit, see

E. Bell's *Social Classes and Social Credit* (Montreal and Kingston: McGill-Queen's University Press 1993).

30 P. Sinclair, 'Class Structure'; see also P. McCormick, 'Reform Party,' 350.

31 M. Canovan, *Populism*, 8–9.

32 Ibid., 294.

33 J. Richards, 'Populism,' 19–20.

34 A. Finkel, *Social Credit Phenomenon*, 202–3; and D. Laycock, *Populism and Democratic Thought*, 19–22.

35 A. Gramsci, 'Prison Writings.'

36 D. Stasiulis, 'Capitalism, Democracy, and the Canadian State,' in D. Forcese and S. Richer, eds., *Social Issues: Sociological Views of Canada* (Scarborough, Ont.: Prentice-Hall 1988), 232.

37 The distinction between conflicts and differences is discussed in E. Laclau, *Politics and Ideology*.

38 A. Gramsci, 'Prison Writings.'

39 See G. Esping-Andersen, *Politics against Markets: The Social Democratic Road to Power* (Princeton, N.J.: Princeton University Press 1985).

40 See P. Dunleavy and C.T. Husbands, *British Democracy at the Crossroads: Voting and Party Competition in the 1980s* (London: George Allen and Unwin 1985).

41 On this point, see C. Tilly, *From Mobilization to Revolution* (Reading, Mass.: Addison-Wesley 1978).

42 Marx and Engels, 'Communist Manifesto,' 224.

43 A. Gramsci, 'Prison Writings.' For concrete examples of organic crises, see D. Gordon, R. Edwards, and M. Reich, *Segmented Work, Divided Workers: The Historical Transformation of Labor in the United States* (Cambridge, Mass.: Cambridge University Press 1982); and D. Chirot, *Social Change in the Modern Era* (Toronto: Harcourt Brace Jovanovich 1986).

44 See Lenin, 'The Heritage We Renounce'; V.K. Yatsunsky, 'The Industrial Revolution in Russia,' in W.L. Blackwell, ed., *Russian Economic Development from Peter the Great to Stalin* (New York: New Viewpoints 1974); also A. Gerschenkron, *Economic Backwardness in Historical Perspective: A Book of Essays* (Cambridge, Mass.: The Belknap Press 1962); T. Skocpol, *Social Revolutions: A Comparative Analysis of France, Russia, and China* (Cambridge, Mass.: Cambridge University Press 1979). For an alternative analysis, see M. Canovan, *Populism*, 59–97.

45 See various works previously cited, particularly J.D. Hicks, S. Buck, R. Hofstadter, E.P. Crapol, L. Goodwyn, and N. Pollack.

46 See L. Panitch, 'The Role and Nature of the Canadian State,' in L. Panitch,

ed., *The Canadian State: Political Economy and Political Power* (Toronto: University of Toronto Press 1977); and W. Connolly, ed., *Legitimacy and the State* (Oxford: Basil Blackwell Publisher 1984).

47 P. Dunleavy and C.T. Husbands, *British Democracy*.

48 The classic texts on disorganization theory are those of E. Durkheim's *The Division of Labor in Society*, (1893, trans. 1933; New York: The Free Press 1966); and *Suicide: A Study of Sociology* (1897, trans. 1951; New York: The Free Press 1951). More recently, see W. Kornhauser, *The Politics of Mass Society* (New York: The Free Press 1959).

49 See C. Tilly's cogent dismissal of social disorganization theory and the case for organizational factors in mobilization in *From Mobilization to Revolution*. The positive relationship between organization and mobilization is stated explicitly M. Pinard, *Rise of a Third Party*, 186:

> Whenever pre-existing primary and secondary groupings possess or develop an ideology or simply subjective interests congruent with that of a new movement, they will act as mobilizing rather than restraining agents toward that movement. And their members will be, not late joiners, but the early joiners of the movement, much earlier than the atomized masses.

50 A.L. Stinchcombe, 'Social Structure and Organizations,' in J.G. Marsh, ed., *Handbook of Organizations* (Chicago: Rand McNally 1965).

51 This point is extremely well enunciated in a recent, unpublished paper, S. Patten, 'Populist Politics? A Critical Re-Examination of "Populism" and the Character of Reform Party's Populist Politics,' paper presented to the annual meeting of the Canadian Political Science Association, Ottawa, 1993. Patten's work makes critical use of certain ideas adopted from E. Laclau.

52 See C. Tilly, *From Mobilization*; also J.D. McCarthy and M.N. Zald, eds., *Social Movements in an Organizational Society: Collected Essays* (New Brunswick, N.J.: Transaction Books 1987).

53 D. Laycock, *Populism and Democratic Thought*.

54 M. Mann, 'The Social Cohesion of Liberal Democracy,' *American Sociological Review*, 35, 3 (1970): 423–39.

55 The progenitor of this belief was R.R. Alford's study of the four English-speaking democracies, *Party and Society: The Anglo-American Democracies* (Chicago: Rand McNally and Company 1963).

56 E. Laclau, *Politics and Ideology*.

57 Figures from A. Hunter, 'The Changing Distribution of Income,' in
J. Curtis et al., eds., *Social Inequality in Canada: Patterns, Problems, Policies*
(Scarborough, Ont.: Prentice-Hall Canada 1988).

58 See D. Forcese and S. Richer, eds., *Social Issues: Sociological Views of Canada*
(Scarborough, Ont.: Prentice-Hall 1988); also J. Curtis et al., eds., *Social
Inequality*.

59 G. Stevenson, 'Federalism and the Political Economy of the Canadian
State,' in L. Panitch, ed., *The Canadian State: Political Economy and Political
Power* (Toronto: University of Toronto Press 1977).

60 See S. Clarkson and C. McCall, *Trudeau and Our Times*; Vol. 1: *The Magnificent Obsession* (Toronto: McClelland and Stewart 1990).

61 R. Logan, 'Immigration during the 1980s,' *Canadian Social Trends*, 20
(1991): 10–13.

62 F. Vallee, 'Inequality and Identity in Multiethnic Societies,' in D. Forcese
and S. Richer, eds., *Social Issues*.

63 R. Bibby, *Mosaic Madness: The Poverty and Potential of Life in Canada*
(Toronto: Stoddart Publishing 1990); see also W. Gairdner, *The Trouble
with Canada: A Citizen Speaks Out* (Toronto: Stoddart Publishing 1990).

64 See J. Richards and L. Pratt, *Prairie Capitalism: Power and Influence in the
New West* (Toronto: McClelland and Stewart 1979); also L. Pratt, 'Whose
Oil Is It?' in L. Pratt and G. Stevenson, eds., *Western Separatism: The Myths,
Realities and Dangers* (Edmonton: Hurtig Publishers 1981).

65 Panitch, *Canadian State*.

66 J. Laxer, *Leap of Faith: Free Trade and the Future of Canada* (Edmonton:
Hurtig Publishers 1986).

67 D.S. King, *The New Right: Politics, Markets and Citizenship* (London:
Macmillan Education 1987), 1.

68 See J. Laxer, *Leap of Faith*.

69 G. Stevenson, 'Federalism and the Political Economy.'

70 See J. Pammett, 'Class Voting and Class Consciousness in Canada,'
Canadian Review of Sociology and Anthropology, 24 (1987): 269–90; R.J. Brym,
M.W. Gillespie, and R.L. Lenton, 'Class Power, Class Mobilization, and
Class Voting: The Canadian Case,' *Canadian Journal of Sociology*, 14, 1
(1989): 25–44.

71 See D.S. King, *New Right*; also N.P. Barry, *The New Right* (London: Croom
Helm 1987); D.C. Green, *The New Right: The Counter Revolution In Political,
Economic and Social Thought* (Brighton: Wheatsheaf Books 1987); M.P.
Marchak, *Ideological Perspectives on Canada* (Toronto: McGraw-Hill
Ryerson 1988), 187–201; and S. McBride and J. Shields, *Dismantling a
Nation: Canada and the New World Order* (Halifax: Fernwood Publishing
1993), especially 5–41.

72 Regarding Germany, see J. Habermas, 'Neo-conservative Culture Criticism in the United States and West Germany: An Intellectual Movement in Two Political Cultures,' *Telos*, 1983, 56, 75–89; regarding Britain, see C. Leys, *Politics in Britain: An Introduction* (Toronto: University of Toronto Press 1983).

73 Regarding the support of liberals for Reagan, and the liberal roots of neo-conservatism generally, see S.M. Lipset, 'Neoconservatism: Myth and Reality,' *Society*, 25, 5 (1988): 30–7; also R. Nisbet, 'The Conservative Renaissance in Perspective,' *The Public Interest*, 81 (1985): 128–41. Lipset quotes Peter Glotz's comment that 'Neo-conservatism is the net into which the liberal can fall when he begins to fear his own liberalism.'

74 R. Whitaker, 'Neo-conservatism and the State,' *Socialist Register* (1987), 1–31.

75 C. Lasch, *The True and Only Heaven: Progress and Its Critics* (New York: W.W. Norton and Company 1991), especially 476–532, provides a sympathetic look at the moral and cultural world-view of American working- and lower-class voters, and the reasons why many of them abandoned the Democrats during the 1980s in favour of the Reagan-Bush Republicans. Lasch contends also that this world-view was cynically manipulated by the latter who wanted the vote but who otherwise cared little for moral conservatism, instead implementing economic and political policies that further endangered traditional families and communities.

76 The term 'excess of democracy' was popularized in the 1970s by the Trilateral Commission, a privately financed think-tank that brought together European, North American, and Japanese corporate interests. See McBride and Shields, *Dismantling a Nation*, 30–1.

77 See P. Brimelow, *The Patriot Game: National Dreams and Political Realities* (Toronto: Key Porter Books 1986), especially 280; also S.R. Barrett, *Is God a Racist? The Right Wing in Canada* (Toronto: University of Toronto Press 1987); and Stasiulis, 'Capitalism, Democracy, and the Canadian State,' 54.

78 S. Clarkson and C. McCall, *Trudeau*, I: 283.

79 J. Laxer and R. Laxer, *The Liberal Idea of Canada: Pierre Trudeau and the Question of Canada's Survival* (Toronto: James Lorimer and Company 1977).

80 See P. Brimelow, *Patriot Game*; W. Gairdner, *Trouble with Canada*.

CHAPTER 2   The Roots of the Reform Party

1 E. Manning, *Political Realignment: A Challenge to Thoughtful Canadians* (Toronto: McClelland and Stewart 1967), 86.

2 Political culture is defined as 'the political vehicle which mediates

perceptions of the issues at stake and the political-economic options available to deal with them.' Quoted from H. Chorney and P. Hansen, 'Neo-conservatism, Social Democracy and "Province Building": The Manitoba Experience,' *The Canadian Review of Sociology and Anthropology*, 22, 1 (1985): 1–29.

3 W.L. Morton, *Progressive Party*.

4 H. Chorney and P. Hansen, 'Neo-conservatism.'

5 Ibid.

6 C.B. Macpherson, *Democracy in Alberta*.

7 S.M. Lipset, *Agrarian Socialism*; J. Richards, 'Populism.'

8 R. Gibbins, *Prairie Politics and Society: Regionalism in Decline* (Scarborough, Ont.: Butterworth and Company 1980; and M. Johnson, 'Failure of the CCF.'

9 M. Johnson, 'Failure of the CCF.'

10 A. Finkel, *Social Credit Phenomenon*.

11 E. Bell, *Social Classes*.

12 H. Palmer and T. Palmer, *Alberta: A New History* (Edmonton: Hurtig Publishers 1990), 138; see also Richards and Pratt, *Prairie Capitalism*.

13 H. Palmer and T. Palmer, *Alberta*, 306.

14 J.D. House, *The Last of the Free Enterprisers: The Oilmen of Calgary* (Toronto: Macmillan Company of Canada 1980).

15 C.B. Macpherson, *Democracy in Alberta*; A. Finkel, *Social Credit Phenomenon*; see also J. Richards and L. Pratt, *Prairie Capitalism*.

16 A. Finkel, *Social Credit Phenomenon*.

17 See S.M. Lipset, *Agrarian Socialism*; J.F. Conway, *The West: The History of a Region in Confederation* (Toronto: James Lorimer and Company 1984).

18 See R. Gibbins, *Prairie Politics*, 130–2.

19 J.A. Lower, *Western Canada: An Outline History* (Vancouver: Douglas and McIntyre 1983), 287.

20 R. Gibbins, *Prairie Politics*, 130–2.

21 J.F. Conway, *The West*, 189.

22 Regarding the *Alberta Gas Trunk Line Company*, see A. Finkel, *Social Credit Phenomenon*, 195. Regarding BC Electric, see D. Mitchell, *W.A.C. Bennett and the Rise of British Columbia* (Vancouver: Douglas and McIntyre 1983).

23 D. Mitchell, *W.A.C. Bennett*.

24 Regarding Bennett, see ibid. Regarding Manning, see A.J. Hooke, *30 + 5: I Know, I Was There* (Edmonton: Co-op Press 1971); J. Barr, *The Dynasty: The Rise and Fall of Social Credit in Alberta* (Toronto: McClelland and Stewart 1974); A. Finkel, *Social Credit Phenomenon*.

25 See ibid.

26 The biographic details of Preston Manning's life that follow are taken from M. Dobbin, *Preston Manning*; P. Manning, *New Canada*; and S. Sharpe and D. Braid, *Storming Babylon*.
27 P. Manning, 'Personal Resume,' part A, section 1, submitted to the Reform Party of Canada, 18 March 1991.
28 P. Manning, *New Canada*, 42.
29 The *Herald* story has been given wide coverage elsewhere. See A.J. Hooke, *30 + 5*, 252–5; A. Finkel, *Social Credit Phenomenon*, 162–3; and M. Dobbin, *Preston Manning*, 29–30 and 34–5.
30 P. Manning, *New Canada*.
31 A. Finkel, *Social Credit Phenomenon*, 157.
32 See P. Manning, *New Canada*, 54.
33 Alberta, *A White Paper on Human Resources Development* (Edmonton: Government of Alberta 1967), 17.
34 P. Manning, *New Canada*, 47.
35 Ibid.
36 E. Manning, *Political Realignment*.
37 Ibid., 63.
38 Ibid., 86.
39 P. Manning, *New Canada*, 49.
40 A.J. Hooke, *30 + 5*; also the author's personal interview with A.J. Hooke, at Sherwood Park, Alberta, 9 August 1991.
41 P. Manning, *New Canada*, 55.
42 J. Barr, *Dynasty*, 170.
43 Ibid.
44 Ibid., 171–2; also A. Finkel, *Social Credit Phenomenon*, 180–1.
45 See J. Richards and L. Pratt, *Prairie Capitalism*; J.F. Conway, *The West*; A Finkel, *Social Credit Phenomenon*; also E. Bell, 'The Rise of the Lougheed Conservatives and the Demise of Social Credit in Alberta: A Reconsideration,' *Canadian Journal of Political Science*, 26, 3 (1993): 455–75.
46 A. Finkel, *Social Credit Phenomenon*, 194.
47 *Alberta Report*, 7 September 1979, 34–5.
48 In 1986 Keegstra ran for leadership of the national Social Credit party, but lost to an Ontarian, the Reverend Harvey Lainson by 67 votes to 38. Lainson's winning platform included the right to bear firearms, opposition to abortion and metrification, and support for a $6^1/2$ per cent ceiling on interest rates. The story is covered in *Alberta Report*, 7 July 1986, 4–5.
49 S.M. Lipset, *Agrarian Socialism*.
50 J. Brodie, *The Political Economy of Canadian Regionalism* (Toronto: Harcourt Brace Jovanovich Canada 1990).
51 A. Finkel, *Social Credit Phenomenon*, 184.

52 R. Gibbins, *Prairie Politics*, 132.
53 H. Chorney and P. Hansen, 'Neo-conservatism.'
54 J. Brodie, *Political Economy*, 42.
55 J.F. Conway, *The West*, 186.
56 See A. Finkel, *Social Credit Phenomenon*, 184; also J. Richards and L. Pratt, *Prairie Capitalism*.
57 H. Strom, *A Case for the West. An Address to the Federal-Provincial Constitutional Conference* (Edmonton: Government of Alberta 1969), 5–6.
58 J. Barr and O. Anderson, eds., *The Unfinished Revolt: Some Views on Western Independence* (Toronto: McClelland and Stewart 1971).
59 H. Strom, *Case for the West.*
60 The term 'symbolic order' is borrowed from H. Hiller, 'The Foundation and Politics of Separation: Canada in Comparative Perspective,' *Research in Political Sociology*, 3 (1987): 39–60.
61 See Conway, *The West.*
62 G. Stevenson, 'Federalism.'
63 G. Grant, *Lament for a Nation: The Defeat of Canadian Nationalism* (Toronto: McClelland and Stewart 1970), 48.
64 See J. Barr and O. Anderson, *Unfinished Revolt*; J. Richards and L. Pratt, *Prairie Capitalism*; H. Chorney and P. Hansen, 'Neo-conservatism.'
65 On the characteristics of the Canadian élite at the time, see J. Porter, *The Vertical Mosaic: An Analysis of Social Class and Power in Canada* (Toronto: University of Toronto Press 1965).
66 A.J. Hooke, *30 + 5*, 221.
67 Author's personal interview with A.J. Hooke, 1991.
68 I. Stewart, 'Global Transformation and Economic Policy,' in T. Axworthy and P. Trudeau, ed., *Towards a Just Society: The Trudeau Years* (Markham, Ont.: Penguin Books Canada 1990).
69 See J. Laxer, *Oil and Gas: Ottawa, the Provinces and the Petroleum Industry* (Toronto: James Lorimer and Company 1983); J.D. House, *Last of the Free Enterprisers.*
70 J. Laxer, *Leap of Faith*; G. Laxer, *Open for Business: The Roots of Foreign Ownership in Canada* (Toronto: Oxford University Press 1989).
71 J. Laxer, *Oil and Gas.*
72 Ibid.
73 See J. Laxer and R. Laxer, *Liberal Idea.*
74 J. Laxer, *Oil and Gas.*
75 C. McCall-Newman, *Grits: An Intimate Portrait of the Liberal Party* (Toronto: Macmillan of Canada 1982), 169.
76 J. Chrétien, *Straight from the Heart* (Toronto: Key Porter Books 1985), 168.

77 All figures from Statistics Canada, Economic Services Section, *Analysis Summary of Federal Government Debt* (Ottawa: Statistics Canada 1991).
78 S. Clarkson and C. McCall, *Trudeau*, I: 179.
79 C. McCall-Newman, *Grits*, 309–10.
80 The biographic material that follows is taken, in the main, from F. Winspear, *Out of My Mind* (1969; revised printing, Victoria, B.C.: Morriss Printing Company 1988); and the author's personal interviews in Edmonton 3 May and 26 July 1991.
81 F. Winspear, *Out of My Mind*, 14–15, italics added.
82 Ibid., 186.
83 *Alberta Report*, 8 June 1987, 5.
84 F. Winspear, *Out of My Mind*, 187.
85 Chief Electoral Officer of Canada, *Report of the Chief Electoral Officer respecting Party Contributions* (Ottawa 1975, 1979, and 1980).
86 See S. Barrett, *Is God a Racist?*; P. Brimelow, *Patriot Game*, 280; and D. Stasiulis, 'Capitalism,' 54; also L. McQuaig, *The Quick and the Dead: Brian Mulroney, Big Business and the Seduction of Canada* (Toronto: Viking 1991).
87 J.V. Andrew, *Bilingual Today, French Tomorrow: Trudeau's Master Plan and How It Can Be Stopped* (Richmond Hill, Ont.: BMG Publishing 1977).
88 K. McDonald, *Red Maple – How Canada Became the People's Republic of Canada in 1981* (Richmond Hill, Ont.: BMG Publishing 1975).
89 J.V. Andrew, *Backdoor Bilingualism: Davis' Sell-out of Ontario and Its National Consequences* (Richmond Hill, Ont.: BMG Publishing 1979), and *Enough! (Enough French! Enough Quebec!)* (Kitchener, Ont.: Andrew Books 1988).
90 The details that follow are taken, in the main, from T. Hughes, H. Fraser, and T. Whelpton, eds., *Who's Who in Canada* (Toronto: International Press 1975–6), 860; N. Fillmore, 'The Right Stuff: Inside the National Citizens' Coalition,' *This Magazine*, 20, 2 (1986): 4–19; S. Barrett, *Is God a Racist?*; and N. Ovenden's column in the *Edmonton Journal*, 20 April 1991, G2.
91 D. Somerville, *Trudeau Revealed* (Richmond Hill, Ont.: BMG Publishing 1978).
92 P. Brimelow, *Patriot Game*, 64.
93 N. Fillmore, 'Right Stuff.'
94 A. Garr, *Tough Guy: Bill Bennett and the Taking of British Columbia* (Toronto: Key Porter Books 1985); also B. Palmer, *Solidarity: The Rise and Fall of an Opposition in British Columbia* (Vancouver: New Star Books 1987).
95 A. Garr, *Tough Guy*, 91–2.
96 See W. Magnusson, ed., *The New Reality: The Politics of Restraint in British*

Columbia (Vancouver: New Star Books 1984); A. Garr, *Tough Guy*; S. Persky, *Fantasy Government and the Future of Social Credit* (Vancouver: New Star Books 1989).

97 In the main, the biographic information which follows is taken from biographical notes supplied to the author by T. Byfield, and the author's personal interview of 1991. The major source of material on the *Alberta Report* is taken from the *Alberta Report* of 28 November 1983, 22–35.

98 P. Berton, *The Comfortable Pew* (Toronto: McClelland and Stewart 1965); T. Byfield, *Just Think, Mr. Berton (A Little Harder)* (Winnipeg: Morehouse 1965).

99 *Alberta Report*, 21 August 1981, 44. Despite its extolling of high moral values, however, *Alberta Report* has often been taken to task by readers dismayed at its apparently prurient interest in news stories, usually accompanied by pictures, concerning beauty pageants, nudist colonies, pornography shops, and prostitution. See, for example, letters to the editor 10 January 1983, 4; 4 April 1983, 2; and 1 February 1993, 3.

100 Ted Byfield editorial in the *Alberta Report*, 14 April 1986, 60.

101 A. Garr, *Tough Guy*; see also S. Persky, *Fantasy Government*.

102 A. Garr, *Tough Guy*, 1; see also W. Magnusson , *New Reality*; B. Palmer, *Solidarity*; S. Persky, *Fantasy Government*.

103 See W. Magnusson, *New Reality*, 281–5, for a full summary.

104 Ibid., 12.

105 Ibid.; A. Garr, *Tough Guy*; G. Mason and K. Baldrey, *Fantasyland: Inside the Reign of Bill Vander Zalm* (Toronto: McGraw-Hill Ryerson 1989).

106 See B. Palmer, *Solidarity*.

107 Ibid.; see also A. Nikiforuk, S. Pratt, and D. Wanagas, *Running on Empty: Alberta after the Boom* (Edmonton: NeWest Press 1987).

108 Mason and Baldrey, *Fantasyland*.

109 M. Lalonde, 'Riding the Storm: Energy Policy, 1968–1984,' in T. Axworthy and P. Trudeau, eds., *Towards a Just Society: The Trudeau Years* (Markham, Ont.: Penguin Canada Books 1990).

110 *Alberta Report*, 21 December 1979, 9–10.

111 See J. Laxer, *Oil and Gas*.

112 E. Knutson letter, *Edmonton Journal*, 22 February 1980, A5.

113 See D. Harrington, 'Who Are the Separatists?' in L. Pratt and G. Stevenson, eds., *Western Separatism*; E. Bell, 'The Western Separatist Movement: Ultra-Conservatism in the Western Hinterland' (unpublished master's thesis, Edmonton: University of Alberta, Department of Sociology 1983).

114 D. Harrington, 'Who Are the Separatists?' 25.

115 *Alberta Report*, 11 January 1980, 11.
116 *Alberta Report*, 6 June 1980, 2–4.
117 E. Bell, 'Western Separatist Movement,' 22.
118 *Alberta Report*, 28 November 1980, 5–7.
119 *Alberta Report*, 6 June 1980, 2–3.
120 R. Gibbins, *Prairie Politics*, 161.
121 *Alberta Report*, 11 December 1981, 12–13.
122 D. Harrington, 'Who Are the Separatists?'; E. Bell, 'Western Separatist Movement.'
123 *Alberta Report*, 21 March 1980, 19.
124 *Alberta Report*, 30 May 1980, 6.
125 'A Vote That Split a Nation,' *Alberta Report*, 29 February 1980, 8–10.
126 'So What If the West Is Absent,' *Alberta Report*, 29 February 1980, 8–10.
127 See L. McKinsey, 'Watching the Separatists,' in L. Pratt and G. Stevenson, eds.,*Western Separatism*.
128 J. Laxer, *Oil and Gas*, 73–4.
129 Ibid., 79.
130 See S. Clarkson, *Canada and the Reagan Challenge: Crisis and Adjustment, 1981–85* (Toronto: James Lorimer and Company 1985).
131 *Oil Week*, 10 November 1980, 76–9, quote on 76.
132 See H. Hiller's 'Humor and Hostility: A Neglected Aspect of Social Movement Analysis,' *Qualitative Sociology*, 6, 3 (1983): 255–65; and 'Novelty Items as Cultural Artifact and Social Assertion: The Case of Western Separatism,' *Journal of Canadian Culture*, 1 (1984): 110–18.
133 J. Ballem, *Alberta Alone* (Don Mills, Ont.: General Paperbacks 1981).
134 The material dealing with the 1982 Constitution is taken primarily from S. Clarkson and C. McCall, *Trudeau*; also A.C. Cairns, *Constitution, Government, and Society in Canada: Selected Essays* (Toronto: McClelland and Stewart 1988); and A. Cohen, *A Deal Undone. The Making and Breaking of the Meech Lake Accord* (Vancouver: Douglas and McIntyre 1990).
135 See R. Whitaker, 'Democracy and the Canadian Constitution,' in *A Sovereign Idea: Essays on Canada as a Democratic Community* (Montreal: McGill-Queen's University Press 1992).
136 Gallup, 19 June 1982.
137 *Alberta Report*, 22 May 1981, 21.
138 *Alberta Report*, 12 December 1980, 2–6.
139 Ibid.
140 P.C. Newman, *The Acquisitors: The Canadian Establishment* (Toronto: Seal Books 1982), II: 368.
141 The biographic details on Stan Roberts are taken from assorted sources,

including undated biographic notes and Mr Roberts's personal notes jotted down on a Feed and Farm Supply Dealer (*Why I Am a Liberal*), which were almost certainly written in 1970, and from which the inset quotes are taken. All of these sources were kindly provided by Pia Roberts. Additional information was gleaned from the *Montreal Gazette*, 2 December 1980, 38; *Financial Post*, 6 December 1980, 11; and *Alberta Report*, 12 December 1980, 2–6.

142 *Calgary Herald*, 30 March 1978, 22.

143 S. Roberts and D. Elton, *A Summary Report on the Proceedings of the Colloquia on Constitutional Change* (Calgary: Canada West Foundation 1978), 1.

144 P. Manning, *New Canada*.

145 A. Finkel, *Social Credit Phenomenon*.

146 A.J. Hooke, *30 + 5*; also author's personal interview.

147 M & M Systems Research Ltd., *Requests for Proposals and Social Contracts* (Edmonton: M and M Systems Research 1970). See also P. Manning, *New Canada*, 55–6.

148 Ibid., 80–1.

149 Canada West Foundation, *A Realistic Perspective of Canadian Confederation* (Calgary: The Foundation 1977).

150 D. Elton, F.C. Engelmann, and P. McCormick, *Alternatives: Towards the Development of an Effective Federal System for Canada* (Calgary: Canada West Foundation 1978), 5–6; see also D. Elton, *Notes from the Speech to Alternatives Canada Conference, March 29* (Calgary: Canada West Foundation 1978).

151 S. Roberts, *A Summary Report on the Proceedings of Alternatives Canada. A Canada West Conference on Confederation* (Calgary: Canada West Foundation 1978), 8.

152 Canada, *A Future Together: Report of the Task Force on Canadian Unity*, co-chaired by Jean-Luc Pepin and John Robarts (Ottawa: Supply and Services Canada 1979).

153 F. Winspear, *Out of My Mind*, 18.

154 The quote and recommendations listed above are taken from ibid., 185–6.

155 Reviewed in *Alberta Report*, 12 December 1980, 2–6.

156 Ibid., 6.

157 Ibid. Most observers would probably agree that the foundation is powerfully influenced by the West's business community and tends as a result to take a somewhat pro-business slant on most issues. Nonetheless, it is far from being simply a right-wing organization and under Elton's able presidency has achieved the well-deserved status as the premier think-tank in Western Canada.

158 *Alberta Report*, 28 November 1980, 2–3.
159 L. McKinsey, '*Watching the Separatists*,' 212.
160 *Alberta Report*, 8 March 1982, 7, and again 14 October 1985, 8.
161 *Alberta Report*, 28 November 1980, 5–7.
162 Ibid., 2–3.
163 *Alberta Report*, 10 April 1981, 6–8.
164 *Alberta Report*, 28 November 1980, 4.
165 *Alberta Report*, 6 February 1981, 6.
166 *Alberta Report*, 27 February 1981, 6.
167 *Alberta Report*, 27 March 1981, 4.
168 Ibid.
169 *Alberta Report*, 10 April 1981, 6–8.
170 *Alberta Report*, 29 May 1981, 6.
171 Ibid.
172 *Alberta Report*, 22 March 1982, 8–9.
173 *Alberta Report*, 10 November 1986, 10–11.
174 *Alberta Report*, 23 October 1981, 8–9.
175 *Alberta Report*, 27 October 1986, 11–12.
176 See *Oilweek*, 3 November 1980, 1; 9 November 1981, 1.
177 See J. Laxer, *Oil and Gas*, 147–51.
178 *Alberta Report*, 11 September 1981, 2–8.
179 *Alberta Report*, 26 April 1982, 6–8.
180 See A. Nikiforuk et al., *Running on Empty*.
181 *Alberta Report*, 14 October 1985, 8.
182 *Alberta Report*, 27 October 1986, 11–12.
183 *Alberta Report*, 3 May 1982, 6–7.
184 *Alberta Report*, 12 July 1982, 8.
185 D. Smith, 'Revolt against the Twentieth Century,' *This Magazine*, 21, 7 (1987–8), 4–5; see also *Alberta Report*, 10 February 1986, 5–6.
186 The Heritage Party was so named because one of its central planks was that the province's Heritage Trust Fund be placed under control of a public board, and that $25,000 be given to each Albertan upon his or her twenty-first birthday. In return, recipients would be ineligible for welfare or unemployment benefits until age twenty-five. The party was otherwise an inconsistent supporter of free enterprise, recommending the selling off of all crown corporations, while simultaneously supporting tax breaks and transportation subsidies for farmers and low-interest loans to farmers and businessmen. Details in the *Alberta Report*, 22 April 1985, 9.
187 Attempts to merge Alberta's right wing during this period are discussed in a number of issues of *Alberta Report*, including 22 April 1985, 9; 14 October 1985, 8; 2 December 1985, 6–7; and 27 October 1986, 12.

188 The Representative Party was created following the 1982 Alberta provincial election by two Independent MLAs, and former Socreds, Walter Buck and Ray Speaker, in an attempt to gain both the status and the perquisites of official opposition status along with the NDP who also took two seats in that election.
189 *Alberta Report,* 27 October 1986, 12.
190 *Alberta Report,* 2 October 1981, 6–8; J. Laxer, *Oil and Gas.*

CHAPTER 3   The Rise of the Reform Party

1 T. Byfield editorial in the *Alberta Report,* 4 August 1986, 52.
2 F. Winspear, *Out of My Mind,* 187.
3 Ibid., 188.
4 The biographic details on Brian Mulroney are taken, in the main, from C. Hoy, *Friends in High Places: Politics and Patronage in the Mulroney Government* (Toronto: Key Porter Books 1987); J. Sawatsky, *Mulroney: The Politics of Ambition* (Toronto: Macfarlane Walter and Ross 1991); and S. Clarkson and C. McCall, *Trudeau.*
5 See L. Gagnon's column in the *Globe and Mail,* 7 September 1991, D3.
6 C. Hoy, *Friends,* 45.
7 All figures from *Report of the Chief Electoral Officer respecting Party Contributions* (Ottawa: Chief Electoral Officer of Canada 1984).
8 The coalition fought the law on the basis that it was an infringement of the right to free expression granted under the Charter of Rights. Ironically, the Charter is opposed by many on Canada's right wing. See, for example, the advertisement of the Alberta branch of the Canadian League of Rights in the *Alberta Report,* 22 May 1981, 21; also W. Gairdner, *Trouble;* and V.W. Forster, Sr, *Conning the Canadians* (Vancouver: Vic Forster Publishing 1989).
9 See N. Ovenden's column in the *Edmonton Journal,* 20 April 1991, G2; and R.M. Lee, *One Hundred Monkeys: The Triumph of Popular Wisdom in Canadian Politics* (Toronto: Macfarlane Walter and Ross 1989).
10 D. Bercuson, J.L. Granatstein, and W.R. Young, *Sacred Trust? Mulroney and the Conservative Party in Power* (Toronto: Doubleday Canada 1986), 5.
11 All figures from CIPO press release, 17 September 1984, reported in C. Adams, 'The COR and Reform Parties: Locations of Canadian Protest Party Support,' paper presented to the Annual Meeting of the Canadian Political Science Association, Kingston, Ont., 1991, 3.
12 B. Mulroney, *Where I Stand* (Toronto: McClelland and Stewart 1983).
13 D. Bercuson et al., *Sacred Trust.*

14 B. Mulroney, *Where I Stand*.
15 C. Hoy, *Friends*.
16 Ibid.
17 J. Simpson, *Discipline of Power: The Conservative Interlude and the Liberal Restoration* (Toronto: Personal Library 1980).
18 C. Hoy, *Friends*; also D. Bercuson et al., *Sacred Trust*; R.M. Lee, *One Hundred Monkeys*.
19 Ibid.
20 See S. Sharpe and D. Braid, *Storming Babylon*, 158, on Preston Manning's view of Quebec politics.
21 L. McQuaig, *Quick and the Dead*.
22 Statistics Canada, Economic Services Section, *Analysis Summary of Federal Government Debt* (Ottawa: Statistics Canada 20 September 1991).
23 C. Hoy, *Friends*.
24 *Alberta Report*, 29 December 1986, 7.
25 D. Bercuson et al., *Sacared Trust*; C. Hoy, *Friends*; R.M. Lee, *One Hundred Monkeys*.
26 D. Bercuson et al., *Sacred Trust*.
27 C. Gray, 'Medicare under the Knife,' *Saturday Night*, September 1991, 10–12, 57; D. Bercuson et al., *Sacred Trust*; R.M. Lee, *One Hundred Monkeys*.
28 *Edmonton Journal*, 20 June 1991, A1; see also L. McQuaig, *Quick and the Dead*; C. Gray, 'Medicare.'
29 See *Alberta Report*, 24 March 1986, 17, and 22 December 1986, 8–9.
30 The biographic information which follows is taken, in the main, from the author's personal interview with Harper in Calgary, 30 October 1991.
31 See D. Bercuson et al., *Sacred Trust*; W. Gairdner, *Trouble*.
32 P. Brimelow, *Patriot Game*, 1.
33 Ibid., 6.
34 Ibid., 7.
35 Ibid., 287–9, italics added.
36 Biographic details taken from C. Berger, 'Introduction,' *Canada and the Canadian Question* (Toronto: University of Toronto Press 1971).
37 See A. Nikiforuk et al., *Running on Empty*, 63.
38 D. Braid and S. Sharpe, *Breakup: Why the West Feels Left Out of Canada* (Toronto: Key Porter Books 1990), 76.
39 *Alberta Report*, 24 September 1984, 8.
40 According to H. Palmer and T. Palmer, *Alberta*, 58, the Ranchmen's Club 'was founded in 1891 on a set of rules based on those of an exclusive men's club, the St. James Club in Montreal.'
41 *Alberta Report*, 24 September 1984, 9.

42 Ibid.
43 A. Nikiforuk et al., *Running on Empty.*
44 *Alberta Report*, 13 August 1984, 13–14.
45 See A. Nikiforuk et al., *Running on Empty*, 152.
46 *Alberta Report*, 29 December 1986, 7.
47 A. Nikiforuk et al., *Running on Empty*, 36.
48 The definition of relative deprivation theory advanced here is slightly modified from H. Krahn and T. Harrison, '"Self-referenced" Relative Deprivation and Economic Beliefs: The Effects of the Recession in Alberta,' *Canadian Review of Sociology and Anthropology* (special issue), 29, 2 (1992): 191–209. The same article provides an analysis of the effects of the 1986 recession upon people in Alberta. For more general discussions of relative deprivation, see H.D. Graham and R.T. Gurr, *Violence in America*; C. Brinton, *The Anatomy of Revolution* (New York: Norton 1938); J.C. Davies, 'Toward a Theory of Revolution,' *American Sociological Review*, 34 (1962): 19–31; and R.T. Gurr, *Why Men Rebel* (Princeton: Princeton University Press 1970).
49 The use of standard deviations to measure economic volatility is borrowed from the innovative work of R.A. McGuire, 'Economic Causes.'
50 R. Mansell and M. Percy, *Strength in Adversity: A Study of the Alberta Economy*, Western Studies in Economic Policy, Pub. no. 1 (Edmonton: University of Alberta Press 1990).
51 Calculated from population figures from the Alberta Bureau of Statistics, *Alberta Statistical Review*, First Quarter (Edmonton: Alberta Bureau of Statistics 1989 and 1991); and GDP figures from Statistics Canada, 'Historical Statistical Supplement, 1989/90,' *Canadian Economic Observer* (Ottawa: Statistics Canada 1990), 102. See graph 3.1, T. Harrison, 'Of Passionate Intensity: Right-Wing Populism and the Reform Party of Canada.' (unpublished doctoral thesis in sociology, Edmonton: University of Alberta 1993), 77.
52 Alberta Bureau of Statistics, *Alberta Statistical Review*, Fourth Quarter (Edmonton: Alberta Bureau of Statistics, 1987, 1988, 1989, 1990). See graph 3.2, T. Harrison, 'Of Passionate Intensity,' 77.
53 See R. Mansell and M. Percy, *Strength in Adversity*, for a fuller exposition of the Alberta situation during this period.
54 A. Nikiforuk et al., *Running on Empty*, 137.
55 See H. Palmer and T. Palmer, *Alberta*, 361; also D. Braid and S. Sharpe, *Breakup*, 75–100.
56 *Alberta Report*, 10 March 1986, 10–16.
57 *Alberta Report*, 17 March 1986, 12–16.

58 *Alberta Report*, 19 January 1987, 10–13.

59 See A. Cairns, *Constitution*.

60 Quoted in *Alberta Report*, 1 September 1986, 6.

61 Figures in *Alberta Report*, 14 January 1985, 8–9.

62 *Alberta Report*, 15 December 1986, 10.

63 Ibid., 10–11.

64 See Gallup poll, 10 September 1987.

65 Not only were the polls suggesting this possibility; the 1986 federal by-election in Pembina saw the NDP's candidate, Ivor Dent, nearly win. Moreover, the provincial election of the same year saw a record sixteen NDP members elected to the Alberta legislature.

66 *Financial Times*, 22 March 1982, 1–2. In a telephone conversation with the author on 7 November 1991, Neil Roberts stated that his father felt that certain officials in the Liberal hierarchy were trying to undermine him.

67 S. Roberts, undated materials, supplied to the author by Pia Roberts.

68 Author's telephone conversation with N. Roberts, 1991.

69 Conversation with G. Gibson, at the Canada West Foundation Alternatives Conference, 28 September 1991.

70 P. Manning, *New Canada*, 91.

71 M. Dobbin, *Preston Manning*, 67.

72 P. Manning, *New Canada*, 92.

73 Ibid.

74 See I. Pearson, 'Thou Shalt Not Ignore the West,' *Saturday Night*, December 1990, 34–43, 74–5; P. Manning, *New Canada*; author's personal interview with Ted Byfield, 1991; author's telephone interview with R. Grbavac, 17 July 1991.

75 Most of the biographic information and quotes on Cliff Fryers are taken from M. McNellis, 'Reform's moneyman,' *The Financial Post Magazine*, September 1991, 18–26; but see also *Alberta Report*, 10 June 1991, 12.

76 M. McNellis, 'Reform's Moneyman,' 23.

77 P. Manning, *New Canada*.

78 The involvement of Poole is mentioned in I. Pearson, 'Thou Shalt Not Ignore the West,' 42.

79 F. Winspear, *Out of My Mind*; R. Grbavac interview.

80 F. Winspear, *Out of My Mind*.

81 F. Winspear, *Out of My Mind*; P. Manning, *New Canada*; author's interview with T. Byfield, 1991.

82 Western Assembly, *Assorted Documents of the Western Assembly on Canada's Economic and Political Future* (Vancouver, May 1987).

83 *Alberta Report*, 10 February 1986, 5–6.

84 Western Assembly, *Assorted Documents.*
85 Ibid.
86 Author's interview with S. Harper; see also P. Manning, *New Canada.*
    Mansell and a University of Alberta economist, Mike Percy, gained fame
    in the early 1980s when their study, commissioned by the C.D. Howe
    Institute, concluded that the NEP had led to an outflow from Alberta of
    nearly $8,000 per capita per year and had intensified the effects of the
    recession (D. Braid and S. Sharpe, *Breakup*, 185–6).
87 Author's interview with S. Harper.
88 P. Manning, *Choosing a Political Vehicle to Represent the West*, A
    presentation to the Western Assembly on Canada's Economic and Political
    Future (Vancouver 30 May 1987), 1.
89 Ibid., 3–5.
90 Ibid., 10.
91 This call for a bringing together of Canadians was reinforced by Stan
    Roberts who pointedly announced, as the assembly began, that an
    interpreter was available for anyone wanting to speak in French (*Globe and
    Mail*, 30 May 1987, A7). It is not known whether any of the delegates
    availed themselves of this opportunity.
92 J. Richards to author, 1 October 1991.
93 *Alberta Report*, 8 June 1987, 8.
94 *Globe and Mail*, 1 June 1987, A2.
95 A. Nikiforuk et al., *Running on Empty*, 85.
96 Telephone interview with R. Grbavac, 1991.
97 P. Manning, *Laying the Foundations for a New Western Political Party*, An
    address to a public information meeting sponsored by the Reform
    Association of Canada (Calgary 10 August 1987), 8.
98 Ibid., 8.
99 See A. Finkel, *Social Credit Phenomenon.*
100 P. Manning, *Letter to J.W. Chomiak*, 5 August 1987.
101 P. Manning, *Letter to J.W. Chomiak*, 11 September 1987, italics added.
102 Ted Byfield editorial in *Alberta Report*, 15 June 1987, 52.
103 *Alberta Report*, 9 November 1987, 15–20.
104 P.B. Waite, *The Confederation Debates in the Province of Canada/1865*
    (Toronto: McClelland and Stewart 1963), v.
105 See also D. Creighton, *Dominion of the North: A History of Canada* (1944, rev.
    1957; Toronto: Macmillan Company of Canada 1972); and P.B. Waite,
    *The Life and Times of Confederation, 1864–1867: Politics, Newspapers, and the
    Union of British North America* (Toronto: University of Toronto Press 1977).
106 P. Manning, *New Canada.*

107 The late A.J. Hooke told the author about the MIDAS Reform Party during an interview in 1991. MIDAS stood for 'Money, Interest, Debt, and Slavery,' and encapsulated the old Social Credit doctrine that capitalism was fine, all that was needed was monetary reform (see MIDAS Reform Party of Canada, *Statement of Beliefs*, undated). Also, author's telephone interview with Oran Johnston, 13 August 1991.

108 P. Manning, *New Canada*, 147.

109 Reform Party of Canada, *Constitution* (adopted at Winnipeg 30 October 1987).

110 See A. Finkel, *Social Credit Phenomenon*.

111 Reform Party of Canada, *Constitution*.

112 *Winnipeg Free Press*, 31 October 1987, 2.

113 *Alberta Report*, 10 December 1990, 18.

114 P. Manning, *New Canada*, 150.

115 S. Harper, *Achieving Economic Justice in Confederation*, Speech given to the founding convention of the Reform Party of Canada (Winnipeg 30 October 1987). All quotes that immediately follow are taken from this speech.

116 P. Manning, *New Canada*.

117 Author's telephone conversation with N. Roberts, 1991.

118 *Alberta Report*, 9 November 1987, 15–20; also P. Manning, *New Canada*.

119 *Alberta Report*, 9 November 1987, 15–20.

120 'Reform Party Candidate Quits, Alleges Wrongdoing,' *Winnipeg Free Press*, 2 November 1987, 1.

121 *Alberta Report*, 9 November 1987, 15–20.

122 F. Winspear, interview.

123 *Alberta Report*, 9 November 1987, 15–20.

124 See, for example, M. Dobbin, *Preston Manning*.

125 See J. Barr, *Dynasty*, 170.

126 See S. Sharpe and D. Braid, *Storming Babylon*, 17–18, on the early Social Credit origins of one of Manning's famous quips.

127 'Blend of Mother Teresa, Rambo Touted for Success,' *Winnipeg Free Press*, 2 November 1987, 1.

128 P. Manning, *New Canada*, 168.

129 Reform's *Blue Book* states the following policy on labour-management relations as adopted at the party's Edmonton convention in 1989 and reaffirmed at the Saskatoon convention in 1991:

   The Reform Party supports the right of workers to organize democratically, to bargain collectively, and to strike peacefully.

The Reform Party supports the harmonization of labour-management relations, and rejects the view that labour and management must constitute warring camps.

This apparently conciliatory and balanced approach is undermined by a third clause that could be viewed as supporting right-to-work legislation:

The Reform Party supports the right of all Canadians, particularly the young, to enter the work force and achieve their potential. Unions and professional bodies may ensure standards, but should not block qualified people from working in a trade or profession or from gaining the necessary qualifications (Reform Party of Canada, *The Blue Book*, adopted at the Edmonton Assembly, 1989 [Calgary: *Reform Party of Canada* 1989]; and *The Blue Book*, Adopted at the Saskatoon Assembly, 1991 [Calgary: Reform Party of Canada 1991]).

It is perhaps worth noting that *56 Reasons Why You Should Support the Reform Party of Canada* (Calgary: Reform Party of Canada n.d.), a glossy brochure produced by the party for popular circulation, repeats the substance of only the second of these clauses.

130 Reform Party, *Platform and Statement of Principles*, Policies adopted at the party convention in Calgary, Alberta, August 1988 (rep. Calgary: Reform Party of Canada 1989). While it is true that Reformers generally frown upon open immigration and multiculturalism and believe that the penal system is too soft on criminals, it is important to understand the context in which these issues gained saliency among many Reform supporters. RCMP uniforms became an issue as a result of a recent federal government ruling that Sikhs would be allowed to wear their turbans in the police force. Supporters of the ruling viewed it as both an attempt to respect the deeply felt religious beliefs of a minority and a practical effort at recruiting Sikhs into the RCMP. Numerous Anglo-Canadians, however, both Reformers and others, opposed the ruling, viewing it as both an attack on Canada's Anglo heritage and a needless intrusion of personal attributes into a ostensibly neutral uniform. At the Reform party's 1989 convention, delegates voted overwhelmingly that RCMP uniforms should remain free of turbans and other religious adornments.

Similarly, the issue of crime became salient as a result of one specific case, involving the capture in Canada of Charles Ng, a man wanted in California for trial on charges involving a particularly heinous crime:

mass murder. A series of hearings into his legal rights under the Charter of Rights and Freedoms held up Ng's extradition to the United States. The hearings dealt with whether Canada, a country without a death penalty, would be infringing on Ng's rights by returning him to California, a state with a death penalty. For many Canadians, the idea of debating the rights of an accused mass murderer seemed absurd. But Ng's case may also have aroused passions for another reason: he is Vietnamese. Hence, the issue brought together several points of concern to the right wing, particularly non-white immigration, law and order, and the controversial provisions of the Charter. The fact that Ng was not an immigrant – he had entered Canada illegally – was immaterial to these right-wing elements, a fact indicated by a draft resolution submitted by the Lethbridge constituency of the Reform party in response to the Ng case, which called for immigrants and refugees to be denied Charter protections. In the end, the Reform party dropped the resolution before it came up for debate (see the *Edmonton Journal*, 12 February 1991, A3, and 24 March 1991, A7). As for Ng, he was extradited to the United States in September 1991.

131 See the review of polls in Gallup, 17 October 1988.
132 The Northern Foundation, *Letter* (Ottawa), November 1990.
133 W. Gairdner, *Trouble*.
134 Northern Foundation, *Letter*; also *The Northern Voice*, 3, 3 (1991), and *The Northern Voice*, 4, 1 (1992).
135 Quoted by columnist Mark Lisac, column in the *Edmonton Journal*, 9 January 1990, A11.
136 See, for example, Link Byfield's columns in *Alberta Report*, 22 October 1990, 4, and 22 April 1991, 2.
137 See G. Potter's letter in *Alberta Report*, 9 September 1991, 5.
138 Author's interview with S. Harper, 1991.
139 The discussion of Meech Lake which follows is taken, in the main, from A. Cohen, *Deal Undone*; but see also P.E. Trudeau, 'The Values of a Just Society,' in T. Axworthy and P. Trudeau, eds., *Towards a Just Society* (Markham, Ont.: Penguin Books Canada 1990); and *Globe and Mail*, 1 June 1987, A5.
140 Gallup, 28 April 1988.
141 Ibid.
142 Reported in the *Globe and Mail*, 26 November 1988, A3.
143 Gallup, 3 October 1988; for a more elaborated discussion of this, see B. Doern and B.W. Tomlin, *Faith and Fear: The Free Trade Story* (Toronto: Stoddart Publishing 1991), 238–42.

144 Concerning the history of free trade between the United States and Canada, see R. Hill and J. Whalley, 'Introduction: Canada–U.S. Free Trade,' in J. Whalley and R. Hill, eds., *Canada–United States Free Trade*, Royal Commission on the Economic Union and Development Prospects for Canada, Research Studies, vol. 11 (Toronto: University of Toronto Press 1985); B. Doern and B.W. Tomlin, *Faith and Fear*; also D. Creighton, *Dominion of the North*; and J.M.S. Careless, *Canada: A Story Of Challenge* (1953, rev. 1963; Toronto: Macmillan of Canada 1983).

145 B. Mulroney, *Where I Stand*.

146 Except where noted, the discussion of how the free trade agreement came about is taken from B. Doern and B.W. Tomlin, *Faith and Fear*.

147 Ibid., 52.

148 Ibid., 29

149 R.S. Khemani, D.M. Shapiro, and W.T. Stanbury, *Mergers, Corporate Concentration and Power in Canada* (Halifax: The Institute for Research on Public Policy 1985), 5; see also R.J. Richardson, 'Free Trade: Why Did It Happen?' *The Canadian Review of Sociology and Anthropology*, 29, 3 (1992): 307–28.

150 J.A. Lower, *Western Canada*.

151 Poll results in Canada West Foundation, *Putting the Cards on the Table ... Free Trade and Western Canadian Industries* (Calgary: Canada West Foundation 1986).

152 The various arguments in favour of free trade can be found in Doern and Tomlin, *Faith and Fear*; J. Laxer, *Oil and Gas*; J. Crispo, ed., *Free Trade: The Real Story* (Toronto: Gage Educational Publishing Company 1988); and Canada, Department of Finance, *The Canada–U.S. Free Trade Agreement: An Economic Assessment* (Ottawa 1988).

153 For the arguments in opposition to free trade, see B. Doern and B.W. Tomlin, *Faith and Fear*; M. Watkins, 'Reservations Concerning a Free Trade Area,' in J. Whalley and R. Hill, eds., *Canada–United States Free Trade*; J. Laxer, *Oil and Gas*; D. Cameron, ed., *The Free Trade Deal* (Toronto: James Lorimer and Company, 1988).

154 J. Laxer, *Oil and Gas*; B. Doern and B.W. Tomlin, *Faith and Fear*; also S. Bashevkin, *True Patriot Love: The Politics of Canadian Nationalism* (Toronto: Oxford University Press 1991).

155 S. Bashevkin, *True Patriot Love*; B. Doern and B.W. Tomlin, *Faith and Fear*.

156 Chief Electoral Officer of Canada, *Report of the Chief Electoral Officer Respecting Election Expenses* (Ottawa 1988).

157 R.M. Lee, *One Hundred Monkeys*, 222.

158 N. Ovenden column in the *Edmonton Journal*, 20 April 1991, G2.

159 See R.M. Lee, *One Hundred Monkeys*; B. Doern and B.W. Tomlin, *Faith and Fear*.
160 See R.M. Lee, *One Hundred Monkeys*.
161 See W.K. Carroll, 'Restructuring Capital, Reorganizing Consent: Gramsci, Political Economy, and Canada,' *The Canadian Review of Sociology and Anthropology*, 27, 3 (1990): 390–416; also B. Doern and B.W. Tomlin, *Faith and Fear*; R.J. Richardson, 'Free Trade.'
162 R.M. Lee, *One Hundred Monkeys*.
163 See Gallup, 25 October 1988.
164 See J. Richards, R. Cairns, and L. Pratt, eds., *Social Democracy without Illusions: Renewal of the Canadian Left* (Toronto: McClelland and Stewart 1991), for public perceptions of the NDP on fiscal matters.
165 Gallup, 17 October 1988, and 19 November 1988.
166 Gallup, 8 December 1988.
167 P. Resnick, *Letters to a Québécois Friend* (with a reply by Daniel Latouche) (Montreal: McGill-Queen's University Press 1990).
168 The CHP presents an interesting comparison to the Reform party. The CHP held its founding convention in Hamilton, Ontario, on 18–21 November 1987 – ironically, at virtually the same time as the Reform party formed in the west. Despite the location of the convention, many of the 520 delegates who attended the event were from the West. Indeed, its leader and founder was Ed Vanwoudenberg an otherwise unknown Surrey, BC, businessman. Like many of the party's members, Vanwoudenberg belongs to the Canadian (Dutch) Reformed Church.

The policies ratified by the CHP at its founding convention, and since reaffirmed, suggest that it is an essentially ethno-centric (English-speaking, western-European), Christian, middle-class party motivated by fears of social and cultural change and with a concomitant desire to return to traditional mores and values. The party's policies on immigration, bilingualism, and multiculturalism are similar to positions taken by the Reform party that emphasize a retention of Canada's historic cultural and linguistic mix. In contrast to the Reform party, however, the CHP tends to be more overtly Christian, with policies frequently justified on the basis of Biblical references. For example, the policy manual's section on economics uses twenty-eight Bible readings to support its espousal of free enterprise capitalism!

With the rise of the Reform party, the base of strength of the CHP has gradually moved into Ontario's rural heartland. The party has also been riven by internal conflicts between those who would like to amalgamate with the Reform party and those who want to remain closer to the party's religious roots. In 1991 Vanwoudenberg resigned as leader. Leadership of the party has since been in turmoil.

169 Calculated from the *Report of the Chief Electoral Officer on the 34th General Election* (Ottawa: Chief Electoral Officer of Canada 1988).

170 Ibid.

171 For details, see tables 3.1 and 3.2 in T. Harrison, 'Of Passionate Intensity,' 107.

172 *Report of the Chief Electoral Officer on the 34th General Election,* 1988.

173 J. Richards and L. Pratt, *Prairie Capitalism*; J.D. House, *Last of the Free Enterprisers.*

174 Reform's Strathcona candidate, Doug Main, subsequently ran – and won – under the Tory banner in Alberta's 1989 provincial election. He was later named culture minister. In the fall of 1992, following the resignation of Don Getty as Alberta premier, Main ran unsuccessfully for the Tory leadership on a platform blatantly attempting to curry support from Reform's constituency. He was subsequently dumped from the cabinet by the winner, Ralph Klein, and then as a PC candidate for the election that followed.

175 *Report of the Chief Electoral Officer on the 34th General Election.*

176 Reform Party of Canada, *The Reformer,* 1, 6 (October 1988): 1.

177 Quoted in R.M. Lee, *One Hundred Monkeys,* 266.

CHAPTER 4   The Legitimation of Reform

1 P. Manning, 'The Road to New Canada,' speech given to the Saskatoon convention of the Reform Party of Canada, 6 April 1991, 2, 18.

2 Details regarding Deborah Grey's background can be found in P. Manning, *New Canada,* 184–5; and S. Zwarun, 'Women and the Reform Party,' *Chatelaine,* March 1992, 46–8, 132–4.

3 For a profile of the other candidates who ran in the Alberta Senate election, see *Edmonton Journal,* 8 October 1989, E2. Regarding Stan Waters's background and views, see *Edmonton Journal,* 28 October 1989, A1, 26 September 1991, A1, and 1 October 1991, A8; also P. Manning, *New Canada,* 202–4. Regarding the financial sources for his Senate campaign, see M. Dobbin, *Preston Manning,* 92.

4 Reform Party of Canada, *The Reformer,* 3, 2 (June 1990).

5 See P. Manning, *New Canada,* 209, regarding the importance which he attaches to the GST issue in Waters's election.

6 Author's interview with S. Harper, 1991, 5–6.

7 Reform Party of Canada, *The Reformer,* 1, 7 (1988), special election issue.

8 P. Manning, *New Canada,* 239.

9 Ibid., 240.

10 Ibid., 223–4.
11 *Edmonton Journal*, 1 January 1990, A8.
12 The following discussion of the events leading up to the collapse of the Meech Lake Accord is taken from A. Cohen, *Deal Undone*.
13 See Angus Reid's analysis in the *Edmonton Journal*, 24 March 1991, A9; also A. Cohen.
14 'Poll Says People Lukewarm to Pack,' *Edmonton Journal*, 13 June 1990, A3.
15 'Reject Meech – Manning,' *Edmonton Journal*, 13 June 1990, A3.
16 *Alberta Report*, 2 July 1990, 10–14.
17 P. Manning, quoted in *Alberta Report*, 24 December 1990, 11.
18 P. Manning, quoted in the *Edmonton Journal*, 1 February 1991, A12.
19 Ibid.
20 Compare Gallup polls of 16 January 1989 and 27 November 1989.
21 See Gallup, 23 November 1989.
22 Gallup, 25 January 1990.
23 Gallup reports for 22 February 1990, 22 March 1990, 19 April 1990, 17 May 1990.
24 Gallup, 18 May 1990.
25 See Angus Reid's analysis in the *Edmonton Journal*, 24 March 1991, A9.
26 *Edmonton Journal*, 21 September 1991, A1.
27 Angus Reid's analysis in the *Edmonton Journal*, 24 March 1991, A9; see also results of CBC–Globe and Mail and Environics polls in the *Edmonton Journal*, 5 September 1991, A3.
28 Gallup poll reported in the *Edmonton Journal*, 21 May 1991, A1.
29 Unemployment statistics taken from Alberta Bureau of Statistics, *Alberta Statistical Review*, First Quarter (Edmonton: Alberta Bureau of Statistics 1991); *Alberta Report*, 8 March 1993, 6; and *Edmonton Journal*, 2 March 1994, A1.
30 See the *Edmonton Journal*, 24 February 1994, A10, describing the decreasing costs of unemployment insurance due to lapsed eligibility.
31 Canada, Department of Consumer and Corporate Affairs, *Statistics on Bankruptcies and Proposals* (Edmonton Bureau: Federal Department of Consumer and Corporate Affairs, 1989, 1990, 1991, 1992); and *Globe and Mail*, 26 February 1994, B6.
32 *Globe and Mail*, classroom edition September 1993, and February 1994, 19, for figures. Regarding the restructuring in general, see also H. Krahn, 'Quality of Work in the Service Sector,' *Statistics Canada: General Social Survey Analysis Series No. 6* (Ottawa: Statistics Canada, Cat 11–612E 1992); and H. Krahn and G. Lowe, *Work, Industry, and Canadian Society*, rev. ed. (Scarborough, Ont.: Nelson Canada 1993).
33 See privatization minister John McDermid's comments in the *Edmonton*

Journal, 9 March 1991, A1; and finance minister Don Mazankowski's comments in the *Edmonton Journal*, 15 May 1991, A4, as reported by Southam columnist E. Beauchesne; also Brian Mulroney's comments in the *Edmonton Journal*, 8 August 1991, A3, predicting a strong inflation-free recovery.

34 *Globe and Mail*, 18 January 1992, D1.

35 *Edmonton Journal*, 2 March 1994, A1. In 1993 GDP grew by 2.4 per cent.

36 H.D. Clarke and A. Kornberg, 'Support for the Canadian Federal Progressive Conservative Party since 1988: The Impact of Economic Evaluations and Economic Issues,' *Canadian Journal of Political Science*, 25, 1 (1992): 29–53.

37 See, for example, K. Ohmae, *The Borderless World: Power and Strategy in the Interlinked Economy* (New York: Harper Business 1990).

38 W. Clement and G. Williams, *The New Canadian Political Economy* (Montreal: McGill-Queen's University Press 1989); M. Porter, *Canada at the Crossroads: The Reality of a New Competitive Environment* (Ottawa: Business Council on National Issues/Supply and Services Canada 1991); G. Laxer, *Perspectives on Canadian Economic Development*; D. Drache and M.S. Gertler, *The New Era of Global Competition: State Policy and Market Power* (Montreal: McGill Queen's University Press 1991).

39 R. Whitaker, 'Neo-conservatism and the State,' 4.

40 Statistics Canada, Economic Services Section, *Analysis Summary of Federal Government Debt* (Ottawa: Statistics Canada, Cat. 68–512 20 September 1991).

41 D. Bercuson et al., *Sacred Trust*; C. Hoy, *Friends*; J. Sawatsky, *Mulroney*.

42 See R. Whitaker, 'Neo-conservatism and the State'; also R. Chodos, R. Murphy, and E. Hamovitch, *The Unmaking of Canada: The Hidden Theme in Canadian History since 1945* (Toronto: James Lorimer and Company 1991).

43 Federal Finance Department statistics released in February 1991 reported in the *Edmonton Journal*, 27 February 1991, A7; see also *Edmonton Journal*, 20 June 1991, A1.

44 See D. Bercuson et al., *Sacred Trust*.

45 J.M. Keynes, *General Theory of Employment, Interest and Money* (New York: Harcourt, Brace and Company 1936).

46 Statistics Canada, *Analysis Summary of Federal Government Debt*.

47 Reform Party of Canada, *The Reformer*, 1, 7, (1988), special election issue.

48 See the federal Tory budget for 1991, reported in the *Edmonton Journal*, 27 February, 1991 A7; also changes in the provisions of the Public Service Reform Act, reported in the *Edmonton Journal*, 19 June 1991, A1.

49 See H.D. Clarke and A. Kornberg, 'Support,' on this point.

50 Canada, Department of Finance, *The Canada–U.S. Free Trade Agreement.*

51 *Edmonton Journal*, 25 June 1992 A1; also E. Beauchesne's article in the *Edmonton Journal*, 5 December 1992, A12.

52 See D. Drache's comments in R. Ziegler's column in the *Edmonton Journal*, 24 August 1991, C1.

53 The issue of a secret side-deal with the American government is supported by L. Martin, *Pledge of Allegiance. The Americanization of Canada in the Mulroney Years* (Toronto: McClelland and Stewart 1993), 131.

54 Canada, Department of Finance, *Goods and Services Tax: Technical Paper* (Ottawa: Government of Canada 1989), 5–6.

55 See the *Edmonton Journal*, 25 February 1990, A1; and follow-up in the *Edmonton Journal*, 21 March 1991, A4.

56 See the *Edmonton Journal*, 3 March 1990, G2, and 10 March 1990, G1; Reform Party of Canada, *The Reformer*, 3, 2 (1990).

57 Gallup, 24 May 1990.

58 Telephone conversation with Statistics Canada, 15 May 1992.

59 Figures in *Alberta Report*, 8 March 1993, 6–11.

60 To many on the left, the debt/deficit 'crisis' is viewed as an excuse manu-factured by right-wing elements to dismantle Canada's social safety net (see S. McBride and J. Shields, *Dismantling a Nation*). They point out that Canada has had a higher debt-to-GDP ratio on several occasions in the past, and that much of the recent rise in the deficit is attributable to the Bank of Canada's interest rate policies and declining corporate tax revenues (see H. Chorney, J. Hotson, and M. Seccareccia, *The Deficit Made Me Do It! The Myths about Government Debt* [Ottawa: Canadian Centre for Policy Alter-natives 1992]). The debate about the debt/deficit centres less on the need to deal with it, than the precise method. For a useful contrast to approaches, see B. Dahlby, 'Canada's Deficit-Debt Problem: Why the Sceptics Are Wrong,' and D. Cameron, 'With a Response: Escaping the Debt Trap,' in *Western Canada: Economic Destiny* (Calgary: Canada West Foundation, 1994).

61 *Alberta Report*, 8 March 1993, 6–11. Far from instilling investor confidence, zero inflation, if actually achieved, might also be viewed as an index of hopelessness in a stagnant economy.

62 H. Clarke and A. Kornberg, 'Support.' Scepticism over Tory acumen was not confined to the general public. Within one week in November 1992 no less than four economic think-tanks – the Conference Board of Canada, Informetrica, the WEFA Group, and Global Economics Ltd. – denounced Tory spending restraints, high interest rates, and tax increases for pro-longing and exacerbating the effects of the recession (see E. Beauchesne's column in the *Edmonton Journal*, 16 November 1992, A6).

63 The Gallup poll for April 1990 gave Reform 6 per cent support. A year later it stood at 16 per cent, and remained in that range over the following year.

64 Gallup, 22 November 1990.

65 See *Financial Times of Canada*, 6 April 1992, 13, regarding the campaign launched by the National Citizens' Coalition against the NDP.

66 D. Laycock, *Populism and Democratic Thought*, 18.

67 The most complete description of Preston Manning's version of Canadian history appears in his recently published autobiography, *New Canada*, 300–5.

68 Ibid., 302–3.

69 See J.M.S. Careless, *Canada*; D. Creighton, *Dominion of the North*; G. Laxer, *Perspectives on Canadian Economic Development*.

70 See D. Creighton, *Dominion of the North*; J.M.S. Careless, *Canada*; J.A. Lower, *Western Canada*. Regarding 'Anglo-conformist' pressures in Alberta in particular, see H. Palmer, *Patterns of Prejudice*; also H. Palmer and T. Palmer, *Alberta*, especially 78–9

71 For a fuller examination of the errors and omissions in Manning's account of Canadian history, see T. Harrison, 'Of Passionate Intensity.'

72 C. Denis, '*Quebec-as-distinct-society* as Conventional Wisdom: The Constitutional Silence of Anglo-Canadian Sociologists,' *The Canadian Journal of Sociology*, 18, 3 (1993): 251–69, provides an excellent discussion of this point.

73 See J. Richards, 'The Case for Provincial Jurisdiction over Language,' in J. Richards, W.G. Watson, and F. Vaillancourt, *Survival: Official Language Rights in Canada* (Toronto: C.D. Howe Institute 1992); and Y. Fontaine, 'A Comment,' in the same text.

74 See Reform Party of Canada, 'Principles and Policies,' *The Blue Book*, Adopted at the Saskatoon Assembly, 1991 (Calgary: Reform Party of Canada 1991), 32–3.

75 P. Manning, *New Canada*, 304–5. Manning appears to suggest elsewhere in his autobiography that, rather than demanding fair treatment from the majority, minority groups should depend upon the sufferance of the majority (pp. 106–7). Some might view this faith in sufferance as rather naive, given the history of atrocities inflicted by majorities upon minority groups in this century. But Manning seems not entirely to believe in the notion of a majority, except in an abstract or numerical sense. Rather, such 'majorities' consist of individuals who may not act coercively as a group. From this classically liberal perspective, it is only organized 'special interests' that tend to act coercively. This interpretation of Manning's view

of individual and group rights is supported by S. Sharpe and D. Braid, *Storming Babylon*, who trace Manning's antipathy to collective rights to his religious belief in personal salvation.

76 H. Palmer, *Patterns of Prejudice*.
77 I.M. Leonard and R.D. Parmet, *American Nativism*.
78 Ibid.; also E.P. Crapol, *America for Americans*.
79 R. Hofstadter, *Age of Reform*.
80 C. Berger, *Sense of Power*; H. Palmer, *Patterns of Prejudice*; and M. Robin, *Shades of Right*.
81 H. Palmer, *Patterns of Prejudice*, 7.
82 See E.P. Crapol, *American for Americans*.
83 C. Berger, *Sense of Power*.
84 See P.B. Waite, *Confederation Debates*; also *Life and Times of Confederation*. That Canada lacked a single unifying identity was bemoaned eloquently by Christopher Dunkin during those Confederation debates: 'We have a large class whose national feelings turn toward London ... another large class whose sympathies centre here at Quebec ... and yet another whose comparisons are rather with Washington; but have we any class of people who are attached, or whose feelings are going to be directed with any earnestness, to the City of Ottawa, the centre of the new nationality that is to be created?' (R.M. Hamilton, *Canadian Quotations and Phrases: Literary and Historical* [Toronto: McClelland and Stewart 1952], 144).
85 F. Underhill, *In Search of Canadian Liberalism* (Toronto: Macmillan Company of Canada 1960), 88.
86 International Labour Office, 'Canada,' *International Migrations, vol. I* (New York: National Bureau of Economic Research, 1929).
87 Canada, *Canada Year Book* (Ottawa: Queen's Printer 1961), 185.
88 R. Logan, 'Immigration.'
89 All statistics calculated from Statistics Canada, *Canada Year Book*. (Ottawa: Statistics Canada 1981), 155–6.
90 Statistics Canada, *Canada Year Book, 125th Anniversary* (Ottawa: Statistics Canada 1992).
91 See J.V. Andrew, *Bilingual Today*; also P. Brimelow, *Patriot Game*.
92 W. Gairdner, *Trouble*, 389.
93 Statistics Canada, *Canada Year Book, 125th Anniversary* (Ottawa: Statistics Canada 1992).
94 R. Logan, 'Immigration'.
95 See D. Braid and S. Sharpe, *Breakup*; S. Sharpe and D. Braid, *Storming Babylon*; M. Dobbin, *Preston Manning*.
96 See tables 4.1 and 4.2 in T. Harrison, 'Of Passionate Intensity,' 138, for a

slightly different presentation of this same data. A more sophisticated analysis of the data also appears in T. Harrison and H. Krahn, 'Populism and the Rise of the Reform Party in Alberta,' *Canadian Review of Sociology and Anthropology*, 32, 2 (1995).

The category 'Anglo-Saxon-Celtic' included all respondents who termed their ethnic heritage as British, English, Irish, Scottish, Welsh, or combinations including at least one of these. The category 'European' included all respondents listing a European heritage, or combinations including at least one European but not including Anglo-Saxon-Celtic. The 'Canadian' category is self-explanatory. All remaining respondents were categorized as 'other.'

97 P. Brimelow, *Patriot Game*, 140.
98 Ibid., 289.
99 *Edmonton Journal*, 29 October 1989, A7.
100 M. Dobbin, *Preston Manning*, 102–7.
101 W. Gairdner, *Trouble*, 3.
102 Ibid., 419.
103 G. Smith, *Canada*.
104 P. Brimelow, *Patriot Games*; W. Gairdner, *Trouble*.
105 See, for example, Ted Byfield's editorials in the *Alberta Report*, 25 January 1982, 52, and 15 March 1982, 60.
106 K. Archer and F. Ellis, 'Opinion Structures of Party Activists: The Reform Party of Canada,' *Canadian Journal of Political Science*, 27, 2 (1994): 277–308.
107 Preston Manning speaking in New York City to the Americas Society, quoted in M. Dobbin, *Preston Manning*, 158. On the issue of American-Canadian political relations, Manning may be somewhat out of step with Reform delegates. In K. Archer and F. Ellis's study, 'Opinion Structures,' 46.7 per cent of delegates to the party's 1992 convention agreed that 'Canada should pursue a foreign policy more independent of the United States.' By contrast, 31.5 per cent disagreed, while the remaining 21.8 per cent were uncertain.
108 Quoted in P. Manning, *New Canada*, 283–4, italics added.
109 See Liberal MP Sheila Copps's comments in the *Edmonton Journal*, 21 November 1991, A3, and the comments of minority group representatives in the *Edmonton Journal*, 31 October 1989, A1.
110 *Edmonton Journal*, 5 February 1990, A8.
111 W. Gairdner, *Trouble*, 393 and 413, respectively.
112 Reform Party of Canada, *Blue Book*, Adopted at the Edmonton Assembly, 1989, 23, italics added.
113 Reform Party of Canada, *Blue Book*, Adopted at the Saskatoon Assembly,

1991, 35. Assimilation is strongly supported by Reform activists. In Archer and Ellis, 'Opinion Structures,' 91.3 per cent of Reform delegates to the 1992 assembly agreed with the statement: 'Newly arrived immigrants should be assimilated into the Canadian mainstream.'

114 *Edmonton Journal*, 30 October 1989, A1, and 10 February 1991, A10.
115 W. Gairdner, *The Trouble with Canada*, Speech given to the Reform party convention, Saskatoon, 6 April 1991; see M. Dobbin, *Preston Manning*, 147, for some quotes transcribed from the speech.
116 *Edmonton Journal*, 7 February 1991, B4.
117 *Edmonton Journal*, 29 November 1991, B13. The derogatory sentence 'Mop Heads in the RCMP' refers to the decision to allow Sikhs in that organization to wear turbans. To their credit, some Reformers have stated their opposition to the party's position on turbans in the RCMP. Most notably, MP Ian McClelland has stated: 'I'm out of step with the vast majority of Reformers and many other people, but I don't care what a person wears on his head. What I'm concerned about is what's in a person's head, not what's on it' (*Globe and Mail*, 29 January 1994, A4).
118 *Edmonton Journal*, 14 October 1993, A4.
119 *Edmonton Journal*, 29 December 1991, A4.
120 *Globe and Mail*, 29 February 1992, A4; see also M. Dobbin, *Preston Manning*, 108–9, on Droege's pronounced support for Reform. The links between the Heritage Front and Reform need to be fully examined. Particularly important are accusations that the Canadian Security and Intelligence Service (CSIS) planted a mole in the Front who in turn encouraged Front members to join Reform. There are intimations that these activities may have been instituted by politically interested groups to embarrass the Reform party (see N. Ovenden's column in the *Edmonton Journal*, 17 September 1994, A10).
121 The expulsions were reported in the *Edmonton Journal*, 11 March 1992, A9.
122 See K. Whyte's column, *Globe and Mail*, 29 February 1992, A4.
123 P. Manning, *New Canada*.
124 M. Weber, *Protestant Ethic*.
125 W. Gairdner, *Trouble*, 44.
126 E. Hoffer, *The True Believer* (New York: Harper 1951).
127 The idea of imaginary identifications is taken from B. Anderson, *Imagined Communities: Reflections on the Origin and Spread of Nationalism* (London: Verso 1983).
128 P. Manning, address to the Saskatoon convention, April 1992, quoted in P. Manning, *New Canada*, viii.
129 Gallup, 19 December 1991.

CHAPTER 5   The Transformation of Reform

1 P. Manning, *New Canada*, 260.
2 V.J. Wiebe letter in the *Alberta Report*, 13 January 1992, 3.
3 *Edmonton Journal*, 8 May 1991, A4.
4 The APA features among its prominent members Reformers such as Dal Brown, a Reform party candidate in 1988, APA founder Howard Thompson, and current APA leader Mark Waters's, Stan Waters's son. See the *Alberta Report*, 5 November 1990, 8–9; and the *Edmonton Journal*, 9 April 1991, A7.
5 Reform Party of Canada, *Delegates Survey* (Calgary: Reform Party of Canada 1989).
6 *Alberta Report*, 19 February 1990, 18.
7 See S. Barrett, *Is God a Racist?*
8 Reform Party of Canada, *Memorandum*, 15 April (Calgary: Reform Party of Canada 1991).
9 P. Manning, *Choosing a Political Vehicle*.
10 *Alberta Report*, 18 March 1991, 10–14.
11 *Edmonton Journal*, 7 April 1991, A3.
12 *Edmonton Journal*, 6 June 1991, A3.
13 *Edmonton Journal*, 19 March 1990, A9.
14 M. Dobbin, *Preston Manning*.
15 P. Manning, *New Canada*, 265.
16 *Edmonton Journal*, 17 August 1990, F16.
17 N. Ovenden's column in the *Edmonton Journal*, 22 September 1990, G2.
18 N. Ovenden's column in the *Edmonton Journal*, 18 September 1990, A12. See also P. Manning, *New Canada*, 251–2; and S. Sharpe and D. Braid, *Storming Babylon*, 106–7.
19 Reform Party of Canada, *Comparative Membership Analyses, 1990 and 1991* (Calgary: Reform Party of Canada 1991).
20 Fifth business: A role that is neither 'Hero nor Heroine, Confidante nor Villain, but which [is] nonetheless essential to bring about the Recognition or the denouement.' Quoted in Robertson Davies, *Fifth Business, The Deptford Trilogy* (Toronto: Macmillan of Canada 1983), frontispiece.
21 On this point, see the *Edmonton Journal* editorial of 11 September 1991, A10, and J. Dafoe's column in the *Globe and Mail*, 14 September 1991, D2.
22 See W. Thorsell's column in the *Globe and Mail*, 14 September 1991, D6.
23 *Edmonton Journal* editorial of 11 September 1991, A10.
24 J. Dafoe's column in the *Globe and Mail*, 14 September 1991, D2.
25 *Edmonton Journal*, 24 September 1989, B2.

26 Polls and quote in R. Ziegler's column in the *Edmonton Journal*, 15 May 1990, B4.
27 Incident reported in A. Cohen, *Deal Undone*.
28 Reported in the *Edmonton Journal*, 5 March 1991, A8.
29 *Edmonton Journal*, 8 April 1991, A1.
30 *Edmonton Journal*, 7 April 1991, A3.
31 *Edmonton Journal*, 7 April 1991, A1.
32 M. Lisac's column in the *Edmonton Journal*, 3 June 1991, A8; also, *Edmonton Journal*, 6 September 1991, A7.
33 *Edmonton Journal*, 18 January 1992, A1.
34 A. Tupper, 'Alberta Politics: The Collapse of Consensus,' in H. Thorburn, ed., *Party Politics in Canada*, 6th ed. (Scarborough: Prentice-Hall Canada 1991); T. Harrison and H. Krahn, 'Increasing Pluralism or Temporary Fragmentation? Federal Politics in Alberta,' *Alberta*, 3, 2 (1992): 87–104.
35 *Edmonton Journal*, 7 November 1991, A3.
36 *Edmonton Journal*, 26 April 1991, A3.
37 *Alberta Report*, 6 May 1991, 10–11.
38 N. Ovenden's column in the *Edmonton Journal*, 20 July 1991, G2.
39 *Edmonton Journal*, 10 August 1991, A3.
40 *Edmonton Journal*, 19 August 1991, A7.
41 *Edmonton Journal*, 10 August 1991, A3.
42 See chapter 4; also, H.D. Clarke and A. Kornberg, 'Support.'
43 H. Winsor's column in the *Globe and Mail*, 4 May 1991, A1 and A4.
44 *Edmonton Journal*, 9 December 1991, A3.
45 *Edmonton Journal*, 29 November 1991, A14; H. Winsor's column in the *Globe and Mail*, 23 November 1991, A1 and A6.
46 *Edmonton Journal*, 13 June 1992, A3.
47 See W.L. Morton, *Progressive Party*.
48 P. Manning, *New Canada*, 24–5.
49 Ibid., 260.
50 See M. Dobbin, *Preston Manning*; S. Sharpe and D. Braid, *Storming Babylon*.
51 In the course of my study, I discovered certain anomalies regarding the Reform's official statements to Elections Canada. My attempts to clarify these discrepancies led me to Dr W. Stanbury who has been studying party finances for the Royal Commission on Election Expenses. Dr Stanbury confirmed my initial findings and explained the major discrepancies as arising in the following manner.

The Reform party has four major sources of funding: memberships ($10 per year), contributions (usually by members), merchandise sales (T-shirts, buttons, etc.), and entrance fees to rallies (usually $10). Although

Reform Fund Canada (the party's official business agent) has reported regularly the revenues received from 'donations and memberships, merchandise sales, assemblies, and other,' the list of contributions appears to have been treated somewhat separately from memberships and merchandise sales. Moreover, it is unclear how or where the money from rallies is reported. Does it remain in the riding? Does it end up in headquarters? Who keeps tabs on this money? According to Stanbury, no one within Reform seems to be able to answer these questions.

A second more serious problem arises out of Reform Fund Canada's relationship to the party's more than 200 riding associations. Financial contributions to the latter are funnelled through Reform Fund Canada so that tax receipts can be issued, and then 95 per cent of the money is returned to the riding. In the past, however, Reform Fund Canada has only reported among its revenues the 5 per cent which 'headquarters' keeps for itself. In short, previous official reports of Reform's financial position may have significantly underestimated the party's funds. With these clarifications and problems in mind, it is nonetheless possible to arrive at an overall picture of Reform's financial situation, and how it has changed over time. For further information, see W. Stanbury, *Money in Politics: Financing Federal Parties and Candidates in Canada*, Research Studies vol. 1 (Toronto: Dundurn Press 1991).

52 Ibid.
53 Ibid.
54 All figures from Chief Electoral Officer of Canada, *Report of the Chief Electoral Officer Respecting Election Expenses* (Ottawa: Chief Electoral Officer of Canada 1988).
55 P. Manning, *New Canada*, 156.
56 Ibid., 214.
57 The 1990 figure is from the Reform Party of Canada, *Comparative Membership Analyses, 1990 and 1991* (Calgary: Reform Party of Canada 1991); the 1991 figure is from *Globe and Mail*, 25 January 1992, A1 and A4.
58 W. Stanbury, *Money in Politics*.
59 *Report of the Chief Electoral Officer Respecting Party Contributions* (Ottawa: Chief Electoral Officer of Canada 1989). *The Reformer* of May 1991 reports, however, total revenues for 1989 of $1,100,096.
60 See P. Manning, *New Canada*, 92 and 229 regarding Mackenzie.
61 *Report of the Chief Electoral Officer Respecting Party Contributions* (Ottawa: Chief Electoral Officer of Canada 1989).
62 Chief Electoral Officer of Canada, *Elections Financing Branch News Release* (Ottawa: Chief Electoral Officer of Canada 1991); also W. Stanbury, *Money in Politics*.

63 See P. Manning, *New Canada*, 229, regarding the Pirie family.

64 *Report of the Chief Electoral Officer Respecting Party Contributions* (Ottawa: Chief Electoral Officer of Canada 1990).

65 Both native groups and fellow academics severely criticize Flanagan's writings regarding Louis Riel, the Rebellion, and aboriginal land claims in Manitoba. See T. Flanagan, *Riel and the Rebellion of 1885 Reconsidered* (Saskatoon: Western Producer Prairie Books 1983).

66 See S. Sharpe and D. Braid, *Storming Babylon*, 8; and F. Luntz, *Candidates, Consultants, and Campaigns: The Style and Substance of American Electioneering* (New York: Basil Blackwell, 1988).

67 S. Sharpe and D. Braid, *Storming Babylon*, 106–7; see also N. Ovenden's column in the *Edmonton Journal*, 18 September 1990, A12; and P. Manning, *New Canada*, 251–2.

68 The quotes from Cliff Fryers are taken from M. McNellis, 'Reform's Moneyman,' 19 and 25; the quote from Gordon Wusyk is taken from the *Edmonton Journal*, 30 May 1992, A3.

69 W. Stanbury, *Money in Politics*.

70 Entire report in the *Edmonton Journal*, 5 October 1991, A3.

71 W. Stanbury, *Money in Politics*.

72 *Report of the Chief Electoral Officer Respecting Party Contributions* (Ottawa: Chief Electoral Officer of Canada 1991).

73 *Edmonton Journal*, 17 July 1993, A3.

74 Ibid.

75 *Edmonton Journal*, 5 June 1992, A1.

76 *Edmonton Journal*, 4 March 1991, D7.

77 *Edmonton Journal*, 22 January, 1992, B13.

78 See the *Alberta Report*, 16 December 1991, 8–13.

79 *Edmonton Journal*, 19 January 1992, A5.

80 M. Dobbin, *Preston Manning*, 148–55.

81 See the *Edmonton Journal*, 12 May 1992, A7, and 26 May 1992, B3.

82 S. Barrett, *Is God a Racist?* See also chapter two.

83 M. Dobbin, *Preston Manning*, 152–3.

84 *Edmonton Journal*, 29 December 1991, A4.

85 *Edmonton Journal*, 19 January 1992, A3.

86 *Globe and Mail*, 29 February 1992, A4.

87 *Edmonton Journal*, 11 March 1992, A9.

88 *Alberta Report*, 9 November 1987, 15–20, and 15 October 1990, 16; *Edmonton Journal*, 13 November 1990, A7; D. Braid and S. Sharpe, *Breakup*; M. Dobbin, *Preston Manning*. The number of former Tories and Socreds is particularly striking: former Alberta PC MLAs Stephen Stiles, Walter Szwender, Marvin Moore, and Ray Speaker, although Speaker's more

notable past affiliation was with the Social Credit party. Burt Brown, the Alberta PC senatorial candidate in 1989, is also a member of Reform. The party also includes several high-profile former Socreds such as former Alberta MLAS Werner Schmidt (who was also the Socred leader for a time), Jim Henderson, and Fred Manderville. Francis Porter, the aged and frail former vice-president of the Alberta Social Credit League, back in the days of Ernest Manning, is a regular attendant at Reform party conventions. Former BC Socred MLA Jack Kempf also is a member of Reform. Finally, Preston Manning himself is not the only child of a prominent Socred; Val Meredith, a former member of the party executive and currently a Reform MP, is the daughter of former Alberta Socred minister of health J. Donovan Ross.

89 'In analyzing the development of parties, it is necessary to distinguish: their social group; their mass membership; their bureaucracy and general staff' (A. Gramsci, 'Prison Writings,' 219).

90 The sample of party executives is drawn from the totality of members elected to the Reform party's executive council in 1987 (n=11), 1989 (n=11), and 1991 (n=16), ignoring replacements due to resignations or other causes. The data are compiled from P. Manning, *New Canada*, *Edmonton Journal*, 13 November 1990, A7; and the Reform Party of Canada, *The Reformer*, 4, 2, (May 1991).

91 See J. Porter, *Vertical Mosaic*; D. Olsen, *The State Elite* (Toronto: McClelland and Stewart 1980); W.W. Lammers and J.L. Nyomarkay, 'The Canadian Cabinet in Comparative Perspective,' *Canadian Journal of Political Science*, 15, 1 (1982): 29–46; and N. Guppy, S. Freeman, and S. Buchan, 'Economic Background and Political Representation,' in J. Curtis, E. Grabb, N. Guppy, and S. Gilbert, eds., *Social Inequality in Canada: Patterns, Problems, Policies* (Scarborough: Prentice-Hall Canada 1988). A comparison of Reform's executive with past federal cabinets is particularly justified by the fact that several high-profile former members of the party executive – Ian McLelland, Diane Ablonczy, and Monte Solberg – won election in 1993 and would almost certainly be cabinet ministers were Reform to form the government today.

92 The description of delegates is taken entirely from Reform's own survey of 2000 delegates to the 1989 Edmonton assembly, reported in the Reform Party of Canada, *Delegates Survey*; reported also in C. McDougall, 'The Reform Party of Canada: A Determination of the Party's Electoral Viability' (honour's thesis in political science, Edmonton: University of Alberta 1990); and the study of delegates to the 1992 Winnipeg assembly reported in K. Archer and F. Ellis, 'Opinion Structures.' See also table 5.2 in T. Harrison, 'Of Passionate Intensity,' 165.

93 Reform's own figures do not add to 100 per cent.

94 Analysis in K. Archer and F. Ellis, 'Opinion Structures.'

95 See J. Lele, G.C. Perlin, and H.G. Perlin, 'The National Party Convention,' in H.G. Thorburn, ed., *Party Politics in Canada*, 3rd ed. (Scarborough, Ont.: Prentice-Hall of Canada 1972); also K. Archer and F. Ellis, 'Opinion Structures.'

96 The membership data reported here is taken entirely from Reform's own 1989 survey of 5000 members, details of which are reported in P. McCormick, 'Reform Party'; and I. Pearson, 'Thou Shalt Not Ignore the West'; and the party's 1991 survey (sample 1784) reported in the Reform Party of Canada, *1991 Membership Survey Initial Results* (Calgary: Reform Party of Canada 1991).

97 All percentages calculated from Statistics Canada, *Census of Canada: The Nation. Occupation and Industry* (Ottawa: Statistics Canada 1986), 1–226.

98 Regarding the Liberal and Tory parties, see N. Guppy et al., 'Economic Background.'

99 The percentage of Reform party members who are unionized workers in the non-agricultural sector is calculated from data in the Reform Party of Canada, *1991 Membership Survey Initial Results*; the Canadian figure is taken from H. Krahn and G. Lowe, *Work*, 243.

100 J. Simpson's column in the *Globe and Mail*, 11 April 1991, A14.

101 The description of supporters is taken entirely from an Environics study of 224 Reform party supporters conducted in May 1991 and reported in Carol Goar's column in the *Toronto Star* 8 June 1991, D1 and D5; Environics' subsequent survey of various party supporters (n=1952), Environics Research Group Ltd., *Focus Canada: Statistical Tables*. Fieldwork dates: 15 July to 15 August (Toronto: Environics Research 1991); and the 1991 Alberta Survey conducted by the University of Alberta (n=1345), reported in T. Harrison, 'Of Passionate Intensity' (see table 5.3, 168). See also T. Harrison and H. Krahn, 'Increasing Pluralism or Temporary Fragmentation?' 93.

102 The disproportionate percentage of Reformers who are Protestants (62 per cent), relative to the Canadian average (38 per cent) is reduced, but not entirely eliminated, if Quebec is left out of the equation. Minus Quebec, the percentage of Protestants in Canada rises to 54 per cent, as calculated from Statistics Canada, *Census of Canada, National Series (4): Religion, Birthplace, Education* (Ottawa: Minister of Supply and Services Canada 1981).

103 C.B. Macpherson, *Democracy in Alberta*.

104 This data is presented somewhat differently in table 5.4 in T. Harrison,'Of Passionate Intensity,' 170; and T. Harrison and H. Krahn, 'Populism and

the Rise of the Reform Party in Alberta.' The 1991 Alberta Survey was particularly well suited to conducting just such an empirical test. Class categories were defined using a modification of neo-Marxist categories as suggested by E.O. Wright, 'Class Boundaries in Advanced Capitalist Societies,' *New Left Review*, 98 (1976): 3–41, and validated by W. Johnston and M. Ornstein, 'Social Class and Political Ideology in Canada,' *Canadian Review of Sociology and Anthropology*, 22, 3 (1985): 369–93; and D. Baer, E. Grabb, and W. Johnston, 'Class, Crisis, and Political Ideology in Canada: Recent Trends,' *Canadian Review of Sociology and Anthropology*, 24, 1 (1987): 1–22. Using a combination of questions dealing with occupational, employment, and supervisory status within the workplace, the authors determined six classes: owners, the petite bourgeoisie, senior and middle managers, semi-autonomous workers, foremen and supervisors, and workers. The petite bourgeoisie was later split into its agrarian and non-agrarian components, a methodological division given tacit support by C.B. Macpherson, *Democracy in Alberta*, 227.

105 A Dunvegan poll of 552 farmers, conducted in March 1992, found that 79 per cent of decided Alberta farmers and 59 per cent of decided farmers in the three Prairie provinces planned to vote Reform (reported in the *Edmonton Journal*, 16 April 1992, E8). A subsequent Dunvegan poll of 576 farmers, conducted in October 1992, showed that 64 per cent of decided Alberta farmers and 49 per cent of decided farmers in all three Prairie provinces continued to plan to vote for Reform (reported in the *Edmonton Journal*, 11 November 1992, D9).

106 Reform Party of Canada, *Delegates Survey*; also reviewed in P. McCormick, 'Reform Party.'

107 See M.W. Conley and P.J. Smith, 'Political Recruitment and Party Activists: British and Canadian Comparisons,' *International Political Science Review*, 4, 1 (1983): 48–56, regarding the motivations of members of the three major parties.

108 See T. Harrison, 'Of Passionate Intensity'; also T. Harrison and H. Krahn, 'Increasing Pluralism or Temporary Fragmentation'; and K. Archer and F. Ellis, 'Opinion Structures.'

109 See table 5.5 in T. Harrison, 'Of Passionate Intensity,' p. 172.

110 It should be considered that the survey was conducted only a few months after the Oka crisis. Hence, native issues were very much salient in the public mind. While the crisis no doubt awoke both guilt and a genuine desire to address aboriginal issues in many non-aboriginal Canadians, a recent survey suggests that Canadian attitudes on the matter are particularly mitigated by such factors as prejudice, perceived group conflict, and economic conservatism. See T. Langford and J.R. Ponting, 'Canadians'

Responses to Aboriginal Issues: The Roles of Prejudice, Perceived Group Conflict, and Economic Conservatism,' *Canadian Review of Sociology and Anthropology* (special issue), 29, 2 (1992): 140–66.

111 T. Harrison and H. Krahn, 'Populism and the Rise of the Reform Party in Alberta.'

112 See R. Ogmundson and J. McLaughlin, 'Trends in the Ethnic Origins of Canadian Élites,' *Canadian Review of Sociology and Anthropology* (special issue), 29, 2 (1992): 227–42.

113 K. Archer and F. Ellis, 'Opinion Structures,' found that delegates to Reform's 1992 assembly had strong beliefs about the influence of certain traditional 'big interests,' including central Canada, the media, and banks. But the federal cabinet and Quebecers were viewed as having the greatest influence, while 'average voters' were viewed as having the least – the latter, a typically populist world-view.

114 S. Patten, *Populist Politics?*

115 See J.D. House, *Last of the Free Enterprisers.*

116 See M. Dobbin, *Preston Manning*; and S. Sharpe and D. Braid, *Storming Babylon.* There are numerous links between the NCC and Reform. Ernest Manning and Eric Kipping, a former New Brunswick PC MLA and current Reform member, were founding members of the NCC. Stephen Harper and William Gairdner also are NCC members, as was the late Stan Waters. His son, Mark Waters, is a high ranking NCC official and, along with David Somerville, has been a formal observer at every Reform party assembly since the party's inception. S. Sharpe and D. Braid quote Somerville as stating: 'The Reform Party has cribbed probably two-thirds of our policy book' (65).

117 Reform Party of Canada, *Blue Book*, 1991.

118 Some Reformers admit the potential danger of corporate influence. In my interview with him, Stephen Harper stated that personally he 'would like to see donations from corporations and unions to political parties prohibited altogether.' More recently, Tom Flanagan has written that Reform should take the bold step of refusing to accept either corporate or union donations, while leading a fight to end all but individual donations to political parties (*Alberta Report*, 13 December 1993, 9). Not dealt with by these otherwise reasonable suggestions is how to curtail corporate efforts to influence election outcomes, outside the party system, as occurred in 1988 in the free trade debate, and in 1988 and 1993 by such organizations as the National Citizens' Coalition.

119 K. Archer and F. Ellis, 'Opinion Structures'; T. Harrison and H. Krahn, 'Increasing Pluralism or Temporary Fragmentation?'

120 *Edmonton Journal*, 28 October 1989, A1.

121 See C. Lasch, *True and Only Heaven,* regarding the notion of limits and the contradictions in the neo-conservative coalition.

122 C.B. Macpherson, *The Political Theory of Possessive Individualism* (Oxford: Oxford University Press 1962).

123 Margaret Thatcher has stated that 'There is no such thing as society' (quoted in S. McBride and J. Shields, *Dismantling a Nation,* 85 n 2).

124 W. Gairdner, *Trouble,* 364, italics in original.

125 P. Manning, *New Canada,* 105. See also M. Dobbin, *Preston Manning;* and S. Sharpe and D. Braid, *Storming Babylon,* regarding Manning's religious beliefs.

126 W. Gairdner, *Trouble,* 80.

127 Environics Research Group Ltd., *Focus Canada.*

128 Reform party figures taken from Reform Party of Canada, *1991 Membership Survey Initial Results.*

129 K. Archer and F. Ellis, 'Opinion Structures.'

130 In the United States, conservative attacks upon state policy as the chief cause of the family disintegration have been around for some time. The thesis has most recently and cogently been stated in Canada in William Gairdner's *The War against the Family* (Toronto: Stoddart Publishing Company 1992).

131 'In America, contrary to what most conservatives argue, it is the untrammelled market and not the state that has done the most damage to civil society. We have the weakest state sector by far among the advanced nations, and the most unregulated markets' (David Popenoe of Rutgers University, quoted in G. Fraser's column in the *Globe and Mail,* 19 February 1994, A7). See also C. Lasch, *True and Only Heaven,* especially the footnote, p. 516, on the incompatibility of the family with the market.

132 *Alberta Report,* 10 December 1990, 18.

133 *Edmonton Journal,* 19 November 1991, A7.

134 *Alberta Report,* 16 December 1991, 8–13.

135 Story and comments in the *Edmonton Journal,* 13 August 1992, D12.

136 Reform Party of Canada, *Official Record of Assembly 1992* (Calgary: Reform Party of Canada 1992).

137 Reform Party of Canada, *Blue Book,* 1991, 29.

138 H. Johnson's letter in the *Edmonton Journal,* 3 July 1992, A11; J. McGillvray's letter in the *Edmonton Journal,* 28 July 1992, A9.

139 Nelson ran unsuccessfully, in the fall of 1992, for the position of Alberta premier to succeed the retiring Don Getty.

140 Reported in the *Alberta Report,* 16 December 1991, 9.

141 *Alberta Report*, 5 November 1990, 9. See also the V.J. Wiebe letter in the the *Alberta Report*, 13 January 1992, 3; and M. Dobbin, *Preston Manning*.
142 *Edmonton Journal*, 9 January 1992, A8.
143 C. Cripps's letter in the *Edmonton Journal*, 21 March 1992, A13.
144 This and the quote that immediately follows are taken from the author's interview with Ted Byfield, 1991.
145 S. Sharpe and D. Braid, *Storming Babylon*, 17.
146 Reform Party of Canada, *Blue Book*, 1991.
147 *Edmonton Journal*, 28 November 1991, A16.
148 Quoted in J. Dafoe's column in the *Globe and Mail*, 15 February 1991, D2. See also *Globe and Mail*, 15 February 1991, A4.
149 P. Manning, *New Canada*, 260, italics added.
150 J. Richards, 'Populism.'
151 The term is drawn from J. Habermas, 'Systematically Distorted Communication,' in P. Connerton, ed., *Critical Sociology* (Markham: Penguin Books Canada, 1976). See also T.A. McCarthy, 'A Theory of Communicative Competence,' in the same text.
152 Quoted in M. Dobbin, *Preston Manning*, 116.
153 Ibid., 120.
154 D. Laycock, *Populism and Democratic Thought*.

CHAPTER 6   The Great Realignment

1 *Alberta Report*, 12 July 1993, 7.
2 See the *Alberta Report*, 2 March 1992, 10–11.
3 *Edmonton Journal*, 30 January 1991, A1.
4 *Alberta Report*, 4 May 1992, 6–9.
5 *Edmonton Journal*, 15 July 1992, A1; 16 July 1992, A1.
6 *Edmonton Journal*, 23 July 1992, A3.
7 *Edmonton Journal*, 17 July 1992, A14, and again 19 July 1992, A3.
8 *Edmonton Journal*, 24 August 1992, A3.
9 The major components of the deal were summarized in the *Edmonton Journal*, 23 August 1992, A3.
10 These and the Angus Reid poll results immediately following are taken from S. Henry, *Public Opinion and the Charlottetown Accord* (Calgary: Canada West Foundation 1993).
11 See T. Harrison, 'Stepping Stone or Pyrrhic Victory? Reform and the Referendum,' Constitutional Forum, 4, 2 (1993): 34–7.
12 *Alberta Report*, 26 October 1992, 9.

13 T. Harrison, 'Stepping Stone or Pyrrhic Victory?' See also *Edmonton Journal*, 22 November 1992, A9.

14 Most of the arguments that follow appeared in T. Harrison, 'Stepping Stone or Pyrrhic Victory?' See also C.V. Ploeg, *The Referendum on the Charlottetown Accord: An Assessment* (Calgary: Canada West Foundation 1993), and poll results in S. Henry, *Public Opinion.*

15 *Edmonton Journal*, 20 February 1993, B6.

16 R. Ponting, 'Public opinion on Aboriginal Peoples' Issues in Canada,' *Canadian Social Trends*, 11 (1988): 9–17.

17 *Alberta Report*, 26 October 1992, 6–8.

18 *Edmonton Journal*, 23 August 1992, A1.

19 Angus Reid poll, reported in S. Henry, *Public Opinion.*

20 *Maclean's Magazine*, 28 September 1992, 22–6.

21 Angus Reid poll, reported in S. Henry, *Public Opinion.*

22 Results reported in the *Edmonton Journal*, 27 October 1992, A1.

23 Gallup, 13 July 1992.

24 Gallup, 13 August 1992.

25 *Globe and Mail*, 24 October 1992, A5.

26 *Alberta Report*, 14 September 1992, 7.

27 See T. Harrison, 'Stepping Stone or Pyrrhic Victory?' See also *Alberta Report*, 14 September 1992, 7.

28 *Alberta Report*, 14 September 1992, 7.

29 *Alberta Report*, 21 September 1992, 7.

30 *Edmonton Journal*, 22 October 1992, A4.

31 *Globe and Mail*, 24 October 1992, A5.

32 The *St. Albert Gazette*, 26 September 1992, 6, reported the complaints of some Reform party members that they had only received their ballots on the day the party's decision on the accord was announced.

33 Edmonton Journal, 2 October 1992, A3.

34 See analysis by C. Cobb, *Edmonton Journal*, 16 October 1992, A3, and the apologetic comments of Reform's director of communications, Laurie Watson, in the *Edmonton Journal*, 24 October 1992, A4.

35 *Edmonton Journal*, 9 October 1992, A3.

36 Gallup, 17 September, 22 October, and 19 November 1992.

37 *Alberta Report*, 28 September 1992, 8.

38 *Edmonton Journal*, 6 October 1992, A3.

39 *Edmonton Journal*, 24 October 1992, E1.

40 N. Ovenden's column in the *Edmonton Journal*, 25 November 1992, G1 and G2, quote on G2.

41 N. Ovenden's column in the *Edmonton Journal*, 14 November 1992, G1.

42 *Edmonton Journal,* 28 October 1992, A4.
43 *Edmonton Journal,* 5 November 1992, A3.
44 See, for example, *Edmonton Journal,* 26 October 1992, A3.
45 Ibid.
46 Prior to stepping down as Reform's policy director, Tom Flanagan stated that, because of the referendum, 'we've now got to put the constitution aside.' Quoted in the *Edmonton Journal,* 24 October 1992, B8.
47 Gallup, 17 December 1992.
48 See *Alberta Report,* 28 December 1992, 13.
49 *Edmonton Journal,* 25 February 1993, A5.
50 Gallup, 16 November 1992.
51 The *Edmonton Journal* of 4 December 1992 reported results of a poll showing that the Tories would surge ahead of the Liberals in popular support if Joe Clark was party leader.
52 A Gallup poll of 15 March 1993, conducted shortly after the announcement of his resignation, found that that 42 per cent of Canadians rated Mulroney as one of Canada's worst prime ministers.
53 A Southam Canadian Business Monitor survey, conducted in December 1992, found that 64 per cent of Canadian CEOs believed that the Tories deserved to be re-elected (*Edmonton Journal,* 30 January 1993, B4). That same month, a Gallup poll showed that only 19 per cent of Canadians were prepared to vote for the Tories (Gallup, 17 December 1992).
54 Most often mentioned were communications minister Perrin Beatty, revenue minister Otto Jelinek, deputy prime minister Don Mazankowski, external affairs minister Barbara McDougall, employment and immigration minister Bernard Valcourt, and minister of industry, science and technology Michael Wilson.
55 Most of the biographic information on Kim Campbell presented here is taken from N. Ovenden's feature in the *Edmonton Journal,* 20 March 1993, G1 and G2.
56 Unquestionably, Campbell's greatest gaffe occurred during a candidates forum in Vancouver in May when she said, 'at the end of the leadership race we will go forward as and defeat not just the enemy of the Progressive Conservative party but the enemies of Canadians.' The statement reminded people all too much of the divisive tactics of her predecessor.
57 Byfield was not alone on the right wing in believing that Campbell was a 'radical feminist.' The *Edmonton Journal* of 10 March 1993, A3, carried a story stating that the anti-feminist group, Alberta Women United for Families, was joining a national campaign by REAL Women to block Campbell from winning the Tory leadership. 'She is left-wing, a captive of

the feminist interest groups and pro-homosexual,' said AWUF head Corry Morcos.

58 *Alberta Report*, 5 April 1993, 10.
59 See K. Whyte's column in the *Globe and Mail*, 17 July 1993, D2. See also *Alberta Report*, 6 September 1993, 8.
60 See Tom Flanagan's comments in the *Edmonton Journal*, 21 August 1993, A3; and 7 September 1993, A3.
61 See *Edmonton Journal*, 20 July 1993, A3; 17 August 1993, A3; and 31 August 1993, A1. Campbell's announcements regarding patronage seemed to many a rather belated attempt to close the barn door. In the final six months of his reign, Brian Mulroney made over 600 patronage appointments. Between 1 April and 3 June 1993 alone, he made 241 appointments (*Globe and Mail*, 5 June 1993, A1 and A2). Several of these were to the Senate – termed by one wag a 'taskless thanks' – thereby ensuring Tory dominance in that body for years to come.
62 For over a year, the Tories had been involved in the purchase of fifty military helicopters at a cost of $4.5 billion. As defence minister, Campbell oversaw the contract and staunchly defended the merits of the deal. Critics complained that the purchase was unnecessary at a time of high deficits. Others charged that the deal was a sop to both the Tory's right-wing military supporters and the province of Quebec, where most of the helicopters were to be built. Finally, it was also noted that the Tories had close ties with lobbyists for the companies involved. See *Edmonton Journal*, 7 February 1993, B6.
63 Regarding Campbell's popularity, see Gallup polls for 19 July and 26 August 1993.
64 See L. Whittington's column, *Edmonton Journal*, 1 September 1993, A8; the expenditure estimate appears in the Edmonton Journal, 25 August 1993, A3.
65 *Edmonton Journal*, 10 March 1993, A3. A Gallup poll in August, reported in the *Edmonton Journal* of 7 September 1993, B14, showed that 41 per cent of Canadians believed that their jobs were at risk.
66 *Edmonton Journal*, 9 September 1993, A1.
67 *Edmonton Journal*, 10 September 1993, A1.
68 *Edmonton Journal*, 17 September 1993, A1.
69 *The Globe and Mail*, 18 September 1993, A1.
70 The NDP's charge was supported by the release of secret government reports showing that the Tories had plans on the table for a massive restructuring of welfare, unemployment insurance, and retirement programs. See *Edmonton Journal*, 24 September 1993, A3; 27 September 1993, A3; and 28 September 1993, A3.

71 *Edmonton Journal,* 1 October 1993, A3.
72 *Edmonton Journal,* 9 October 1993, A1.
73 See analysis by E. Greenspon, R. Howard, and S. Delacourt in the *Globe and Mail,* 16 October 1993, A6.
74 Regarding Tory infighting, see the *Edmonton Journal,* 18 October 1993, A6; 20 October 1993, A3; and 30 October 1993, A1.
75 *Edmonton Journal,* 21 October 1993, A1; and the Angus Reid/Southam News-CTV poll in the *Edmonton Journal,* 22 October 1993, A1.
76 *Edmonton Journal,* 19 October 1993, A3.
77 Gallup, 30 August 1993 reported that 46 per cent of Canadians disapproved of the FTA while 58 per cent disapproved of NAFTA. Afraid, however, of what an outright abrogation of the agreements might mean, most Canadians simply wanted them changed. This was what the Liberals promised. On the issue of trade and its relationship to voting in the 1993 election, see J. Pammett, 'Tracking the Votes,' in A. Frizzell, J.H. Pammett, and A. Westall eds., *The Canadian General Election of 1993* (Ottawa: Carleton University Press 1994).
78 See N. Ovenden's article in the *Edmonton Journal,* 18 October 1993, A4.
79 Reform's budget solution to Canada's financial crisis was revealed in April 1993. It called for reducing the annual federal deficit to zero over three years. This would be accomplished by axing $18 billion from government spending, on the one hand, and relying on an annual rate of economic growth, after inflation, of 3.5 percent, on the other hand, to generate an additional $16 billion dollars in government revenue. Government spending cuts would involve transfers to individuals and governments, for example, unemployment insurance, welfare, and equalization payments. According to Manning, health care, education, child benefits, guaranteed income supplements, and veterans' benefits would be untouched. See *Alberta Report,* 5 April 1993, 6–10.
80 *Edmonton Journal,* 13 October 1993, A3.
81 *Edmonton Journal,* 22 October 1993, A3.
82 See J. Pammett, 'Tracking the Votes'; also, *Globe and Mail,* 26 March 1994, D1.
83 See Gallup's post-election poll of 11 November 1993.
84 See the *Edmonton Journal,* 26 September 1993, A3, and 7 October 1993, A3.
85 See Preston Manning's statement in the *Edmonton Journal,* 18 September 1993, A3. Like the Tories, Reform propounded an economic formula that stated: lower deficit = lower taxes for business and individuals = increased investment = job creation (see P. Manning's formulation in the *Edmonton Journal,* 17 September 1993, A4). By contrast, the Liberals and NDP contended that: increased employment = less social spending +

increased tax revenues = lower deficit. The general public wanted both deficit reduction and jobs, a combination that the Liberal plan, in the eyes of many voters, seemed best able to offer (see J. Pammett, 'Tracking the Votes,' also Globe poll results in the *Globe and Mail*, 16 October 1993, A1 and A8).

86 *Edmonton Journal*, 14 October 1993, A4. See chapter four for a more complete rendition of Beck's remarks.

87 Hard-core western separatists, such as Doug Christie of the WCC and Elmer Knutson of COR, have for some time been estranged from Reform (see *Edmonton Journal*, 5 November 1990, A9, and 17 May 1993, A3). At the same time, one should not underestimate the amount of quasi-separatist sentiment underlying much Reform support in Alberta and British Columbia. A poll of 710 westerners conducted by Environics Research in March 1992 found that 42 per cent of respondents agreed with the question: 'Western Canada gets so few benefits from Confederation the region might as well be on its own' (*Alberta Report*, 28 September 1992, 7; 8 November 1993, 8). I would speculate that many of the 'agreeing' respondents also are federal Reformers.

88 G. York's article in the *Globe and Mail*, 12 February 1994, A4, describes Reform as now presenting a 'dual personality,' one a western (Albertan) regional party, the other a national party more interested in accommodating the interests of Quebec.

89 See *Globe and Mail*, 18 December 1993, A4 for a list of perks renounced by Reform; see *Edmonton Journal*, 6 April 1994, A11, regarding Manning's expense account.

90 *Edmonton Journal*, 25 September 1993, A3. Some traditional conservatives also see Manning's resolve weakening on such issues as homosexual rights (see *Alberta Report*, 6 September 1993, 8).

91 The role of the NCC within Reform has previously been mentioned. In the 1993 election, the NCC spent over $50,000 dollars attacking the incumbent PC, Jim Hawkes, in the riding of Calgary West. Ostensibly singling out Hawkes because of his parliamentary role in leading the fight to control election spending by special-interest groups such as the NCC, the latter's actions almost certainly had the effect of lending support to the Reform candidate, Stephen Harper, a staunch member of the NCC (see K. Whyte's column in the *Globe and Mail*, 2 October 1993, D2).

92 See Tom Flanagan's column in the *Alberta Report*, 13 December 1993, 9.

93 The day after the election, Reform was embarrassed by the written statements of John Tillman, Reform's campaign manager in Halifax West. In a letter to a defeated Tory candidate, Tillman criticized government

support for the 'so-called disadvantaged.' 'Gone are the days,' wrote
Tillman, 'of catering to radical womens' groups, minority groups, etc.
Gone are the days of protecting these and other parasites of society.'
Although Tillman was eventually expelled from the party, the incident
reinforced Reform's negative public image. Moreover, Tillman's expulsion
created new problems for the party, pitting moderates who felt that he
had gone too far in using the term 'parasites' and more right-wing
supporters who felt Reform was caving in to 'political correctness' (see
Edmonton Journal, 30 October 1993, A3, and 8 November 1993, A3; *Alberta
Report*, 29 November 1993, 8).

94 Manning has specifically stated that he wants to expand Reform's support
among ethnic minorities, women, and young people (see G. York's article
in the *Globe and Mail*, 12 February 1994, A4).

95 Reform's other seats were won in Saskatchewan (four), Manitoba (one),
and Ontario (one).

96 See K. Whyte's column in the *Globe and Mail*, 9 April 1994, D2; regarding
the Reform's caucus revolt, see J. Crockatt's article in the *Edmonton
Journal*, 23 July 1994, A8; and E. Greenspon and G. Gherson's article in the
Globe and Mail, 23 July 1994, A1, A4.

97 *Edmonton Journal*, 23 February 1994, A1.

98 The fall of 1993 and spring of 1994 saw massive layoffs of public sector
workers in Alberta, including teachers and nurses. Five per cent wage cuts
across the board became the order of the day. Thousands of hospital beds
were closed and numerous government services privatized. Hours of
publicly funded kindergarten were cut in half. University tuition fees
increased substantially, and some university departments closed altogether. User fees (essentially a flat tax) were implemented or increased for
numerous government services. Tens of thousands of welfare recipients
were driven off public rolls and the benefits of several thousand more
were cut. At the same time, corporate tax rates remained virtually
nonexistent, and unelected advisers from the business community were
given a prominent say in formulating government policy.

CHAPTER 7   The 'Problem' of Populism Revisited

1 C. Lasch, *True and Only Heaven*, 532.
2 M. Canovan, *Populism*, 15.
3 J. Richards, 'Populism'; D. Laycock, *Populism and Democratic
Thought*.
4 J. Richards, 'Populism,' 19–20.

5 D. Laycock, *Populism and Democratic Thought*.
6 C.B. Macpherson, *Democracy in Alberta*.
7 E. Bell, *Social Classes*.
8 C.B. Macpherson, *Democracy in Alberta*, 227.
9 R. Hofstadter, *Age of Reform*.
10 E. Laclau, *Politics and Ideology*, 163.
11 Ibid.
12 See, for example, E. Laclau, and C. Mouffe, *Hegemony and Socialist Strategy: Towards a Radical Democratic Politics* (London: Verso 1985).
13 H.D. Graham and T.R. Gurr, *Violence in America*. See also chapter three.
14 C. Tilly, *From Mobilization*; and J. McCarthy and M. Zald, *Social Movements*.
15 M. Dobbin, *Preston Manning*.
16 S. Sharpe and D. Braid, *Storming Babylon*.
17 A similar conclusion arises from studies of the 1993 election results. See J. Pammett, 'Tracking the Votes.'
18 B. Anderson, *Imagined Communities*.
19 Quoted in M. Dobbin, *Preston Manning*, 120.
20 M. Weiler, 'Neo-conservatism: A Study of Ideological Argument,' *Journal of the American Forensic Association*, 24 (1987): 37–47, quote from 44.
21 See J. Richards, 'Populism.'
22 J.D. Davidson and W. Rees-Moog, *The Great Reckoning: How the World Will Change in the Depression of the 1990s*, 2nd ed. (Don Mills, Ont: General Publishing 1993); J.K. Galbraith, *The Culture of Contentment* (Markham, Ont.: Thomas Allen and Sons 1992).
23 In 1985, multinationals comprised 46 of the largest economies in the world. The largest of the multinationals, General Motors (eighteenth place), had a larger volume of sales than the GNP of Sweden, Switzerland, and several other prominent countries (H. Veltmeyer, *Canadian Corporate Power* [Toronto: Garamond Press 1987], 78–9). By 1991 multinationals made up 47 of the top 100 economies. Although General Motors had slipped to twentieth place on the list, several other multinationals, including Ford Motor Co., Exxon Corporation, and International Business Machines, had risen against the position of various nations (*Edmonton Journal*, 16 December 1991, c4).
24 A. Toffler, *Power Shift: Knowledge, Wealth, and Violence at the Edge of the 21st Century* (Toronto: Bantam Books 1990), 462.
25 C. Lasch, *True and Only Heaven*, 532.
26 In terms of globalization, neo-conservatism might be better termed 'neo-liberalism,' the basic tenets of which involve notions of comparative advantage and free trade drawn from Ricardian economics. My point here

is that traditional conservatism believed in the notions of community and that there was something worth 'conserving.' Neither of these beliefs is found particularly strongly in liberal doctrine.

A COMMENT ON METHODS AND SOURCES

1 Useful discussions of the historical sociological approach can be found in T. Skocpol, ed., *Vision and Method in Historical Sociology* (Cambridge: Cambridge University Press 1984); S.M. Lipset and R. Hofstadter, eds., *Sociology and History: Methods* (London: Basic Books 1968); C. Tilly, *As Sociology Meets History* (Toronto: Academic Press 1981); C. Tilly, *Big Structures, Large Processes, Huge Comparisons* (New York: Russell Sage Foundation 1984); and S.A. Kent, 'Historical Sociology,' in E. Borgatta and M. Borgatta, eds., *Encyclopedia of Sociology*, vol. 2 (Toronto: Maxwell Macmillan Canada 1992). I would also recommend the entire issue of *Sociological Methods and Research*, 2, 4 (1992).
2 A. de Tocqueville, *The Old Regime and the Revolution* (1856; New York: Doubleday 1955); K. Marx and F. Engels, 'The Communist Manifesto'; M. Weber, *Protestant Ethic*.
3 E.P. Thompson, *The Making of the English Working Class* (Harmondsworth: Penguin 1968); B. Moore, Jr, *Social Origins of Dictatorship and Democracy: Lord and Peasant in the Making of the Modern World* (Boston: Beacon Press 1966); T. Skocpol, *Social Revolutions*; D. Chirot, *Social Change*; and G. Laxer, *Open for Business*.

Index